The Great North American
SKI BOOK

The Great North American SKI BOOK

I. WILLIAM BERRY

*A completely revised
and updated third edition of*
America's Ski Book

CHARLES SCRIBNER'S SONS   NEW YORK

First Charles Scribner's Sons paperback edition 1984

New and revised material copyright © 1982 I. William Berry
Copyright © 1958, 1959, 1960, 1961, 1962, 1963, 1964, 1965, 1966, 1967, 1968, 1969,
1970, 1971, 1972, 1973 Universal Publishing and Distributing Corporation

Library of Congress Cataloging in Publication Data
Berry, I. William
    The great North American ski book.

    Rev. and updated ed. of: America's ski book / by
the editors of Ski magazine. Rev. ed. 1973
    Bibliography: p.
    Includes index.
    1. Skis and skiing.   2. Skis and skiing—United
States.   I. America's ski book.   II. Title.
GV854.B377 1982   796.93'0973   82-6029
ISBN 0-684-18207-6

1 3 5 7 9 11 13 15 17 19   F/P   20 18 16 14 12 10 8 6 4 2

Printed in the United States of America.
Portions of this book were originally published in SKI Magazine, Skiing, Skier's
Advocate, *Robert G. Enzel's* White Book of Ski Areas *(Inter-Ski Services, 1981), and*
John Howe's Skiing Mechanics *(Poudre Publishing, 1982). Reprinted by permission.*
Other portions appeared previously in different form in I. William Berry's Skier's
Almanac *(Charles Scribner's Sons, copyright © 1978 I. William Berry), and* Kids on
Skis *(Charles Scribner's Sons, copyright © 1980 I. William Berry). All rights reserved.*

To the writers and the marketeers:
Adversaries, friends, and (often unwitting) partners
in the growth and refinement of the sport.

And as always, to Dee, Greg, and Alix,
who keep me interested and entertained.

Also by I. William Berry

WHERE TO SKI
THE SKIER'S ALMANAC
KIDS ON SKIS

Contents

Foreword

You are about to be entertained by one of the truly inspired sports-history writers of our time, I. William Berry. (I. William Berry? Should it be J. Claude Killy—"Hello there, Claude?"—I think not.)

Perhaps it should be I *am* William Berry, because the man who *is* Mr. Berry is unique in his field. He is a deft painter of the written word who, with his legal training, can take on any assignment and develop an imaginative and appealing approach. His writing spans the spectrum of our ski world, from lifting the veil of the most complicated maneuverings of back-room ski politics in a disarming but not disenchanting style, to expressing the simplest elements of a limited-scope subject (like a ski trail) in terms that make it appear almost heroic in proportion.

Berry's comments are insidiously incisive yet thoughtful, regardless of the subject; and the narrative images that evolve are a delight. He has that unusual ability to discern the common thread of understanding in all of us and can inject even the most mundane aspects of skiing with elements of intrigue and interest.

I. William Berry perhaps has broader knowledge of all sides of the ski industry than anyone else in the trade. He understands planning and development as if he were in the business himself. His insights and intuition concerning the financial/operational field are respected by bankers and owners alike. And, ultimately, he understands the consumer (the lifeblood of the sport), the expectations, the experiences, the frustrations, and because of this understanding Berry can weave the fabric of the story the way it should be woven, straightforwardly and honestly but with humor and consummate sensitivity.

I. William Berry has developed an intriguing work about our winter life-style. In so doing he has provided us a great service. Perhaps someday we will have the opportunity to return the favor and write about Bill Berry.

James R. Branch
President, Sno-Engineering

Preface and Acknowledgments

Probably evidence of the biggest change in the American ski scene since 1973 can be seen in the change in title and in the revised contents of this book. Although the first two editions, in 1966 and 1973, were called *America's Ski Book*, they contained major sections and photographs devoted to European skiing. As recently as 1973, American skiing was still regarded as derivative and American skiers were considered an export commodity. But this edition, with the new title of *The Great North American Ski Book*, refers only passingly to European skiing and even then, only in an historical context. By 1982, to put it another way, American skiing had come of age, and American ski resorts were attracting slightly more Europeans than the European resorts were attracting Americans.

Furthermore, as the seventies drew to an end, American ski instructors were acknowledged to be the world's best, having won the major European competition known as Interski and created the important innovations in advanced-skiing workshops and children's programs. "Bend Zee Kneez" became, if anything, a joke rather than an emblem of superiority.

Yet oddly, since 1973, the Europeans have extended their domination of the ski sport—and industry—in what should be an American zone: equipment. The French, Germans, and Austrians controlled bindings, and a small zone in

Italy produced most of the boots. Only in the production of skis did the United States *almost* hold its own against the Austrians and French. (Even stranger, the Japanese have failed to penetrate this American and worldwide market despite their producing good skis at reasonable prices. Taiwan and Korea, however, have a large piece of the clothing business; skiing isn't totally immune to worldwide trends.)

The succession of principal authors on the three editions of this book further underscores the Americanization of skiing. The first edition (1966) was written and edited by John Henry Auran, a native of Europe then serving as editor of SKI Magazine (and now as senior editor on *Skiing* magazine). The second edition (1973) was written and edited by John Fry, a native French-Canadian then serving as editor-in-chief of SKI Magazine (and now as editor-in-chief of SKI's Cross-Country Guide). This edition is written and edited by a native of the United States (no matter what the rest of the country says about people born and reared in Brooklyn, New York), for more than a decade a contributing editor on SKI Magazine, the equipment editor of *Skier's Advocate*, and a writer for numerous other publications.

One point I feel is particularly important—namely, to explain just how "completely revised and updated" this edition is.

As an editor, which I was for more than a decade before becoming a full-time writer in 1971, I was never addicted to or afflicted with what I call the Kilroy Syndrome: the need some insecure editors have to change copy just to prove "they were there." I'm still not, and the second edition of this book contained whole, long tracts by John Fry that didn't need a pencil laid on them, so I left them alone. Other sections needed revision not because John had been "wrong" but rather because the whole subject—equipment, resorts, instruction—has been reevaluated in the past decade and new conclusions have been drawn. I'd have done the same as I've done with this book had I revised my own written in 1974.

Further, John is a better student of ski history than I am, and he's much closer to the world of competition. Conversely, I'm closer to the resort and equipment people; just a difference in personality and interest.

However, in all sections, anything pertaining to events, trends, people, philosophy, or outlook that occurred after 1973 is strictly mine, as are all projections for the next few years. And since I had the final authority to decide what remained and what was changed, I'll take final responsibility for that, too.

Besides, I've always had a strong respect for John's knowledge about and scholarship in the overall world of skiing, even where we've disagreed. This has been personal as well as professional: we've both been involved with SKI Magazine forever, or so it often seems. So, insofar as possible, I've tried to blend our outlooks; where I've had to change anything, I feel it's clearly marked.

Not too long ago, a noted Swiss ecologist pronounced that skiing was the worst plague of the twentieth century. Even allowing for the tunnel vision of most environmentalists and for the immunity of many Swiss to such disasters as the flu epidemic of 1918 and the Nazi pestilence of the thirties and forties, the statement was inane even within the speaker's narrow frame of reference: How much damage to the ecosystem has skiing done compared with the excesses of the petro-auto-aero-highway combine, the DDT salesmen, the heavy-industry manufacturers, or, for that matter, the "dogs of war"? Yet for all that the statement was patently ludicrous, it underscored one important concept: Skiing generates very strong feelings, pro and con.

The feelings are often stronger than the sport's, or industry's, role or power. Skiing, after all, is nothing more than a minor component in the recreation/travel/leisure business, and while that industry is of awesome importance to the fiscal health of most nations (including Switzerland), it's not a controlling one: Its leaders lack the clout "on the inside" of those who speak for agriculture, finance, or heavy manufacturing. Which is only right: Those three forces direct the destiny of mankind, while tourism and leisure only keep it placated and pacified. So why does skiing provoke that ferocity of feeling? It's hard to explain rationally.

Yet I see it in myself. I generate roughly half my income by writing about business and finance, yet it's been years since I felt personally involved in one of those articles: How excited, after all, can you get writing about a multicontract commodities spread or different theories of managing cash flow? You do your research thoroughly, write carefully, get paid, and, unless you're dumb enough to follow your own investment advice, you forget about it. I cannot think of a financial editor who ever "inspired me to greater effort" or to whom I owe more than professional respect and responsibility, and my only really negative experience there was based on a personality clash rather than conviction.

In contrast, I feel strongly about ski writing. I can still remember some articles I wrote as long ago as 1970, and get much more involved in my research and writing: I'm a participant, after all, not just a reporter. Ski writing has remained a potent force in my life since I joined SKI Magazine as executive editor back in 1969, and it shows no signs of waning; other interests have come and gone.

So my first acknowledgment is to skiing itself.

My second is to the editors I've worked with over the years, who've pushed me, fought with me, supported me, and occasionally driven me up a tree (I suspect that's mutual) but who have never left me bored. Among those editors who've allowed my writing (and therefore me) to grow are John Fry and, more recently, Dick Needham of SKI; Evie DiSante, a real comer at *Skier's Advocate;* Debbye Naber at *Ski Industry Letter;* Mike Moore at the late and very lamented *Mountain Gazette;* and Judy Greer and now Bob Gillen at *SKI Business.* All of them have expanded the range and definition of ski writing, and you better believe it takes a certain amount of guts to do that in the face of more than occasional opposition from the industry they cover.

Further, since most writers (especially this one) are also voracious readers, I'd like to acknowledge the insights and courage of two editors for whom I don't write, David Rowan of *Ski Area Management* and Don Metivier of *Ski Racing.* Even when I haven't agreed with them they've gotten my thinking processes working, which in some (but not many) ways is more important than a paycheck.

My next group of acknowledgments is to the writers themselves, at least to those who have pushed me outward and, I like to think, upward. Back in 1969 when I first joined this world of ski writing, the best of the breed, I felt, was John Jerome, then writing for *Skiing:* a man of skill, style, insight, and humor, he never lost his balance and perspective. His series "On Mountains," run in the late seventies, added something important to our insights and generated a book by the same name that, while not strictly (or even predominantly) about skiing, should be on every skier's "must" list.

When John, for personal reasons, quit ski writing a few years ago, his crown fell on the head of Charlie Meyers, the hard-hitting and knowledgeable columnist on the *Denver Post* as well as a perceptive writer for SKI, and *SKI Business.* (His only weakness is an inability to stop seeking the Harold Hirsch Award; most of us stop after one.) I read his work regularly because he's always on top of what's happening.

Charlie benefits from having a strong rival on the opposing paper, Mike Madigan of the *Rocky Mountain News,* much as I did when I wrote the ski column for the *Long Island Press* until it folded. Dave Knickerbocker, another former Hirsch winner and ex-president of Eastern Ski Writers who had the column in *Newsday,* always kept me on my toes, and on a few occasions we squared off; if nothing else, we kept Long Island's hordes of skiers entertained and informed. But unlike Charlie, I also had to contend with the incredible Archer Winsten of the *New York Post* and the irascible Jerry Kenney of the *New York Daily News* across the river. This kind of friendly warfare tends to improve the writing and perception of all the combatants and to cause more than a few ski-area marketing directors to complain, give us a break, huh? (Incidentally, I'd like to add a special acknowledgment to Archer, who, now in his mid-seventies, continues to write and ski with the zest of a teenager and gives all of us "kids" something to shoot for. In addition, he still writes the most perceptive movie reviews in New York.) Winsten, Knickerbocker, and Kenney give New York the kind of reportage all skiers should get, much as Meyers and Madigan do in Denver; I wish that level were more common.

Speaking of raising the level of the craft: Abby Rand has probably done more to improve the quality of ski-travel writing than everyone else combined (and no one can equal her in quantity). Although travel writing hardly generates a lot of respect among professional journalists—ski writers make it a point of honor not to be confused with *them*—Abby continues to seek the new way and to push us away from the cliché.

Even more challenging is writing about equipment, not only because the craft itself is more difficult than travel writing (take that on faith, because I do a lot of both) but because advertiser pressure is far more intense. Doug Pfeiffer, when he was editor-in-chief of *Skiing* in the sixties and early seventies, defined the scope of what it could be, but these days no one wends his way through this jungle better than Seth Masia. No one on SKI has a tougher job, and only his fellow professionals appreciate the snares and snakes in his path.

In all honesty, I don't think any of us yet does a Class A job of writing about instruction, and conversely I don't think there's a subject we've worried about more and worked on harder. I'd like to acknowledge the work of James Major and Olle Larsson in *World Cup Ski Technique* as pointing the way we have to go, but unfortunately, as is always the case, the pictures are better than the words. The old gag about early ski writing is that we had only two stories to tell—how to turn left, and how to turn right—but we still can't do either very well. Maybe this year. . . .

Probably the toughest type of ski writing to *sustain* is humor, but one guy who gives that a shot twenty times a year in a nationally syndicated column, "Ski Tips," is Craig Altschul. In the last year or so Craig has elevated

xviii/ *Preface and Acknowledgments*

the column from simple humor to satire, which in turn has elevated him to high on the list of targets among the ski-industry marketeers.

Equally difficult to maintain is the reputation as *the* enfant terrible, the perpetually outraged innocent decrying the fall from purity of the ski experience and doing it with a professional snarl and snap. Dick Dorworth staked out that role a decade ago—we were stable mates on *Gazette* then as we are on SKI now—and no one even challenges his preeminence anymore.

Two other front-line writers who are lesser known than they deserve are Paul Robbins, a first-rate journalist with range and insight, and Peter Miller, a strong stylist with a quirky and often biting bent as well as a real sensitivity to skiing and competition. (He's better known, however, as a photographer.)

At the other end of the spectrum is Bob Enzel, who edits and publishes *The White Book of Ski Areas,* an annual compendium of facts and crucial data that has become the bible for any serious writer covering the ski-area/resort sector. In addition, he's another of the increasingly large number of writers with a strong financial background who've drifted into ski writing the past several years, both presaging the future and reacting to the increasingly large number of marketing people with MBAs who've also drifted into the ski business of late. I believe the applicable cliché is send a thief to catch a thief. . . . The fact is, the increasing sophistication of management within the ski industry demands a parallel professionalism among the writers who cover it, and as always, supply follows demand, art follows life

For all that, ski writing didn't suddenly emerge full grown in the late sixties and seventies. Sure, the improvement in it in just the past five years or so has been almost revolutionary; today's routinely competent columnist would have been a star, a hero, in 1972. And sure, many of the pioneers were unabashed boosters of the sport rather than reporters; often, in the changeover period 1970–75, they took offense at the consumer approach some of us newcomers preferred—sometimes as much offense as the industry people themselves. But let's not forget that they broke the ground for our craft.

Chief among these pioneers was the late and great Lowell Thomas; I can add nothing meaningful to his legend. But a bare half-step behind him were such writers as John Jay, Hal Burton, Bill Berry (no relation), Frank Elkins, and Mike Strauss. Among the forerunners of the current approach are Mort Lund and John Henry Auran, both of whom are still very active on SKI and *Skiing* respectively, and Bill Tanler, who probably leads the league in innovation. The earliest prickly pears among the newspaper columnists were Jay Hanlon, Burt Sims, Monty Montgomery, and, of course, Archer Winsten.

Actually, another group of journalists really inaugurated the consumer approach: the broadcasters who fought for honest reports about ski conditions, often at some cost in terms of sponsors and good relations. The all-time leader here, without challenge, is Roxy Rothafel; the best of the new breed is John Hamilton. The ultimate accolade for Roxy is that thanks to his decades-long battle the war has been won: listeners today can get a reasonably honest account.

So, to the degree that all of these writers have led and/or joined the fight to enlarge, refine, redefine, and expand the scope and quality of ski writing, I acknowledge my debt—and the debt of all skiers.

But writers do not live by sweat and skiing alone; we have to rely on responsible news sources within the industry to keep us apprised of "what's comin' down" in many sectors. The group that keeps us informed is largely and generically referred to as "marketing," although public/press relations would be a more accurate description.

Much like ski writing itself, "marketing" has evolved and improved significantly in the past decade and the pattern is accelerating. Initially, the promoters and developers did their own wheelin' and dealin' to a responsive, boosterish press corps, but once that began to vanish so did the pure hucksters. Even the group that would still prefer to "tell it like they wish it was" has gotten the message that one short-term "win" equals a long-term loss and today many—albeit still a minority—of the marketing/PR people "tell it as it is."

My first acknowledgment in this arena goes to the National Ski Areas Association. Since Cal Conniff took control of it, the NSAA has not only been consistently responsive to writers' queries but, more important, has often taken the lead, under press aide Kathe Dillmann, in pushing both financial and technical coverage . . . in a sense, forcing some of the writers to ask the questions they should have thought of by themselves. The NSAA conventions, and virtually all committee meetings, have aggressively been opened to press coverage, and the association compiles and releases data that, like that of the auto industry, don't always reveal skiing in a positive light (unless, as many of us feel, honesty is the most positive light). This, in turn, has prompted many area operators to talk about all aspects of skiing, warts and all.

In addition, the resort sector has produced, over the last twenty years, three marketeers who charted the proper route and defined what a good marketing director is and does: Bob Parker, Paul Pepe, and Foster Chandler, as different as they can be from each other in approach and personality.

No one has ever had a better intuitive sense of the needs of both skiers and writers than Parker—and no one sensed more quickly when those needs began to change. Possibly even more than Pete Seibert himself, Parker "created" Vail and, over the years, has solved more problems than the kid who wins the math medal. He was also the first to be willing to tip writers to impending problems, and he could present his side of the issue without trying to preempt the writer's objectivity—to the degree that he'd often tell you who was the best spokesman for the other side. When he was "kicked upstairs" to become senior vice-president of operations, Vail had to hire no fewer than *three* marketing directors to replace him. Parker also has no hesitation in crossing pens with any writer with whom he disagrees, and at different times he's challenged many of us in print—without, however, disturbing the underlying relationship, no mean feat. He's the only marketing director ever to receive the U.S. Ski Writers' prestigious Golden Quill Award. His handling of the fatal gondola crash and the battle for Beaver Creek stand as models in the industry.

Despite that, no one has defined better how to work with writers than has Paul Pepe. Not in the least obsequious—I once described him as the "cigar-smoking Godfather of Hunter Mountain"—he *knows* writers, because he studies our work and understands which of us will be most responsive to a certain type of story, and he doles out "exclusives" with a mastery some in Washington should learn to emulate. "Worst" of all, in thirteen years of close dealings with him I've never caught him out on a tough question.

About as far in the opposite direction as you can get is Foster Chandler, whose personal dealings with most writers vary from nil to negative but whose sense of marketing strategy is unsurpassed: not for nothing did Killington and Mount Snow generate 1.2 million skiers in 1981–82. Reclusive where Parker is open and Pepe gregarious, Chandler has the unerring instinct for putting together the programs that no responsible writer can avoid covering. He'll offer shrewd analysis when you ask the right question, but he definitely lacks the Pepe-Parker tact when you ask the wrong ones.

Coming up quickly to join that select company is Jerry Jones, who ramrods the Keystone/A-Basin program and could well challenge Parker as king of the Rockies. Almost as acerbic as Chandler, he also has an excellent sense of program and of what his team can and can't do. He has no hesitation in pointing out the strengths and weaknesses of his competition, and he's definitely not one to "go along with the gang" if he thinks the others are wrong; as a result, Keystone/A-Basin posted a huge increase in 1981–82 when virtually all other major resorts in the Rockies struggled (and often failed) to stay even against their best previous season. Also as a result, Jones is not always very popular with his fellow marketing directors in Colorado, which doesn't bother him at all.

Among the leaders of the newer breed (the potential challengers, if you prefer) are Bruce McCloy of Mount Snow, Rick Owen of Loon, Bob Kunkel of Winter Park, the Bob Schaeffer–Chan Weller team at Sugarbush, Raivo Puusamp of Utah, Tom Britz of Indianhead, Kent Myers at Steamboat, Kathy DeGree at Mount Bachelor, and Scott Van Pelt at Stowe. Also among them, although (temporarily, I hope) out of the ski-area business, are Bob Foster, Dan O'Connor, Garry Mitchell, Gene McMasters, and Gary Andrus.

The picture is not quite so rosy on the equipment front. Unlike NSAA, Ski Industries America has remained a closed-door operation even though its current (1981–83) president, Bob Tarrant of Aris Gloves, has worked hard to change this. What makes this more than an intramural problem is the fact that so few writers (maybe a dozen) cover the equipment scene, while virtually all three-hundred-plus ski writers do a credible job in travel and resort coverage and many do a decent job with competition. While at first this seems to speak poorly of most writers' abilities to seek out stories for themselves, the fact is that writing about equipment demands a lot of technical knowledge that only a few writers have the time, inclination, and educational background to learn. A similar problem on the area side would be snowmaking, but on this topic NSAA has done an excellent job of education, which in turn has generated many informative articles and columns that benefit readers of all media. In contrast, equipment coverage is centralized in a few magazines. Although cooperation at this level is far better (and improving) under Executive Director Dave Ingemie than it had been under his predecessor, a move toward wider communication with the press is necessary.

Fortunately, a few companies have seen the need to innovate in this educational process. The first was Salomon, under Carol Cone, who convinced several writers that there were, indeed, good stories about equipment to be written. Since then, the Head-Tyrolia-Raichle group has also moved aggressively into this theater under Bob Mignone, who will get added support now that John Brandt has signed on to handle PR. This trio is currently doing the type of pioneering work that Parker-Pepe-Chandler were doing in the sixties and early seventies, which maybe says it all. Among the others pushing to meet writers' needs here are Jean-François Lanvers, now with

Lange after nearly a decade with Look; Rick Howell at Geze-Elan; and Keith d'Entremont of Fischer-Dynafit.

So much for the acknowledgments. No writer lives in a vacuum, and all of these people—in different ways at different times—have helped me research and write this book, enjoy this sport, and understand that I am far from the only person with strong feelings about what we do and what we are.

And so, to blazes with Swiss ecologists (and, for that matter, many of the American ones as well). The only thing worse than strong feelings, pro or con, is no feelings at all.

Preface to the Second Edition

Until 1966, no comprehensive ski book—one encompassing every facet of the sport, including its history, equipment, resorts, instruction, and competition—had been published in America. In that year, the Editors of SKI Magazine collaborated with Charles Scribner's Sons to produce the first edition of *America's Ski Book*. The book was an unequivocal success. The editors were able to distill in its pages all of the knowledge of the sport acquired in publishing the oldest ski publication in America.

SKI Magazine started up in 1936. Most observers now agree that this was the starting era of modern alpine skiing in America. The first chair lifts were erected, and skiers began to adopt the modern form of parallel skiing. The first downhill and slalom events were included in the 1936 Winter Olympics. Since then, the sport of skiing has grown to the point where it now numbers almost 4 million participants and more than a thousand lift and tow-served areas in North America.

The second edition of the *America's Ski Book*—seven years after the first appeared—is long overdue. In some respects, this is almost totally a new book. With the exception of most chapter headings, basic advice, and historical sections which appeared in the original edition, almost every other part of the book has been revised. It is not surprising. Skiing is perhaps the most rapidly changing sport in the world. In 1966, for example, the following did not exist, except mostly on the drawing boards: wet-wrap fiberglass skis, plastic boots, highback and custom foam fitting of boots, antifriction devices for bindings, and cracked edges. The words *avalement, GLM,* and *hotdog* were unknown. The resorts of Snowmass, Kirkwood, Alpental, Copper Mountain, Breckenridge, Keystone, Waterville Valley and La Plagne did not exist. An American male skier had yet to win a gold medal in world championship skiing. All that has changed. And it is presented in this book.

The original writing for *America's Ski Book* was done by John Henry Auran, former editor of SKI and presently an editor at *Skiing* magazine. Many of his words, and much of his style and thought, remain from the first edition. The revised second edition has been prepared by John Fry, the present editor-in-chief of SKI Magazine. Fry is a prolific writer on the sport. In addition, he is credited with developing the idea for NASTAR, the National Standard Ski Race, now run at some eighty areas across the United States. Under his editorship since 1964, the magazine has pioneered the Nations Cup, introduced avalement to Americans for the first time, and coined the term *GLM* to describe short-ski teaching.

The expertise in this book would not have been possible without the outstanding technical authorities who contribute to SKI and to the dedicated photographers and artists who have created the graphics of the sport. Special thanks are due to Michael Brady, SKI's Nordic correspondent in Oslo, who edited the sections dealing with cross-country skiing and who, with Jakob Vaage, Director of the Ski Museum at Holmenkollen, Norway, provided the chapters dealing with the very early history of the sport. Much of the technical thinking about ski instruction which appears in the second edition arises out of the many contributions made by Georges Joubert to SKI Magazine over the years. Thanks also are due to SKI's travel editor, Abby Rand (herself the author of two books of ski travel) for helping with the section "Where to Ski"; to John Perryman, technical consultant to SKI, for his contributions to the section of "Equipment"; to Henry Tauber, former U.S. Women's Coach, for checking Appendix F; and to Pat Doran, SKI's fashion editor, for checking the chapter on "Apparel."

The Editors of SKI Magazine

Introduction and Symposium: The Future of American Skiing

What will skiing be like ten years from now?

I suppose that's a funny way to begin this book, but skiing—as a pastime, business, and way of life—has changed so much these past ten years. And it will probably change even more in the next ten. The past, increasingly, isn't even a prologue. It borders on the irrelevant.

Nothing drove that truth home harder than a trip I took a week before Thanksgiving in 1980. On a beautiful Saturday (following a heavy early season snowfall that week), my son Greg and I tossed the gear into the hatchback (skiracks waste gas) and rolled up the New York Thruway to the Catskills and Hunter Mountain. The area, which can justify its claim as "the Snowmaking Capitol of the World," had combined the production of its armada of snow guns with a foot of natural snow to keep 3,200 people busy skiing all day— proof that despite the underlying economic and energy malaise skiers would ski. Yet as I drove home that night I couldn't help but put things into perspective:

• Expert snowmaking had in the East become routine rather than the emerging gee-whiz craft form it had been in 1973. Approximately ten areas were open and functioning efficiently that pre-Thanksgiving weekend in 1980, and the five-month ski season, mid-November through mid-April, had become commonplace. Two major Vermont resorts, Killington and Sugarbush, had pushed out to a seven-month season, mid-October to mid-May, with others following this lead as the decade matured: Mount Snow hit a six-month season in 1981–82 and ran third just in Vermont! In Oregon, Mount Hood runs a twelve-month season.

    •   But the price for this performance is high. Snowmaking takes large amounts of energy and trained manpower—it's both capital- and labor-intensive—and the cash has to be committed long before the first day-ticket revenue rolls in. The snow can also vanish quickly in a late-fall thaw—money literally poured down the drain—or be polished down to an icy sheen by a heavy rain and/or two days of high skier traffic, after which the expensive grooming equipment comes rolling out. Because today's successful area operator is a businessman first and an evangelist a distant second (if at all) and has an obsessive desire to see a profit come May and a positive cash flow come Christmas, this does wondrous things to the price of a day ticket.

    •   Thus, the $20 lift ticket emerged for 1980–81, at Stratton, Vermont, and at Jackson Hole, Wyoming (if you use the tram), and $18 and $19 were common. At $15, Hunter was probably the most underpriced ticket among major areas in the region, yet even there, tickets for dad and son cost $25. (Now the $25 lift ticket for *one* skier is on the horizon, and Hunter, at $19, is still at the low end of the price range in the East. Food ate up another $10 (although we usually resort to brownbagging when all four of us go skiing).

    •   Gas and tolls devoured another $20, which did not include any amortization factor for new wheels and snow tires and wear-and-tear on the machine.

    •   Equipment cost each of us $7.50 a day. Not rentals; just amortization of my hardware at list price—$240 for skis at 50 days ($5 a day), $240 for boots at 150 days ($1.50 a day), and $135 for bindings at 150 days ($1 a day), not to mention poles and goggles and the like. (Although children's and junior equipment costs less, it survives about half as long.) Clothing is harder to amortize because we all wear much of it for nonskiing uses and would probably buy something to serve the same purpose, but $5 a day is a reasonable estimate. (By 1982–83, those list prices had risen to $750 and the per diem to $9.)

The day therefore cost $80—without dinner and with a fairly short roundtrip. You crank that up to a weekend in Vermont—lodging and food included—and you're well in the $250 range for two people. You do that ten weekends a year and you've committed a fair amount of money to skiing. And these costs will do nothing but increase in the next eight years.

Yet on balance, skiing remains an inexpensive *sport*: A skier logging a full nine-to-four day even at $20 is spending less than $3 an hour, which is below minimum wage and usually produces a rather low return on investment for resort owners—well below that of certificates of deposit or money-market funds and much less than that from speculative or high-risk investments. The only time the owners make a real profit is when they sell out, and the truth is that most of them don't want to.

But owners are being forced to sell, for a multitude of complex reasons we'll discuss in Chapter 5, and the new owners are big corporations like 20th Century-Fox that have very little emotional or historical reason to try to hold the line on prices. This, combined with the U.S. Forest Service's movement toward deregulation of lift-ticket prices (the USFS is steward of the land on which virtually all major resorts in the Rockies and Sierra are located and has significant control over pricing and operations because it issues restricted permits to use the national forests), should bring an escalation in the cost of skiing.

Furthermore, the leveling effects of supply and demand don't apply because the environmental movement of the early seventies has persisted in throttling new development and severely limiting supply. Who then knows where ticket prices will be in the next ten years? We're already conceding that the $30 ticket "isn't too far away."

Yet, as the perceptive among you caught immediately, the lift ticket isn't the leading cost factor in a day or weekend—and even less so in a ski vacation. One person driving alone will spend more for gas than for a lift ticket; two will roughly break even when you include amortization and service on the car (which we discuss in Chapter 20). Lodging, whether you own or rent your own house or take a room at the inn (see Chapter 12), will be higher by far than a season pass or a weekend of day tickets. And even though equipment amortizes at less per diem than the ticket, it demands a high front-end commitment since very few ski shops let you pay it off at $7.50 a day—and even in that figure is the assumption that you ski frequently and take care of your hardware (which itself adds to the cost).

Since these costs are generally escalating faster than the price of a lift ticket, the ratios will probably increase. In short, the *cost* of skiing isn't merely the *price* of skiing, and in the final analysis it doesn't really matter. You and I have to think in terms of out-of-pocket expenses or the bottom line, which will continue to soar.

And these increasing costs will no doubt change the face of skiing. Since no one person can predict the future no matter how smoothly he says the sooth,

I've asked some of the "best minds of our generation" to offer their projections, which are included in the symposium on "The Future of American Skiing" that follows this introduction. If nothing else, it should define the parameters.

What makes this trend all the more amazing is—according to a series of well-financed, well-documented, and well-publicized studies—that this sport, at this price level, is attracting 12 million Americans every year. True, some of us—in intramural battles in the trade press—have disputed that figure on technical grounds far beyond the scope of interest of a recreational skier, but I've long suspected that the real cause for doubt is how so many people can afford to go skiing.

It's a puzzle that remains unsolved, because many people do ski and, more to the point, they tend to ski at the most expensive areas and resorts; only the small, low-priced areas lack adequate volume. Typically, if you put two areas close to each other and one charges more for a better experience but the other has totally adequate facilities, the former will get the business. Stratton bumped its price to $20 for the 1980–81 season without so much as a by-your-leave, and it did more business than the prior season; whereas areas nearby that charged $10 to $15 waited in vain for skiers. Until it all caught up with them with a thud in 1981–82, following the previous year's drought and poor marketing during the summer of '81, resorts in Colorado charging $100 a day *and up* had to continue to build condominiums at boom-town speed to handle the mobs pleading for entry. Those condos, with prices ranging from $150 to $400 per square foot, were "sold" before the first shovel was turned. Airlines stopped offering sizable midweek skier discounts because they didn't have to. Skiers kept coming at any price, tolerating the foul-ups at the incredibly inefficient Stapleton Airport in Denver, battling for exorbitantly overpriced rental cars, pumping high-priced gas into those guzzlers, fighting the snow and ice over the passes and through the tunnels, snarling at the mess at the lodging offices (if they were even open), wrestling with bulky equipment, and stocking up on overpriced breakfast/lunch food.

Why? Beats me. After all my years of involvement in this weird pastime, I can only conclude we're all nutty. When I think of the creative energies, the brainpower, the money, and the effort that have been pumped into something as essentially useless as skiing—a devotion to yo-yoing up and down a mountain on uncomfortable chairs and unpredictable skis, often battered by weather and conditions that a polar bear is smart enough to avoid—I'm at a loss to explain it, to justify it, and to defend it.

So I won't.

All I can say is that when you're standing on top of a ridge, battered by sleet and a minus-40 windchill, goggles and glasses so fogged you can't see where the crud becomes ice or where the snow groomer left golfballs and frozen tracks—when you do that and yell "Let's go for it," and the three other idiots with you go flying off that ridge with equally big grins, well, then you know the answer. It isn't explicable or justifiable or defendable, but it's the answer.

And we haven't even discussed new light powder at 20 degrees under a sunny, cloudless sky. Why bother?

Now let's give the other experts their shot.

THE FUTURE OF AMERICAN SKIING

Technology. That dastardly influence on all of us. It will seriously affect the future of American skiing. Bet on it. Count on it. But don't try to understand it.

You think today's skiing technology is advanced? Hogwash (as they say in places where hogs are still washed). Look how long it took for a fellow with a belly bigger than mine to attach a cable to his bindings so they'd snap into place after he fell, thus saving future generations from the effort of bending down. That is the seriousness level of modern ski technology.

Tomorrow (by the year 2125), look for a "Snow-Processing Center" to be marketed by IBM, Xerox, or Exxon (choose one).

You'll sit on your living-room sofa and push a button on your home computer unit. This will automatically plug you into your regional Snow-Processing Center.

The programming will be highly sophisticated. The computer will speak to you in dulcet bleeps: "Stay home today, dummy, it's raining . . ." "Deep powder awaits you, fella. Get off your rear end."

On your personal computer screen, you will be able to accomplish impossible tasks. For example: Wake up early in the morning as usual and push a button. Your favorite ski mountain comes into view. There's Jane Pauley with the lift-line report. (OK, so by now maybe it's her daughter.) You don't like the looks of the line, and you program the computer carefully so that at exactly the time you arrive on the mountain (10 A.M.) the entire picture is erased. Poof. No more lift lines.

The biggest technological advance of all will arrive sometime during the twenty-first century. Remember the old saw about how America was built by men who could move mountains? Well, technology will become so advanced in the future that men will actually do it. They'll bring the mountains to us.

Thus, no more snow tires. What's futurism for if it can't be helpful?

—Craig A. Altschul
Writer of the nationally
syndicated "Ski Tips"
column and president,
Eastern Ski Writers
Association

Because America is endowed with many of the finest ski mountains in the world, with snowfall that is usually abundant and with a free enterprise system that allows us to be innovative, creative, and sensitive to change, the future of American skiing will always remain bright.

The dynamic appeal that the sport has for people of all ages is so great that it helps ensure a bright future for skiing. In a society such as ours that is often complex and fast paced, there is no better tonic than to be high atop a mountain on a crisp winter morning amid the beauty of nature enjoying the exhilaration, challenge, and excitement of a run down the mountain. It's a good feeling when your only care in the world is where to carve your next turn. Everyone needs this feeling now and then, and skiing can offer it like no other sport.

Indeed we do have some problems in the ski industry today, but I'm confident that eventually they will be solved. The ski industry has the ability to adjust to change, if indeed change is desired by skiers. We have come a long way in the past forty years, developing close to 700 ski facilities in thirty-seven states, thus bringing the sport of skiing within reach of millions of people. No where in the world is the opportunity to ski so readily available to so many people.

Just as we have met past challenges in order to bring skiing in America to where it is today, we will meet the challenges of the future and, in so doing, move the sport and the industry to an even higher plateau of enjoyment and excellence.

—Cal Conniff
Executive Director,
National Ski Areas
Association

After much pondering and frustration (and a certain amount of cursing), I'll have to admit that I have no predictions, wise thoughts, or even serious ideas about the future of American skiing. I do, however, have something to say about the present of American skiing and some factors that will undoubtedly help shape the industry in the future.

As most anyone who's been skiing lately will recognize, skiers are no longer a homogeneous group. It used to be that you could say the word *skier* and everyone got a fairly similar picture of cap, goggles, parka, and so on in their minds. That's no longer true. Now you say *skier* and what do you see? A kid in blue jeans and a tattered parka? An elegant lady in a fur-trimmed parka, with sparkling capped teeth and monogrammed sunglasses? Or some muscle-bound fanatic scaling an impossible cliff for the sheer fun of catching untracked powder on the way down?

The point is: We no longer have one reasonably similar class of skiers—but three classes of skiers: the masses, the exclusives, and the crazies.

The ski areas that will fare best in the future have already begun to recognize—and market to—these separate sources of ski income.

The masses, of course, are where most of us belong. These are the hordes of reasonably well off but not wealthy skiers who spend a bundle on a ski vacation once a year and the rest of the time tend to patronize lower-priced local ski areas or areas offering discount programs. Naturally I'm somewhat biased in this direction, but I'd bet that for most ski areas these will continue to be the bread-and-butter skiers and that in the future there will be an increasing number of discount programs aimed at luring the masses to the slopes.

The exclusives, as their name suggests, are the really wealthy folks, the people who show up in $1,000 outfits and turn ski-shop clerks into instant charm-school graduates. Now the exclusives, being a somewhat inbred group, don't like to mix much with the masses, and so large parts of the ski industry are breaking off to cater to, and make their living from, the exclusives. Anyone doubting the place of exclusives in American skiing had better look at the plans for Beaver Creek in Colorado—an unabashed "exclusives" setup. Or consider the many heli-skiing operators who during the past several years have learned to love—and thrive on—the exclusive skier.

Finally we have the crazies—a growing group that has yet to earn its own place in the marketing plans of the American ski industry. The crazies, as their name suggests, are those skiers who will ski anywhere, anytime, on just about anything. They're the folks you see tracking off into the wilderness with Ramer boots and bindings; the impossibly healthy people who climb up mountains for the sheer glory of skiing down; the ski fanatics who spend most, if not all, of their disposable income on skiing. The crazies are hard to deal with; they include so many different types of people. But if I had to make one prediction about the future of American skiing it would be this: Someday, somebody will develop a marketing program especially for the crazies. And that somebody will open a whole new profit center for the ski industry.

So what does it all mean? Simply that skiing is becoming big business— and, like most big businesses, it's also becoming fragmented. And in the not-too-distant future, we can all look forward to Madison Avenue types "positioning" us to fit into the fragments that fit into the industry that used to be so simple.

> —Evie DiSante
> Editor, *Skier's*
> *Advocate*

Skiing has a great future. Give us a few years of excellent snow through-out the United States, and IBM will want to diversify into the growing sport of skiing. But with every poor year of snow, more and more mom-and-pop operations are knocked out of business. It's not just the lack of income for one year but the tremendous overhead of insurance, debt service, and upkeep. Once out, the chances of a return to ski-area use are poor.

Even though each poor year of ski weather causes a decrease in the number of ski areas, numbers here are as deceiving as saying that in 1928 there were sixty-four automobile manufacturers and today we have only four. The picture is still focusing. The bigger areas are getting larger, and capacity continues to increase. Evidence Vail, Keystone, Aspen, Sugarbush, Boyne USA, Stratton, and Killington, which among them can account for eighteen or nineteen areas, most of which are of significant size.

Skiers are coming despite the cost increases in lift tickets. After all, what hasn't increased in our economy, and why should skiing be different? Skiers are getting more for their dollars—slopes are groomed by $100,000 machines; the rope tow has been replaced by sophisticated $250,000 (and up) chair lifts; day lodges are superb and cater to après-ski activities and have little innovations like indoor plumbing. (Oh, you think this was always indoors for skiers!?!)

Faults aside, the ski industry is dedicated to its sport. It is a determined industry that will continue to promote and expand even though hindered by conservationists and cost considerations. The big may get bigger, smaller areas may fall by the wayside, costs will certainly increase—but skiers will continue to come.

Remember, very few industries depend on the weather as much as skiing does. The sport needs snow for its image—not contrived but real. Skiers need snow, lots of snow, and whatever the skier count is—6 or 14 million—a few good snow years will make it seem like 16 to 40 million. Give us snow and the IBM's of this world will wonder why they haven't discovered this beautiful (and lucrative) industry earlier.

—Robert Enzel
Publisher,
White Book
of Ski Areas

The author of this book—a talented, incisive, first-rate ski journalist (OK, Bill, now do I get paid?)—asked me to do a little crystal-ball gazing on the ski sport. Now Bill can make some pretty decent ski turns, particularly those unintentional ones, but he certainly does not have a grasp on things when he asks me to look into the future. Because the future, no matter how we try to screw it up, will always be a surprise, and I'm all for that. What I mean is if skiing were to be so bloody predictable, we wouldn't be into it in the first place, right?

How about those things that will never change?

- Pay toilets in the base lodge and all you have is a $20 bill.
- "Meet you at Chair Two at three? I thought you said meet you at Chair Three at two!" (I can't claim that one, it's Warren Miller's.)
- 300 miles by car into ski country and you forget your boots.
- You bring some great ski films to the ski house only to learn that the projector bulb is burned out.
- An icy day on the touring tracks—and all you brought was klister.
- You're facing an elevator shaft of icy crust and your teenage son, who borrowed your skis last weekend, tells you that, uh, he blew out an edge.
- It's a great spring-skiing day and you're wearing a down-filled one-piece powder suit.
- Your lift partner, discovering that you are the editor of a ski magazine, tells you about his and his wife's first experience on skis and wonders "Now don't you think there's a dandy story there?"
- Brownbagging lunch for four adults and seven kids and you're the only one with a backpack.
- Your lift partner, discovering that you are the editor of a ski magazine, tells you that you must meet his hot skiing buddy, who is certainly

worth a profile in SKI. We find him in the patrol shack, his leg being set.

Then there are those Murphy maxims (compiled by Murphologist Arthur Bloch) about situations that will always prey on skiers, which I will take the license of adapting to our beloved sport here.

- The car that passes you on the access road is the one that gets the last area parking space.
- The challenge of the trails your friends will choose will vary inversely with the intensity of your hangover.
- To err is human; to really foul things up requires a lodging-reservations computer.
- Teamwork, when packing for a ski vacation, is essential. It allows you to blame someone else.
- In any ski house, there will always be one person who knows what is going on. This person must be replaced.

—Dick Needham
Editor, SKI Magazine

After rocky going through recent seasons of little or no snow in many parts of the United States, who could blame any skier for seeking out the comfort of a climate-controlled bowling alley? But skiing is a game played out of doors and, as frustrating as poor snow seasons might be, it's all part of the experience and agony. The hardy will continue to enjoy the challenge of a sport that gives us a taste of risk.

Improved snowmaking techniques and careful preservation of the crop will help create more potential skiing in the future under even marginal conditions. The cost of ski equipment will continue to climb, but the value received for the dollars spent will also improve. The strongest manufacturers of ski equipment have already invested heavily in more sophisticated production equipment capable of turning out better-performing and higher-quality gear.

Skiing never has been, at least since the exit of the rope tow, an inexpensive sport. It's unlikely to ever become a mass-participant sport. The trend may be for skiers to ski less frequently but to seek out better-quality ski experiences. The complete resort with full resort facilities will be the vacation choice of the typical skier who is willing to pay more, ski less, and hope to enjoy the sport more.

Although the cooperation of nature to provide ample natural snow and temperatures necessary to create artificial snow will continue to be the key to the health of our ski future, the costs of transportation and the uncertain availability of unlimited supplies of fuel will also encourage skiers to seek out skiing closer to home. The trip to Europe or to another part of the country will be reserved as a very special occasion.

—Bill Tanler
Senior Editor
and creator,
*The Ski
Industry
Letter*

Skiing started in this country as a two-pronged pastime of nostalgic Scandinavians and the idle-rich axis between Sun Valley and St. Moritz. Dartmouth undergrads put their toe in the door. It continued as a hype of the railroads, then the buses, and exploded into mass participation because individuals and families had discovered its magic.

Now, as inflation gets in its solar-plexus blow to the pocketbook while skiing itself has experienced the elephantiasis of skis, boots, clothing, release bindings, gloves, goggles, socks, duofold underwear, and extras totaling in the $1,000 bracket—while the poor customer is sold trips to Europe and the West in terms of Paradise Available (only another $1,000)—some turn hopefully to cross-country, and some, with families or incomes less than six figures, seek alternative sports like TV-watching, jogging, and ice-skating.

Eastern cross-country drop-intos find themselves in the dead-ends of no snow, or too much ice, or trails groomed at the cost of a daily fee.

The beginnings of a solution are glimpsed in half-day reduced lift tickets, pointing the way to two-hour or quarter-day tickets. Style mavericks can join the blue jeans set, and those who refuse to follow the crowd can seek out little-known, cheaper, local areas.

It is, of course, quite unthinkable for a skier to give up the sport completely. The real dilemma is the choice between one shoot-the-works winter vacation and weekly one-day or two-day, one-night safaris. Carrying your own lunches, sharing the rides, and hitting small areas for half-days can stretch your shrinking dollar. The times call for stern measures. Let them eat peanut butter on health-food bread.

—Archer Winsten
Ski columnist,
New York Post

The Great North American
SKI BOOK

PART ONE

THE STORY
OF SKIING

Introduction

I've always viewed the development of the sport, industry, and way of life called American skiing as a three-period sequence:

- The Pioneer Period, running from the thirties to the beginning of World War II.
- The Golden Age, running from 1945 to 1969.
- Environmental Era, running from 1969 through the present.

Now, the breakpoint between the latter pair wasn't selected just because I happened to join SKI Magazine that fall. Rather, it was a funny coincidence (or "karma," if you prefer). I'd spent the prior twelve years in "hard-news journalism," a sequence of daily newspapers and newsmagazines, and had more than my share fold along the way (including the *New York Herald Tribune*). When the last one—a newsmagazine covering the education field—went down the tube abruptly one Friday afternoon, I felt I'd earned a year off from serious journalism. When I heard the number two slot was open on SKI, I decided that was the ticket: play for a year, skiing free and getting the best lessons "on the house," even though it meant taking a rather sizable cut in pay.

Well, I hadn't warmed the chair yet when the Mineral King case erupted in California, and I still remember John Fry walking in and saying, "You're a lawyer, do you understand this environmentalism stuff?" Since no lawyer—

much less one from Yale—would ever admit not knowing everything about everything, I said, "Sure," and one way or another I've been covering the hard news of skiing ever since.

Thus, Mineral King, the breakpoint in the history of the development and growth of skiing, just happened to occur that first week I was on the job, and so much for play (although my wife tends to disagree).

The Many Joys of the Skier

*He saw the pine grove behind and below him, on his right,
turned again toward it, and with a quick descent reached the
laden trees; they stood in a wedge-shaped group, a vanguard
thrust out from the mist-screened forests above. He rested
beneath their bows and smoked a cigarette. The unnatural still,
the monstrous solitude, still oppressed his spirit; yet he felt
proud to have conquered them, brave in the pride of having
been measured to the height of surroundings such as these.*

The Magic Mountain, THOMAS MANN

Enough Americans have become intrigued with skiing in the last twenty years
to make it this country's most popular winter sport. From a few thousand
pioneering devotees before World War II, the sport has grown to where it now
can count over twelve million enthusiasts in its ranks. And their number grows
by as much as 10 percent every year (although this volume dropped by 4
percent in 1980 and flattened in 1981).

These figures are cited not to demonstrate what an impressive number of
skiers there are but as evidence of the powerful appeal of this seemingly simple
sport. Although earlier generations preferred to stick by their fireplaces during
the winter, Americans have discovered, through skiing, a whole new world—a

world once thought frigidly forbidding but now, thanks to skis, at least as enjoyable as the playgrounds of the more temperate seasons.

"It's as if sunspots had altered the climate," skier-philosopher James Laughlin once wrote on the startling growth of skiing. "Winter suddenly became a different season—as exciting as summer—in which we could be outdoors having fun on weekends and on vacations."

There is no question that at least part of skiing's appeal lies in the test it provides for man against nature. Even as we accumulate more leisure time and become ever more insulated against the vagaries of wind, sun, and storm, we seem to need a certain amount of assurance that we can still prevail without the conveniences provided for us by twentieth-century technology.

The need to be outdoors—whatever its overtones of play—is no small matter. Volumes have been written on the benefits of outdoor recreation, a great deal of which was summed up by the Outdoor Recreation Resources Review Commission, the so-called Rockefeller Commission, in its final report to the President:

"Outdoor activity, whether undertaken lightly or with serious intent . . . is essentially a 'renewing' experience . . . The fact that we live in a world that moves crisis by crisis does not make a growing interest in outdoor activities frivolous . . ."

Skiing provides the "renewing" experience in a special way. As a participant in one of a limited number of winter outdoor activities, the skier does not have to wait until spring or summer to "renew" him or herself. Whether the skier tries a few runs on the weekend at a local ski area, takes a vacation at a major ski resort, or goes on a ski tour in the wilderness, skis provide a freedom in the snow-covered outdoors that no other activity can match. And with its possibilities of downhill speed, skiing becomes an experience of unusual exhilaration.

Reinforcing this exhilaration is the powerful appeal of the mountains. They can be rolling midwestern hills or the craggy peaks of the Rockies or the Alps. Snow endows them with a simple beauty few can resist. The reaction of the skier may run from the lyrical to the laconic, but mountain beauty is never dismissed. The fact that skiers are never mere onlookers at scenery but actually come into meaningful contact with the mountains heightens their perception and stimulates their appreciation of what they see.

This very perception that skiers so quickly cultivate also forces them to see the mountains as a challenge to their skill, as an obstacle to overcome, and, particularly in the high mountains, as a possible threat to their survival.

Probing this strange paradox in an article on cross-country racing, SKI Magazine once noted that "it is one of the ironies of modern civilization that

man, in order to remain man, must of necessity make a sport of what used to be of necessity to his survival. The more the products of his genius smooth his path, the more he feels he should walk, should exercise, should run to keep alive those instincts and muscles which enabled him to reach his state of ease in the first place."

That we should get pleasure and satisfaction out of skiing probably defies wholly rational explanation. But Dr. Ernest Dichter, the motivational researcher who originated the term "survival sports" for outdoor activities such as skiing, mountain climbing, sailing, and skin diving, says that the benefit of skiing is that it puts the participant on his mettle. And while we are long removed from the Lapland peasant who had to ski to get from place to place, or to hunt, simply to stay alive, nevertheless "There is a feeling of immediate achievement. At a certain point skiing is self-rewarding. You enjoy it while you are doing it. You know how well you did it. And you don't have to wait for anybody to tell you."

There is no doubt that the challenges of skiing and the feelings of achievement they make possible are tremendously powerful attractions.

The challenges are for all practical purposes unlimited. There are trails and slopes of almost every gradation and with great variations in length, width, steepness, and terrain configurations. It is nearly impossible to make the same run twice on the same trail or even on something as confining as a slalom course. Although most ski terrain seems solid enough, it is constantly being altered by wind, sun, and snow and, above all, by the skiers themselves.

Whatever the challenges of any one area, there is ever greater variety in the challenges of the more than one thousand ski areas in the United States and Canada, and beyond them the areas of Europe, Japan, Australia, New Zealand, and South America. And in addition to the skiing to be found in organized areas, there is the endless terrain open to those willing to dispense with lifts and to tour in the forests or in the high mountains.

It is hardly necessary to seek the challenges of skiing on so grandiose a scale. The average skier finds it challenge enough simply to move through the ranks from raw novice, through intermediate, to expert. The technical feat of mastering the variations of parallel skiing under a wide variety of conditions can in itself be a fairly sizable goal. It is one of the charms of skiing that one does not have to be an absolute master to enjoy the sport. Providing the skier is reasonably adept at a few basic fundamentals, there is no reason why he or she cannot experience most of the sensations of the expert.

It is not uncommon to find many pursuing the sport well into their sixties, and beyond. The popular 70-plus Club now numbers several hundred

members. Even without the excitement generated through the clash of competition, skiing simply refuses to get dull.

Underlying the challenges is the need for personal courage, and this applies on all levels of skill. The expert, skiing so flawlessly down a difficult trail, may seem fearless. But one has only to talk to a racer to realize that he is quite conscious of the risks involved. His fear may differ in emphasis from the fear experienced by the beginner, but it is fear nevertheless. Beginner or expert each have to make a deliberate decision to take the run and, with it, all its risks.

What distinguishes skiing from most other risk sports is that it cannot be experienced vicariously. Except for an occasional big race or jumping meet, an Olympics or a World Championship, skiing is not a spectator sport. There is no way of delegating the risks to someone else, as in auto racing, professional football, or bull fighting, and still get enjoyment and satisfaction out of the spectacle. Ski racing is interesting, occasionally even thrilling, but its excitement, its satisfying sensations, and even its daring are not apparent to the spectator. The very best competitors tend to be the most unspectacular. The only way to experience what skiing has to offer is to try it yourself.

Anyone who has been on skis for a while becomes sharply aware that the challenges of skiing are quite personal. In the absence of a score or other competitive factors, it is up to each skier to determine his objective: what he wants to get out of his day on the slopes or out of a particular run. It may be a modest series of linked snowplow turns or to ski "like Killy." It doesn't particularly matter. No one will ever really know. But this very privacy of decision aso demands self-honesty that allows no rationalizations. It explains why, on the one hand, skiing has been called, despite all the people who crowd the slopes, a lonely sport, and why, on the other hand, skiers as a group are so delightfully ebullient. There are few sensations so thoroughly satisfying as a self-set challenge successfully met.

Skiing is a relatively easy sport to learn and doesn't require a long period of apprenticeship before its thrills and pleasures become apparent. It is an open question as to who gets more excitement from the sport: the expert who makes run after flawless run, or the beginner who for the first time has negotiated the bunny slope without a fall. While the expert has greater expectations, the panorama facing the novice or intermediate is really no less exciting.

Although there is no question that challenge and achievement are vital aspects of skiing, there is always the temptation, particularly on the part of skiers themselves, to overstress the sensation of survival. "I crashed," "I was hip deep in powder," and similar notations are common items in the skier's conversation.

Actually, thanks to modern, lightweight insulated clothing, on-mountain shelter, and lifts, skiing is not excessively demanding physically or even particularly chilling or dangerous. Although skiing can be carried to hazardous lengths, the skier is not basically like the mountain climber, to whom high danger and extreme physical effort are stocks in trade. The skier does not even require the stoic acceptance of bone-chilling cold of the ice fisherman. While skiers can never ignore the possibilities of extreme cold, heavy storms, or a painful fall, these threats remain for the most part in the background and are merely part of the spice of their endeavors.

In point of fact, skiing is among the most sophisticated of sports. This applies to its technical aspects as well as the peripheral activities associated with it. Skiing is not a natural act, such as walking, running, or throwing, the basics of most other sports that are usually learned without instruction. There is no such thing as an instinctive skier, because instinctively people dislike the sensations of falling, of leaning forward on a hill, and of fighting centrifugal force—all of which are essential elements in skiing. To live with these instinctive dislikes, the skier must have a high level of concentration and self-control, even a certain amount of intellectual discipline.

The taste for skiing must be cultivated. Because it emphasizes quick thinking and coordination and actually defies sheer applications of brute strength, it has a strong appeal to those with a sophisticated turn of mind. This sophistication becomes most apparent in the activities that accompany skiing and in the resorts that cater to skiers. As Archer Winsten, ski columnist of the *New York Post,* once wrote, "No matter how good [the skiing] close at hand, skiers have a well-developed yearning for far-away places and strong convictions that the snow is deeper and lighter elsewhere."

It may seem somewhat spurious to claim that skiers receive some special benefit from travel, but comparing them with other tourists, one cannot help but be struck by the difference in the attitudes and impressions that skiers bring back.

The difference is due to having a reason for traveling at all. They go to ski and will spend a week or two at a particular place. Even though their main objective is to ski, the fact that they stay in one place, come into close contact with local people and absorb the atmosphere, provides them with a full experience of far greater value than the fleeting impressions of place after place received by the average tourist.

Sir Arnold Lunn, a British philosopher and one of the true pioneers of the sport, has said that one of the main reasons to go skiing is "to absorb mountain culture." This culture may have been diluted by the very internationalism that skiing has fostered and by the many city amenities that have found their way to the mountains. But through travel the skier can still be exposed to a rich variety of experiences.

Even beginners, making their first turns in some foothill area, quickly become aware of the sport's involvement with travel and the international atmosphere that pervades it. American skiers may find that their instructors

have an accent—Austrian, German, French, Swiss, or even Norwegian (though there are also more American instructors than ever before). Furthermore, they invariably find, even if the instructor is native-born or Canadian, that they are being taught in a sort of code, easy enough to understand, but one that transcends any language barrier. And it isn't long before they speak the code themselves, so that a short exposure will enable them to take lessons in any ski country they choose to visit.

But the accents are not confined to the instructors. Since the number of topnotch places to ski is relatively limited, it is not unusual to find a scaled-down version of the United Nations at most major ski resorts. And the hotter and more unlikely a place of origin, the more enthusiastic its skiers— which might explain why Texans seem to take to skiing with the same enthusiasm they show for oil wells.

The élan of a high-speed sport, the variety of experiences it has to offer, the sophistication of its milieu, its internationalized language, and its rather sardonic sense of humor—these are the ingredients in the joyful world of the skier. Yet they merely indicate, rather than explain, what skiing is all about.

Many have tried to explain, including some of the world's best writers. All have failed. The reason for this failure was once pinpointed by John Fry, then editor-in-chief of SKI Magazine, who asked his readers to recall a moment when their skiing was absolutely right:

> What made that moment of skiing so right? The answers perhaps are many. But one thing is certain in my own mind: The less you talk about it the better. The joy of that original moment lies precisely in its subjectivity; it is valuable because it is private to you. You betray it with each inevitably unsuccessful attempt to describe it to others. After all, they should know; they may have experienced it themselves.

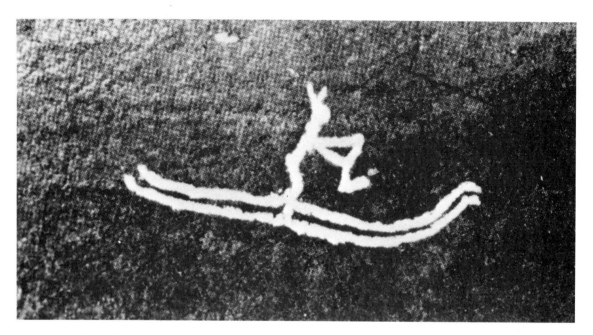

Four-thousand-year-old rock-wall carving from the island of Rodoy, Norway, showing a man on skis.

The Ovrebo Ski, found in a Norwegian bog, is estimated to be 2,500 years old and rests in the Ski Museum at Oslo, Norway.

How It All Started

Although skiing as a sport is little more than a century old, the origins of skiing can be traced back to the Stone and Bronze ages. These early beginnings have been substantiated by discoveries of skis in bogs and marshes in Finland, Norway, Sweden, and Russia and of rock-wall carvings in Norway and Russia. Archeologists report that some skis found in Finland and Sweden are 4,500 to 5,000 years old—the oldest yet found. Ethnographic experts date a rock carving of a skier on the island of Rödöy, just south of the Arctic Circle in Norway, to be about 4,000 years old.

Most prehistoric skis were more like snowshoes than like the skis we use today. The 4,500-year-old Hoting ski from Sweden is an excellent example of this snowshoelike construction. The 2,500-year-old Övrebo ski from southern Norway, however, has a turned-up, pointed tip and resembles a modern ski. These old skis are preserved in museums—the Hoting ski in Umeä, Sweden, and the Övrebo ski in Oslo, Norway. A few other collections can be found in the larger museums of Finland and Russia.

One of the first written mentions of skiing appears in the *Sagas*—the classic literature of the Viking period. The Norwegian Vikings were said to be excellent skiers, and the *Sagas* describe several kings living around A.D. 1000 as superb skiers. Skiing was so much a part of Viking life that a god and goddess of skiing, Ull and Skade, were objects of worship. The Vikings were not the

An 1853 painting by K. Bergslien of the flight of the "Birchlegs" with the infant King Haakon Haakonsen in the 1206 Norwegian Civil War.

most peaceful of people, and wars and battles were often described in the *Sagas*, though not employing skis. The first account of the use of skis in wartime occurs in a report of the Norwegian Civil War in 1206. King Sverre sent two scouts, called Birchlegs because they wrapped their legs with birch to protect them against the cold, to carry the infant royal son, Haakon Haakonson, over the mountains in the middle of winter. This feat is commemorated in Norway today by the annual Birkebeinerrennet (Birchleg race), a cross-country event that follows the same thirty-five-mile course taken by King Sverre's scouts more than 750 years ago.

Skiing has played such a large part in Scandinavian life that it is sometimes difficult to separate sport from history. Norway's Birkebeinerrennet has its counterpart in Sweden—the annual fifty-three-mile Vasaloppet cross-country race. In 1521 the Swedish King Gustav Vasa fled from his country to Norway on snowshoes. He was overtaken by his own men, who persuaded him to return to fight the Danes, who were then ruling Sweden. The Vasaloppet race follows the original route, celebrating King Gustav's victory. Today more than 8,000 skiers participate in this fifty-year-old test, making it one of the great sights in sports as the skiers all surge forward in a mass start.

Skiing is several thousand years old, yet very little improvement occurred in ski technique until the last two centuries. This lack of progress was due mainly to the early bindings and boots. Bindings were just single, loose toe straps of willow or leather, and boots were usually simple hide or leather shoes. With such a loose connection between boots and skis, it was not possible to jump or turn while in motion. Skis, therefore, were merely a means of transportation and were used chiefly by hunters and woodsmen. They were also used by doctors, midwives, priests, and undertakers in nineteenth-century Norway. Norway's first skiing postman made his rounds in 1530.

In 1721 a ski company was formed in the Norwegian army, and twelve years later regular ski drills were held as part of maneuvers. These soldiers were the first to use a leather strap around their heel, in addition to the toe strap, to keep the skis from falling off when skiing downhill. But even these bindings were too loose to allow for any real control. So a single solid pole was used as a brake downhill and as a "pusher" to increase speed on flat ground. Skis of this period were as much products of local fancy as of technique. Every valley and country village had its own type of ski. The most common type, used in eastern Norway, Sweden, and parts of Finland, was one short ski (six to seven feet) and one long ski (nine to twelve feet). The short ski was used to push off or kick (much as one kicks a scooter), whereas the long one was the gliding ski. In some areas fur was added to the running surface of the short

Drawing of a ski jump, 1862. Jumps were often made from walls or embankments.

kicking ski to give it better bite. Many areas had special types of skis suitable for jumping or turning.

Later in the eighteenth century, ski competition began to appear. Military ski competition began in Norway in 1767, but the development of skiing as a recognizable sport, even in Scandinavia, was slow. The event now known as the Holmenkollen originally started in 1866. In 1879 the jumping meet was moved to Huseby and in 1892 to Holmenkollen in Oslo.

Late in the stick-riding era, skiing was exported from Europe for the first time, specifically to the midwestern United States, California, and Australia. Norwegians were much in demand as miners, and their ability to get about in the mountains during winter was an unexpected if highly useful fringe benefit. The man who did most to dramatize the use of skis was John A. "Snowshoe" Thomson. Born Jon Thoresen Rue, he was brought to America from Telemark by his parents in 1837 at the age of ten. He joined the gold rush to Diamond Springs and Hangtown (later Placerville) in 1851, and after a fling at panning for gold he took up ranching.

In 1856, Thomson, recalling the use of "gliding shoes" in his native Norway, responded to a plea by the Sacramento postmaster for someone to carry the mail between Placerville, on the west side of the Sierra Nevada, and Genoa, Nevada, on the east—a distance of ninety miles. Two snowshoers, "Daddy" Dritt and "Cock-Eye" Johnson, had attempted the trip three years earlier, but without success. Yet Thomson was able to reach Genoa in three days and return in two, and he made the trip numerous times during the next thirteen winters, until the Central Pacific railroad was completed in 1869. During the Civil War years, Thomson was the only midwinter postal connection between California and the Union.

Thomson's feats, in themselves remarkable enough, were further embroidered by the miners. It wasn't long before mountain California was in the grip of the "snowshoe" craze. Competition, a pleasant diversion in the long winters of the isolated mining towns, quickly followed. The rules were simple: the men lined up at the top of the hill and the first man to reach the bottom on both skis was the winner.

As racing grew more popular, ski teams and clubs were organized. The first club in the United States was formed in La Porte in 1867. Port Wine, Poker Flat, and La Porte became hotbeds of competitive skiing, and there were numerous entries from other mining communities. It was inevitable that with money and community pride at stake, attempts would be made to coax a little more speed out of the "snowshoes." The first of these innovations was a racing crouch that minimized wind resistance. The miners also developed waxing to

A 1790 drawing of a Norwegian ski soldier on Osterdal skis (one short, one long).

Lithograph by J. Pettersen, Trondheim, of the Norwegian Ski Company on winter maneuvers in 1822.

the point where the "dope" makers became as important as the racers. Len France of Port Wine and Ed Pike of La Porte were famous throughout the Sierra for their concoctions, and their recipes were closely guarded secrets. "Dope" was usually applied over a coat of burned tar and consisted of beeswax, sperm, spruce oil, and other ingredients. The "snowshoes" so treated made speeds up to sixty miles an hour commonplace.

When gold played out in California after 1875, interest in "snowshoeing" played out with it. In the 1930s, Bill Berry, ski editor of the Fresno *Bee* (and no relation to this author) started to research the origins of Sierra skiing and ran into a blank wall when he sought out "skiers" in Plumas County. Only when he referred to "snowshoers" was he able to tap a surprisingly rich vein of newspaper clippings and personal recollections of the era when skis were the major form of transportation in the snow-covered Sierra. A match race was held in 1938 between the best of the new generation of California skiers and the few "snowshoeing" old-timers left in La Porte. Using skis and a "dope" formula dating back sixty years, white-haired Ab Gould, then in his seventies, had no trouble defeating the youngsters.

Although there was widespread use of skis for practical purposes before the twentieth century, their recreational potential was circumscribed by lack of a suitable technique for turning and control. Speed was checked by riding the

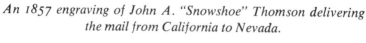

An 1857 engraving of John A. "Snowshoe" Thomson delivering the mail from California to Nevada.

single pole. This lack of a bridge between recreational needs and hell-bent-for-election downhill racing accounted for a temporary decline in skiing once the principal need for skis was superseded by the railroads.

THE TURN IS BORN

Skiing as the widespread, widely practiced recreational and primarily non-competitive sport we know today has its roots as much in mountaineering as in its original Scandinavian form.

Starting in the middle of the nineteenth century, there was a constantly accelerating interest in virtually all forms of sport and recreation throughout Europe and North America. It was this period that saw the emergence of most survival sports.

During this time, the English started to make the Alps, especially the Swiss Alps, almost their own by systematic assaults on every major peak. As the peaks were scaled and rescaled by increasingly difficult routes, it was only natural for climbers to try to find means to scale them in the winter.

Since 1865 these mountain climbers had been looking longingly at the Alpine summits during the winter. Then one day, four Englishmen were wagered by their St. Moritz host, Andrea Badrutt, that they could not withstand a month of the rigorous Swiss winters. Of course, he knew he would lose. Even before the Englishmen arrived in St. Moritz, they were shedding mufflers and sweaters, and after their return to their fogbound isle, bronzed and fit after a month of good living, they had little trouble convincing their fellows to accept previously scoffed-at reports of hot winter sunshine and dazzling clear days high in the mountains.

In the latter part of the nineteenth century, the Arctic and Antarctic regions were the last frontiers of man's geographical knowledge. The barriers of ice, snow, wind, and extreme cold and the unavailability of any food made these regions seem impenetrable. Impenetrable, that is, until in 1888 Fridtjof Nansen showed how to cope with Arctic conditions by crossing the Greenland ice cap with skis in forty-three days. The feat itself generated tremendous excitement as a giant step toward the eventual solution of the mysteries of the Arctic and Antarctic, but it was the mountaineers who were to benefit most from the dramatic use of skis in the crossing. The publication of Nansen's book, *Paa Ski over Grönland* (*Crossing Greenland on Skis*), in 1890 inspired mountaineers in every alpine country to experiment with skis with such dedication that skiing rapidly became a movement of international proportions.

Among the young boys playing on skis in the hamlet of Morgedal in Telemark, Norway, in the early 1800s was one destined to be the father of "modern" skiing. As a young man, Sondre Norheim became a master on skis. He could jump farther than the others, and he dared go higher than anyone had thought possible. To add to the fun, Norheim made turning and twisting tracks when he skied downhill. In the dialect of Telemark, these tracks on the hillside were known as Slalom (*Sla*, "slope"; *Lom*, "ski track"). Norheim soon found that loose leather bindings were of little use, and so he fashioned combination toe-and-heel bindings from twisted birch root, wet-formed to shape, dried and drawn tight. With these "stiff" bindings, he became the first man to control his skis. He could jump and turn. Modern skiing had seen the light of day.

The impulse given by Norheim's binding was all but explosive. As a poor sharecropper, Norheim couldn't afford many luxuries, yet he began experimenting with skis. To make the skis turn better, he made the tips broader than the tails and gave the skis a side camber. With his revolutionary bindings and skis, Norheim became in 1850 the first man to do a parallel turn. He also developed a turn with the inside ski in a half-plow position. Jumpers of the day used these two turns to stop after landing. In 1901 the first ski-jumping rules

An 1881 drawing by J. Berg (Norway) shows Telemark turn and Telemark costume.

The first "stiff" binding made by Sondre Norheim about 1850, mounted on a Telemark ski.

committee gave them names: christiania for the parallel turn, and telemark for the half-plow turn, to honor the capital (now Oslo) and Norheim's home county.

In 1894 another Norwegian, Fritz Huitfeldt, further improved bindings with the invention of toe irons. Huitfeldt's binding left the heel free to move up and down for walking, but held the toe firmly to allow for a vastly improved control over the skis.

Although this innovation was to be a source of continuing controversy, it opened the field to improvements in the technical aspects of alpine skiing. To Mathias Zdarsky of Austria goes the credit for the first systematic exposition of the dynamics of skis on snow and the possibility of a technique based on these dynamics. Zdarsky was something of an eccentric and lived in hermitlike isolation in a house he built himself near Lilienfeld, not far from Vienna. After reading Nansen's book, he saw skiing as a solution to his annual problem of getting to town in winter. He ordered a pair from Norway, but they came without the benefit of instruction. His subsequent difficulties inspired him to develop a technique.

Sir Arnold Lunn, the British scholar whose own fertile mind contributed greatly to the development of skiing, calls Zdarsky "something of a genius . . . with the zeal of a schoolmaster and the iron discipline of a Prussian drill sergeant." Zdarsky built his technique on the use of stemmed skis and a single pole. He paid relatively little attention to either the christiania or the telemark. While this limited the scope of his skiing, it did provide the basic mechanics of complete control on alpine slopes of all types.

Zdarsky didn't have the field to himself for long. Col. Georg Bilgeri, an Austrian army officer, evolved at almost the same time his own stem system; it was based on two poles and a far wider stem. In lieu of stick-riding on the steeper slopes, Bilgeri advocated widening the stem. The resulting controversy, among the followers of the Zdarsky, Bilgeri, and the Norwegian schools and later involving other innovators, was to rage until after World War I.

What tends to be forgotten by those who attempt to evaluate the contributions of Zdarsky and others is that all of these pioneers considered skis as a means to move about in the mountains during the winter. Bilgeri, and to a lesser extent, Zdarsky, maintained that the day's sport was the climb—not the downhill rush. Both stressed the danger of rapid descent and, rightly, the need for safety.

Limited as these techniques were, they resulted in some remarkable ski ascents. All but the most difficult alpine peaks yielded to skis before World War I. The mountaineer found he had as much freedom in the winter as in the summer. And he discovered there was an added thrill in the run down.

Hannes Schneider combined safety and speed in organizing a logical system of ski instruction.

The transformation of skiing from a means to an end, from a mountaineering aid to a sport in its own right, was not the work of one man. But one man looms so large in this evolution that he overshadows all others.

Hannes Schneider was an important innovator, as important as any of his contemporaries. But what distinguished Schneider, a native of Stuben, Austria, from his peers was a far-seeing vision, a deep analytical ability, a colorful sense of the dramatic, and, above all, an ability to put himself in the skier's, particularly the beginning skier's, boots. To Schneider—first instinctively, then consciously—speed was the attraction in skiing. He had barely been exposed to the problems of teaching when he told a companion, "I am going to put speed into everyone's skiing. And I am going to make it reasonably safe. It's speed, not touring, that is the lure."

Schneider solved the problem of safety at high speed by developing a crouch that lowered the skier's center of gravity without putting him back on his heels. Then he added more speed by perfecting the stem christiania, progressively reducing the stemming portion until the skis were almost parallel throughout the turn. Finally, he organized the various maneuvers into a logical system—much as it is taught today—in which the pupil learned one maneuver, then another one more advanced, and so on up the ladder.

What transformed Schneider's Arlberg system (named for the region in Austria) from a purely personal method into a universally accepted technique was Schneider's sense of the dramatic. Even as a youth he participated in races and jumping meets in order to publicize his system. And in the aftermath of World War I, in collaboration with the German documentary filmmaker Dr. Arnold Fanck, he pioneered ski movies. The movies were classics of their kind. They made thousands of converts and established the Arlberg technique as a universal ski standard.

RACING TOUCHES OFF A CRAZE

With the decline of interest in skiing in the California–Colorado mining country, the sport had to be reintroduced to North America. This time the carriers were the Norwegians, who provided the manpower for the lumber camps in northern New England, the Midwest, and Pacific Northwest and the iron mines of Michigan. And it was the latter part of this immigration that brought jumping to the United States in the 1880s.

Skiing for these Norwegians was a clannish affair. Their ski clubs—the first in the modern era of skiing—were formed not so much to propagate the sport as to provide means of organizing jumping meets and congenial, ethnic socializing. By 1904 there were enough of these clubs to justify forming the National Ski Association (NSA). The group, however, was dominated by Norwegian members. One of the organizers of the U.S. Eastern Amateur Ski Association (now the Eastern chapter of the U.S. Ski Association) recalled in that group's official history that when the Eastern tried to join NSA in 1925, the more or less official philosophy of the National was that only Scandinavians could ski. There was an overwhelming emphasis on jumping, and none at all on recreational downhill (or alpine) skiing.

Despite this attitude, skiing did manage to become popular. During the 1880s and 1890s, there were reports of skiing in almost every section of the country that gets snow, including one in New York City in 1888. But this activity amounted to little until the infusion of collegiate enthusiasm provided by the outing clubs of the Ivy League colleges.

The outing club had a precise beginning. The first club was organized December 7, 1909, at Dartmouth, and the man responsible was Fred Harris. Harris, in suggesting the creation of a ski and snowshoe club to relieve the tedium of Hanover's long winters, wrote to the student newspaper: "Dartmouth might well become the originator of a branch of college-organized sport hitherto undeveloped by American colleges."

Although the ski activities of the outing clubs had a distinct Nordic character in jumping and cross-country, downhill running quickly found its place thanks to the delightful upper-middle-class institution of that period—the *wanderjahr*. It was the custom of the well-to-do to send their sons to Europe for a year between high school and college, and these young men brought back the new message of skiing and a rough approximation of its technique.

These were essentially germinating years. In the absence of formal ski instruction, there was a great deal of trial-and-error learning, which was further slowed by a complete lack of facilities. But there was noticeable progress. College and community winter carnivals brightened the long winters

Norwegian skiers in Red Wing, Minnesota, 1891, the first team in the U.S. Left to right: *Paul Honningstade, Mikkel Hemmesteveit, Torjus Hemmesteveit, Ludvig Hjermstad.*

The Canadian Pacific ski train arriving at St. Marguerite Station in the Laurentians in the early thirties.

and gave a boost to skiing. There was enough interest in the sport so that C. A. Lund, a Norwegian immigrant, felt justified in founding the Northland Ski Company in 1911. And across the border, the Canadians, led by the example of McGill University, closely paralleled American development.

For almost two decades after the organization of the Dartmouth Outing Club, American skiing developed without any significant transatlantic influence. A few American competitors were exposed to European skiing in the first two Olympic Winter Games—Chamonix in 1924 and St. Moritz in 1928—but these games excluded downhill and slalom, and no startling lessons were brought back.

Late in the 1920s North American skiing demonstrated that skiing had commercial possibilities. In the winter of 1926–27 Oscar Hambro of Boston opened the first ski shop—and survived. The Canadian Pacific ran weekend snow trains from Montreal to the Laurentians and found no difficulty in drumming up customers. American skiing was building up a fair head of steam. All it needed was a good publicist. It found him in the person of Otto Eugen Schniebs.

A watchmaker by trade, a disciple of Hannes Schneider, and the Dartmouth ski coach, Schniebs had a basic message: "Skiing is a way of life."

What gave the message special charm and appeal as he delivered it to audiences throughout the Boston area were the Bavarian-accented assaults on the English language that carried it. Much of what Schniebs is supposed to have said is pure fabrication, but his message left its mark and formed the basis for the élan that marks skiers to this day.

Schneider's Arlberg technique did more than establish skiing as a sport in its own right. It created new competitive concepts in the 1930s—downhill and slalom—which divorced skiing from its Nordic origins; it established winter tourism as a major economic factor in the Alps; it was responsible for the changing of ski-making from a craft to an industry; and it provided a platform for further advances in technique.

The event that established alpine skiing and fixed its essential character was the Arlberg-Kandahar. Here, too, Schneider was closely involved, but the original idea for the race came from Sir Arnold Lunn. Sir Arnold had long been irritated by the refusal of the Scandinavian–dominated Federation Internationale de Ski (FIS) to recognize down-mountain racing, the only branch of the sport at which the British excelled. He also wanted to find a permanent niche for slalom, a personal creation of his. He found a kindred soul in Schneider, who had always objected to the curious double standards that

Otto Eugen Schniebs, a disciple of Hannes Schneider and advocate of skiing as a way of life.

Sir Arnold Lunn originated the Arlberg-Kandahar races. He was knighted for his contributions to skiing and to Anglo-Swiss relations.

prevailed in the treatment of professionals. Frequently, as a professional, he was asked to give exhibitions—without pay—while the amateurs would not only get trophies but under-the-table payments too.

The first A-K in March 1928, featuring most of the top racers in the Alps, had its desired effect. Its success was reflected by imitation in every mountain country, and it created a great wave of interest throughout Central Europe. Within two years the FIS was forced to recognize downhill and slalom as world-championship events and, in addition, to accept ski instructors as bona fide competitors. This latter concession was to prove a source of serious dispute within the International Olympic Committee in future years. In one guise or another, this issue persisted until the late seventies within IOC, especially vis-à-vis FIS. Then, oddly, it subsided, for reasons that will be discussed in the chapters dealing with racing.

The elevation of alpine competition to world status had immediate impact. It further stimulated the already growing interest in skiing. Of more immediate importance, however, was the spur it provided for the improvement of equipment and technique.

The invention of the steel edge in 1928 by Rudolf Lettner of Austria was probably one of the most important developments in ski equipment. This simple innovation—which Nansen had originally experimented with in his crossing of Greenland in 1880—had a profound effect on every phase of skiing. While the original function of the steel edge was thought to be merely protective—the reason why Lettner never bothered to patent it—it actually provided the basis for the narrow-tracked, precise running and turning we take for granted today. Before the edge, even the most expert skiers had a constant struggle to hang on to the hill. Control was precarious, and only the fact that most skiing was done on soft snow prevented wholesale disaster. On hard snow, only an awkwardly wide stance could assure that the skier remained upright. The edge had the immediate effect of springing the Arlbergers out of their deep crouch. Control improved and skiing speeds rose, not only for racers but for all skiers who adopted the edge. This was the start of a chain reaction of major developments in equipment and technique that continues today.

The Thundering Thirties:
The Pioneer Period

The 1930s was one of the most fruitful decades in the history of skiing. These years between the invention of the edge and the start of World War II set the groundwork for everything now considered fundamental in alpine skiing. The old ski instructor who says "It's been done before" is not really far wrong.

The impetus for these developments was provided by the sport's growing popularity. A rather aristocratic, exclusive, and esoteric pastime was being transformed into a mass movement. Skiing changed from being a tool of the winter mountaineer to a sport in its own right, attributed partly to the proselytizing activities of ski clubs, the impact of the Schneider-Fanck films, and the growing interest in competition. But perhaps as important as all these factors together was the development of uphill transportation.

"One can regard lifts as one will," Prof. Stefan Kruckenhauser, head of Austrian ski teachers, wrote in 1958. ". . . The fact that skiing pupils can today advance in skill about four times as fast with the help of small lifts as without them is an advantage that cannot be exaggerated. This helps attract thousands to the sport every year." Lifts not only brought more people to skiing, they also changed its dimensions and character.

For the most part the already existing mountain railways of the Alps were useless to skiers. Even the first *téléferiques* were built with summer tourists in mind (which explains why many of the older European runs end some distance away from the base terminal). But the lifts were welcomed by skiers and after 1930 a brisk construction program was under way in most major Alpine ski centers.

By bringing more people to skiing, the lifts also changed the condition of the snow. Where one major run a day used to be par, four, five, or more runs were the rule with a lift. The resulting traffic packed down the runs, requiring new technical skills of the skier.

With the popularization of "downhill-only" skiing, there was no longer any need to leave the heel free for walking. The development of bindings with "down-pull," which peaked with the introduction of the Kandahar cable binding in the thirties, allowed unprecedented control over the skis and made further advances in ski technique possible.

The first attempt to change the technique to take advantage of the new control was made by two Austrians, Dr. F. Hoschek and Prof. Friedl Wolfgang. They rejected the snowplow and the stem in favor of the "direct way to swinging," emphasizing shoulder rotation and upward unweighting. This approach would not have caused the sensation it did had it not been for the racing successes of Anton (Toni) Seelos, an Austrian ski instructor. Seelos was the unchallenged master of slalom in the mid-thirties, having arrived

Austrian Toni Seelos was the unchallenged master of slalom in the mid-thirties. His technique was characterized by parallel skis throughout the turn.

independently at what Hoschek and Wolfgang essentially advocated. Seelos's technique was characterized by upward unweighting, rotation, and, most important of all, parallel skis throughout the turn.

The Hoschek-Wolfgang-Seelos system drew a cool reception in Austria but struck a responsive chord in France, which was then emerging as a major ski power in Europe. Seelos was brought to Chamonix, where he coached the French team, which, under the leadership of Emile Allais and Paul Gignoux, further refined the parallel technique. It differed from the Austrian version primarily by unweighting with a down-and-forward motion (a precursor to avalement?) and by what is called the ruade, a lifting of the tails of the skis in a horse-kick type of motion.

Even while rotational skiing was reaching its peak, a small but prophetic group of Swiss and Austrian ski technicians were developing a parallel system based on counterrotation—that is, the twisting of the upper body in a direction opposite to the legs and skis. This system has dominated modern skiing. Based on an analysis of motion, it was invented by the Austrians Toni Ducia and Kurt Reindl and by the Swiss Giovanni Testa and Eugen Matthias. Ducia and Reindl published their counterrotational thesis, *Le Ski d'Aujourd'hui*, in France in 1935. Testa and Matthias published their first edition of *Natürliches Skilaufen* in Munich the following year.

"What was set forth in these books was for that time fundamentally new, and in fact difficult to grasp," Kruckenhauser wrote. ". . . Looking back, we now realize how far ahead were these four authors and their fellow workers."

Despite the slalom victories of Rudolf Rominger, a powerful downhiller who became the world's best slalom racer with the new technique, an attempt made to institute reverse shoulder in St. Moritz just before World War II was only partially successful. The emphasis of the day was too much on pure parallel, and the beginning maneuvers of counterrotation were still based on the *passé* stem and snowplow.

The introduction of new techniques had an important influence on equipment, particularly on boots. Prior to 1930, ski boots were little more than glorified walking or mountain boots. But with the growing need for precise control, boots began to change. They became progressively stiffer, both in the sole and the uppers. The soles were stiffened to bear the growing tensions generated by the new cable bindings and the uppers for rigid support of the ankles so that they could transmit every motion to the skis. The Scandinavian skier of a century or more ago would have had no difficulty in recognizing the functions of the various items of equipment used by skiers in 1930. But just ten years later, he would hardly have understood any of it without considerable explanation.

Meanwhile, skiing in the United States and Canada was developing rapidly. At Dartmouth, Otto Schneibs was giving Americans a taste of the potentials of skiing. The subsequent enthusiasm led Peckett's Inn of Franconia, New Hampshire, to bring over Sig Buchmayr from Hofgastein, Austria, to head the first organized ski school in America in 1929. That same year the Boston and Maine Railroad sponsored a ski train in the United States, running it to Warner, New Hampshire, and Franconia.

The railroads, with their vast publicity power, truly boosted the sport. Another aid was the invention of the rope tow. The brainchild of Alex Foster of Shawbridge, Quebec, the rope tow first saw the light of day in 1932 and was to provide the bulk of uphill transportation for almost twenty years. It was a solution eminently suited to the times—simple, economical, and swift. Even in its most primitive form, it had a remarkable hourly capacity, ideal for the huge crowds brought in over the weekend by the ski trains.

With the existence of the rope tow and ski trains, the pattern of the weekend ski trip emerged. Unlike their European counterparts who went to the mountains for a vacation and only coincidentally to ski, Americans went primarily to ski. "The Europeans," said Fred Iselin, the Swiss-born ski-school director of Aspen Highlands, "go up on the lift in the middle of the morning, they lie in deck chairs like seals to get brown, or they take a bottle of wine and a salami and go on a picnic. Then they come down on skis. This they call skiing. We don't do that here [in the United States]. The American is geared for technique, for hard sport, and the average American skier is two classes

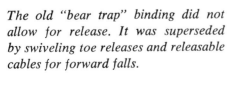

The old "bear trap" binding did not allow for release. It was superseded by swiveling toe releases and releasable cables for forward falls.

The world's first rope tow, at Shawbridge, Quebec, 1932. Powered by an old four-cylinder Dodge with a jacked-up wheel, it was invented by Alex Foster and was originally referred to as "Foster's Folly."

ahead of the European." (This is beginning to change as Europeans get more serious about skiing—especially as more of them visit U.S. ski areas.)

Iselin, a witty elf of a man who died in 1971, was only half joking. Particularly in the early days of the rope-tow era, there were no deck chairs at the top of the tows and little to be seen that couldn't be viewed just as well from the bottom. What has often been described as "yo-yo skiing" was primarily brought about by the limited range of the rope tow.

Following the introduction of the rope tow into the United States at Woodstock, Vermont, in 1934, skiing spread swiftly throughout New England and upstate New York. Snow trains to these regions became commonplace. For the first time, skiing could boast of a substantial following outside the small hard core of super-enthusiasts.

Skiing, and winter sports in general, benefited greatly when the third Olympic Winter Games were held at Lake Placid in 1932. Lowell Thomas, who skied occasionally, broadcast an account of the games and was to write later that "it was the Olympics at Lake Placid that sold me on skiing." His frequent broadcasts about skiing and ski areas in subsequent years were important publicity for the sport.

All that skiing needed at this point was a touch of glamour. It was provided in 1936 with the opening of Sun Valley. Modeled after an alpine village, Sun Valley was the inspiration of W. Averell Harriman, then president of the Union Pacific Railroad. The atmosphere, however, was the creation of Steve Hannegan, the famous publicist who later was Postmaster-General under Franklin Roosevelt.

Much of what is standard equipment today at major ski resorts was first introduced at Sun Valley. Chair lifts, swimming pools, private cottages, high-style dining and entertainment, and a clientele studded with society names and movie stars gave skiing a prestige previously reserved for yachting and polo. More important, although it wasn't stressed in Hannegan's promotion, Sun Valley offered ski terrain and snow conditions few European resorts could match.

Governor Roosevelt conducts opening ceremonies at the 1932 Winter Olympics, Lake Placid, New York.

Averell Harriman, founder of Sun Valley, Idaho.

One of the first two chair lifts in the world was built at Sun Valley in 1936.

Enthusiastic crowds attended ski exhibitions at Madison Square Garden in the late thirties.

There was a need in the mid-thirties for competent instructors. With Europe teetering on the edge of war, many Swiss and Austrians, inspired by Buchmayr and Schniebs, emigrated to the United States. Sepp Ruschp came to Stowe, Hans Hauser and Friedl Pfeifer to Sun Valley, Luggi Foeger to Yosemite, Benno Rybizka to North Conway, Walter Prager to Dartmouth, Fritz Loosli to Quebec, Hans Georg to Southern California, and Hans Thorner to Franconia. There were also many others a good deal less competent. These were the ones who gave rise to the phrase "Bend zee knees, two dollars pleez." By 1937 skepticism about ski instruction had reached such a point that the Eastern Amateur Ski Association ordered the first certification examinations. These were held at Suicide Six at Woodstock in February 1938. Of the seventeen candidates who took the certification examinations, six passed, ". . . showing all too clearly," as reported by certification chairman Ford K. Sayre, "that many of those now giving instruction need further training in skiing as well as in teaching."

The 1936 Olympics Ski Team thirty years later. Left to right: *Clarita Heath Bright, Grace Lindley McKnight, Helen Boughton-Lee McAlpine, Betty Woolsey, Marian McKean Wigglesworth, and Mary Bird Young.*

The certification idea spread rapidly. It thrived in great part because no attempt was made to establish a unified system of ski instruction. The only demand was that an instructor show skiing competence in his chosen system and an ability to explain it to his pupils. Each system had its own strong advocates. Louis Cochand and Hans Georg had brought over the reverse shoulder of the St. Moritz School. Loosli was an early advocate of the all-parallel school of Emile Allais. Thorner and Prager taught traditional Swiss methods. Yet, despite these various heresies, Schneider's Arlberg method remained the accepted standard of what good ski technique was supposed to be. His personal lieutenants—Foeger, Lang, Pfeifer, and Rybizka—were not only superb skiers and teachers but they were also highly articulate, and their message during this area of technique confusion was strongly supported by a number of influential American skiers.

North American skiing made impressive strides from 1936 to 1939. Major lift installations were built at Alta, Utah; Sugar Bowl, California; Belknap (now Gunstock) and Cannon, New Hampshire; Stowe, Vermont; and Mt. Tremblant, Quebec; as well as hundreds of rope tows on less imposing hills in every snow region of the United States. Thousands were learning to ski under competent instructors—and being rescued from occasional follies by members of the National Ski Patrol System, an organization inspired principally by Minot Dole and formally recognized in 1938. And American racers were closing on the Europeans. A remarkable group led by Dick Durrance planned to go to the FIS World Championships in Norway in 1940; as it turned out, most of them, as well as hundreds of others, volunteered for the ski troops instead.

Colonel Rolfe of the Tenth Mountain Division and "Minnie" Dole; Dole argued for the formation of the Tenth and was a founder of the National Ski Patrol System.

The Tenth Mountain Division specialized in mountain and winter warfare and contained many of America's best skiers of that time.

The War and the Postwar
Golden Age of Skiing

The rapid-strike capabilities of the Finnish patrols in the Russo-Finnish war made a deep impression on certain tacticians in the U.S. War Department. In the bitter winter of 1939–40, the Finns, taking maximum advantage of the mobility of skis, were able to bring the Russian Army to a dead stop, using hit-and-run raids on vulnerable supply and communication lines. Not until the snow left the ground were the Russians able to bring superior fire and manpower to bear and break the Finnish resistance.

But the point had been made. At the urging of Minot Dole and a few other American skiers who saw that the United States might shortly be involved in the European war, the Army activated the Eighty-seventh Mountain Infantry Regiment at Fort Lewis, Washington. For the first time in American military history, the Army had a unit specializing in mountain and winter warfare. Initially composed only of volunteers who had demonstrated ability on skis, the Eighty-seventh drafted a good portion of the best skiers in the country. And even though this quality was diluted when the regiment was expanded into the Tenth Mountain Division, throughout the war the unit remained one of the Army's elite corps.

The Tenth saw its first action in the Aleutians in 1943 when it was used to regain the island of Kiska from the Japanese. The operation was carried out in a dense fog, and all the division casualties were self-inflicted because intelligence had failed to note that the Japanese had abandoned the island.

The division trained for two more years before it saw action again, this time in Italy during the closing phases of the war. The Germans were firmly entrenched along the Gothic Line, guarding the agriculturally rich Po Valley. The anchor point of this line was Riva Ridge on Mt. Belvedere, a 1,200-foot rock ledge that blocked entrance to the Po Valley. By scaling Riva Ridge without artillery preparation, members of the Eighty-sixth Regiment were able to surprise the defenders in a dawn attack. The following day, led by the Eighty-seventh Regiment, the division took Mt. Belvedere and, despite many casualties, held the position against heavy counterattacks, thus opening the way to Austria.

On the home front, skiing remained at low throttle "for the duration." Gas rationing precluded much travel, and material shortages discouraged expansion of facilities. Skiing might well have died out had it not been for the concentration of skiers in the Tenth Mountain Division, who provided much of the manpower for the expansion during the two decades following the war. Many of the leading names in skiing today were in the personnel rosters of the Tenth Mountain Division. Sadly, they're phasing out as the 1980s emerge.

Equally important to skiing immediately after the war was the vast amount of surplus ski equipment. Originally intended for the division, it was of remarkably high quality and, with virtually no modification, was adaptable to civilian sport. It was possible for people who availed themselves of this equipment to take up skiing for about $25, and that includes oversized parkas and pants. Thousands seized the advantage.

The postwar decade was a curious mixture of status quo and experimentation. A comparison of racing styles, for instance, showed little difference between prewar and postwar masters. In many cases they were the same men. Only among the German and Austrian ski masters did the war take a substantial toll. Nor was there much change in ski instruction. The Austrians, although using many of the foundation maneuvers of the Arlberg technique, had adopted sideslipping and a great deal of rotation from the French. And while the French still emphasized their no-stem approach, they were not nearly as dogmatic about it as in former years. The rivalry between the two systems flared briefly after the war when Emile Allais came to the United States, but generally there was little difference between the top practitioners of the two systems.

Equipment changed slightly. Initially the plastic bottoms made little impression and an overwhelming number of skiers followed the waxing ritual as before. And with few exceptions, skiers as a whole spurned the few release (then wrongly called safety) bindings coming on the market.

Opposite:
An indirect result of mechanical lifts, moguls are caused by large numbers of skiers making turns in the same spots. Outer Limits Trail on Bear Mountain at Killington, Vermont, tests skiers with a seemingly endless progression of huge moguls and pitches up to 62 percent.

What was changing radically, however, was the sport's popular acceptance. And the growing number of skiers brought about changes in technique. The effect of a large number of skiers on a slope gave rise to a condition called "moguls," probably a Tyrolean or Bavarian corruption of the German word *hügel*, meaning small hill or hillock. (Other derivations have been advanced, but it no longer matters because now we generally call them bumps.) Moguls are caused by skiers turning continuously in the same spot. Whole fields with these bumps began to appear in the late forties, requiring tighter turning instead of the long, swooping curves skiers were used to cutting. Particularly on trails carved out of the forests and on steep narrow slopes, the skier's choice of turn became more limited. Theoreticians began to talk about a phenomenon called *gegenschulter*, an application of reverse shoulder used with occasional success by racers that allowed them to get as close as possible to the inside pole of a slalom gate. However, there were few instructors who took it seriously, believing it to be meaningless for recreational skiers. Two men who did not take this attitude were Dr. Stefan Kruckenhauser of Austria and Georges Joubert, a physical education professor at the University of Grenoble, France.

The very number of skiers also influenced changes in ski areas. Rugged outdoorsmen became a decreasing percentage of the ski population. The new skier began to demand better facilities—better lodging, better food, better entertainment. And to cope with the growing lift lines, high-capacity, high-speed lifts were developed, of which the double chair lift was the first. It was also during this period that slopes were first mechanically groomed. Less experienced skiers found the going much easier at those areas that cleared and packed their slopes, and they flocked to them.

During these years skiing also became a more graceful sport. By 1954 *gegenschulter* was no longer a stylistic aberration of a few top racers. Not only were all of the good racers using it, but a large number of expert recreational skiers as well. These sinuous dancelike movements were officially endorsed the following year with the introduction of the New Official Austrian Ski System at the International Ski Instructors' Congress held in Val d'Isère, France. Its ultimate form—continuous turning down the fall line—was called *wedeln*.

The new system, although seemingly more complex than the older rotation, moved like an avalanche through the ski world. The reasons for this rapid propagation are several. Many skiers had advanced sufficiently to be capable of *wedeln*. Metal skis, easier to turn than the old skis, were seen on the slopes in increasing numbers. Furthermore, precise control of the skis

Prof. Stefan Kruckenhauser of St. Christoph, Austria, directed the creation of the official Austrian ski teaching system in the postwar era.

had been considerably enhanced by the improvement in boots. Double boots, developed by the French during World War II, were introduced into the United States in the late forties. By the time *wedeln* became official, even the lowliest skier had a better linkage with his skis than the experts of the old era.

Adding greatly to the glamour inherent in the new technique was the introduction of stretch pants in 1955. These made the technique more obvious and attractive. What before had been a sea of navy, tan, and black, suddenly became a palette of every conceivable color. This fashion factor, along with the new socializing possibilities of the sport, is frequently underestimated as a contributor to the startling growth of skiing.

Ski racing too underwent important changes. Winners in major international meets were acclaimed worldwide. Toni Sailer, Stein Eriksen, Jean-Claude Killy, Nancy Greene, and Billy Kidd became household names.

The decade of the 1960s brought changes to skiing on a scale that few could have anticipated. The era of the mega-resort began. The money it cost

Two of the greatest champions of modern ski racing: Jean-Claude Killy of France (above) won all three gold medals in alpine skiing at the 1968 Winter Olympics; Anne-Marie Moser-Proell of Austria has won the World Cup six times and was the 1980 Olympic Downhill champion.

A lift line at Mt. Snow in the 1960s. The pattern of the maze is different today, and high-speed lifts shorten the waiting periods significantly.

to start Vail, Colorado, in 1962—about $5 million—probably represented the value of all the major American ski areas at the start of World War II. Yet, by the summer of 1971, Vail was spending almost $20 million, quadruple its initial investment in facilities, just on expanding the resort. Other resorts started or expanded on an equally ambitious scale: Steamboat, Keystone, Breckenridge, and later Copper Mountain, and even old Winter Park, all in Colorado; Park City and Snowbird in Utah's Wasatch Mountains outside of Salt Lake; Sugarbush, Killington, Mount Snow, Stratton Mountain, Sugarloaf, and Waterville Valley in New England; and the coming of skiing to the South in the form of areas like Beech Mountain, North Carolina.

By the end of the 1960s, ominous signs already existed that unrestricted growth of ski areas—particularly on the most prevalent, publicly owned available land—would not continue forever. In this regard, the landmark case became that of Mineral King in California, a planned resort to be developed by the Disney Corporation, which was blocked by the legal action of the preservationist Sierra Club. This case set the tone and climate for the entire decade of the seventies.

Changes in ski equipment were no less radical. The metal ski that ushered in the sixties was virtually obsolete by the time the decade ended. By the beginning of the 1970s, most ski manufacturers had shifted to fiberglass or fiberglass/metal laminate construction. The shift to synthetic materials was

Howard Head (left) *of Baltimore, Maryland, designed the world's first successful metal ski. Another American, Robert Lange, developed the first plastic ski boot. Both are gone from their companies, which are now owned by foreign firms, but their names linger on.*

even more pronounced in boots: At the beginning of the decade, all ski boots were made of leather; by the end of the sixties, almost all boots were made of plastic, and they rose higher on the leg and were much stiffer. Custom fitting, by injecting foam into an inner bladder surrounding the skier's foot, began (and died, fortunately) in the 1970s. Cable bindings, universally used in 1960, were completely obsolete by 1970, replaced by the safer step-in release binding.

The radical changes in equipment fostered equally radical changes in ski instruction and technique. After sponsoring a successful experiment at Killington, Vermont, in 1966—in which beginners improved more quickly by starting on short skis and progressing to longer ones—SKI Magazine coined the term *Graduated Length Method*, or *GLM*, to describe this new approach to teaching. The 1960s also brought the publication of Georges Joubert's *How to Ski the New French Way*. Joubert described the new technique of avalement, by which the skier swallows up irregularities in the terrain by retracting

Georges Joubert, author and coach, revolutionized modern ski technique with his early analysis of the jet turn and avalement. He and French Ski Team Director Jean Vuarnet also invented the egg position in downhill racing.

his legs and sitting back momentarily. In introducing avalement to the North American public for the first time in 1967, SKI called it "the technique which demolishes a sacred cow," because previously all ski instruction had emphasized the skier getting his weight forward over the skis. Today, history has swallowed avalement, the sacred cow is on all fours again, and skiers are upright and forward. Until the next change.

Bob Beattie, the coach who dominated U.S. amateur ski racing throughout much of the 1960s by his flair for creating programs and finding the money to fund them, was "retired" by the end of the decade. He successfully launched professional racing with rich cash prizes to the winners.

A promising omen for American racing in the 1960s was the creation of a National Standard Ski Race, NASTAR. Launched by SKI in 1968, it is a program tailored to recreational skiers who want to race and get a meaningful measure of their ability. It now encompasses some 120 ski areas and participation by more than 180,000 skiers annually, many of whom are small children.

5

The Environmental Era

The birth of modern skiing burst upon us like a jet taking off: a slow acceleration, a growing surge, and a whoosh and a roar as it zoomed free. By the end of the seventies, modern skiing often seemed to be cruising at Mach 1.

In the past two decades, Summit and Eagle counties in Colorado have become the largest ski-destination locale in the country, with six major ski resorts—and a growth in skier visits from roughly 100,000 to nearly 4 million. This doesn't even include Winter Park, the next resort to hit the million-skier mark (probably in 1982 or 1983), or Steamboat Springs, currently in the midst of a major resort-development phase. Colorado, which in the late fifties barely existed in skiing's "great scheme of things," had the top three multi-area destination resorts in 1980. Only one other *state* topped the combined Summit–Eagle volume: California. Only one other was about equal to Summit–Eagle: Vermont. No other state—not Utah or New Hampshire or New York—was even close.

Yet Colorado, America's leading ski state today, owes its success not only to the Golden Age but, more importantly, to its ability to survive and thrive in the Environmental Era—despite the disasters of Aspen and Adam's Rib and the delays at Beaver Creek.

Let's back up a bit, though, to put this into perspective. The Golden Age focused on the pampering of the intermediate skier and thus gave us Mount Snow and Vail. These were the dominant forces of the sixties, as

Stowe and Sun Valley had been for the thirties, forties, and early fifties. It also gave us two of the nation's more interesting ski impresarios—Walter Schoenknecht and Pete Seibert—who invaded Vermont and Colorado respectively with their unique dreams, aggressive visions, and dynamic personalities. Both were World War II veterans, Schoenknecht a tall, skinny ex-Marine and Seibert a wounded veteran of the fabled Tenth Mountain Division; both also shared long experience in skiing and a commitment to its future appeal to the mass of Americans. (Oddly, within close proximity in the mid-seventies, both would be run out of their creations by newer business-oriented owners, and both would try to do it again from scratch on their own: Schoenknecht in Connecticut, Seibert in Utah.)

Although Vail has certainly become the bigger, Mount Snow initially was the more important. Walter Schoenknecht's philosophy and immediate success in 1955 led quickly to the development of Stratton, Killington, Sugarbush, Waterville Valley, Loon, and Hunter—and, by the mid-sixties, to the exploding popularity of skiing in the East. (It's hard to remember and accept this, but as recently as the early seventies Vermont still led Colorado in skier visits.) This burgeoning in the East (and the Midwest) created the traveling skiers who've been responsible for Colorado's current dominance.

Mount Snow and Schoenknecht proved that the atmosphere and terrain at Stowe (and the smaller Mad River Glen) were self-limiting and that most Americans would never tolerate the (expressed or implied) arrogance that went along with that Pioneer Period. Only the expert, Stowe decreed, could be a *skier*, and therefore only the expert would be allowed to *enjoy* skiing. All others, confronting the convoluted, badly designed, and poorly maintained serpentine cuttings on Mount Mansfield, would fail—"payin' their dues" as we said in a later time—until either they persevered and mastered, as a few did, or quit, as most did. Schoenknecht thought this was nonsense; he felt that everybody should enjoy themselves as much the first day on skis as they would later as experts. (Siebert felt the same way at Vail.) So, where Sepp Ruschp and his pals had cut corkscrews through the tree cover at Stowe, Schoenknecht bulldozed wide, gentle swaths not merely at the bottom, as the Stowe crowd did with disdain, but right from the top.

He also realized that skiers—especially the novice and intermediate—do not live by skiing alone. Nor do they want to be intimidated and scorned by the more competent. Rather, they want to be welcomed and entertained and coddled, and since they're paying the money they should get what they want.

While this was heresy to the dogma of the Pioneer Period, Mount Snow proved that the intermediate was the future and that the future was now.

Ski impresario Walter Schoenknecht, at Mohawk Mountain, Connecticut.

Whether the idea itself would have caught on as quickly had Walter Schoenknecht been self-effacing is moot, because he was never that. He had a zealot's belief coupled with a hyperactive spirit and a snake-oil-salesman's soul. The fact that he was six-foot-nine, skinny as a ski, with a rapid-fire delivery and dark-black snapping eyes that made him the terror of the ski club circuit didn't hurt either. The skeptics tried and became converts, and they came back again with their friends. Those flapping flags around that heated outdoor pool, the goldfish in the wall-sized tank at the bar, the palm trees around the indoor pool, f'gosh sakes—how could anyone not laugh at the foolishness of it since, after all, it mirrored so perfectly your own foolishness at trying to slide down a snow-covered hill on two skinny boards? And lord, how the money rolled in.

Seibert, if anything, went Schoenknecht one better. Seibert's vision, while equally intermediate and fun oriented, was aimed as much as the affluent investor as at the middle-class skier: He was selling not just the pastime but the promise of owning a piece of a luxurious, controlled, self-contained resort. Where Schoenknecht built a massive, colorful *ski area* and dreamed of a huge resort interconnected by innovative lift networks, Seibert built that massive,

Mount Snow, Vermont.

colorful *resort* at Vail. He conceived the modern American Ski Town not as a retrofit mining town like Aspen or (in time) Breckenridge, not even as a rich man's hideaway (Sun Valley); he conceived it as a place where anyone could be comfortable.

How successful was he? When he was to replay that hand twenty years later at Snowbasin, virtually all twenty-five limited partners (at $75,000 a pop) came from Vail, and the other general partner was the mayor of Vail. And in most cases, that investment in Snowbasin came from "loose cash" from their investments in Vail.

Or, how successful was he? In one way or another all the succeeding popular resorts—Keystone, Copper Mountain, even Steamboat and Snowmass —followed the same basic profile in their early stage of development during the seventies—as Sugarbush currently is.

Or, how successful was he? By 1970, less than a decade from the day it was opened, Vail had become the queen of American ski resorts. It was so complex in structure that it had split into three separate organizations: the ski-area company (Vail Associates), the Resort Association, and town government, which by the middle of the seventies had shattered any illusion that it was a captive "company town" as it increasingly became a contrary and, fortunately, often a limiting force. Because if Seibert's creation had a weakness, it was his *lack* of vision: Vail had become far bigger, a sprawling megaresort nearly ten miles long and a mile deep, than anyone could ever have anticipated or planned for. It had simply exploded past the limits of anyone's vision circa 1960. It happened because Seibert, like Schoenknecht, had been *right*. This was what skiers wanted and this is where they came.

Ultimately, the bubble had to burst.

Killington was the first in the East to challenge Mount Snow's emerging supremacy. Started in 1957, quite soon after Mount Snow, under the equally legendary (albeit far more reclusive) Preston Leete Smith, Killington at first seemed more a throwback to the older areas with its difficult, cold, erratic trails and distinctly unfriendly lodges; to some degree this perception survives today. But Killington promoted the ski-instruction programs far more than Mount Snow did, especially the total ski-week concept. The skiers were spread better throughout the seven-day week, where Mount Snow continued to peak on weekends, producing crowds so massive that no one noticed how little the facilities were being used midweek. Killington also pioneered by ignoring the "big-name" ski-school director, choosing instead to integrate teaching into its total ski-week program without the temperamental obstructions other areas faced. Killington was the first to key snowmaking and grooming to

Pete Seibert, and a nighttime view of the Vail he created.

midweek ski-school usage as the students matured day by day, and it packaged lodging (some of which it owned) and equipment (which it rented) with tickets and lessons into one overall price. In time the resort came to be known as Big Green Ski Machine, but the "green" applied to cash as well as to the mountain range. The contrast was interesting in the sixties: Schoenknecht sold fun and games; Smith sold experience and learning. Schoenknecht sold chaos; Smith sold order. Schoenknecht relied on natural snow and accepted the vagaries of some weekend crowds' being better than others, whereas Smith relied on snowmaking and accepted advance reservations.

In the final analysis—at this juncture in time, anyway—Smith had the better idea, so much so that when Mount Snow faltered in the "bad years" of the early seventies, Killington bought it and is now resurrecting it as a curious hybrid of the two.

As an oddity, the other ski company that seriously considered buying Mount Snow was Hunter Mountain in New York's Catskill Mountains—a previously little-known area that exploded into prominence during the 1973–74 gas-and-snow-drought season by performing better under adversity than anyone else in the East. Begun as a weekend diversion by a group of Broadway personalities in 1960, Hunter was taken over by the Brothers Slutzky, who ran a road-building company, when the Broadway boys went belly-up and couldn't pay their construction bills. Younger brother Orville Slutzky began playing with and improvising on snowmaking, and by 1973 Hunter had the best snowmaking and grooming in the East and better proximity to the New York market—and presto, it became the third most popular ski area in the East. By 1979–80, the Second Great Eastern Drought, Hunter had become number two in popularity, edging ahead of Sugarbush/Glen Ellen (renamed Sugarbush North) and Stratton/Bromley but not nearly catching Killington, which is almost as reliable and runs a far longer season.

Thus, as we enter the eighties, we begin to see the shape of the future: dependability (snowmaking became crucial also in the Rockies following the drought there in 1976), packaging (including the learn-to-ski experience), and the self-supporting ski town. (Plus, as we'll discuss in Chapter 13, the big corporate owner.)

But other trends, somewhat subtler to spot at first, were equally important—thanks to the incursions of the Environmental Era.

The Environmental Era hit with more stunning quickness than did the Golden Age—more like a jet landing on a carrier—simply because it was a reversal rather than an escalation. Two generations' worth of belief in the inexorability of skiing's growth was shattered in five years, beginning with California's Mineral King episode in 1969 and peaking with the 1974 election of Dick Lamm as governor of Colorado. Between those years virtually every major skiing state was hit with varying degrees of severity, especially Vermont, Utah, Michigan, Maine, New York, and the entire Northwest. New ski areas and resorts emerged in the seventies only where they'd been planned and approved well in advance, and even large expansions ran into delays. New resorts starting from scratch after 1969–70, when the National Environmental Policy Act was passed and the Environmental Protection Agency established, could not be placed on U.S. Forest Service land, where virtually all Rocky Mountain and Sierra resorts are located. (Deer Valley and the Snowbasin expansion are on private land.) Vermont's infamous Act 250 (1970) cracked down with even more brutal severity; several years were to pass before even a new chair lift or a snowmaking installation would be approved without screaming hassles, and the first *major* expansion in the state—the proposed interconnection between Sugarbush and its neighbor, the former Glen Ellen, bought by Sugarbush and renamed Sugarbush North—is running into California-type warfare.

And California is where it all began. In 1969 the Sierra Club instituted a lawsuit to block development of Mineral King, a proposed $50-million four-season resort to be built by the Disney Corporation. However, while Sierra eventually lost the court battle, it began to perfect the Chinese-defense strategy of losing the battles but winning the war by exhausting the developer's resources through expensive and extensive delays (known as the "cash-flow blues"). It refined this technique even further in another Disney proposal, Independence Lake, by seeming at first to cooperate in the planning before swinging the ax and by participating or providing the inspiration to similar environmental groups elsewhere.

Another successful attack hit in Maine, where the much-needed Bigelow Mountain development—near the existing Sugarloaf and Saddleback ski areas —was thwarted by a combination of a tough environmental code and a small group of elitists. The same thing happened in Utah, where the planned expansion of Snowbird to include necessary intermediate terrain was halted by the Wasatch Mountain Club (aided by Sierra Club), the federal Wilderness Act, and the EPA. In Montana, where Big Sky became the last resort to open in the United States on national forest land in 1973, after a lengthy fight, the preservationists learned the lessons and blocked Ski Yellowstone three years later. The Aspen Skiing Corporation lost a major battle in Washington State over Early Winters (this one's still alive, albeit just barely), and Clay Simon waged war for years in Oregon before he got approvals to expand Mount Hood Meadows. Arizona, because of a unique situation with the Indians (thanks to devoutly antiskiing Rep. Mo Udall), nearly lost not only the expansion but the *entire ski area* called the Snow Bowl.

Still, through it all, Colorado, like New Hampshire, seemed serene, able to ride out what many thought was going to be a short squall. Colorado about that time was one of the nation's leading ski states, a tad ahead of Vermont and still trailing California in total skier visits, but coming on faster than either of them. It seemed that somehow Colorado—that bastion of the American West with its mining heritage and free-silver culture—had drawn a pass on the California/Vermont/Utah blockade.

Except for the Olympics. Oh, maybe not; perhaps if it hadn't been for the Olympics, targeted for Denver in 1976, it would have been something else. But those Winter Olympics became the rallying cry "Don't Californicate Colorado," and when the voters KO'd the games during the summer of '72 they created a new folk hero named Dick Lamm. Two years later he rode that one-issue campaign into the state house and, seemingly within seconds after being sworn in, issued a moratorium on future development and created the Winter Sports Council, the Council of Governments, and a bureaucracy in Denver that, in one stroke, rivaled those of far longer standing in Albany and Sacramento and aped the worst of the one in Montpelier. In a day Adam's Rib was fractured and Beaver Creek dammed.

Yet, in all truth, it wasn't completely one-sided. In many locales—southern Vermont and Tahoe being probably the most glaring but far from unique—slovenly development stole the beauty of the natural environment. Cheap neon-lit cinderblock and A-frame structures cluttered the access roads, polluted the streams and the air, and threatened to destroy the fragile ecosystem of the high alpine tundras. Worse, ski-area owners either bluntly didn't care or gave lip-service to the need for solution and subtly didn't care. Virtually no one *did* anything, preferring to rely on the sad old cop-out: It's not my land, I do the best I can at the area, but how can I tell other property owners what to do with theirs? The result was that the governments stepped in, prompted by a small group of preservationists, and told everyone what they should and could and would do—or *not* do, which became the more common reaction. And the gates slammed shut.

Whether the cure was worse than the ailment depends on the eye of the beholder. But the net result was that as the decade wore on crowding at ski areas became *over*crowding, creating increasingly dangerous conditions on the trails, discomfiting ones in the towns, and finally degrading the "ski experience." Something had to be done.

Had the "movement" created an aura of reason and compromise, forcing the excesses to be removed and generating better planning for the future, the Environmental Era would, on balance, have been a "good thing," as I commented in major articles in 1969 and 1970 in SKI Magazine. But, of course, "things" never stop at their natural resting places; unscrupulous politicians got hold of a "hot" issue and ran for daylight against a weak, unorganized group of opponents. The National Ski Areas Association didn't become the effective lobbying and industry-reform group it now is until late in the decade, when Jay Price of Boreal Ridge, California, and Phil Gravink of Loon, New Hampshire, took over as successive presidents. Skiers remained totally unorganized; the U.S. Ski Association, which could have done that job, proved totally inept, uncaring, and concerned only with racing (aside from its Far West chapter, which actually got so fed up with the national organization that it resigned for a short time). In contrast, organizations like the Sierra Club, the Wilderness Society, the Audubon Society, and ad hoc groups in the Wasatch and Adirondacks and Gallatin Valley and Bigelow region got their acts together and guaranteed the vote; the rest was inevitable.

As the Environmental Era evolved, a whole new group of leaders emerged to replace the Ruschps and Schoenknechts and Seiberts—people like Chuck Lewis of Copper, Roy Cohen of Sugarbush, Jim Branch of Sno-Engineering, Bob Maynard of Keystone, Phil Gravink of Loon, Cal Conniff and Dave Cleary of the National Ski Areas Association, and Joe Prendergast of the American Ski Federation, each representing different aspects and philosophies of the "new ski-resort business." But in the first major battle that the ski industry won (after five successive years of defeats on a variety of fronts), the general was one of the "old-timers": Bob Parker, a veteran of the Tenth Mountain Division and a man regarded by insiders as being as much the essence of Vail as Seibert himself. Parker effectively took a leaf from the Sierra handbook and reversed it: Where the preservationists previously had perfected the Chinese defense, Parker went them one better and "conferenced them to death." Come, let us reason together, he would say. These are our plans, and you can tell us where we could make them better. We need your input. Tell us. Show us. Help us all. And in time, the federal and state and local officials and the elitist forces of preservation talk themselves into exhaustion, a strategy that enabled Beaver Creek to go through the planning mill "without changing one jot or tittle of the original plan." (Others have since taken much of the credit, but you can believe it was Bob Parker who held the field command in the "North Africa" of the Environmental War.)

But as with most campaigns, winning the Battle of Beaver Creek was expensive. It cost Vail Associates an additional $7 million in planning and permit and land-acquisition costs over initial projections, not even considering the inevitable drain as projected revenue failed to appear. The Creek, after all, had been due to open for the 1976 Olympics, but it didn't open until 1981 and then on a very moderate scale: no resort facilities, which were further delayed until 1982–83. Overall, the cost to open was roughly $50 million, and many experts wonder if Vail can ever earn it back.

It also cost Vail Pete Seibert, who simply ran out of fiscal resources to fight the environmental war—especially after the old gondola at Vail crashed and killed four skiers in the spring of '76. Seibert's departure—while bitterly and justifiably resented by the residents and old-time investors/promoters of Vail, a mood that hangs over the town to this day—was inevitable. No town the size of Vail (or possibly, no state the size of Colorado) could contain two such powerhouses as Seibert and Harry Bass, the president of the Goliad Oil Co. Bass and Goliad Oil took control of Vail Associates—the company that runs the ski area, as compared with the resort and town—and put an end to the efforts by other companies to "raid" VA stock. He had been one of the original investors and simply bought up a controlling interest, which left Seibert's position somewhere between awkward and untenable. (The same pattern would soon confront Walt Schoenknecht vis-a-vis Pres Smith and the Sherburne Corp. at Mount Snow.) Many in Vail feel Bass could have resolved it in a "nicer fashion" (as Smith, in fact, did), but the result was inevitable because for Vail, as elsewhere, the "Day of Goliad Oil"—all the Goliad Oils—had clearly come.

If the Environmental Era had one coldly demonstrable result, it was that developing, expanding, and running a major resort had become very expensive. The shoestringers couldn't do it anymore. The old days of "building what you could until the money ran out in July or September or the 13th of November" were gone, and those great stories of Schoenknecht adding two-thirds of the second level of Snow Lake Lodge in the Summer of '64 (or whenever) had joined the Bunyonesque and Runyonesque. To "make the resorts happen," as they say, you needed long-term financial resources and an ability to make accurate cash-flow, return-on-investment, and earnings-per-share projections to prove to investors that you could survive a series of reversals and delays that seemed inherent in the new approval process—which generally took five years! You needed, in short, a very fat-and-happy parent corporation aswim in liquid assets and thin in accounts receivable. (For details, see Chapter 13.)

The Environmental Era also created a wicked spiral in the real-estate market at existing or already-approved resorts; nothing like finite supply and expanding demand to shoot the prices higher than Independence Pass. Condominiums, which have become the staple second-home unit west of the Divide, blew from $40 per square foot to $75 to $150 to $225 to $300 and occasionally, in Aspen, as high as $400. Housing developers either got rich quick or went broke quicker as they tried to reap the whirlwind, judge the market, juggle the cash flow, and pray for the snow to hold off and for the labor market to hold out and for the approvals to hold up. Exacerbating the spiral were floods of Europeans and Latin Americans and Middle Easterners and Japanese, anxious to get their money out of home base and to take advantage of the declining dollar. Equally predatory were the hordes of Americans playing the inflationary trend and figuring they could pay off their high debt with ever-cheaper dollars. Fortunately for everyone's sanity—except for the few developers who got caught in the final squeeze—this overheated market cooled during the credit-crunch/recession of 1980 and hit the deep freeze, at least in the Rockies, by 1982.

This boom, coupled with the permit process that evolved during the Environmental Era, did several good things:

- It began to attract to the ski-area business a large number of intelligent management people with MBAs, LLBs, and engineering degrees; the industry could finally afford to pay decent salaries and offer interesting business and legal problems to solve.
- It underwrote the development of highly skilled consulting firms employing diversified talent.
- It finally compelled both groups to learn how to retrofit the old, declining resorts of the Pioneer Period to absorb the growing demand for skiing.
- It demanded sophisticated marketing-research programs to underwrite the large loans suddenly necessary to build *anything*, thanks to the ever-lengthening periods required to get permits.

Two other major forces emerged in the Environmental Era that contributed both to the problems of ski-resort management and to its increasing sophistication—the "energy crisis" and the "liability crunch." The energy mess needs no explanation here—we've met it in too many other situations—but it's safe to say that the ski-area people reacted to the warnings of 1973–74 with as much long-range perception as Detroit did. Fortunately, under NSAA's increasingly professional guidance, the owners reacted far more quickly to the scare of the summer of '79 and, aided by those bright young executives, got solid conservation and transportation programs incorporated into management philosophies in time for the 1979–80 season. Also, thanks to the potent lobbying skills of its new umbrella organization, the Washington-based American Ski Federation, skiing helped to thwart the proposed weekend-closing legislation and to form the Congressional Travel and Tourism Caucus, on which ASF plays a role far larger than its size would seem to warrant. Skiing, in short, was growing up.

The "liability crunch" hit with equal suddenness in 1976 as the energy crisis did in 1973. For more than two decades the ski-area owners, especially in the East, had believed that any skier who falls and hurts himself had assumed that risk when he bought the lift ticket. That had, in fact, been the law, but late in the spring of 1976 a judge in a state court in Vermont thought this just wasn't right and awarded $1.5 million to a paraplegic named Jim Sunday who'd been injured skiing at Stratton. The ensuing panic was inevitable; yet on balance it was beneficial because it forced area operators to reexamine all preconceptions about safety on the trails, including snowmaking, grooming, and marking. At the same time, the safety of the ski lifts came under tighter scrutiny, and with it came the creation of a new, more sophisticated national standard for lift safety and inspection—prompted, in no small part, by the fatal gondola and tram accidents at Vail and Squaw Valley during the latter part of the decade.

Thus, no matter how you look at it, the decade of the seventies was probably the most important in the history of ski-resort development. Under all those diverse pressures—environmental, financial, energy, safety—the industry's leaders either matured or left. The new heroes weren't the pioneers of the thirties and forties like Sepp Ruschp or even the spellbinders of the Golden Age like Walter Schoenknecht and Pete Seibert. Rather, a new group emerged, keynoted by people like Chuck Lewis who, in addition to developing and promoting Copper Mountain, chaired the Colorado Tramway Safety Board, used his accounting and MBA background to create tight budgetary controls, and moved quickly from "young Turk" to president of NSAA in 1981. Or like Jim Branch, president of the powerful Sno-Engineering consulting firm, who expanded ski-resort design from the old days of focusing only on lift-and-trail networks to a modern theory that includes the social, the political, the financial, and the environmental/energy issues as well.

Sno-Engineering's existence antedated Branch; the firm was formed by the now-legendary Sel Hannah, one of the great designers of ski-area terrain dating from the late thirties. He focused mostly in his native Franconia region in New Hampshire—Loon, Waterville Valley, Cannon's Peabody Slopes are among his best—and had an incredible "feel for a mountain." (He's also a great raconteur, and I wish we had the space for his "early tales.") But much like the Seibert and Schoenknecht days, Hannah's era ended not because of a lack of perception—he foresaw earlier and more accurately than most what the Environmental Era would lead to—but because to Sel Hannah, as with all the pioneers, skiing was and always will be "the mountain." He appreciated the need for financial and political and social planning and in many ways pioneered this evolution; but *he* just didn't want to do it. However, Jim Branch, one of Sel's appointees to the firm in the late sixties, did want to get involved—as did other associates—and in time, Sel semiretired amicably to his farm and Branch took over. (Skiing gets no pass from the Corporate Inevitable either.)

Branch and his ever-widening group of special-expertise associates began to attack all aspects of planning: getting the special permits needed under federal and state environmental laws; running the political/marketing campaign that "sold the locals" on the need for resort development or expansion; considering political/social/economic constraints on development as superseding in importance the capacity of the mountain; designing the five- and ten-year financial models that developers need to attract investors and to run the operation long enough to make a profit; and coordinating airports and highways with accommodations and lift capacity. Today there's hardly a new resort even in the dream stage in which Sno-Engineering—or one of the other firms now following the same pattern—isn't deeply involved. This, too, contributes to the overall maturity of the industry.

Thus, if you were to summarize the seventies in skiing, you'd have to say that it was dragged, somewhat reluctantly, from its teens to early adulthood; it was matur*ing*. And the process will continue, at times willingly and at other times reluctantly and painfully, as the forces that rise continue to converge.

Snowbasin, Pete Seibert's future kingdom.

Still—let's admit it—most of us are rooting hard for Pete Seibert to "make it big" at Snowbasin, to prove that there is still room for the Lone Ranger in the Golden West on the frontiers of skiing. When I wheeled into that virtually nonexistent base area at Snowbasin in March 1980 and saw the rudimentary lodge and the two trailers serving as offices, I couldn't help but remember Chuck Lewis starting at Copper and Max Dercum at Keystone and the stories about Seibert's early days at Vail—before I'd even begun to ski. For the first time in several years the view brought back the romance and the drama and the whole crapshoot soul of skiing that dates back to its earliest days. Because no matter how much we like and respect and enjoy today's new heroes, we have a special corner of our souls we reserve for the Ruschps and the Schoenknechts and the Seiberts. And if you want the truth, so too have the "new heroes"—and virtually to a man they're also rooting for Seibert to go one up on Harry Bass.

PART TWO

WHERE TO SKI

Introduction

What struck me the most as I reread the "Where to Ski" section from the last edition of this book was the naivete about the nature, quality, future, and essence of the ski-resort business. Convinced that I had been sharper, I reread my own book published about the same year, *Where to Ski*, and was quite disappointed. I hadn't been! We were all guilty of refusing to perceive skiing as business. That was too bad, because it left the skier—you—unaware of what was really happening. So let's try to rectify that—as, in fact, *SKI* and *Skier's Advocate* are now doing.

What were the main errors of that perception?

• The geography was wrong. With a typical eastern bias most ski writers have (because most of us are from the East), discussion of the areas usually ran from east to west and gave equal time to the five regions. The problem is, there aren't five regions; there are three—and they aren't weighted equally. The Rockies are first, foremost, and by far the most popular and important; the Northeast and the West Coast are about equal in volume and vitality to each other and, cumulatively, to the Rockies. The other two—the Midwest and Southeast—are small, trivial, and irrelevant to the true future of skiing in the United States except that, like the minor leagues of baseball in a bygone era, they produce the skiers for the serious regions. In 1979–80, for instance, the Rockies produced more than 20 million skier visits, the East and

West Coasts about 10 million each (the East was severely depressed by a bad snow season and properly should produce closer to 12 million), and the Midwest and Southeast about 4 million each.

• The projections were wrong. Although most of us realized privately by 1973 that the decline in relative position (if not volume) of two of the nation's three world-class resorts—Aspen and Sun Valley—was inevitable and that even the third, Vail, could be in trouble unless patterns were arrested, we tended to give them undue prominence. Aspen had already grown into what I felt was the smuggest, most arrogant, and generally the least pleasant major ski resort in the United States, but in those days we didn't say that kind of thing. Sun Valley, more by dint of location (access problems) than that same overbearing undertone, was about to become irrelevant rather than merely passé. Vail barely avoided the same type of implosion and unpleasantness only because one Tenth Mountain Division veteran, Bob Parker, reemerged into the top position circa 1980 and arrested the decline in pleasure. Today the story of the Rockies focuses instead on Summit Country—especially Copper Mountain and Keystone—and Winter Park, Steamboat Springs, and Vail/ Beaver Creek in Colorado, plus Little Cottonwood Canyon (Alta and Snowbird), Park City (town and multiarea resort hub), and Snowbasin in Utah. And, not incidentally, both Vail and Aspen are now seeing actual declines in volume.

• Both coasts were in trouble. No-growth patterns at the area and resort levels had already emerged and plagued us all decade, and many continue to do so for this decade—although 1981–82 saw the start of a reversal in the Northeast! California's a disaster: overcrowded on weekends, generally underdeveloped as resorts (and, therefore, lacking ambience), and totally blocked by preservationists. The Northeast (New England and the Mid-Atlantic) is almost as overcrowded, but it is saved from the après-ski dreariness of California only because it inherently has a more pleasant environment: lovely old inns and good restaurants and bars. Neither region has seen a major new ski development since the sixties, and the only hopes for the eighties are expansions in New Hampshire and Vermont and Oregon and California. I suppose we still had vague flickers of hope in the early seventies that that could be altered; we really don't now.

• The subject wasn't emphasized enough. Where to ski is the most important issue in skiing, against which the others—equipment, instruction, and certainly competition—pale by comparison. Let's face it, if you don't find a place where you like to ski you're not about to indulge in buying, learning, and racing. Furthermore, if you can't afford to ski the other aspects of the sport become totally irrelevant.

So now let's take a look at where to ski circa 1985 and the years that follow.

Skiing—ski areas and resorts—may not truly have become "big business" by the standards of the automotive industry, but increasingly, as I'll detail later, it's become the captive of big business. As I mentioned in the general introduction, the Tenth Mountain Division is slowly fading into history and the people at the helm of the important resorts work for large corporations. This is an irreversible trend—and, on balance, probably a good one—and these people look to the bottom line. In time the result will be that fewer people will ski but will enjoy it more (and pay a lot more for it). The only reason the businessman gives any thought to the cheap-ticket ski-club types is that a few of them will evolve into the high-paying customers of tomorrow. Therefore, the big resorts will eventually have to buy a few satellite small areas on which to deposit and entice the future clientele, but by the middle of the decade most skiers will find it hard to make a reservation at or afford a top resort.

Initially, this pattern will appear in the Rockies, first in Colorado and then in Utah. But as these resorts turn away business the trend will overflow into the expanding resorts on the coasts: Mammoth and Tahoe in California, Bachelor and Mount Hood in Oregon, Ski-93 (and the Mount Washington Valley, if anyone there ever wakes up) in New Hampshire, Sugarbush and Mount Snow (initially) in Vermont. In addition, large areas on both coasts that are reluctant to commit to the resort concept will find themselves in fiscal trouble and, in turn, will be purchased by large corporations willing and able to make the commitment.

A major component of this future is what one resort marketing director in New England called "the $200,000 ski vacation": buying a condominium. I once described the difference between a ski area and a ski resort as being this: An area has a base lodge; a resort has a real-estate office. Increasingly, resort developers are bringing condo construction "in house" and reaping all the benefits (as well as expanding their risk or "exposure"); the more they control their housing and satellite operations, the more they're going to turn the screw and sell "packages" rather than lift tickets.

To make the $100-a-day ski-trip price tag more palatable (and thus sell condos), resort owners will make skiing more pleasant. How? By eliminating the biggest problem: overcrowding on trail and lift. For most of the seventies, area operators figured the easiest solution was to build bigger and faster lifts, widen trails, improve snowmaking and grooming, and, generally, increase a mountain's capacity to absorb skiers. Without belaboring the reasons and causes, this just hasn't worked: Lift lines may have become shorter but the trails became lethally overcrowded, especially at the intermediate level (which, as they say, is the "money market"). The next solution? Limit ticket sales harshly—more and more areas on the coasts have already begun doing this—and jump the day-ticket prices significantly (while absorbing part of this increase in the ski week/vacation package price). Even some nonresort "day" or weekend areas will learn that 200,000 skiers a season at $30 a person generates a far better *profit* than 400,000 skiers at $15.

What will exacerbate this pain in the pocketbook is the rapidly escalating cost of "getting there." We'll be able to amortise the cost of gasoline far better over the course of a week's vacation than for a day or weekend trip, unless we drive short distances with a full car. Thus, day-trip ski areas in the Berkshires and Catskills, near Big Bear Lake or on Snoqualmie Pass, or hiding in Big Cottonwood Canyon, will continue to do fine, but small or midsized areas four and five hours away from *anywhere* will shrivel and die or be absorbed into larger empires.

And that's one vision of the future. Who knows? Maybe Aspen and Sun Valley will finally realize they're in the service business and that their persisting arrogance will simply put them out of the resort business. Let's hope so; we all hate to see such lovely ski terrain spoiled because a few of the self-anointed think it's their private preserve.

Aspen aside, Colorado continues to lead the nation in all facets of skiing. In fact, Colorado has grown so solidly, consistently, and inexorably that it has created a major access problem: Stapleton Airport can't handle the volume on a busy weekend, and the recently built I–70 highway isn't adequate for the traffic when it snows. This has already begun to limit the growth potential and may get worse.

Utah will be the top contender in the eighties, a trend that will become more pronounced as skiers continue to become older and better. For much of the sixties and seventies, Utah's great problems were fairly difficult mountains —tougher than Colorado's, on balance—and a reputation for being "dry" in an alcoholic as well as powder vein. But now, the importance of being able to buy drinks in a bar has ebbed since liquor is easily available and since today's skier just isn't as hooked on the need for booze. In addition, he's capable of skiing Alta and Snowbird and, in fact, has forced Park City to add tons of expert terrain to its previously intermediate mix. When both Snowbasin and Deer Valley emerge, by mid-decade, as major resorts in their own right, Utah could well push past California as number two in popularity; in any event, it will nudge Colorado in the "quality" and price arena, which in the long run may become the more important.

California is in serious trouble, as we've suggested, and the needed new areas and resorts just aren't emerging. Mammoth, so aptly named, will expand mightily by mid-decade and become the nation's largest ski hub by far—it already runs even with Vail. Heavenly, Squaw, Alpine Meadows, and Northstar anchor the highly popular Lake Tahoe region, but don't look for major growth or expansion there for years to come: The preservationists have stopped it cold.

Vermont continues to lead the East in volume, although New York has emerged as a potent force in raw skier-day volume and New Hampshire is beginning to offer a better ski experience. In Vermont, Sugarbush and Mount Snow will become the top resorts in terms of quality and growth. Killington will continue to lead in skier visits and expanse of terrain but may lag in sprucing up its resort operation. Killington also owns Mount Snow, which in the long term may become the company's leader, especially in the resort phase, because it's the more pleasant and compact of the two and has grown quickly to regain its prior image. Stowe, for all its random and occasional expensive surges toward a return to prior greatness, has too much Aspen/Sun Valley about it and probably won't quite make it again as either an area or a resort.

New York remains a puzzle, because although it leads the nation in sheer number of ski areas it boasts few major mountains—compared with Vermont and New Hampshire to the east—and two of the three it does contain, Whiteface and Gore, are owned by the state. The only large, well-run ski mountain in all of New York is Hunter, which puts an awesome burden on one company.

Like Utah, New Hampshire is the comer in its region, the Northeast. The Granite State also tends to offer more challenging mountains and a lower-keyed but very pleasant après-ski experience. The state's top complexes are along I–93—Waterville Valley, a full-service resort in the southern core, and Loon-and-Cannon, two disparate areas drawing close together to create a major resort surrounding the beautiful Franconia Notch region. The parallel valley to the east, named after Mount Washington, has one of the best resort towns in the country, North Conway, and a superior high-difficulty mountain, Wildcat; alas, owners of the other areas in the region have failed to produce competitive areas for the eighties.

The Midwest? We have to mention Boyne and Lutzen and Indianhead, and so on—so regard them as mentioned. Mostly, the Midwest produces

Colorado's (and increasingly Utah's) skiers and has begun funneling some into northern New England.

The Southeast is the next coming region, although like the Midwest it functions more to generate skiers for other regions after they have learned the skills on the mountains of North Carolina and West Virginia. The Southeast is the only region that has a record of consistent growth for the past four years.

Although perceptions about the relative merits of different resorts must, perforce, be subjective, they can be reinforced by watching growth patterns: If the resorts and areas you like tend to have the largest and most consistent increases in skier visits year after year, you can't be too far off base. The correlation isn't perfect because other factors besides high-quality experiences and management can generate growth: improved access, better proximity, a major expansion, even a new area nearby. Similarly, a snow drought or gas shortage can dry up the crowds at even the best areas/resorts. However, these gains or losses tend to be short-run; gains and losses based on quality tend to be enduring.

Now, how can you quantify—or at least identify—quality? Are there demonstrable criteria? What are they?

• Full-service facilities. A resort or large-scale area should contain a decent sit-down restaurant in addition to its cafeteria, a nursery within easy walking distance, a ski shop with good repair expertise and a fair range of "demo" equipment, and a free shuttle to lodging. Some also offer free, or quite reasonable, transportation to and from the airport or train station, a service that will become more widespread.

• Total integration. Although some well-run *areas* haven't achieved this, almost all first-rate *resorts* have. This means that one company owns and runs everything: mountain (snowmaking, lifts, grooming), ski school, food service, ski shops, nursery, lodging bureau (and increasingly, the lodging itself). The more a resort "franchises out," the more it cedes control over the quality of the facility. A plea by a resort company that "we're only in the uphill transportation business" should be greeted with a call to the next resort on your list. I've run into very few operations where the subcontractors equal the quality of the mountain operation.

• One-price shopping. The resort that can sell you a ski week that includes lifts, lessons, equipment rentals (if you want them), lodging, most food, and ground (not necessarily destination) transportation has its act together. The more those pieces fall away into a separate-pricing format, the more the total operation is fragmented. Take it from there.

In addition, front-line areas and resorts have large fleets of grooming equipment, high-capacity snowmaking systems (even in Colorado and increasingly in Utah), and well-developed lift-maintenance programs. The problem is that there's no way you, the recreational skier, can check that yourself, but Bob Enzel's *White Book of Ski Areas* does an excellent job.

A good resort or large-scale area also offers a wide range of terrain to handle all levels of skiers comfortably. For one thing, this tends to produce a first-rate ski school; for another, it means that everyone in your group can find some comfort and challenge.

Finally, a good resort should offer a pleasant "walking village" complete with restaurants, bars, a few shops (it doesn't have to be Vail), and some facilities for other sports (it doesn't have to be Sugarbush).

Costs, of course, are usually high. Even the racing establishment is committed to the premise that only the wealthy need apply for a place on the U.S. Ski Team, as evidenced by the fact that the team decreed, in 1980, that parents of all members of the Development Team—the official feeder or "farm" system—had to fork over $8,000 apiece. No scholarships.

A few large areas, like New York's Hunter Mountain, Utah's Alta, and virtually every place in the Northwest, make a serious effort to keep the price of skiing relatively low. Most don't, and most will move within the next few years to push the prices up as high and fast as they can without hurting the bottom line. Ski clubs, bus-tour operators, regional and national associations will find it increasingly difficult to book into first-line areas or resorts at bargain rates, except for low- or off-season bookings (early December, January, late March, and April). Their leverage will decrease as the major resorts fill their rooms—which will occur by mid-decade even at those Rocky resorts that are fizzling now.

Still . . . how expensive is "high"? Many market people complain that the press focuses too much on the day ticket and underplays the ski-week package or the season pass. (Most areas and resorts still offer the latter, and in fact for the serious weekend/day skier it's the only way to go, especially if you have a family. But that serious family of four is going to lay down $2,000 for a season anywhere worth skiing by 1985.)

So why talk about "*usually* high"? Because some bargains exist: The ski-week package is the best buy in skiing at the overwhelming majority of ski resorts and areas—$100 or less for five days of lifts and (usually) lessons, sometimes even including rentals. You can often get all that plus lodging (and occasionally some food) for a bit more than $200—not much more than you'd spend for the same thing on a weekend. Why? Because the ski industry is in the process of changing your skiing habits, and there's no way to do that better than by offering a good price incentive.

So take it. Change your habits. You're going to have to, sooner or later, and so start going with the flow.

It's possible for a couple from either coast to spend a full seven-day week (even eight or nine days) in the Rockies for $1,000, including airfare, if they know what they're doing in dealing with the airlines and the resorts. It involves long-range planning and commitment and some comparative shopping among carriers and resorts. You can almost halve that amount by staying in your own region, and cut it even further by doubling the size of your party and renting a larger condo, cooking some of your meals (breakfast and a few dinners), and accepting the realities of life. For a little while longer, you'll be able to ski inexpensively on a ski-week basis if you're willing to make the effort. But if you persist in your day/weekend habit, you're going to pay the price.

The High and the Mighty: The Rockies

The Rockies are an embarrassment of riches. Quite simply they offer the best skiing in America (some say the world), as demonstrated by the fact that they attract twice as many skiers as any other region. Even those who love eastern or Sierra skiing feel obliged to defend their choice against what the Rockies have to offer, whereas people in the Rockies feel no need to defend their preferences at all.

For skiing purposes, the Rockies have been defined as Colorado and the six little sisters: Utah, Montana, Wyoming, Idaho, New Mexico, and Arizona. Utah, though, is making a serious effort to get out from under that Centennial cloud; the others also get a bit restive on occasion. The problem is that three are one-resort states—Jackson Hole, Wyoming; Sun Valley, Idaho; Taos, New Mexico—and all three are keyed to the advanced and expert skier (no matter what they say). Montana has two serious resorts—Big Mountain and Big Sky—and two of the fine "sleeper" areas, Bridge Bowl and Red Lodge. So when you come down to that well-known bottom line, the Rockies are Colorado, the emerging Utah, and five little sisters.

COLORADO

Colorado, as we said in the introduction, dominates American skiing. Period. In 1979–80, for instance, it had three resort complexes that topped one million skier visits—Summit County, Vail, and Aspen—and seven areas that topped 600,000 visits: Vail, Winter Park, Breckenridge, Steamboat, Snowmass, Keystone, and Copper. That's seven of the nation's top ten areas in terms of volume—and possibly of the top eight, since figures from California tend to be less reliable.

Sometimes, though, it's hard to figure out how this happened. Even as recently as the last edition of this book, Colorado had barely nudged ahead of Vermont and still hadn't caught California; now it outstrips them both by a lot. Its airport access is far from ideal and getting worse; Salt Lake City's airport is better. Furthermore, Stapleton Airport is nearly two hours from the best Colorado skiing—Summit/Vail/Winter Park—and more from Steamboat and Aspen. In contrast, Salt Lake is easily within an hour's drive (or bus ride) from Alta, Snowbird, and Park City; Snowbasin will fall into the same time frame when the new highway exit is completed. Finally, Utah tends to have lighter, drier, deeper powder, at least equally impressive mountains, and a fascinating culture.

Despite all that, Colorado is still king.

Why? No state offers more diversity of skiing than does Colorado; no two areas or resorts are interchangeable in terrain or personality. The good Denver skiers have their favorites: Either they ski Breckenridge *or* Copper *or* Winter Park/Mary Jane. (Vail is slowly phasing out of that "day" market despite its protests to the contrary, and Steamboat is just that little-bit-extra-too-far-to-go, although it's starting to do a good weekend business à la Vermont.)

Plus—maybe more important—every major area in the state has an awesome quantity of novice and intermediate terrain, even Ajax at Aspen. Many of Colorado's ski mountains are predominantly easy right off the summit. And while few areas in the state ever get that Utah-like dump of three feet of bottomless powder overnight—which can defeat all but an expert skier—they do get adequate quantities quite frequently, and its slightly wetter texture packs out to a better novice and intermediate surface: money snow rather than ego snow.

Those Colorado mountains are big, wide, rolling, and expansive: It would take three days of dawn-to-dusk skiing to cover every trail at Vail or Snowmass and two each for Copper, Winter Park, Ajax, Breckenridge, and Steamboat. That's skiing each trail *once*. Several of those mountains top 3,000 feet of vertical, and all the rest easily exceed 2,000. They all have plenty of lodging nearby—most within walking (and/or free shuttle bus) distance of the lifts—plus an adequate-to-excellent range of restaurants, bars, shops, drugs, and sex close at hand. True, the Northeast tends, on balance, to have better restaurants (and, like California, holds its own in the drugs-sex-booze category), but nothing else touches the totality of the Colorado experience.

While we all recognize that Summit County is number one in skier visits and diversity, the problem is there really isn't a Summit County ski experience (although there is an interchangeable ski week lift ticket and a countrywide free shuttle bus). You've got three-and-a-half different ski experiences: Breckenridge, Copper, and Keystone, plus A-Basin, owned by and run from Keystone but a totally different type of mountain.

Breckenridge, town and mountain, is a small-scale Aspen, which is no surprise since the ski area (Peaks Eight and Nine) is owned by the Aspen Skiing Corporation and the town is owned by everyone else—none of whom seems to agree about anything except that the "Ski Corp." is a bad guy. The town is wild and wide open with a basically laissez-faire outlook on life and love and development—just so long as everyone keeps it cool on Main Street. A couple of the restaurants are fine and most are OK. The skiing is diverse, chaotic, often very challenging but mostly intermediate. On balance, it's the kind of place you start off liking and slowly get disenchanted with.

Copper, by acclamation, is the "skier's mountain," mostly because of the incredibly tough eastern section known as the A-B Lift circuit. The west side of the mountain is strictly novice and low-intermediate. The core, right down the middle, is pure intermediate, edging, on occasion, toward the advanced: It is the closest thing in the United States to a perfectly organized mountain. The support facilities are equally good; but the resort complex has taken the better part of a decade to emerge, and for much of that it resembled the Ardennes Forest after the battle. It began to fill in nicely as the eighties arrived, anchored by the huge Club Med, and will have a visual affinity with Vail when it's done. However, the departure in 1982 of Chuck Lewis, its initial developer and moving force, leaves its future open.

Keystone, basically, is a four-star (in the *Mobil Guide*) resort/hotel complex with a pair of ski mountains attached: Keystone, a lovely, gentle novice-intermediate gem (with a few advanced-to-expert trails to keep you honest); and A-Basin, that hoary monster harkening back to the forties and featuring the famed Pallivicini trail. This is one of three Rocky Mountain resorts whose restaurants will give the East a good run, and overall may be the best-managed resort in the Rockies, and certainly one of the most pleasant ski experiences.

Over the pass from Copper is the legendary Vail, which has withstood a lot of grief—environmental fights, gondola accidents, town-mountain-county

A lone skier challenges "Drainpipe" from the summit of Copper Mountain.

civil wars—only to reemerge, virtually unscathed, as the Queen of Colorado. It deserves the title. It runs nine miles edge to edge, can handle 25,000 visitors and 15,000 skiers of all ability levels at any given time, and even manages to keep the "Wild Side" hidden underground. You could do a whole chapter just on the range and diversity of the skiing and another on its nearly one hundred restaurants. It may have become too big for its own good, however: the ambience is diminishing, as are the crowds.

Circling two hours southwest out of Vail brings you to Aspen. What's there to say that you haven't heard before? No two people see it the same way. It has four mountains (Ajax, Buttermilk, Highlands, and Snowmass) and two

Skiers pause to enjoy the view of Dillon Lake from the summit of Keystone Mountain.

towns (Aspen and Snowmass), loosely tied together by a slew of marketing operations, and whether you love it or hate it you won't be bored. Each mountain is unique; skiers like Ajax, tourists prefer Snowmass, beginners love Buttermilk, and no one can quite define Highlands (least of all Highlands, the only area in the complex not owned by "Ski Corp." or its parent, 20th Century-Fox). Despite (or perhaps because of) all this, Aspen—even worse than Vail—has slumped in business during the 1980–82 period, and seems to need a good shakeup.

Had you swung northwest rather than southwest out of Vail you'd have found Steamboat, the Cowboy Capital of Skiing. This is a most interesting

Soaring above Aspen, a competitor in Aspen's Winterskol carnival jumps for form and distance.

resort, with separate real and resort towns and a great, big, meandering, chaotic lump of essentially intermediate mountain—something of a surprise, really, given its renown as the home hill of such famous racers as Buddy and the whole Werner clan, Billy Kidd, Hank Kashiwa, Lonnie Vanatta, and Moose Barrows. It labored through growing pains under its owner, the giant LTV Corporation, in the seventies, but a new consortium has gotten the luxurious-type resort complex rolling; however, it has a solid wild side, anchored by the Tugboat Bar.

East of Steamboat (or north of A-Basin) is Winter Park, one of the last of the great sprawling ski complexes in search of a main village (I never have found it—or at least, I hope I didn't). The old Winter Park, dating slightly prewar, is a lovely novice-intermediate complex; the new Mary Jane is a mean, steep, moguled monster. Take your choice—or ski both, on the same ticket. Incidentally, a new master plan unveiled early in 1982 finally promises a real resort town.

Heading ten miles due west out of Vail brings you to Beaver Creek, owned by Vail. Although the complex is far too new to evaluate yet, it bears a solid resemblance in feel and skiing to Vail—as you'd expect. It's big, still raw and ungentled, with only the hint of resort to come, but it skis long and happy in the fall line. Initial "notices," however, have been poor to fair, and crowds are still thin to nil for the size of the investment.

And we haven't even discussed Crested Butte, Telluride, Monarch, or the other denizens of the powder belt of southwestern Colorado. They're all worth skiing—and would be giants in any other state.

UTAH

Can Utah's Wasatch Front challenge this murderers' row lineup? Not in quantity—not yet, and probably never—but it can hold its own in quality and diversity of skiing. Furthermore, Park City is as well developed and free-wheeling a resort town as you'll need, and Snowbird and Alta each offer distinct experiences. Snowbasin is the "comer."

Park City is the state's giant, a former (and still functioning) mining town anchored by one of the most rapidly expanding ski mountains in history —it seems to grow new terrain and vertical, like a teenager—and the only one that has matured from novice-intermediate only a few years ago to an up-front expert killer today. (One of the biggest challenges, alas, is figuring out how to get back down.) Only a mile away, served by the same town, is the

Park City's Jupiter and Scott Bowls at the ten-thousand-foot-level overlook historic old mine buildings.

Opposite:
The smooth, light powder of Alta.

new Deer Valley, a high-priced ski experience on a well-designed mountain complex. A mile the other way is ParkWest, a lower-priced but interesting mountain. Together, the mélange almost equals Aspen (albeit with a more pleasant ambience) in terrain and good restaurants. And despite what you've heard, the bars are good, too, just BYO.

Alta, up in famed Little Cottonwood Canyon (why "famed"?—try to drive it in a snowstorm), may be the best ski mountain in America. That simple. Its reputation is for being highly expert—and it is, it is—with a tendency to corner light powder; but Alta hides a huge amount of superb intermediate terrain and a few lovely novice slopes. As a resort, however, it's a tad weak; it has a few pleasant family-style inns, a couple of which offer decent food (great by Utah standards), but it has no central hub and certainly nothing that resembles "action."

A mile south in the Canyon is Snowbird, which runs mean for mean with Alta but yields badly in the novice and intermediate levels. However, it's a far more sophisticated resort—high-rise in the French fashion, high-priced by any fashion—and concedes that boys and girls occasionally like to meet and mate. (Many people prefer to stay at Snowbird and shuttle up the road to Alta.)

Still, *the* sleeper in Utah is Snowbasin, which has much of the feel of Alta with a very Colorado-like master plan—no surprise, since its owner is Pete Seibert, creator of Vail. When (and if) it is built out as projected, the expanse will be endless and the expense will be high, but the product will justify both. Like much of Utah, Snowbasin offers—and will continue to offer—a predominantly bowl-skiing experience; but where the current area is advanced to expert, the new section will offer a large variety of intermediate as well.

WYOMING, IDAHO, AND NEW MEXICO

The three main resorts throughout the rest of the Rockies are worth trying—if you can get there. Especially Jackson Hole.

Jackson Hole, Wyoming's claim to fame, is the largest ski mountain in the country at 4,100 vertical feet and, on balance, probably the toughest (even including Mansfield). Its development during the past decade focused on producing a large quantity of intermediate terrain on the lower and middle sections on the big mountain, Rendezvous, and the program has worked. But no intermediate can take the tram to the top—that expert!—with any chance of getting down comfortably. This is the home of Corbett's Couloir, where we take all those great photos of "getting air," and some say that isn't

Jackson Hole, Wyoming.

Vista of the Sawtooth range near Sun Valley, Idaho.

even the toughest run there. The housing complex has developed nicely and, generally, it's a good resort for good skiers.

Sun Valley, Idaho's big-league entry, isn't any easier or more tolerant and also ranks among the nation's toughest mountains. It has an excellent lift network, thanks to recent additions and replacements, and lift lines are all but nonexistent. The village, however, hasn't changed from its old Averell Harriman/upper-crust heritage and doesn't seem to have realized that its halcyon days are long gone. Frankly, anyone willing to hassle the travel to get to the northern Rockies would probably be better advised to head for Jackson, especially coming from the East.

Taos, the New Mexican champ, is one of those resorts described as "unique"; the bossman, Ernie Blake, "does it his way." If you find him more puckish than arrogant, you'll love it; if you can't you'll hate it. Skiing, as at Jackson and Sun Valley, is essentially expert with even less concession to intermediates. Like Alta, everything after skiing centers on a group of family inns—and like Alta again, Taos loyalists are fiercely protective and its detractors vociferous. It is, however, quite a ski experience.

All three, incidentally, have excellent ski schools. They have to.

MONTANA

Over lunch one fall, Abby Rand glanced around the table at the other contributing editors of SKI and pronounced to Doug Pfeiffer, "It's your turn to 'discover Montana.' The rest of us already have."

Yet despite SKI's (and *Skiing*'s) earnest efforts, Montana remains the great secret in American skiing. Why? Who knows?

True, not many have chosen to "discover it" in January, when it tends to get a mite cold even by New England standards. But during March, its Big Four are worth skiing.

Big Sky gets the ink because it still looks like a Colorado resort that got lost. It has a first-class hostelry, a pleasant village (two, in fact, separated by one of the meanest access roads in skidom), and some good low-end skiing—

A Big Mountain "snow ghost," caused by freezing fog.

but until recently it lacked the challenging terrain that justified making so long a trip. However, that has been largely solved. The resort/area's major weakness does persist: It's Anywhere, U.S.A. and lacks character and uniqueness. But it does its job well.

"Just the other side of Bozeman" (by Montana standards; an eon by human scale) is Bridger Bowl, a small-scale Alta and one of the true discoveries. Alas, Bridger—a powder-hound's pleasure—is the jealous preserve of "the locals," who fired an otherwise excellent general manager just because he wanted to make it famous. No resort village of any kind exists (Bozeman's a neon wilderness and fifteen miles away at that), but the area does boast a nice, small inn at the base.

"A few miles to the east" (less than a day's drive, anyway) is Red Lodge, town and area, connected by six miles of access road that rivals Big Sky's and that has dumped graders over the edge. The town is one of those little gems you happen upon (the word is *serendipity*), and the Carbon County Coal Company is one of America's great bars, complete with a vicious stud-poker game (legal in Montana). The area leaves a bit to be desired—namely, novice and easy-intermediate terrain—but its expert stuff is expert, not merely advanced, and some of the "trails" are barely demarked blazes in the tree cover.

Finally—and this is near absolutely nothing else even by Montana or Texas standards—Montana offers Big Mountain, the area that produces those great snow-monolith photographs. The resort is very pleasant, if small by southern Rockies standards, and the skiing is good to very good (not quite on a par with Bridger but better than Big Sky). On balance, it's a nice place for families who ski—"OK but not super."

And that's the Rockies. That's a lot. That's the guts of American skiing.

Where Snowmaking Is King: The East

In the fall of 1980, I wrote a short introduction to "The East" section of Bob Enzel's *White Book of Ski Areas*. It reflects my feelings as tightly and accurately as anything I've ever written.

Let's hear it for the East and to hell with Utah and being defensive. Sure, we all sneak out to the Wasatch every couple of seasons, but a week of that perfect-powder-and-blue-skies monotony is all we can take. Out there, if the skiing crowd sees two whole clouds in the blue eternity it stays home; in the East, we have *skiers* who brave the elements and face nature in its raw state—minus 22 and *raining*, not unusual in a New Hampshire January—and return the following weekend to tangle with plus 50 and machine-made slush. And where, until March, the skies are not shining all day.

The East, where American skiing began fifty years ago, still yields nothing in the size and challenge and diversity of its mountains. Not to the Rockies or the Sierra or the Northwest. More than a score of areas top 2,000-foot vertical; Killington, Vermont, and Whiteface, New York, hit 3,000 feet, and Sugarbush, Vermont, and Sugarloaf, Maine, exceed 2,500. Those four plus Stowe (Mount Mansfield) and Mad River Glen, Vermont; Cannon and Wildcat, New Hampshire; and the west side of Hunter, New York, are as demanding on expert skiers as anything Alta or Jackson Hole can offer—even when the

Panoramic views greet skiers as they begin their descent from the summit of Killington Peak in central Vermont.

snow conditions are ideal, which happens at least one day in March every third season if you get there by 10 A.M. Yet we also have as many easy-riding, ego-soothing intermediate runs as Colorado.

Over the past decade, we eastern skiers have taken a strongly defensive posture talking to our Rocky Mountain cousins. Can't figure out why, either. True, our condominiums don't cost $400 a square foot yet and we don't have to hang in the air for two hours to land in Burlington, Vermont, or Springfield, Massachusetts (and two more to learn our skis were misshipped to Siberia), and we don't have to make reservations three days in advance for the honor of waiting an hour to get seated at a mediocre restaurant and . . . but you see, there we go again, getting defensive. Someone once said the Pilgrims landed on their knees at Plymouth Rock and then landed on the Indians and that their descendants now land at Stapleton and ski Colorado to see where the Indians went. Nonsense. A few of the rich ones go out there to visit their investments, but they come back home to *ski*.

Eastern skiing is a challenge, but sometimes it seems more of one to the ski-area public-relations folk than to the paying veterans. The PR types coin funny phrases like "Vermont powder," which has as much credibility among the cognoscenti as "We're from Washington and we're here to help you." Eastern skiing conditions fall between the rock and the hard place, and even the good intermediates talk knowledgeably about flex patterns and Rockwell grades and tuning skis, which means be-sharp and very-flat. You tend to pay a lot of attention to hand position and standing tall on the inside edge of the turning ski and not getting psyched when the refried ice has a 4000 Rockwell. The amazing thing is that after a while you get to like it. You feel something's missing when you can't hear the edge. You get worried when the pole tip sinks into rather than bounces off the snow; roughly 37.4 percent of eastern skiers don't know why poles have baskets.

Sometimes, of course, it doesn't snow much in the East, at which time we rely on machines. Machines to make it, machines to smooth it. It's no surprise that some of the owners and presidents of the most successful eastern areas are veterans of the road-construction business rather than the real-estate trade (which populates the executive suites in the Rockies), because in midwinter, grooming an eastern ski mountain resembles nothing so much as regrading a highway, and you better know how the hardware works. In the winter of 1979, when it no-snowed in impressive no-quantity all season long, at least twenty areas offered good skiing top-to-bottom by mid-January. Two areas independently coined the phrase "Oreo-cookie skiing": white in the middle, brown at the edges. Sure it was tough and crunchy and dicey but even in 1980–81, the worst in a century, 75 percent of the skiers came.

Then, making the winter workouts worthwhile, spring arrives. Starting roughly at Washington's Birthday and often running well into April (in 1981–82, Mount Snow and Sugarbush battled until mid-May and Killington hit June), the East explodes with some of the best slidin'-and-turnin' you'll find anywhere. The sun returns from Florida, and the hats and goggles get shelved, and the cooking oil and bright colors reappear; the snow softens and the bumps grow and everyone surreptitiously resurrects the soft skis and is very happy he's in top-flight shape from winter's ice skating so he can bound with abandon down the black-diamond trails. Picnics in the sun, wine in the skins, kids in bright vests, and the jury at the base, beer in hand, ruthlessly rating your skill and daring, and woe betide the bomber who gets a "9.5 for a great head-plant." He buys the next round.

But as with the sliding sport elsewhere, eastern skiing does not live by mountains alone. We have at least five ski towns in New England and the Catskills—Hunter, Killington, Stowe, Manchester, and North Conway—that will give Aspen a run in the sex-suds-and-sound scene and ten restaurants that'll make the veterans of Vail weep in envy. Those skiers from Manhattan and Westchester aren't blinded by the candlelight or snowed by the sizzle. Last time we heard, some enterprising developer from Summit County was trying to lure Charlie Lovett's and the Horse and Hound, two of the best white-clapboard inns-and-restaurants in skidom, from Franconia Notch, New Hampshire, to Colorado. And you'll hunt a long time in Utah without finding a Common Man (Warren, Vermont) or an Inn at Saw Mill Farm (West Dover, Vermont). What gets three stars in Montana gets sent back in the Catskills . . . and I won't even mention those three gourmet experiences in the Berkshires right in the shadow of Butternut Basin, one of those beautifully run small areas in which the East abounds.

So . . . what is eastern skiing? Hard sliding, soft living, a sense of antiquity unequalled elsewhere, and a soft, comfortable glow after a day, a weekend, a week, or a season well spent. Ski areas run by professionals not baffled by ice or drought, lodges and inns owned by people who abjure the condo coldness and the microwave cliché. And vistas: Can anyone ride the new eighty-passenger tram at Cannon or the sparkling gondolas at Loon or Wildcat without feeling the same heart-stopping sense of awe at the majesty of New Hampshire's White Mountains and the famed Mount Washington as he would at the Front Range or Wasatch? We easterners think not—which is why a week in the West is a fine visit, but a season in the East is where we live.

Funny thing was, several eastern executives—mostly in Vermont, of course, the land of thick-furred woolly bears and thin-skinned area operators—voiced minor displeasure that I had not indicated that all was perfection in northern New England. Well, it isn't—not by a long shot. Snow conditions remain tentative and snowmaking is king. The areas that show the best consistent rates of growth—such as Hunter, Killington, Loon, Sugarbush, some of the smaller mountains in the Berkshires—prosper because of their skills in making and grooming artificial snow. (I enjoy those few operators who insist "It isn't 'artificial,' it's machine-made." It reminds me of that old gag line: "It isn't fake fur, it's real Dynel.") Both producing it and skiing on it are the crafts of eastern skiing, and it's no accident that eastern (and midwestern) skiers who learn and survive on this surface are among the world's best.

Competing grooming vehicles at Stratton, Vermont, during annual National Ski Areas Association trade show.

Nor is the East unique; it's just the most honest about this situation. (For this purpose, we can include the Midwest, which has the same weather patterns, snow quality/predictability, and dedicated skiers and yields only, albeit significantly, in vertical feet). The giants of the Rockies are increasingly committed to snowmaking: Copper, Keystone, Winter Park, Vail, Park City, even Aspen have serious installations these days, and they crank up the guns as early and heavily as anyone in the East, save Killington. Frankly, the heavy skier traffic at the popular Rockies resorts make snowmaking mandatory—and again, it's no surprise that the Easterners are often the best on the hill when the snow in Colorado and Utah packs down hard (as it does, with increasing frequency).

So let's not get defensive about eastern skiing. It is what it is: technically and physically demanding and a lot of fun. Preston Leete Smith, president of the Sherburne Corporation (Killington and Mount Snow), once said that the challenge of skiing is meeting and mastering all the different conditions and neither expecting nor wanting perfection every day. There's something very soul satisfying about hanging a good carved turn on frozen granular; it means you know what you're doing with, and on, the edges of a pair of skis. It is why, I suspect, eastern skiers never get bored and remain committed to skiing for decades.

VERMONT AND NEW HAMPSHIRE

The principal eastern ski corridors are Route 100 in Vermont and I–93 in New Hampshire (although Route 28 in New York is emerging).

Vermont remains the leader in the Northeast. On or near Route 100 are those household names in skiing (from south to north): Mount Snow, Stratton, Bromley, Okemo, Killington, Pico, Sugarbush, Stowe, and Jay Peak. Stratton has bought Bromley, Killington has bought Mount Snow, Sugarbush has bought the old Glen Ellen (and will add Mad River Glen one of these days), Stowe has allied loosely with Smugglers' Notch, and Jay is essentially a Canadian ski area with few real ties to the U.S. of A. Only Okemo and Pico remain truly independent, and Okemo was almost taken over in the late seventies. Eastern skiing, especially in Vermont, is going the way of big-corporate Colorado.

Although the Sherburne Corporation continues to lead the Northeast in skier volume, with some 1.1 million visits between the two *areas*, it's the least *resort*-oriented company among the state's major complexes; the company prefers to put its money onto the mountain to upgrade the skiing. Both Stratton and Sugarbush are pushing ahead faster into the high-quality skier-village format, although Stratton seems to be struggling, while Smugglers' probably has the most highly developed resort village in the state (although its mountain operation remains mediocre). Stowe, however, is battling hard to overcome its Aspen-like ambience of arrogance and to modernize Mount Mansfield, unquestionably one of the two toughest mountains in the East (and possibly the country). By the mid-seventies, Stowe had lost any claim to its old title of "Ski Capital," and the chances of its regaining it are roughly equal to Muhammad Ali's of winning a fourth crown. The Sugarbush complex has displaced Stowe among the expert and advanced skiers and should widen the gap under its more aggressive and imaginative management, especially when the new village is finally ready.

Opposite:
Tackling knee-deep powder on the North Face at Mount Snow.

Stratton and Mount Snow, both battling for leadership of the southern Vermont intermediate league, do an excellent job of servicing their slightly different clientele (Stratton the more affluent), and both are getting better every season. You'd have to look long and far to find two areas with better children's and junior programs, totally integrated from nursery through racing. (All these areas, not incidentally, have excellent and very different ski schools. You'll learn how to *ski* in a week at any of them.) As of 1981–82, Mount Snow had surged into a huge lead and was expanding faster than Stratton. Also, it remains one of the most ego-pleasing areas in the nation.

Still, Killington leads the East in volume—the only area east of the Divide to make the national top ten—and as the old saying goes, it has to be doing something right. It is not warm and cuddly; it is not luxurious and affluent; it is not compact and easy to maneuver in. But Killington is efficient: It has one of the most organized learn-to-ski programs in the nation; its access road, sprawling as it does, contains more swinging-singles action than anywhere in the East (save, possibly, Hunter); it has large quantities of all levels and types of skiing, from wide and supersteep (Bear Mountain) to glades to twisting trails to one of the best learning slopes in the nation—Snowshed. It does the job.

The two sleepers in the state are Okemo and Pico, both 2,000-vertical-foot areas with little of the ol' pizzazz but a lot of first-rate skiing, and a lot more being developed. These are the areas that draw a high ratio of serious skiers—in a funny way more akin to the New Hampshire than to the Vermont experience, even though little of the terrain is truly expert.

An interesting difference, by the way. A good friend commented that Ralph DesLauriers of Bolton Valley was the only native Vermonter running an area in the state, and while it's not completely true—the managers of Pico and Okemo are also natives—it makes the point: Vermont skiing is alien, and few locals ski. In contrast, almost every owner in New Hampshire is a native, and the state produces a far higher ratio of natives who ski seriously and often. The result is that while residents in Vermont often view ski-resort development hostilely, the people in New Hampshire regard their areas and resorts as just other local businesses and respond rationally. Furthermore, since they are locals, they demand far fewer frills and voice more concern with what we currently call "the quality of the ski experience": turning the skis.

Thus, by and large, New Hampshire offers a lower-keyed (and lower-priced) skiing and vacation experience: People go there to ski. The old-time, white-clapboard inns are still highly popular, especially in the Franconia Notch region (Cannon and Loon) but also in the Conway and Sunapee zones, while

The three-and-one-half-mile Killington Gondola, longest ski lift in North America. Trails up to five miles long challenge skiers on the return descent.

condos have caught on only at Waterville Valley, still the state's only "planned resort." Loon, however, is now making moves into the condo market also.

The best—and most popular—skiing in the state is up that I–93 corridor, starting with Gunstock and running through Waterville, Loon, and Cannon. Cannon, run by the state, had the first aerial tram in ski country (1938) and replaced it in 1980 with a huge eighty-passenger version that covers the 2,100-foot vertical in five minutes—and drops you onto some of the toughest, most demanding ski terrain you'll ever want to ski. Cannon is linked, by free bus through the Notch and an interchangeable ski-week ticket, with Loon, one of the smoothest, most professionally run areas in the country with a wide array of excellent intermediate cruising trails (plus a trio of high-expert runs for *those* days). In between, inns like Lovett's and Horse and Hound are worth the trip. Half an hour south is Waterville, the state's leader in volume (although Loon is closing fast), which offers a good range of challenge, a superb ski school (from nursery through expert-adult), and a tight, compact, well-organized village.

The best skiing in the neighboring Mount Washington Valley to the east is up at the famed Wildcat, another tough, demanding mountain, with snow-

The base lodge facility at the Mt. Tecumseh ski area, Waterville Valley.

Hunter provides good skiing even in a snowless season (1980–81) with an extensive snowmaking operation.

making now covering the full 2,100-foot vertical. The other major areas surrounding North Conway—the largest resort complex in the state—vary from slim (Cranmore) to nil (Attitash) in snowmaking and provide interesting skiing only in good snow seasons—a major weakness in New England.

In the southwest, the state's other first-rate large area, Sunapee is finally installing snowmaking, and offers beautiful intermediate runs on a 1,500-foot vertical. Pat's Peak is the best small area in the state, with excellent snowmaking and a fine junior racing program.

NEW YORK

New York offers three first-line ski mountains—Hunter, Gore, and Whiteface —in order of preference. Hunter is the only privately owned mountain of the three and is by far the best managed. No area is more apt to produce good skiing in a snowless season, with the vast majority of the 1,500-foot-vertical mountain covered by snowmaking, and few areas can boast Hunter's scope of skiing—from super-gentle (Hunter One) to almighty expert (Hunter West). Gore, however, boasts potentially the best skiing terrain in the state, on a

2,100-foot vertical, if the state (which owns it) ever commits itself to running a first-line ski area. Whiteface, site of the 1980 Winter Olympics and the other major state-owned area, is the biggest (3,100-foot vertical) ski mountain in the East ,the other "toughest" (besides Stowe) has one of the best managers in the nation—and even he can't get the state to run it properly. So right now New York offers only Hunter Mountain as a major, first-line ski experience (and one of the wildest ski towns in captivity), although nearby Windham is finally awakening, with its 1,500-foot vertical, and could make it two.

MAINE

The "other" Northeastern state of any vertical stature is, of course, Maine, which translates into the magnificent Sugarloaf—2,600 vertical feet of tough, sometimes-above-timberline skiing and a well-developed resort village/program/ski school—plus Saddleback and Sunday River. Saddleback has probably seen more broken dreams than Las Vegas, a pleasant mountain that just hasn't generated enough business for a succession of owners. Sunday River —recently sold by Sherburne Corporation when it decided to concentrate on Vermont—is a good, prototypical family area with a small, efficient condo program. The only problem with Maine is that you can't get there. . . .

The Northeast also offers some fine 1,000-foot ski areas: West, New York; Butternut Basin and Jiminy Peak, Massachusetts; King Ridge, New Hampshire, and Bolton Valley, Vermont.

And that's the East.

Opposite:
Skiing at Sugarloaf.

A heavy snowfall at the lodge at Indianhead Mountain, Michigan.

Small Hills, Big Interest: The Midwest

The Midwest is something of a skiing anomaly. It has a longer continuous tradition of skiing than any other section of the United States, yet it came to alpine skiing relatively late. In terms of enthusiasm, there are few groups who can match the midwestern passion for skiing, yet its ski areas are something less than impressive; one wonders how the small hills could generate that enthusiasm for the sport.

Yet strange as it may seem, Midwesterners are as a whole remarkably proficient skiers and are totally unawed by the mountains they encounter elsewhere. They acquire this proficiency on those much maligned hills of Michigan, Wisconsin, Minnesota, Illinois, Indiana, and Ohio.

Midwestern ski areas compensate for their deficiencies first by featuring strong ski schools; second, by lifts and tows by the dozens; and, third, by the gusto of their after-ski activities. Nor are most Midwest ski-area owners bashful about the lack of vertical drop.

Boyne Country, near Boyne Falls in northern Michigan, features four areas and at least a dozen chair lifts. The area's owner, Everett Kircher, claims "even on a packed weekend it is possible to take twenty-five to thirty rides a day for more than 15,000 vertical feet of skiing"—above average for even the largest areas of the Rocky Mountain West or Europe. (However, for all that, Kircher couldn't wait to buy his own Rocky Mountain resort at Big Sky, Montana, in the late 1970s.)

There's a diversity of facilities at midwestern areas. One of the best-planned complexes, Schuss Mountain in northern Michigan, has nearby landing facilities for private planes, as does Boyne. Devil's Head Ski Resort, near Merrimac, Wisconsin, opened in 1972 and now has eight chair lifts. Alpine Valley at East Troy, Wisconsin, has no less than twelve chair lifts and a rathskeller. Mount Telemark in Wisconsin holds an annual Maple Sugar Feast at which Chippewa Indians cook and serve food. Michigan's Indianhead Mountain (an excellent little hill) financed its expansion by selling shares to skiers who got free lift passes in addition to their investment. (This has been done quite a bit in Vermont, also, although bonds are more common.)

Midwesterners have been aided in their passion for practice by growing clusters of ski areas in the suburbs of Detroit, Chicago, Milwaukee, and Minneapolis–St. Paul. Thanks to snowmaking and the bone-chilling cold to be found throughout much of the Midwest in December, January, and early February, these areas offer reliable skiing if not massive mountains.

After-ski life at some midwestern areas has tended toward the Germanic and Scandinavian. That means a lot of jolly beer drinking and group singing

View of the ski hill at Big Powderhorn, Michigan.

still exists accompanied by the accordion. A notable departure from this tradition is the Playboy Club resort at Lake Geneva, Wisconsin. Skiing is a prime attraction at the big Lake Geneva facility and, of course, the after-skiing is thoroughly stamped with the style of Hugh Hefner. Care for a hot rum served by a Bunny? Incidentally, Playboy is not alone among the midwestern resorts in offering lavish lounges and entertainment. Some midwestern areas are reported to have spent as much on their cocktail lounges as they have on uphill lifts. (Telemark may have spent more, especially recently, which could be one reason it battled through Chapter 11.)

The shorter but frequently steeply pitched hills of Mid-America are ideal for slalom racing practice, and it is no accident that some of the better slalom technicians on American teams have hailed from this region. NASTAR, the National Standard Ski Race, was conceived to add spice and variety to small-hill skiing. Again, it is no accident that Midwesterners participate in huge numbers in NASTAR races (although Colorado does more). A prime NASTAR sponsor is the Milwaukee-based Joseph Schlitz Brewing Company.

Until the end of World War II, lift skiing was a distinct oddity in the Midwest. Skiing meant jumping. Then, in a little less than a decade, downhill skiing became the midwestern rage to such an extent that it threatened to overshadow jumping completely. Only the formation of strong junior programs prevented jumping from disappearing in the Midwest.

The lift skier who wants to mix downhill skiing with jump spectating finds plenty of opportunity in the Midwest. There are jumping hills almost everywhere, with major jumps at Iron Mountain, Ironwood, and Ishpeming in Michigan. Ishpeming has an additional attraction: the Ski Hall of Fame.

Heavy Crowds, Heavy Snow: California and the Northwest

CALIFORNIA

The West Coast means mostly California, with oases of skiing in Nevada, Arizona, Oregon, and Washington. Were it not for the tempting offerings in the Rocky Mountains, several California resorts would loom much larger in the national ski scene than they do. As it stands, West Coast skiing needs no apologies. (Well . . .) There are several areas built to true California scale.

Skiing in California is concentrated in two relatively small sections of the state. Within a hundred miles of Los Angeles is a cluster of about a dozen or so areas catering mostly to residents of that city. The other cluster is to be found in the Lake Tahoe region in the center of the High Sierra. About halfway between these widely separated complexes, like a balance point on a scale, is Mammoth Mountain, California's most famous resort and a hotbed of racing talent.

Although they seldom figure in the ski-travel plans of any but Los Angelenos, the southern areas are substantial. Several feature vertical descents of more than 1,200 feet with highly varied terrain. When there is snow, these areas are good. But this is precisely their problem: In the south of the state snow is a highly unpredictable commodity. It may not come at all. It may come at unexpected moments, and it may disappear just as quickly as it came. Furthermore, temperatures can be such that snowmaking becomes almost impossible, although several areas have the equipment.

More specifically geared to the vacationing skier are Lake Tahoe's areas. They have rapidly developed into one of the most densely developed ski complexes in the United States. Most of them are large, capable of accommodating the vast crowds pouring out of the Bay Area, and lodgings for the skier are not hard to find. The Lake Tahoe region is a popular summer resort, and on the Nevada side there is the year-round attraction of legalized gambling. There is a choice of motel, hotel, or lodge for every taste.

The newest are Kirkwood and Northstar, while the most famous is Squaw Valley, site of the 1960 Olympic Winter Games. It was largely developed by a transplanted eastern socialite, Alex Cushing, who was instrumental in winning the games for Squaw. Like many California areas, Squaw is endowed with so much natural beauty, terrain, and abundant snow that it has been able to survive occasionally haphazard management. Lifts keep sprouting up to capitalize on a seemingly endless amount of fresh ski terrain. The area is not one mountain, but rather several peaks. In addition to its many chair lifts, Squaw is home to one of the largest aerial tramways in the world of skiing as well as the giant ice arena left from the 1960 Olympics (though this is not in such great shape). California skiers keep hoping that Squaw Valley's terrain will be linked by lift some day to that of neighboring Alpine Meadows, another Tahoe area that is not as large and is more geared to the family skier. Alpine today is the real "comer" in the region.

At the south end of Lake Tahoe, hard by the gambling casinos of Stateline, Nevada, is Heavenly Valley. Heavenly has been compared to an upside-down saucer: Its bottom slopes are steep, far steeper than the upper slopes. As a result, beginners and many intermediates journey to the top for skiing and ride down the lower part of the mountain on the tram. Heavenly's skiable terrain reaches on and on; in fact, its best powder skiing is on the Nevada side. From the top you can stare down at the fantastic blue expanse of the lake, on the other side at the desert extending eastward. Many consider Heavenly the most photogenic of all the North American ski areas. There is also a stunning contrast at night when the massive neon strip of Stateline's main drag lights up. Gambling is definitely part of the après-ski scene. Many are the ski racers who come to Heavenly to compete and have to wire for money to get home.

Another Tahoe area, the Sugar Bowl, offers a rather staid contrast to Heavenly. The oldest area in the region (1939), the Sugar Bowl makes its own entertainment, much of it in the superb mountain homes of prominent members of San Francisco society. The resort is probably the snobbiest in American skiing.

To the south of the Tahoe region, reached through Mark Twain's Calaveras frog-jumping country, is a little gem of a resort, Bear Valley, which supports skiing at nearby Mt. Reba. It is far more secluded than other California ski areas and therefore much sought after by second-home owners and skiers anxious to escape the trampling throngs. Still, the most pleasant resort in the southern region is Kirkwood, which has a nice ambience and the highest base.

Mammoth Mountain, about 150 miles to the south, has the second longest ski season of any American area (Mount Hood, Oregon, has the longest). Skiing starts in the early fall and extends into July, so great are its snow depths. Many summer racing camps are held here. Owner Dave McCoy has coached two of his own children to U.S. Olympic ski teams and has helped dozens of other youngsters develop into first-class racers. Accommodations in the area are plentiful but not plentiful enough. Every weekend, thousands of Los Angelenos stream up the desert side of the mountains to throng Mammoth's slopes, producing some of the worst crowds in the country. However, this is where all short-term future development in California will occur.

Snow conditions in the High Sierra region of California are unusually reliable, so reliable that there is more apt to be too much snow than too little. At least once a year, the Sierra resorts are overwhelmed by a massive snowfall that may drop as much as two feet an hour for days at a time. So there is always a certain risk that you will get snowed in. There is also a good likelihood that the snow will be on the wet side. Warmed by the brilliant Sierra sun, it can make for sticky going, particularly in the latter part of the season (starting in January).

Standing alone in the northern part of California, Mt. Shasta looks down from every direction like a massive white deity. Until the 1850s Shasta was an active volcano, and the Indians believed that the great spirit had made the mountain his wigwam and built a fire in its center. The area has managed to maintain an atmosphere of solitude and beauty despite the network of lifts and facilities that are still being added. High above timberline, Shasta offers open-bowl skiing with many different routes of descent and a season that runs from late November to the beginning of June. Panoramic skiing, friendly people, and informal living all help make Shasta a prime ski area. Alas, preservationists have made development highly unlikely.

For as much as the eastern and Rocky Mountain areas have changed during the past ten years, so have those in California remained the same. It's

Lake Tahoe as viewed from the Heavenly Valley tram.

sad: The state needs new ski areas badly, possibly more so than any other region. But the preservationists—not merely conservationists or environmentalists—have won and will probably, for much of the eighties, continue to win.

What makes it sad isn't merely that California skiers have had to suffer overcrowding and its related ills more than others; Easterners don't really get all bent out of shape about that, to tell the truth. Rather, California has imposed on the rest of the nation a sense that *anti*skiing is the movement of the good guys, a view many skiers themselves often share (as letters to SKI Magazine disclose, rather surprisingly). This has forced skiing—the industry and its spokesmen—to take either a defensive or a counteroffensive posture that only reinforces the erroneous premise. Colorado Gov. Dick Lamm, who rode into office on an antiskiing (anti-Winter Olympics, to be precise) platform, once asked why skiing seems to be allied with development forces—

oil, timber, and so on—rather than with those of conservation. The answer is rather simple: Thanks to Mineral King and Independence Lake (Disney's second and equally abortive effort to develop a new resort), the preservationists put skiing there, and no one knew quite how to counter it. That's the legacy of California skiing.

Yet this has produced a strangely positive result as well: California skiers, consumers rather than owners/operators, began to react as a strongly militant group, fighting against the Sierra Club and others. For most of the seventies, the only chapter of the usually moribund U.S. Ski Association (USSA) with any credibility was Far West (FWSA), which combined an effective travel program (they had to get out of California *some*how if they wanted to ski) with political activism, and so well did they do the job that by the decade's end they were larger than the other eight USSA chapters combined. Unfortunately, the group began to overvalue its importance and became shrill rather than effective. Like the Sierra Club, they fought, they believed, and they were the anoited and could tolerate no other voice, opinion, or organization. And in one of those marvelous paradoxes, their credibility sagged just as they assumed control of USSA—and only underscored the validity of the new and more moderate consumer organization, the American Ski Association.

THE NORTHWEST AND ALASKA

For most of the seventies, the Northwest—Oregon, Washington, and Alaska—remained every bit as undeveloped as California, albeit with more dignity. Washington State quietly—with ruthless efficiency—shot down the Aspen Skiing Corporation's proposed Early Winters resort, while nothing even got *that* far in Oregon or Alaska. However, as the decade ebbed, developers at Mounts Hood and Bachelor, Oregon's two major ski complexes, finally got plans for major expansions approved and funded. Today Oregon is about as bullish as any ski state in the nation, save possibly Utah, and offers the only hope for West Coast skiers to see a significant quantity of new ski terrain.

If there is a central condition to skiing in the Pacific Northwest, it is that its two largest cities, Portland and Seattle, are within an hour's drive of the snow-rich Cascade Mountains. The two cities are well known for their damp climate. Next to Midwestern skiers, the Pacific Northwest species is one of the most joked about and one of the hardiest of the breed. Most of the jokes originate in the Northwest, and one suspects that skiers of the region take a certain masochistic delight in describing their suffering.

Opposite:
High on the slopes of Mt. Shasta in northern California.

Actually they don't suffer too much. The snow may occasionally be on the damp side, but it comes early, stays late, and is deep. Thousands of skiers may scrape away at it, but because it is wet and packs well, it resists these abrasions admirably.

Northwestern skiing has the advantage of being eminently available. The Seattle or Portland skier merely has to throw his skis in the car or bus and drive for an hour or so to get all the skiing he wants—a choice of four areas each on the flanks of Mount Hood if he lives in Portland, or in Snoqualmie Pass if he lives in Seattle. The only difficulty the skier is likely to encounter is finding a parking space: One out of ten residents of these two cities skis.

If there is a drawback to this convenience, it is that it has left facilities on the skimpy side (Washington more than Oregon, which is the more civilized of the two). Although there are signs of change, you are expected to go and return on the same day. Après-ski consists mostly of what Portland and Seattle have to offer in the way of night life.

An exception to this state of affairs is Timberline Lodge on Mount Hood, one of the most massive mountain hostelries ever built. It has survived long years of mismanagement, but is now efficiently run, if slightly awesome. If summer skiing is your wish, you are most likely to find it there. The slopes from the lodge on up are rarely without snow. (However, the better skiing is located at the neighboring Mount Hood Meadows area, now in the midst of a major expansion.) The lodge is also headquarters of a summer racing school.

One of the best of the Pacific Northwest ski areas is Crystal Mountain in the shadow of Mount Rainier, about eighty miles from Seattle. Not only is Crystal elegantly equipped with lifts, but it has sprouted good restaurants and a wide range of accommodations. Alpental, a bit farther away, offers some of the best expert skiing in the region.

Perhaps the most competition-minded area in the Pacific Northwest is Mt. Bachelor, near Bend, Oregon. Bachelor owes much of its reputation to its close identification with racing. It is also one of the larger areas in the Northwest, with a wide variety of terrain, much of it geared to more advanced skiers—though of late it's become much more intermediate and has a cluster of first-rate après-ski and vacation-oriented inns. It, too, is expanding seriously.

While vacation-type offerings are becoming more diverse in the Pacific Northwest, Northwesterners still make up the majority of guests at Sun Valley. These days, Big Mountain, Montana, is also getting a lot of this crowd.

Although it has a reputation as the land of snow and ice, Alaska was late in its ski arrival. Rapid strides have been made since snowshoes and dogsleds were the favored mode of winter transportation. Alyeska, not far from

Summer skiing on the west slope of Mount Hood.

First run of the morning at Mt. Bachelor, Oregon.

Anchorage, is a major area by any measure and has lots of snow, a long season, and surprisingly mild temperatures. The site of a 1973 World Cup race, Alyeska has many open slopes and dramatic vistas. The sourdough atmosphere is prevalent, but there is also a considerable international flavor, since Anchorage is a major stop of the transpolar airlines. In 1980 the Japanese finally established a solid beachhead in Alaska—after those tentative moves toward Kiska and Attu early in World War II—when one of their megaconglomerates bought Mt. Alyeska. It seemed to satisfy everyone's yen, and Alyeska is sure to become even more international.

Sylvain Saudan near the summit of Mount McKinley, Alaska.

The sparsity of the population has prevented other major developments in Alaska, but the incredible mountains of the state are receiving more and more recognition as targets for ski adventures. In the spring of 1972, Sylvain Saudan, a daring Swiss mountaineer, climbed to the 20,000-foot level of Mt. McKinley, highest peak in North America, and then skied down a difficult route that had never been climbed, let alone skied, before. Alaska has other magnificent glaciers and peaks awaiting future challenges from skiing mountaineers.

10

The Boom that Leveled Off: Canada

If skiing can be described as popular in the United States, it positively exploded north of the border in the sixties—although it has cooled down recently. Canada has many more skiers per capita than the United States. In Canada, if there's a hill near a town, it is almost certain to have a ski lift. Nor does the skiing know any boundaries. Canadian skiers flock to northern U.S. resorts like Whiteface, New York, and Jay Peak and Stowe in Vermont.

But a big lure is for the American to journey north. At first glance, the hills of Quebec's Laurentians hardly seem worth it. Few, except Mt. Tremblant, have as much as a thousand feet of vertical. But that is not where the answer lies. French-speaking, French-cooking, French-partying Canada is the attraction. And if it's ski lessons you want, Canadian instructors are skilled teachers, challenged perhaps by the fact that so few of their compatriots seem to take lessons. So the American skier is much sought after.

If Canada's eastern skiing has a special ethnic attraction, its Rockies offer scenic beauty comparable to Europe's Alps. Banff, of course, is the best known. Located on the Canadian Pacific's transcontinental railroad and a ninety-minute drive from Calgary's airport, Banff's skiing is on Mt. Norquay. The most attractive place to stay is the huge Banff Springs Hotel operated by the railroad. Alberta liquor laws somewhat restrict nightlife (frankly it's deadly), but there are exotic hot mineral baths to soak in. For the one- or two-week vacationer, Sunshine Village is something special. A bus takes you

up the rugged road from Banff to Sunshine and deposits you in beautiful scenery, deep powder, and a well-run, attractive hotel (also dull, unless you BYO).

Banff is also the headquarters for ski-mountaineering guide Hans Gmoser. Gmoser has pioneered a kind of skiing that is unique in the world. He takes skiers—mostly Americans—across the Great Divide into British Columbia and then lifts them by giant helicopter to the tops of scores of peaks in the wilderness ranges of the Bugaboo and Cariboo mountains. Some skiers call it the nirvana of the sport. Each run is on a new mountain. Each run is through a field of unbroken powder, sometimes descending 4,000 vertical feet at a time. And always the helicopter at the bottom is waiting to take you to a new peak. The cost is high, now in the range of $1,000 per week and up—but if the weather is fine, few begrudge the expense.

About forty miles northwest of Banff on the main rail and highway route is the Lake Louise ski region. There are a number of excellent lodges with accent on the informal. A gondola lift takes you up Mt. Whitehorn for morning skiing. As the sun shifts, skiers move to the slopes of Temple, a ski circuit reminiscent of those in the Alps.

On the British Columbia side of the Rockies, there is fine-powder skiing at Tod Mountain, an hour's drive from Kamloops. Here is North America's longest chair lift (9,413 feet) and a vertical drop greater than at Vail. Lodge life is pleasantly informal and personal, and lift times are short.

Vancouver has skiing in its backyard, literally. Grouse Mountain can be reached with ease by means of the city's bus system. When the weather is right—Vancouver suffers from the Pacific Northwest syndrome—you get a magnificent view of the city and the harbor area. The ski area is well equipped to handle the large crowds it attracts. Snow is plentiful, if occasionally wet.

Only sixty miles from downtown Vancouver is Garibaldi Park and Whistler Mountain. The area possesses a big vertical drop (only half of which, until recently, was really skiable) but frequently has inclement weather. With its huge snow depths, it has good late-season skiing and offers a summer racing camp. A few years ago, government officials ended an eon-long moratorium on Whistler, the base village, and the neighboring giant named Blackcomb, underwritten by the Aspen Skiing Corporation. The new resort, when even partially built, will be awesome.

At the opposite end of the country, the province of Quebec has acquired so many lifts it gets more difficult every year to count them—plus snowmaking machinery, limited-access highways, and motor inns. Despite these changes, skiing in the province seems to have lost none of its foreign allure to eastern American skiers. They are nostalgically determined that somehow they

Opposite:
Skiing down Mt. Norquay at Banff, Alberta. Mt. Rundle is in the background.

Night scene at Grouse Mountain overlooking Vancouver, British Columbia.

Aerial turn through the glades at
Whistler Mountain in British Columbia.

View of Hill 70 at St. Sauveur des Monts in the Laurentian Mountains north of Montreal. This was one of the first tow-served hills in the world.

will still be met at the station by a horse-drawn sleigh complete with a pipe-smoking old *habitant* who will fill them with home-brewed pea soup on arrival at the simple rustic lodge heated by a glowing cast-iron stove. That little of this still exists in the Laurentians seems to deter no one. After all, an exotic French continues to be spoken, the food is great, and the tables are flecked with the foam of overflowing steins of Molson's ale. And it is still necessary to make reservations two years ahead if you want Christmas accommodations at Mount Tremblant Lodge or Gray Rocks Inn. Nor have the resort names lost their allure: Chantecler, Manoir Pinoteau, St. Sauveur, Mont Gabriel.

With the exception of Mont Tremblant, a half-dozen of Quebec's bigger ski mountains are not in the Laurentians but in the Eastern Townships region to the southeast of Montreal, just north of the Vermont line. In fact, they share a common lift ticket with Vermont's Joy Peak. Finally, for the ultimate in Quebec charm, you can visit the areas around historic Quebec City, Mont Ste. Anne, a frequent site of World Cup races, is not far from the cobbled, narrow streets of Quebec's capital.

Ontario is a gigantic regional complex, much along the lines of the Midwest. There are more than one hundred areas in the province, mostly served by rope tows and T-bars. The denizens of this region have strong tendencies to spend their ski vacations at areas other than those in Ontario. Nevertheless, or because of it, Ontario areas have in recent years acquired luxury touches, such as chair lifts, swimming pools, airstrips, first-class accommodations, and a thriving after-ski life. Some of the most popular Ontario areas are at Collingwood—Blue Mountain, Georgian Peaks, and nearby Talisman.

Overall, Canadian skiing offers dependable snow at the occasional risk of very cold weather. Take an extra sweater and also your driver's license for border identification. Otherwise you'll need nothing extra to enjoy Canadian skiing.

11

A Resort Wrap-up

THE FUTURE

Well, why not make a few educated guesses? It runs with the franchise. During the seventies I had a good track record in this area—provided, of course, you ignore the many times I was wrong.

The eighties will see four major new resorts open:

• Beaver Creek, Colorado, ten miles west of Vail: ski area in 1980–81 (that's safe), resort village in 1982–83. It's run and developed by the people who currently give us Vail. The terrain is highly commercial, which isn't pejorative so much as predictive: Most skiers will like it and return for more. It has a good supply of intermediate terrain with few unpleasant surprises, plus an adequate inventory of advanced and expert skiing and plenty for the beginner/novice.

• Deer Valley, Utah, one mile from Park City: ski area in 1981–82, resort slowly thereafter (although the current Park City will supply most of the resort base for several years). Much the same analysis of the terrain as for Beaver Creek, albeit slightly more difficult overall.

• Whistler-Blackcomb, British Columbia, eighty-five miles north of Vancouver: skiing has long existed on Whistler, and Blackcomb opened in 1980. The resort village, also long existent if rudimentary, is developing rapidly as a full-fledged major-league facility. Whistler, at 4200 vertical feet, the

120

Opposite:
Beaver Creek, Colorado.

largest in North America, offers primarily high-intermediate to expert open-bowl skiing. Blackcomb will have a more commercial trail-and-glade network on a 4000-foot vertical. Both areas are served by lifts running from the new base resort. In time, this should become the major ski-destination resort on the West Coast, surpassing Lake Tahoe, and could even threaten some of the giants in the Rockies. Not surprisingly, 20th Century-Fox/Aspen Skiing Corporation owns Blackcomb and is a partner in the resort village—covering its bets, as they say.

• Snowbasin, Utah, an hour from Ogden: skiing already exists at the current area; no resort base exists at all. This development falls into that gray area between "massive expansion" and "new resort." Current skiing is excellent, largely open-bowl terrain for intermediate through expert with interesting diversity; proposed new skiing is, if possible, even better—largely intermediate and advanced open-bowl, but with more a rolling-rambling feel than the Alta-like challenge of the current mountain. The combination should be breathtaking. So too is the challenge of developing the new much-needed resort base, which will turn on getting good financing and a new highway access from the airport; both look feasible by 1985.

Other major development proposals exist: Little Annie and Burnt Mountain at Aspen; Adam's Rib in the general Vail–Beaver Creek region; Ski Yellowstone (reviving after total defeat in the mid-seventies) in southern Montana; Early Winters (Aspen Skiing Corporation) in central Washington State; perhaps another one or two here and there. Each has suffered delays of magnitude for one or more serious reasons. I doubt any will appear before 1985; odds are no better than even money they'll debut before 1990.

A few significant expansions are on the boards for the early eighties:

• Vasquez at Winter Park, Colorado: Like Mary Jane, a separate but interconnected mountain, it will expand the already massive ski terrain by 50 percent. Unlike the advanced-to-expert Mary Jane, though, it will be largely novice and intermediate. When completed—hope for 1985 but don't reserve your tickets yet—Vasquez will make Winter Park one of the megaresorts on the scale of Vail and Mammoth: one-million-plus skiers per season.

• Slide Brook at Sugarbush, Vermont: When Solon bought Glen Ellen and renamed it Sugarbush North, it noticed that between the two areas—located on the same broad ridge that also includes ancient Mad River Glen—is a delightful natural bowl that both interconnects the two areas and increases the intermediate ratio of the total complex. It also provides a natural base area to develop a full-service, tightly controlled resort village to counter the current resort sprawl—but alas, the scope of the project provides a natural target for Vermont's now-disaffected preservationists who are annoyed at the creeping expansionism elsewhere in the state. Stay tuned, but 1985 seems a good target.

• Everything at Mammoth, California—or perhaps, who-knows-what at Mammoth? Californians more than anyone in the country need new terrain, but Mineral King and Independence Lake and just about everything else is dead. Thus, the great white hope is to triple the size of Mammoth, to handle about 45,000 to 50,000 skiers a day, or four times the number at Vail. How much will happen? Who knows? When will it happen? You tell me. What are the probabilities? Remember that the last two governors in this state have been Ronald Reagan and Jerry Brown, and *you* create a predictive pattern from that!

• Significant changes in Oregon. The biggest appears to be at Mount Bachelor, which completed Phase One in 1981 to add 40 percent more terrain and which will begin Phase Two in 1983: a massive expansion that will increase the skiable vertical from 1,700 to 3,100 feet, triple the skiable acreage, offer skiing on all exposures of the mountain, and keep the complex open year round. However, housing will continue to be contained in Bend, a town some twenty miles away. At Mount Hood, the Meadows area is planning an expansion of similar scope with some lodging involved, while ancient Timberline is getting a major facelift.

And that's it. Maybe it's not a whole lot, but it's a lot more than we saw as the seventies waned.

PERSONAL FAVORITES
(Alphabetical order, by type and region)

INTERMEDIATE[1]

Northeast	*Rockies*	*West Coast*
Hunter, N.Y.	Alta, Utah	Alpine Meadows, Cal.
Loon, N.H.	Copper Mtn., Colo.	Kirkwood, Cal.
Mount Snow, Vt.	Keystone, Colo.	Mount Bachelor, Ore.
Pico, Vt.	Vail, Colo.	Mount Hood Meadows, Ore.
Waterville Valley, N.H.	Winter Park, Colo.	

[1] All ski areas listed as "Intermediate" also have strong quantities of expert terrain. Alta, Copper Mountain, and Winter Park (at Mary Jane) are especially noteworthy at the expert level as well. (Areas marked "Sleepers" are primarily rated for the intermediate terrain, although Beaver Creek and Deer Valley get very expert in places.) The converse isn't necessarily true, although the only area marked "Advanced" that doesn't have a reasonable amount of intermediate terrain is Snowbird.

ADVANCED

Cannon, N.H.
Sugarbush, Vt.
Wildcat, N.H.

Bridger Bowl, Mont.
Jackson Hole, Wyo.
Snowbasin, Utah
Snowbird, Utah

Alpental, Wash.
Squaw Valley, Cal.[1]

SLEEPERS

Butternut Basin, Mass.[2]
Okemo, Vt.
Sunapee, N.H.

Beaver Creek, Colo.
Deer Valley, Utah

Timberline Lodge, Ore.[3]

[1] This area has had a poor history in lift safety, but its incredible terrain makes the risk worth taking.
[2] Possibly the premier small ski area (1,000-foot vertical) in the country.
[3] More for its fantastic lodge than the skiing.

12

Housing, Food, and Transportation: The Nuts and Bolts

Unless you're an inveterate member of that dying breed called the day skier, much of your ski trip and budget will focus on those mundane matters that involve getting to and surviving at a ski area or resort. And the critical issue focuses on lodging, since this controls everything else you do.

Serious skiers are more inclined to buy a second home rather than to rent space in a condo, a motel, or an inn. I learned this very early, during the first three-day ski weekend my wife and I ever took way back in 1968 in southern Vermont. Even sleeping at a motel in Bennington, the cheapest and least gemütlichkeit locale we could find, we spent $200 plus. (I'd hate to price it today.) "This is ridiculous," I said. "If we're going to pursue skiing seriously we have to buy a house somewhere in this region." Within six months we had located a lovely small farm nearby in New Hampshire—still a better locale on a price-for-quality basis than Vermont—and through the years it's become as much our home as anywhere else. Without even factoring in the value of the rapidly increasing equity, it costs us less to run that house for a month than it would cost us to lodge elsewhere for a weekend—which we do once a season for fun (and to keep tabs)—and our food costs are just what they'd be if we'd stayed home in Westchester County. In essence, especially when you consider the equity growth, we ski free vis-à-vis housing and food. In addition, we use the house in the spring, summer, and for those glorious fall weekends of New England foliage.

A second home needn't be a farm or townhouse; during the seventies, the "condo"—condominium apartment—replaced the farmhouse in skier popularity, especially as the latter became scarce and condos quite plentiful in all recreation locales across the country. If you choose well, the equity value in a condo can increase even faster than in a house and, in Colorado anyway, resale prices can zoom: At Copper Mountain, for instance, prices increased in three years from $40 a square foot to $120. This produces a better *investment* medium, but I've never fallen in love with condos as a *living* medium. They tend to be smaller in real space than their urban counterparts, even more poorly constructed, and too prone to marry you to one ski area or complex. (In typical contrast, nearly a score of good areas are within reasonable driving distance of my New Hampshire farm.) However, you don't have to worry about paying for heating or painting the outside or mowing the @#$% lawn —at least, not directly—and many are literally within skiing distance of the lifts, which means you don't have to use your car once you get there. If you put your unit into the rental pool at the right resorts and limit your use, you can *almost* cover your out-of-pocket expenses for the season. Still, one cannot: the condo market can *drop*, also, as it has in a few locations in Colorado.

But whichever route you go—house or condo—you'd better realize you're not involved in a "skiing decision," aside from location. You're involved in a "real-estate transaction," an investment medium, and you better know what you're doing. One word of warning: Do NOT buy anything ten minutes after you've come down off the mountain on a beautiful blue-sky day in March. Your judgment will be, as they say, impaired. Buy in the late spring, when the mud is at its peak, the flaws are exposed, and the realtors are a bit anxious to unload the season's remaining inventory and get down to Mexico.

Still, rational people don't go a-buyin' the first weekend they ski (although we came pretty close, I must admit). A better program, especially in these days of intricate real-estate marketing systems, is to rent lodging early in your ski career until you find *the* place you want to call (second) home. Initially, this means the weekend motel/inn bit; then you shift to the season rental on a "trial basis"; then, finally, you buy.

Also, unless you have money to burn and heavy expertise in real estate, your second home should *not* be where you *vacation*: Colorado or Utah, for instance, if you live in New York or Chicago or Los Angeles. If you plan to vacation regularly for a week or two every winter in the Rockies, rent a condo or take a room at the inn. For the vacationing skier even more than the weekender, the ability to bounce around is crucial. Two seasons at Vail may be quite enough, especially when you start becoming curious about all those stories you hear about Snowbasin or Snowbird or Jackson Hole or Whistler-Blackcomb or Summit County or Deer Valley. The real advantage of that one-week vacation every winter is that you can try the new and expand your experience and pleasure. *Buy* only in your "home region," where you'll use it as a frequent ski house (and more).

What are the current rental options? Although they vary widely, they fall into four general categories:

Inns

Staying at inns is by far the best option for random ski visits, especially at the good ones: Charlie Lovett's in Franconia, New Hampshire; Snowy Owl at Waterville Valley, New Hampshire; Sugarbush Inn at Warren, Vermont; Inn at Saw Mill Farm near Mount Snow, Vermont; SkiTip Ranch in Dillon, Colorado; Peruvian at Alta, Utah; Bridger Mountain Inn at Bozeman, Montana; Timberline Lodge at Mount Hood, Oregon; maybe another dozen here and there in New England and Oregon, which seem to corner the market in numbers. What they offer is ambience and character, good food, pleasant bars, and an easy way to meet other skiers free from the hassle of the "bar scene." Inns, however, are generally oriented more to married than to single skiers. The prices tend to be on the high side, and you're less free to try local restaurants because you've already paid for dinner. You are also usually locked into meal schedules. The plumbing occasionally is a tad primitive, if you want to know the truth. But on balance some of my best ski weeks have been spent with good people I've met at those small inns.

Condos

The best rental choice for the independent, the small groups, or those on a tighter budget is the condo. You can cook your own breakfasts and pack your lunches and decide freely on a night-by-night basis whether to eat dinner "home" or at a top restaurant. Total freedom, usually combined with good access to skiing, are the strong points, but you can find it very difficult to meet other skiers unless you're aggressive and extroverted. The plumbing and fireplaces usually work, and the furniture is new if mundane.

Motels

Only if all else fails or nothing else is available. Why belabor the obvious? It's a bed, a shower, and a TV set.

Houses

This option is popular more for season-long than for ski-week rentals, although sometimes a large group can find a house for a week or two. These have the cook-your-own advantages of condos, but they usually lack the lift access. On a season-long basis, it's the next best thing to owning one.

There is really no way to offer guidelines on price ranges for accommodations these days. Providing any kind of "ball-park" price would be irresponsible. You can find something somewhere at any price, from $100 or less to $1,000 or more a week, from sleeping-bag barracks to suites with butlers. Colorado and Vermont tend to be higher than Utah and New Hampshire, but you've got low-priced locales in the former pair and some tariffs at the latter pair that would make an oil man wince. Tell your travel agent what you want to spend; and if you want to keep the price down, be sure to do it no later than August. Lodges in Summit County and Vail, Colorado, are usually booked by the prior Christmas.

As for restaurants and the like, the problem is that this book will be around for a while and the chef may not. I'll name four restaurants circa 1982 (in addition to those inns above) that offer fine food—Horse and Hound, Franconia, New Hampshire; The Common Man, Warren, Vermont; Garden Room, Keystone, Colorado; and Pepi Gramshammer's, Vail, Colorado—but I can recall four excellent ones circa 1975 to which I wouldn't send anyone today.

I do have a strong bias concerning breakfast before skiing: Carbohydrates are better than protein—such as pancakes rather than fried eggs, some home fries with the eggs if that's what you must have—augmented by such natural sugars as juice and/or fruit in significant quantity. You need the quick hit and mid-speed energy when you're cranking along, and breakfast has to carry you a while.

Lunch? There's this marvelous invention nearly a century old: the big, heavy, brown paper bag. There's a slightly newer one called a Thermos. Fill them with whatever you and yours like.

Getting there, as I've noted in other publications, is *not* half the fun, although sometimes it can eat up half the cost. Currently, your options are limited to four, either alone or in combination.

The Car

We discuss this in Chapter 20, but all too often the car is the course of last resort: You check every other possible combination of "alternative means of transportation," and then you screw the rack on the car and toss the boots in the back and off you go. We talk a whole lot about needing those other methods of getting to ski areas, but the reason we persist in having an energy crisis is that we have a forty-year history of neglect and a shortage of mass transportation. All too often you can't get there from where you are except by car.

The Jet

It tends to get you *most* of the way there, quickly and often inexpensively if you plan and book ahead (although prices are zooming again). Alas, the skiing at Stapleton Airport leaves much to be desired, which often tends to revert us to a variation on the first option called the "rented car" (and often called far less polite things when you try to get it over the pass or through the tunnel). Small planes have a habit of landing close to, but not quite at, the small airports, especially during snowstorms.

The Bus

The only really viable here-to-there alternative to using a car is taking a bus. Increasingly, resorts run shuttle buses from the airports, and they often get to the resort before the lodging bureau shuts down. More and more tour-bus operations and public-carrier lines are running regular city-to-area routes from New York, Boston, Chicago, Denver, Salt Lake City, Portland, Seattle, and others. Where possible, this is the way to go.

The Train

Our ultimate fantasy. The only ski resorts in the country that make this work are Winter Park, Colorado, and Big Mountain, Montana. We keep talking and talking and talking, but until you've been dumped off the train at Santa Fe, New Mexico, or Reno, Nevada, or Rock Springs, Wyoming, or Essex Junction, Vermont, and tried to get to the resort, you don't know what frustration is. ("Rent a car.") Some day . . . ?

13

American Skiing and the Resort-Ownership Profile

It's the only way to attract responsible capital to skiing.
BOB MAYNARD, Ralston Purina/Keystone Resort, Colorado

It's the only way to establish economies of scale and operation.
ROY COHEN, Solon Automated/Sugarbush Valley, Vermont

It's the only way skiers are going to get new resorts.
JIM BRANCH, Sno-Engineering, New Hampshire/
Colorado/British Columbia

It is the fact that the veterans of the Tenth Mountain Division, fabled in song and story as the creators of the modern American ski-area business as we know it, no longer control much of that business: the big corporations do. And the trend will continue to grow, as inexorably as the increasing price of a lift ticket or a room at the inn.

It also is the growing tendency of one company to own more than one ski area—in some cases a corporation solely in the ski-resort business, such as Vermont's Sherburne Corporation or California's Alpine Meadows Corporation, but more commonly one of those giants like 20th Century-Fox.

And finally, *It* is unquestionably a "good thing" for big business and the ski "industry," which more than most from the thirties to the early seventies was a prime example of that old gag: "We weren't organized as a not-for-profit company; it just worked out that way." This was proved all too glaringly in that first economic/energy/drought squeeze of 1973–75, when many of those early entrepreneurs with long dreams and short cash wandered around singing, "Brother can you spare a dime so I can take the next step, whatever that is." Yet during the far worse economic/energy/drought squeeze of 1979–80, the by-then corporate-dominated ski-resort business simply shrugged it off as a natural cyclic downturn, reviewed the cash-flow and return-on-investment projections, tapped the parent company's till, and opened for business as usual in the fall of 1980.

This is generally viewed as so positive a trend for the ski business that even "independents" like Copper Mountain's Chuck Lewis—who described himself as "surrounded by all those giants"—offered nothing but praise and encouragement for the movement during the summer of 1980. He was so convinced of its validity that he and the other stockholders sold Copper to an oil/real estate/recreation conglomerate that fall for an impressive $24 million.

But is all this inherently a good thing for you and me, the recreational skiers? In Dwight Eisenhower's time, the heyday of the Tenth, a fellow named Charlie Wilson achieved a certain fleeting notoriety when he intoned, "What's good for General Motors is good for the nation." Without passing judgment on that—sometimes it's more true than at other times—the fact is that what *may* be true for GM isn't necessarily true for Ford or Chrysler or AMC or even Toyota or VW or Fiat.

And that's what we recreational skiers face: Corporations are no more interchangeable than veterans of the Tenth. Some do a more responsible job in the ski-resort business than others. Several—Ralston Purina at Keystone, Solon at Sugarbush, Goliad Oil at Snowbird, and others—are committed to providing a high-quality ski experience, not because of any inherent aesthetic appreciation of skiing (although that, too, on occasion) but because of a conviction that quality, in the long run, outsells schlock in the high-income market.

Others are more committed to short-term quarterly reports, a *right-now* approach to financial accountability and investment evaluation, and you'd better believe that "Hit-and-Run, Inc." is just as apt to cut corners on lift maintenance and trail grooming as the most cash-poor/big-dream/small-plan entrepreneur of the sixties—and with far more malice, since Hit-and-Run has the cash. However, the "ski establishment"—including state tramway boards— tends to be far more rigorous in penalizing Hit-and-Run than one of its own, and so even there the skier gains. Furthermore, local, county, and state zoning and environmental boards tend to apply the same logic: If you've got it, we're going to make you spend it to do it "right" whether you want to or not. So everyone, skier and nonskier, gains again.

Now, what are the real advantages of corporate ownership for the skier?
• *Development of new resorts.* Name one resort that has any prospect of coming on "live and strong" in the early eighties and you've got a big corporate sponsor: Goliad at Beaver Creek, Royale Street at Deer Valley, 20th Century-Fox at Whistler-Blackcomb. In addition, Solon is backing the major expansion at Sugarbush, and Moore & Munger is behind the one at Stratton. Pete Seibert, the last great independent entrepreneur, who gave us Vail, is trying the same route at Snowbasin—but will probably meet major delays because he still lacks a big corporate sponsor. Don't be surprised if one suddenly surfaces.
• *Major renovation and expansion of existing areas.* Ralston Purina at Arapahoe Basin; Little America at Sun Valley; Goliad at Vail; Solon at Glen Ellen; Waterville Valley at Onset/Bobcat (since renamed Crotched); American International Group at Stowe (Mount Mansfield); Sherburne at Mount Snow; Alpine Meadows at Park City; Boyne County at Big Sky—the list is long and impressive. In a few cases the condition of the lifts was deplorable and trail grooming nothing more than a line in an annual brochure before Daddy Bigbucks arrived to save the day (and many skiers). The improvement in every one of those ski areas "under new corporate management" was significant and occasionally infinite. A few might not have been able to open for the next season without new capital, and a couple might not have been allowed to open without rebuilding the lifts.
• *Long-term commitments.* This is not universal; a few, seeing protracted expansion plans that needed heavy investments, bailed out (e.g., LTV at Steamboat, Colorado). But generally the big corporations are the only ones who can afford to fight and win the environmental wars, with all the delays and negative cash-flow situations those battles create. Without Goliad's resources Dick Bass couldn't continue to press Snowbird upward and Harry Bass couldn't have developed Beaver Creek. Chrysler needed all its clout (and that of its corporate consorts) to win at Big Sky before selling out to Boyne County. Roy Cohen will need all of Solon's leverage to outlast the preservationists in Vermont in his battle to build a new resort at Sugarbush. Fox is persevering at Early Winters, Washington, which even the Aspen Skiing Corporation couldn't afford to do, and Moore & Munger will push ahead on the new Stratton resort. Without AIG, Stowe would never have seen the new snowmaking-and-lift system it needs to compete in the eighties—but whether

Big Daddy is willing to be committed fully to the total retrofitting remains to be seen. But if it does, it's probably because Solon, Sherburne, and Moore & Munger are applying too much pressure for Stowe not to respond!

    • *Responsible capital.* This term is tough to define quickly in a non-financial publication because it means different things to different people and isn't as precise a term as *cash flow* or *return-on-investment* (which occasionally also have divergent interpretations). In general, *responsible capital* means that when a big company is investing its own money in an ownership (*equity*) position rather than merely lending money or buying bonds (*debt*), it tends to watch how the company performs more closely, and even more tolerantly, to the point where it may advance additional money at favorable rates. (We'll ignore the technicalities here.) It can also mean, less commonly, that because of that big company's investment, coupled with its ability to raise money based on its other assets (*leverage*), a bank is more willing to lend money for expansion—often at quite favorable terms. Translation: A ski area in short-term financial trouble will be able to bail out more easily if it has a fat sugar daddy.

But there are also inherent weaknesses in the corporate-ownership situation.

    • *Absentee ownership.* The more removed the parent company is from the ski-area operation, the less it perceives the short-term problems or hears the reaction from skiers. Ski-resort-*only* companies such as Sherburne, Alpine Meadows, or Waterville Valley avoid this; on-site managers at Mount Snow, Park City, and Crotched were trained in the home office and confer regularly. Smaller broad-based corporations like Solon and Moore & Munger often see the chief executives (Cohen and Frank Snyder) taking "hands-on" roles in daily management. But companies like Fox, Ralston Purina, Goliad, Little America—the giants—tend to have subsidiary presidents with essentially limited authority vis-à-vis the budget (although this varies widely among the companies) and operations and who often face intense pressures to meet cash-flow commitments and investment-return projections. In other words, they're corporate, and their jobs are on the line. In a few instances—such as Bob Maynard at Keystone—they bought themselves a lot of maneuvering room by doing the job well on both objective and corporate criteria.

Which leaves you and me, the recreational skier, exactly where? Dependent on the kindness of strangers. In the final analysis, as Jim Branch of Sno-Engineering has noted, we need the big corporations—and their access to "responsible capital"—if we're ever going to see those new resorts or massive expansions necessary to relieve the ever-increasing problems of overcrowding. To a small degree, expansions at a few government-controlled ski areas— Winter Park, Colorado; Cannon, New Hampshire; and Whiteface, New York —can satisfy some of this need; but ultimately the bulk of the financing and commitment must come from companies whose revenue sources are sufficiently broad based to shrug off a bad snow season or a temporary dislocation in gas-line supplies. Even the biggest of the ski-only multiarea companies— Sherburne, Alpine, Boyne—must react negatively to a short-term decline in skier revenues, while a Fox can keep plunking in the shekels as long as *Star Wars*' Empire perseveres. Also, let's face it, a Goliad or a Solon or a Moore & Munger can get banks to agree to more favorable terms than even a Sherburne can; that's the nature of the business world. How does this shape up in the major states?

Colorado

Every major resort along the Denver–Aspen corridor and its offshoots—about 5.5 million skier visits' worth—is owned or controlled by corporations, partnerships, or consortiums whose principal source of income is not skiing based (aside from Winter Park, which has a complex fiscal relationship with the city of Denver). No major independents remain.

Vermont

The "last hope" of the ski romantics. All the major areas are owned by large corporations, but half are ski only (Jay Peak, Killington, Mount Snow) while the others are broad based (Stowe, Stratton, Sugarbush). By 1985 we should know if even a major ski-only corporation like Sherburne can withstand the greater financial leverage of Solon and Moore & Munger. My guess is yes, but who knows?

California

Hopeless. The big corporations, mindful of what happened to the giant Disney Corporation at Mineral King and Independence Lake, have given this state a semipermanent pass.

Utah

The most interesting situation. Goliad continues to underwrite Snowbird (no ski-only company could afford to) but can't quite overtake the independent and ageless Alta. Alpine-owned Park City leads the state and seems to be working cooperatively with the on-coming Royale Street–owned Deer Valley. Only Seibert is trying to prove that the sole entrepreneur can "make it alone" at Snowbasin. No line yet; we'll look anew in 1985.

New Hampshire

There's no big-corporation involvement here, mainly because skier volume at most areas is quite low. The state owns Cannon and Sunapee, and Waterville Valley is developing its own small multiarea company. The rest, even the on-rushing Loon (loosely allied with Cannon), are still independents. No change is anticipated by 1985, and not much significant growth, except at Loon-Cannon.

THE BOX SCORE

When 20th Century-Fox bought the Aspen Skiing Corporation for $48 million in 1977, it handled the whole venture with true Hollywood fanfare as if the *Star Wars* folk had invented the wheel rather than just the Empire. However, it remains by far the record purchase; Apex Oil is a distant second at $24 million for Copper Mountain.

Western resorts generally sell in the high teens or roughly $30–40 per skier visit the best season in the past three (with additional consideration for developable land); Eastern resorts run at $20 per skier visit, again adding the value of developable land and subtracting certain types of long-term debt.

As best we can determine, the first investment in a ski area by a major corporation was by American International Group (which includes American Home Insurance) at Stowe (Mount Mansfield) in the thirties. Several lumber companies developed ski areas on their holdings during the immediate postwar-to-sixties period.

The first major multi-area ski company was Aspen, which developed Snowmass and Buttermilk in the sixties and bought Breckenridge in the early seventies. The Sherburne Corporation (Killington, Vermont) added Sunday River, Maine, while Boyne absorbed and developed three areas; both companies evolved in the sixties.

The movement really flourished, however, following the recession/gas crunch/snow drought of 1973–74.

- ASPEN SKIING CORPORATION, by 20th Century-Fox: Ajax, Breckenridge, Buttermilk, and Snowmass ski areas, 1977, $48 million.* Interest also in Whistler-Blackcomb, British Columbia; Fortress Mountain, Alberta, and Early Winters, Washington.

- COPPER MOUNTAIN, by Apex Oil Company: ski area plus resort village, 1980, $24 million.
- PARK CITY, by Alpine Meadows Corporation (S): ski area plus part of resort village, 1975, for $20 million** in complex transaction.
- VAIL ASSOCIATES, by Harry Bass (Goliad Oil): Vail and Beaver Creek ski areas plus Beaver Creek resort, 1976, controlling interest for $18 million.** (Goliad also effectively controls Snowbird, Utah, through Dick Bass.)
- SUN VALLEY, by Earl Holding (Little America, Arco): Sun Valley ski areas plus resort village, 1977, for $15 million.**
- STEAMBOAT SPRINGS, by Colorado-based consortium of businessmen: ski area plus resort village, 1978, for $15 million.** Note: purchased from LTV.
- BIG SKY, by Boyne Country (S): ski area plus resort village, 1976, for $10 million.** Note: purchased from Chrysler Realty Corporation.
- SUGARBUSH VALLEY, by Roy Cohen (Solon Automated Services): ski area, 1977, for $4.5 million;* GLEN ELLEN (renamed Sugarbush North), ski area, for $2.3 million;* plans to connect the two and build new resort village.
- MOUNT SNOW, by Sherburne Corporation (S): ski area plus small resort, 1977, for $4.5 million.**
- JAY PEAK, by Mt. Ste. Sauveur (S): ski area plus resort village, 1979, $4 million.** Note: purchased from Weyerhauser.
- STRATTON CORPORATION (includes BROMLEY), by Moore & Munger: two ski areas plus small resort village, 1980, for $3.1 million.* Note: Stratton had purchased Bromley ski area in 1979 for $2.2 million.**
- BOBCAT (previously named ONSET), by Waterville Valley (S): small ski area, 1979, about $200,000.* Effective merger with long-established Crotched Mountain ski area on same mountain as joint venture.

* Announced price.
** No announced price; best estimate.
(S) Ski-area/resort-only company.

PART THREE

EQUIPMENT

Introduction

Nothing describes what's happening in the wacky world of equipment better than an account of a scene in March 1980 at the annual hardware/fashion trade show in Las Vegas, which I attended under the auspices of *Skier's Advocate*.

Hidden away in a little sequestered room in the huge Geze display was The Thing, The Next Generation: a step-in binding with an upward toe release. To get into that room you had to be not a mere ski writer but a ski writer with full accreditation in equipment, and The Thing was displayed—no kidding—under glass. Surrounding it were the acolytes, all clad in white as if they were about to perform brain surgery (maybe they were at that), and the silence would have done credit to a TM session. Finally someone was escorted in and introduced in whispered tones as Herr Doktor something or other (I think he owns the store), and he goes through this rrrrap (only Peter Sellers could have done it justice) and slowly fades away. Standing next to me are the editor in chief and the equipment maven of *Brand X* magazine, both of whom are highly expert about bindings and not above casting a random aspersion, and they are nodding sagely and asking bated-breath questions. I didn't say a word. As we're all being led away from the viewing ("No cameras, pleez"), a good friend of mine, the binding company's technical rep for northern New England, remarked about my unusual silence. "What did you think?" he asked.

"Well," I replied, "if you mount a 105-millimeter recoilless rifle on it, it would be even-six against a Patton battle tank."

"It won't affect the ski's flex," he said.

"True," I conceded, "but it will flatten my car's tires when I put the skis in the rack."

Nor is Geze, one of the more responsible manufacturers, unique—or even rare. The whole equipment situation has far transcended its true value and complexity, thanks to an overemphasis on the technical by both major magazines. However, lest you think that's a one-way road, the response of readers who demand more-more along these overtechnical lines has left the editors with little choice but to comply. I remember commenting a few years ago when I was talking with the equipment editor of one magazine, "Those are good charts this year." "You understand them?" he asked. "Yup," I said. "We can't have that," he said, "we'll have to change them next year." Why? Because that's what the readers really seemed to want: a highly, overly complex approach.

Personally, covering the equipment scene for *Skier's Advocate* for a few years, I've preferred to take a functional and practical tack, on the theory that anyone reading my articles will already have OD'd on the charts in *SKI* or *Skiing*. I prefer to focus on the important and common items—the lines you'll actually see in the ski shops and on the slopes—and downplay the esoteric unless (1) it's innovative, and (2) the company has enough of a market share to put some product on the market somewhere.

Why? I have this recurring nightmare that one day I'd walk into a ski shop at an area and say "My Moog is malfunctioning," and the mechanic would turn to me in all honesty and say "How can you tell?" (Not to mention not having repair parts on hand.) So in the final analysis, even though I suspect that Geze makes the best binding among the step-ins, I tend to use Tyrolia or Salomon because the safety and functional differences between them and Geze are essentially insignificant and any ski shop in the country can repair—or replace—a heel, toe, or brake on either of them since between them they control roughly 70 percent of the market. Even shops where the owners have distinct alternative preferences (often for Look) tend to carry either and usually both lines.

"Essentially insignificant"? Yes. Based on several confidential (and occasionally conflicting) studies of release-retention characteristics I've seen, any of the top five step-ins (Geze, Look, Marker, Salomon, and Tyrolia) will "work" 95 percent of the time for 95 percent of the skiers, assuming you don't "peg the binding"—nail it down at its maximum setting rather than following the approved setting—and that you do keep it maintained. The purported "best" units, Geze and the Marker rotamat, *may* move up to 97 percent—and the remaining problem isn't at the top end. It's at the bottom, where novice skiers take slow, twisting falls that don't develop much torque (twisting force). As far as I'm concerned, the best—maybe the only—binding for a novice/low intermediate is the Burt; but for aggressive, competent skiers, all of today's major, top-of-the-line, step-in bindings work well enough.

Alas, that's not much of a magazine article, is it?

The situation doesn't hold for skis or boots. Not that they don't *work*; rather, it's that most of them may not work *for you*. Differences between/ among skis and boots are significant. You've got a zillion companies making boots and a half-zillion companies making skis, and most of the companies offer a wide range of models and each of everything is different. You've got different fits and flexes and torsions and materials and sidecuts and cambers and buckles and adjustments—not to mention lengths—and most of the companies have effective advertising/marketing types who can weave convincing tales. Here the magazines *subtly* try to do a good job in the charts, if you can read biomechanics as a second language or if you're a fugitive from the NSA cipher school and can read between the lines of the descriptive text. (Some charts and descriptions are included in Chapter 15.)

What bothers me about equipment coverage in magazines is the lack of discrimination. Every serious equipment writer knows which five to ten boot and ski lines are selling in any significant quantity and, therefore, which ones are apt to show in most ski shops. The average shop carries three to five lines of each, with Rossignol and Nordica virtually ubiquitous. So we should cover those ten to twenty brands in depth and touch the others only glancingly, if that, unless a product is unique or truly innovative.

What makes this important is that selecting the right ski equipment is absolutely critical to your survival, enjoyment, and improvement. Pick the wrong binding and you'll spend a lot of time reading. Pick the wrong boot and you might as well try tennis. Pick the wrong ski and you'll never get better than intermediate. The problem is that it's not so easy to pick the right item for you.

Even worse, the intelligence gets dated faster than yesterday's newspaper. The equipment charts published last season in *SKI* and *Skiing* are barely relevant today. Equipment, in short, resembles nothing so much as the automotive and fashion industries. Which is good and bad.

No point dwelling on the bad: the evils of built-in obsolescence and declining durability/increasing costs are obvious, real, inevitable, and inexorable. My 1980 Mustang is vastly inferior on all levels (except *slightly* in gas mileage) to my 1968 Mustang, and it cost a lot more to buy (and even more to maintain). But there's nothing we can do about it.

Fortunately, unlike the automotive situation, you'll get a lot more ski equipment for your lot-more money. Most of today's skis, boots, and bindings —even poles—are so far superior to what was available even five years ago on a *performance* basis that I'm willing to overlook the skis' often-annoying lack of durability, need for more frequent maintenance, and overall the significantly higher price tag. But higher priced they are: were you so imprudent as to buy new, top-of-line equipment all at one stroke at list price you'd drop $750— $250 to $300 each for skis and boots, $150 for bindings, and $50 for poles. The last three items would last through 100 to 150 days of use, assuming adequate care, and skis about half that (except in the Rockies, where you might equal the same 100). If you're a little-old-lady-in-tennypumps-who-skis-only-on-novice-trails-when-the-snow-is-soft-and-deep you'll do a lot better, and if you're a teenage freestyle/racer type who feels that keeping the skis on the snow is a sign of weakness you won't do half as well; but for normally aggressive, experienced skiers those are reasonable projections.

That means that topline equipment will cost you roughly $7.50 a day, which doesn't include maintenance and tuning (about $2.50 a day). True, if you buy properly and bargain aggressively and do your own maintenance, you can slash those costs considerably—under $7.50 per diem totally—but that's up to you.

Now, what do you get for all this money besides pretty graphics and that soul-satisfying feeling of being "with it"? The answer is quite simple: performance—the ability to make a carved turn, as we'll discuss in the section on instruction. The fact remains that equipment and instruction are so inter-related you really can't separate the two, no matter how hard the magazines try. (Sigi Grottendorfer, who runs the ski schools at Sugarbush, Vermont, and Portillo, Chile, and owns the ski shops at Sugarbush, makes that point in an interview starting on page 000.) The reason why intermediate and advanced skiers ski so well today is that the equipment lets them. The boots are quick and skis are quicker, and they're both designed to let you stand on the inside edge of the turning ski—and because of that, so is the new technique/learning theory. (For that matter, so are ski-area grooming techniques.) You try to make some of these new turns—with their absence of unweighting and rotation—with an old Head Standard and Lange Pro and unless you're an incredibly good skier, as in super-expert, they're going to carry you off into the trees.

TO BUY OR TO RENT?

This once-burning issue has largely been resolved over the last few years:

- Consider buying boots fairly early in your career.
- Ignore skis and bindings until you're a solid intermediate.

Boots are the only truly personal piece of ski equipment; a good boot has to fit *you* well, and the chances of getting that in a rental boot are, as they say, slim to nil. Too many people with different sizes and shapes of foot, weight distribution, and skiing technique pound the innards of even the best boot into a misshapen lump within a few weeks; and believe it, rental boots are rarely among the best of the breed. Thus it would seem a good idea for you to invest in boots fairly early.

But do you know how a boot should fit? Sure, the big and small magazines and every ski book worth its ink and paper offer a slew of rules, but no article or book can tell you how it's supposed to *feel* on your foot *in the shop*; unlike skis, boots are rarely available on a try-before-you-buy basis. Even most experienced intermediates tend to buy their boots too large, and novices inevitably opt for comfort—or what *appears* to be comfort—at the expense of control. Thus the key word in Rule 1 above is *consider*, as in *be careful*.

Buying skis early in your career is a waste of money; it's cheaper to rent until you can use top-of-line hardware, and you'll probably be using equipment from the rental operation during that era superior to what you'd be prone to buy. (Those discount-store bargains are, by and large, junk, a fact you could discern by comparing the prices charged by those same chains for top-line equipment: the same, if not higher, than charged by specialty ski shops!) Today the good skis produced by most companies are in the two top-of-line categories, "racing" and "performance." A good intermediate can and should use one of those; a notch or two lower and you're not only throwing money away but inhibiting your rate of improvement.

Buying bindings is even more troublesome. No skier should use a unit lower than the company's second line—for example, the Salomon 637, the Tyrolia 280D—and children, in fact, should use only the company's first-string junior model. The problem is, as we mentioned earlier, even the best step-in bindings are less than perfect at the lowest settings. On the other hand, the two best bindings in the rental market—the Burt and the Spademan, in my order of preference—have a near infinity of release angles and can be set for very low torque. But both bindings (for different reasons) tend to reduce a skier's sensitivity to his skis and snow conditions, and the higher up the ability ladder you go, the more you're apt to trade a small margin of safety for significantly better performance. Lest you miss the point, though, that Burt/Spademan margin of safety is far higher at the beginner level; what reduces the margin up-scale is the higher speed (and torque) a good skier develops and the greater predictability of his angles of release. Some very good skiers do opt for the safety of the Burt, but not that many.

Finally, most instruction programs use some variation of GLM or ATM (see page 238), at least into the mid-intermediate range, so why waste your money buying short skis? When you've reached a full-length ski and a solid base of competence, *then* invest knowledgeably in skis and bindings. Until then, rent.

PERSONAL FAVORITES

Although equipment writers make an honest effort to remain as neutral as possible, we do make personal selections for our own use when we're skiing— and those selections are based on the results of testing. This doesn't mean that these items are the best but rather that they are the ones on which we feel the most secure and relaxed and with which we therefore ski the best. In addition, our feelings change: I began the 1981–82 season firmly convinced that the Rossignol FP (gray) was the best slalom ski in the world, but as the year progressed and I logged more time on the Head SL I found myself reaching for the quicker and more responsive (albeit less versatile) Head rather than the Rossi on marginal days. Finally, as I shifted to giant-slalom skis for all-purpose use and relied less and less on a slalom model except for extreme-ice conditions, my preference for the Head became absolute. So our choices are subject to change also.

With that disclaimer, here is my choice for "best" as the 1982–83 season began:

- Slalom skis: *Head SL*; runner-up, Rossignol FP (gray cosmetics; the new blue-topskin model isn't as good).
- Giant-slalom skis: *Fischer SuperCompetition*; runners-up, Elan RC08, Dynastar MV5. (Overall, this category probably has the highest number of excellent skis now on the market, including the Blizzard Firebird, Head GS, Rossi SM, and Atomic Bionic.)
- Boots: *Lange XLS*; runner-up, Raichle Flexon-5.
- Bindings: *Tyrolia 380RD*; runners-up, Geze 950, Look 99 (my first rotamat in a decade).

Although I've personally dismissed the "performance/super-sport/soft-racing" models from my lineup (I feel that today's GS skis do all of that better and more positively), I can understand that people who don't ski fifty days a season or who don't like to have to "stand on their skis all the time" might decide otherwise. Not surprisingly, the best of the softer, high-performance skis are made by those same companies (why should it be otherwise?): Head SC, Fischer Superlite, Dynastar Omesoft, Elan RC02, Blizzard Racer. However, if you like Rossignol for some reason, stick with the SM unless you like to ski 203 cm or longer. For 1982–83 I tested SL and GS at 200.

14

All About Boots

Ski boots are essentially a corrective device to remedy an oversight of nature. Man's feet and ankles did not evolve with modern skiing in mind. If they had, they would have been a great deal stronger, with much better circulation.

Ski boots have three basic functions: to transmit the motions of legs and feet to the skis; to give support to feet and ankles when they are under stress, as in a turn; and to keep the feet warm. The modern ski boot fulfills these functions admirably, although at a relatively high cost: top models today range between $250 and $325.

There is no other footwear like a ski boot. Although fashion has invaded skiing in force, the boot remains largely functional. It is not a thing of great beauty, yet it is the topic of more ski conversation than any other item of equipment. "I love my boots. It feels so good when I take them off" is only one of the many jokes about boots, whose "clump, clump" heralds the arrival of the skier long before he or she comes into sight.

Ski boots were known as such with the coming of alpine skiing, but they did not develop as a species distinct from mountain boots until the development of cable bindings in the 1930s. Even the rigid box toe was developed as much for mountaineering as for skiing. The box toe not only helped keep toes warm but prevented them from being squeezed and chafed by the straps of toe irons and crampons.

One of the first consequences of the cable binding was that its tension buckled the soles of existing ski boots; thus, the heavy half-inch sole was developed. But this was only the beginning. With full control over the ski established by the cable bindings, skiers began to demand more support from their ski boots, a demand that developed the high, stiff boots of today. In addition, the rapid increase in the number of lifts made walking an almost incidental adjunct of skiing.

The trend toward the modern boot sharply accelerated the introduction of sideslipping as a formal part of skiing technique, which required strong support of wobbly ankles. Rigid lateral support of the ankle and the lower leg gives the skier greatly increased leverage to apply edging power to his skis on ice and hard snow. As long as leather boots were in use, however, this lateral rigidity was hard to maintain because leather tends to break down in use. Now that all boots are made of rigid plastic material that maintains its stiffness even after several winters of hard skiing, the problem has been eliminated. In fact, progress in making high laterally stiff boots has had a lot to do with getting rid of the exaggerated positions of body angulation that skiers once were compelled to learn in order to obtain edge bite on ice. Thanks to the modern boot, today's skiers can adopt a more natural, better balanced position over their skis.

Modern ski technique evolved from a second important design change in boots: the high back. One of the aims of the modern ski boot is to make use of the tail of the ski, although this has moderated from its peak in the mid-seventies. The first racers who discovered this effect, Frenchmen such as Patrick Russel, had to settle for high backs—jet sticks, as they were called—that were added to the boot, much as you buy an extra gadget for a car. Now, many of the boots for advanced skiers have very high backs running up the back of the lower leg.

Many people—skiers and nonskiers alike—often wonder why ski boots are made so high and stiff. But the reasons are perfectly valid once you understand modern ski technique, as we discuss later (Part Four).

A LOOK AT THE OUTSIDE

When buying a pair of ski boots, divide your attention between the two essential elements that make up the modern boot: the outer shell, and the inner lining or bladder, which determines how it fits.

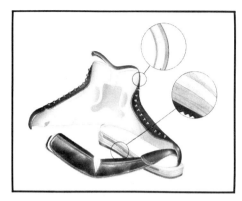

The evolution of the modern ski boot. As late as 1965, the laced leather boot (top photo at left) *was still king of the slopes. It was built around a last—a wooden foot-shaped form. The construction required much hand work and stiching. As labor and leather costs soared, designers started to look for other materials that were cheaper, more durable, and more rigid. The solution was plastic* (second photo at left), *which was further refined by substituting buckles for laces. However, the first plastic boots were virtually impossible to modify for better fit, so the next stage* (bottom photo at left) *saw the evolution of the removable liner. The first product in this system was the foamed bladder, into which soft, hot gunk was blown while the skier's foot was encased in it; but this died a merciful death as more sophisticated forms of chemicals, known generically as "flow," accomplished the same goal more pleasantly. Currently* (see diagrams at right), *this evolution has produced the Lange boot, probably the most traditional among the top sellers, with close attention now being paid to many different facets of design, fit, and comfort. (These diagrams, produced by Lange, are obviously self-promoting, but they illustrate the concepts.) At the same time, other companies began to design new types of boots, featuring rear rather than front entry and relying on far fewer buckles; the most popular are the Salomon and Hanson. It's all a matter of taste, but virtually all the boots on the market today are vast improvements over not only the old lace-and-leather numbers but over the first plastic-and-buckle designs as well.*

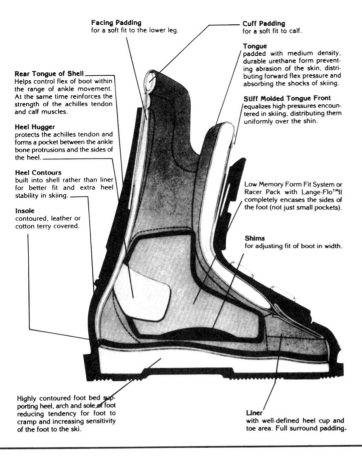

Facing Padding
for a soft fit to the lower leg.

Cuff Padding
for a soft fit to calf.

Rear Tongue of Shell
Helps control flex of boot within the range of ankle movement. At the same time reinforces the strength of the achilles tendon and calf muscles.

Heel Hugger
protects the achilles tendon and forms a pocket between the ankle bone protrusions and the sides of the heel.

Heel Contours
built into shell rather than liner for better fit and extra heel stability in skiing.

Insole
contoured, leather or cotton terry covered.

Tongue
padded with medium density, durable urethane form preventing abrasion of the skin, distributing forward flex pressure and absorbing the shocks of skiing.

Stiff Molded Tongue Front
equalizes high pressures encountered in skiing, distributing them uniformly over the shin.

Low Memory Form Fit System or **Racer Pack** with Lange-Flo™II completely encases the sides of the foot (not just small pockets).

Shims
for adjusting fit of boot in width.

Highly contoured foot bed supporting heel, arch and sole of foot reducing tendency for foot to cramp and increasing sensitivity of the foot to the ski.

Liner
with well-defined heel cup and toe area. Full surround padding.

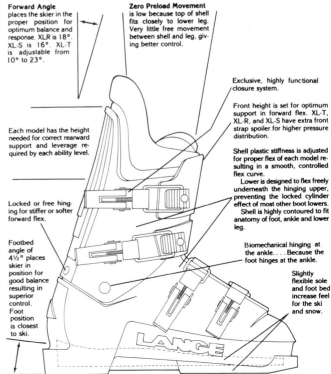

Forward Angle
places the skier in the proper position for optimum balance and response. XLR is 18°. XL·S is 16°. XL·T is adjustable from 10° to 23°.

Zero Preload Movement
is low because top of shell fits closely to lower leg. Very little free movement between shell and leg, giving better control.

Exclusive, highly functional closure system.

Front height is set for optimum support in forward flex. XL·T, XL·R, and XL·S have extra front strap spoiler for higher pressure distribution.

Shell plastic stiffness is adjusted for proper flex of each model resulting in a smooth, controlled flex curve.
Lower is designed to flex freely underneath the hinging upper, preventing the locked cylinder effect of most other boot lowers. Shell is highly contoured to fit anatomy of foot, ankle and lower leg.

Each model has the height needed for correct rearward support and leverage required by each ability level.

Locked or free hinging for stiffer or softer forward flex.

Footbed angle of 4½° places skier in position for good balance resulting in superior control. Foot position is closest to ski.

Biomechanical hinging at the ankle.... Because the foot hinges at the ankle.

Slightly flexible sole and foot bed increase feel for the ski and snow.

LANGE

The outer shell can consist of as many as four parts molded from plastics, often polyurethane. It is hard and stiff, so that any forgiveness to your feet and ankles must come from the inner padding of the boot. The way the outer shell is designed pretty much governs what it will do and how it operates:

- It determines how you get in and out of the boot.
- Together with the number and type of buckles, it determines how the boot closes around your foot and locks you in for skiing.
- The way the upper shaft of the shell is pitched forward determines how you will stand over your skis.
- Its hinging, or lack of it, governs the forward flexing of your knees as your shins press against the front of the boot.
- It may, or may not, offer a means of adjusting the angle at which your foot and leg are canted in relation to the ski.

Unlike a shoe that your foot enters through the top, a ski boot offers two modes of getting in and out. In most models you enter the conventional way; through the front. But there are excellent boots designed so that the part behind the heel hinges back and you enter through the rear. For some reason, this concept hasn't quite become as popular as it should, possibly because it creates too stiff a forward-flex pattern.

The number of buckles a boot has is really irrelevant. The more conventional shells have four buckles, but the trend is to have fewer. In rear-entry boots, the number of buckles is usually one. There is considerable convenience in having fewer buckles, provided you can still get a good fit and are able to adjust or relieve pressure points, but many of the best boots continue to use four.

Since the normal position for skiing is with knees bent and body pitched slightly forward, the collars or upper shafts of boots reflect this. The more expert models tend to have more of a built-in forward lean, including raising the heel inside the boot. Some models have an adjustment by which you can vary the forward lean of the shell.

The amount of forward hinging in a boot is a matter of individual taste among expert skiers. On the one hand, a skier wants a certain amount of play in the ankle joint to gain a better feel of his feet for the snow. On the other hand, to much ankle-joint articulation is undesirable. In order to apply vigorous forward pressure on the front of the skis in carving a turn, the skier must feel a resistance from the boot to forward flexing. For slalom racing

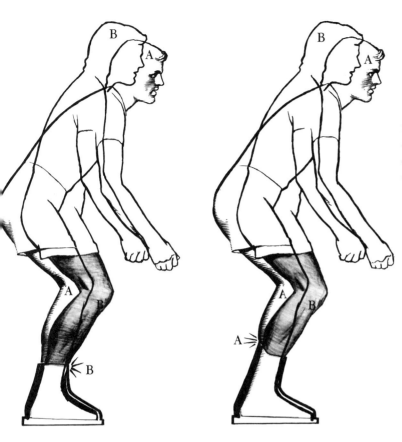

There is no one single correct stance on skis. Within a limited range, people of different natural stances can ski correctly. Some skiers are more up-right with less forward knee bend; others are more forward leaning. This posed less of a problem with older, flexible boots. But it can result in pressure points and discomfort with the new, high, very rigid, unflexing boots. Skier A is comfortable in a fairly straight-shafted, rigid boot (left), but a high-backed, forward-pitched boot (right) will pinch the rear of his leg. Skier B has a naturally forward leaning ski stance. He is comfortable in a forward-leaning boot, but a more upright rigid plastic model will press hard and constantly against his shin.

particularly, skiers want virtually no hinging action: They rivet or lock the boot hinges shut. In order to create the best of two worlds, some boots come with locked and unlocked hinges, and others offer a means of adjusting the amount of forward flexibility.

CANTING

One of the most obvious and least considered facts about skiing is that your skis, in normal running, should be flat on the snow. A flat ski is critical to good technique and safety in skiing. The relationship of boots to your bone legs structure and manner of standing can easily set you constantly on the edges of your skis even though you may not be aware of it. The result may be that you are suffering unnecessary falls from catching your edges on the snow.

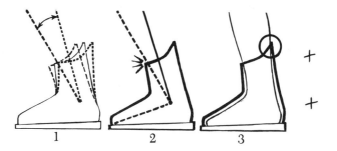

(1) Every boot has some ability to flex forward. (2) Ideally, it should flex forward enough to allow ankle flexion without shin discomfort at the front of the boot, but it shouldn't flex so far forward that the ankle will hurt or be injured by too severe bending. (3) When the skier is relaxing—for instance, standing in a lift line—the unflexed boot shaft should allow the leg to rest in a comfortable position without an acute pressure point behind.

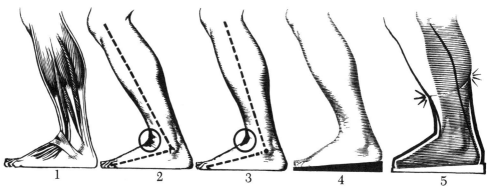

How far forward should your ankle bend? Figure 1 shows normal angle of ankle bend for general skiing, 2 shows a skier who has a fairly supple forward ankle bend, and 3 a skier with limited ankle bend. Figure 4 shows how placing a wedge under the heel of the boot to cant it forward allows a skier with limited ankle bend to lean forward more. Figure 5 shows a poorly fitting boot with an overly large upper that will allow the skier to flex and unflex his legs easily. But if, like the new plastic boots, it is rigid, it eventually will cause sore points on the lower leg.

High boots initially accentuated the problem. As the boots climbed higher on the leg, any bowing of the leg, for instance, was translated into excessive pressure on the outside edges of the skis. To remedy the situation during the mid-seventies, it was necessary to insert a wedge, called a cant (one-eighth inch is a typical thickness), along the inside of the boot, between the boot and the ski. However, by the end of the decade boot designers began "canting" the upper portion of the shell (see p. 153). Today, most boots come precanted, thereby partly taking the problem into account. Some even come with adjustable canting.

To relieve your anxiety about the problem of canting, consult your local ski retailer. Many ski shops have testing devices that enable them to determine how much, if any, canting you need.

Sideslipping and edging with low, soft boots contrasted with modern, high, rigid boots. At left, the skier is wearing a low, soft boot that allows him to sideslip his skis by a single lateral bending of the ankle joint inside the boot. To create the same flattening of the ski on the snow to sideslip, a high, rigid-booted skier must allow the knee to move out laterally.

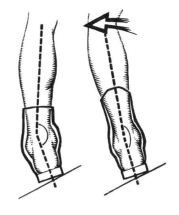

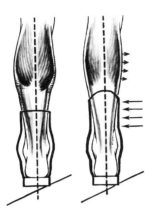

The feel of edging with low, soft boots and high, rigid boots is quite different. To edge at left, the skier in a soft, low boot must apply strong muscular effort around the ankle joint (make it rigid) to keep the ski on its edge. At right, the skier with a high, rigid boot is able to use the leverage of his lower leg against the high, stiff side of the boot to edge the ski with minimal muscle effort.

The old-style soft boot allowed fairly free lateral movement of the lower leg. Similarly, a modern, rigid plastic boot with a shaft that is too wide for the leg will allow lateral ankle bending like a loose hockey skate.

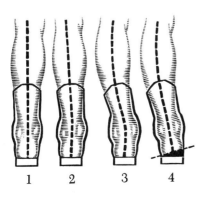

1   2   3   4

The modern rigid ski boot takes different leg structures into account by lateral tilting or canting. Figure 1 shows a straight-up boot shaft. In Figure 2 the shaft is canted slightly to accommodate a bowed leg. Figure 3 shows a severely canted shaft used by a skier with a pronounced arc of the lower leg. In Figure 4, a straight-shafted boot has been canted by a wedge under the boot to allow a bowlegged skier to gain even distribution of his weight on the ski edges.

Note how leg configuration is important in the type of boot you buy, particularly the lateral canting of the boot. These illustrations show three typical leg structures: straight, knock-kneed (frequently typical of women), and slightly bowed (typical of many men). The illustrations indicate the pressure points that can develop when each skier is fitted in a straight-shafted boot (top row) and what happens when he is in a boot with an outward canted shaft.

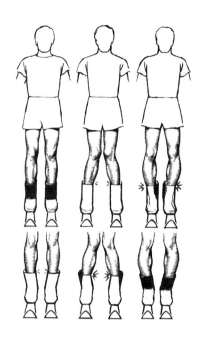

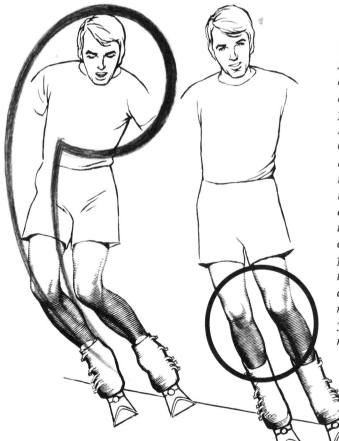

With the advent of the modern high-shafted ski boot, the exaggerated comma or angulated position (left) of a few years ago is disappearing (right) from skiing. The skier at left has low, soft boots with ankle play inside them. Consequently, he must tilt his upper body at a considerable angle to his legs to get his skis on edge. The skier at right has high, rigid boots with no ankle play inside, and he can simply use knee pressure and lower leg muscles to control his edges without need for much upper body angulation. More than any changes in ski design, the development of the modern boot has revolutionized ski technique in recent years: It has moved us into an era of more natural, relaxed body position.

The modern ski is designed to make use of both its forebody and the afterbody. But the skier's ability to transmit pressure instantly to the front and tail of the ski would not have been possible without the development through plastics technology of the high, rigid boot. Forward pressure of the shin against the boot, with limited hinging of the boot, causes an instant transmission of force to the forebody of the ski. Any straightening of the ankle exerts a pressure on the back of the boot; if the highback boot shaft is rigid, the pressure is transmitted instantly to the tail of the ski.

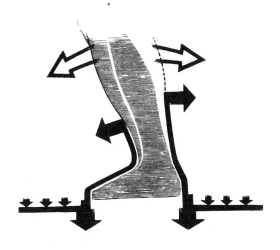

THE BOOT MARKET TODAY (AND TOMORROW)

The big bopper in boots is Nordica, which controls roughly 40 percent of the market. Yet this is a bit deceptive, because much of this is achieved by a total dominance of the low-end and women's markets. At the top end—high-intermediate through expert—Nordica is just another popular, first-line, competitive company against which Lange, Caber, Raichle, Dolomite, the rapidly emerging Salomon, and a couple of others hold their own. It's a tough market up there, because word of mouth and what your instructor uses often "outsells" expensive advertising. A couple of seasons of poor models, as Lange suffered in the mid-seventies while then-parent Garcia struggled through hard financial times, are tough to overcome—and until Lange came up with its excellent XL1000 and 800 series the company was in decline. Now it's on the way up again and is probably number one in the advanced-skier market.

What makes it a tough market is the durability problem. Today, any bootmaker could produce a polyurethane shell that would last forever, and the buckle systems used by Lange (and several other firms) are almost as enduring. Design concepts are so sophisticated that even a good advanced skier uses hardly any of the performance the boot offers until he's been in it for a season—and even then he's got a long way to go before he outgrows it (if he ever does). Frankly, a boot could last the average skier for a decade.

So what's a manufacturer to do? We all remember what happened to Chrysler after they made those incredible enduring models of the forties and early fifties, don't we? The Feds just bailed them out.

A few forces converge to bail bootmakers out of that bind—and put the buyer in one.

· The price of oil soared, and since plastics are petrobased and poly-urethane is a high-priced plastic, some manufacturers went to cheaper thermoplastics, either totally in cheap boots or partially, in some components of the complex three- and four-piece models. However, the bindings companies have kept the pressure on by insisting on PU bootsoles to assure reliable release.

· Ullr invented the liner or innerboot, which often seems to have the life span of a fruit fly and which gives manufacturers the freedom to re-design the boot frequently, discontinue the current innerboot, and report as "unavailable" replacement liners when the shell is still virtually unscarred or unsoftened.

· Marketing experts conceived an infinity of conflicting fitting systems, aided and abetted by orthopedists and the like, that totally confused all efforts to make order out of conflict.

GETTING THE RIGHT FIT

The problem is that fitting is everything. A boot that doesn't fit properly doesn't work. Period. According to Doug Pfeiffer, who writes the Clinic Column for SKI, between 50 and 80 percent of American skiers use a boot that's at least a full size too large. So how should a boot fit? Let me pick up part of an article I wrote in 1980 for *Skier's Advocate*.

Start with one concept: You're got five criteria for picking boots. The first three, to paraphrase an old real-estate gag, are fit, fit, and fit. The fourth is forward flex. The fifth, so far down the priority line you could ignore it because differences among the boots are quite minor, is lateral flex.

FIT, FIT, and FIT: Friends often ask me if I also dig leather and whips, because I've been skiing Lange boots since the days of the original black-liner, Lange-bang Iron Maidens, where you had to develop a karate-like layer of callous on your instep each season before you could "get it on." The reason I like them is simple: I've got a long, narrow foot and heel, and Lange always had—still has—the narrowest last on the market. (A last is the basic foot-shaped design a shoe/bootmaker uses to make his outer shell molds.) There's no way anyone with a narrow foot can enjoy, much less evaluate, boots like Nordica or Dolomite that use wide lasts, while someone with a wide foot screams in pain at the very thought of a Lange or Trappeur. So which company makes the right last for you? How could I possibly know? It's your foot.

In the old days (the sixties), you could feel quickly if the last was the right one for you. The bootman at your favorite shop would eyeball your foot, blow the hair dryer into the flo material, buckle you up, and zap, in fifteen minutes, you'd know the boot wasn't too tight if your foot didn't turn black. If you could lift your heel more than a quarter-inch or roll your ankle at all you'd try another size or brand, and when you left the shop you knew the boot fit.

No more. Around the turn of the decade we had visited upon us the great boot-foaming disaster, and although that charade (to be kind) died quickly, its legacy lingers on. Bootmakers learned that if they jiggered extensively with the innerboots they could make fewer lasts and molds for the outer shells—molds for an inventory of twenty-plus sizes are expensive—and today, the same shell may carry as many as two full sizes and three widths, with all variations covered by the innerboot (just as if, in fact, you were being foamed). That's one reason innerboots are removable today: to accommodate the bootmakers and retailers.

How do you make this work for you? If a shell, for instance, covers sizes 11 and 12, you'll get a better fit if your foot is 12 rather than 11. The more slop that has to be filled by the soft material of the liner, the more you'll have to "play" continually with modifying that liner for the life of that boot. What this means is that if two boots "feel right" on your foot when you try them on, ask the shop owner which *shell* is closer to your real foot size. (And yes, he knows.)

Still, since no one has two feet exactly the same size, you'll have to enter phase two: the fitting process. These days, with the immense variations among bootmakers in methods and theories of designing innerboots, boot fitting has become, like abstract physics, a perfect match of pure art and precise science. Or, to put it another way, we're being hustled into believing we can make little ones out of big ones. Today the guy selling boots has a master's degree in physical engineering, a doctorate in podiatry, and the soul of a pro-football trainer. It also helps if he has ten years' experience selling ice to Eskimos.

The moment he sees you about to remove a pair of swimming pools, he walks over with this kit he could use to get a Cowboy offensive tackle ready for the tenth game and says, "Awright, let's get to work. Where doesn't it fit right?" He pulls out this mess o' stuff—moleskin and duct tape and pads and cutouts and different insets and wedges lined with goo—and as he wields a pair of scissors from *Psycho* he also mentions (oh, so casually) the special they're running that week on orthotics and sporthotics and the fact that Dr. Scholl's sells a good line of innersoles. By the time he gets finished working with that boot, how could you *not* buy it?

I'll give you a clue: If it doesn't feel right almost immediately, don't go for the song and dance.

In reality, we've reached an age of Neo-Rosemountism (remember those, oh ancient mariner?). Those were a brand of boots, popular in the late-sixties through the mid-seventies, with scads of itty-bitty pockets into which you jammed bags of goop until everything fit perfectly. For a day. Then, as the weather changed or you skied harder, they'd loosen up and you'd jam in more bags of goop. I know many really fine skiers who lament the day those vanished from the scene because, the cardinal sin in skiing, they weren't sexy like those Screaming Yaller Zonkers (Nordicas).

The key was—and it has returned—Rosemountism demanded a large amount of do-it-yourself retrofitting. But whereas all you needed then was a supply of little bags of goop, today you need a total survival kit. You think I'm kidding? I almost got busted one March at Stapleton Airport when the X ray disclosed Excalibur, my scissors, in my boot knapsack, together with the wedges and moleskin and all that stuff. The only thing that saved me was my press card; they figured anyone silly enough to write about this sport would be silly enough to carry foot-long scissors. They even gave them back in New York.

Despite all this Neo-Rosemountism, the key elements in fit remain the same: The heel shouldn't move upward, the ankle shouldn't roll, the piggies should have lots of breathing room, the pain across the instep should be bearable, the arch should support your foot properly, and the cuff shouldn't let your leg rotate freely. Your foot, in short, shouldn't move inside the boot.

By now, most of you should know how heel, ankle, and ball of the foot are supposed to feel: tight, tight, and loose respectively. But do you know how *long* the boot should be?

You should be able to feel the end of the boot—the *shell*, not the liner —when you stand up with the boots unbuckled. Why? If your foot can slide forward, you'll slide out of and *lose* that tight heel-ankle lockdown. Over the years I've found that the boots that ski best for me are those that feel tight to the point of discomfort when I first buckle them up in the shop, assuming I can wiggle my toes. If they're comfy in the shop, they're sloppy on the snow, because the liners compress quickly.

Don't go to the other extreme and reach the point where your toes curl— from fit, not fear—or you'll get ingrown toenails and bruised toes. Just make sure you can feel the tip of the shell with your longest toe before you crank the buckles.

15

On Buying Skis

A fact too frequently forgotten is that skis are basically extensions of the feet. Their function is to distribute the weight of the skier over a larger surface. It is this change in weight distribution that enables the skier to travel over snow without breaking through. For instance, a 150-pound man with size ten feet exerts a pressure on the snow of about two and one-half pounds per square inch. With the right pair of skis on his feet, the pressure is reduced to three-tenths of a pound per square inch.

But the modern ski has more complex functions than the reduction of the load on the snow. It must be able to turn and to track at various speeds. And although it appears to be simple, it actually is one of the most complex structures in engineering.

EVALUATING SKIS

Methods of evaluating skis are almost as varied as the number of brands sold in shops. The aim is to determine which skis will best suit your needs, because the choices can be as different as a snowplow is from a seventy-mile-an-hour schuss.

Some ski makers place a lot of emphasis on racing results to determine the designs of skis they produce. Others use computers to solve complex

Side Cut

Built-in arc on each side of a ski, as viewed from the top, enables the ski to carve a turn in the snow when it is edged, weighted, and sliding forward. The solid line represents the lesser side cut of a downhill model, a ski used predominantly in straight running and long arced turns. The dotted line represents a more severe slalom cut, narrower at the waist, permitting quicker turning action.

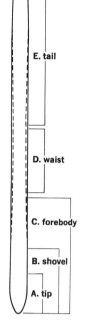

E. tail

D. waist

C. forebody

B. shovel

A. tip

Camber

A *As viewed from the side, ski has a bowed shape. This bottom camber distributes a skier's weight evenly over the snow, and the stiffer the ski the* lower *the height at* **A**.

B *The dotted line represents the most common way of determining length, but some companies mark it as if the ski were totally flat instead of having a turned-up tip.*

Flex

Variation in stiffness or bending properties throughout the length of a ski; thicker and stiffer at the midsection, thinner and more flexible tip and tail. The solid line illustrates a ski with an even flex curve. The dotted line depicts the uneven flex curve of a ski with a stiff tail relative to its forebody.

equations in designing skis. Another allows recreational skiers to try its products and offer advice—although this theory has become essentially useless.

The information confronting you about skis can be bewildering. One company will tout its cracked edge. Another points to the advanced side cut of its ski. One promotes the sideways flexing of the ski, another its twisting properties or side profile. Some ski makers measure frequency of vibration of the ski; some can't tell you what theirs is.

To cut through these cross-currents of claim and counterclaim, both SKI and *Skiing* introduced systems of evaluation common to all skis. SKI's, for instance, was called Ski Performance Prediction, or SKIpp for short. The aim was to assist the skier in selecting the right ski for his or her ability, height, weight, and style of skiing. SKIpp was a combination of bench testing and on-snow evaluation of the skis, and by learning the SKIpp terminology you could understand a great deal more about why a ski is made the way it is and how it performs on snow. In time, both magazines developed the highly sophisticated systems in vogue today (see pp. 165–75).

The analogy between a ski and a piano often has been made, but it bears repeating. The ski is a highly tuned machine in a constantly dynamic state when it is being skied. As with a piano, altering one string or property can put

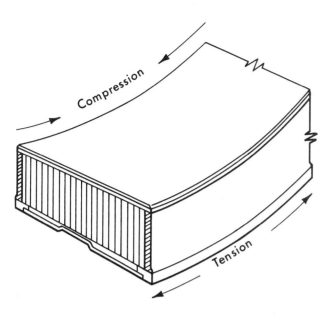

Typical sandwich construction of many skis. A relatively neutral core of wood or foam is sandwiched between top and bottom skins of epoxy-fiberglass material or aluminum alloy or a combination of the two. When the ski is flexed, as when it crosses the trough between two bumps, the bottom skin is highly stressed in tension, while the top skin material becomes highly compressed. Ability of the ski to withstand these forces, repeated tens of thousands of times, adds to its life.

Example of a skier in a forward sideslip. A good performing ski should be able to skid easily, as in this maneuver, and also carve precisely on its edges as the skier demands it.

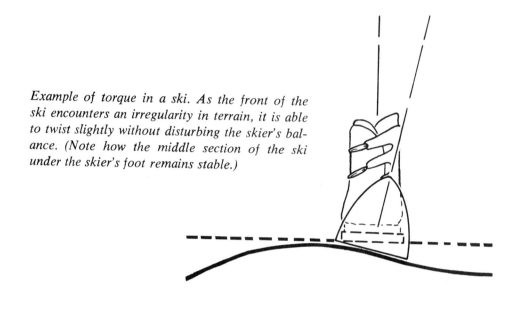

Example of torque in a ski. As the front of the ski encounters an irregularity in terrain, it is able to twist slightly without disturbing the skier's balance. (Note how the middle section of the ski under the skier's foot remains stable.)

the whole instrument out of tune. Every property is intimately related to every other property. Alter a ski's side cut, for instance, and you change the way in which its torque and flex distribution act upon the snow.

The measurements that describe some of the complex set of interrelationships are as follows.

Effective Torsion

Torsion or torque is the ability of the ski to twist on its longitudinal axis. Some skis are fairly soft torsionally; others are quite stiff. In determining how a ski will perform on snow, it is useful to combine the measurement of its torsion with the side camber or cut. The side cut of the ski refers to its waisted shape when observed from the top: it is wider at the tip, narrow under your foot or binding, and it flares out again at the tail. The relationship between torsion and side cut, called Effective Torsion, has been found to profoundly affect the turning character of a ski and its edge-holding on hard snow and ice.

Effective Compression

Every ski has a certain amount of bottom camber. That is, observed from the side, it is bowed like an archery bow. On a flat table, the ski will make contact at the tip and tail, and the mid-point of the ski will be raised off the table by a half-inch to an inch-and-a-quarter or more. It will take a certain amount of pressure or force to press the middle of the ski flat on the table. The combination of this force and the amount of camber is called Effective Compression. This is the key factor in determining how your weight is distributed over the snow. If a ski has too much camber and resistance to compression, the tip and tail will tend to ride hard on the snow and this "catchiness" at the extremities will make the ski difficult to turn. If a ski has a small camber and little resistance to compression, there will be insufficient weight distribution at the extremities and the skis will tend to "swim" about, lack stability, and lack overall even edge distribution in a turn. One of the benefits of the modern ski, compared to twenty years ago, is that it can be made with less camber while controlling the ski's resistance to being compressed flat.

Just as important as bottom camber to distribute a skier's weight over the length of a ski is the ski's resistance to being compressed flat. One of the positive features of modern ski manufacture is the ability to design a ski with a relatively small amount of bottom camber but with a high resistance to compression.

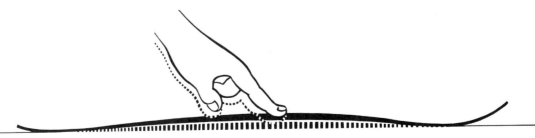

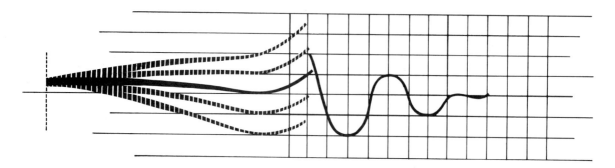

Vibration waves set up by a flexed ski are shown in this chart. The natural frequency of vibration of a ski (indicated here by the diminishing amplitude of the wave) is important in promoting ski-snow contact. The more the ski stays in contact with the snow, the better its vibrations are damped.

Damping

This represents the ski's ability within its own structure to suppress vibration. Reduced vibration, up to a point, is desirable in a ski because it promotes more continuous contact of the edge with the snow—a critical factor in getting a grip on hard snow and ice. Actually, the most effective damping comes from contact with the snow itself. A ski with a desirable natural frequency of vibration will maintain excellent ski-snow contact even when it lacks much internal damping. In the illustration above, the diminishing size or amplitude of the wave indicates the ski's damping; the distance between the waves determines the natural frequency of the vibration of the ski.

The old metal ski lacked damping, but it still is one of the best skis for deep powder and soft snow, which is a natural damper of vibrations. The fiberglass ski, on the other hand, has superior vibration damping, but this alone will not make it a good ski on hard snow and ice; it must also have a good natural frequency of vibration.

Swingweight

Another fairly important property of a ski is its weight distribution. Most skis weigh between eight and eleven and one-half pounds a pair, but more significant is the way that weight is distributed. Too much weight at the tips and tails of the skis can be felt in unweighted turns, where there will be undue resistance to your feet twisting the skis in a new direction. A good swingweight makes skis easier to pivot.

Ski Length

The emphasis on the Graduated Length Method (GLM) and Accelerated Teaching Method (ATM) forms of instruction means that most beginners start out on short rental skis and advance to the longer ski they will buy. Because of age, disability, or timidity, some skiers will prefer to stay with the short ski they learned on. Most skis purchased today are 200 centimeters (6′8″) or less in length. Consult your ski shop and follow reports in the ski magazines. Your skiing ability, height, and weight—but most important, the speed at which you like to ski—must all be considered in the choice of length.

The energy level of a ski is most important in determining the ski you select. Some 185-centimeter (6′2″) skis are as stable as some 200-centimeter (6′8″) skis. This is because their energy level is as high as the longer skis. Expert skiers do use higher-energy skis in lengths as short as 170 and 180 centimeters, particularly for deep-powder skiing and for acrobatics, but they have returned to long skis—195 to 207 centimeters for hard snow and are beginning to edge upward in powder as well. Frankly, the short-ski craze has just about ended.

SKI AND *SKIING* EVALUATE SKIS

The systems of evaluation used in the early seventies have evolved into the complex and detailed comparisons made today. Both magazines use outside laboratories to run the tests and compile the data, although each magazine assigns its equipment staff to write the analyses.

The pair of charts reprinted here appeared in the October 1980 issues of the respective magazines. *Skiing*'s chart had thirty-five skis rated, SKI's included ninety-four. For simplicity, we've only shown the twenty-five skis that were evaluated on both charts, together with the explanations of what the criteria mean. Following this are evaluations of four skis from the two magazines, written by Bill Grout for *Skiing* and Seth Masia for SKI.

RACING SKIS

(Data supplied by Ski Testing Program, College of Engineering, Univ. of Utah)

Make & Model	Suggested Retail Price	Advertised Test Length (cm)	Contact Length (cm)	Weight Per Ski (kg)	Waist Width (mm)	Sidecut Angle (degrees)	Overall Stiffness (N/cm)	Flex Distribution Shovel/Middle/Heel (N/cm)		Torsional Stiffness (Nm/deg.)
Atomic ARC Cup HV	$215	200	177	1.8	67	Medium (.44)	37	Med./Med./Med.	(7.4/55.7/8.0)	Med. (1.07)
Blizzard Firebird Competition Pro	$285	200	175	1.9	66	Medium (.46)	42	Med./Med./Med.	(7.3/61.8/7.9)	Med. (1.75)
Century 5.0	$335	205	183	1.6	68	Medium (.45)	33	Med./Soft/Firm	(7.7/44.8/12.3)	Soft (0.99)
Dynamic VR 17 Equipe S	$290	204	184	2.1	69	Shallow (.43)	32	Med./Soft/Med.	(6.7/47.9/7.1)	Med. (1.50)
Dynastar Acryglass	$270	203	181	2.1	69	Medium (.46)	40	Firm/Med./Med.	(8.4/60.6/8.8)	Firm (2.86)
Elan RC-04	$245	200	180	1.8	66	Deep (.50)	32	Soft/Med./Med.	(6.2/50.9/7.0)	Soft (0.97)
Elan RC-05	$250	205	181	2.0	66	Deep (.52)	34	Med./Med./Med.	(7.0/49.3/8.6)	Med. (1.19)
Fischer Target	$210	205	182	2.2	67	Medium (.47)	37	Med./Med./Med.	(6.8/55.9/7.9)	Med. (1.24)
Hagan Flight	$190	200	176	1.9	66	Medium (.48)	40	Med./Med./Med.	(7.3/55.1/8.3)	Med. (1.07)
Hart HC Comp SL	$260	200	181	1.6	67	Shallow (.43)	24	Soft/Soft/Soft	(4.1/39.4/5.7)	Soft (0.90)
Head SR 90	$240	205	187	2.0	66	Medium (.46)	37	Med./Med./Med.	(6.8/52.3/8.4)	Med. (1.75)
Hexcel HDS-1 Splitail	$325	205	186	1.9	68	Medium (.44)	36	Med./Med./Med.	(7.9/54.2/7.8)	Med. (1.99)
K2 710-FO	$250	204	183	2.0	66	Medium (.48)	37	Firm/Med./Med.	(8.2/52.1/9.5)	Med. (1.96)
K2 810-FO	$275	204	183	2.2	66	Medium (.49)	36	Med./Med./Soft	(6.5/59.2/6.4)	Med. (1.92)
Kästle RX Performance Team	$230	205	181	2.0	66	Deep (.51)	41	Med./Firm/Med.	(6.7/66.6/7.4)	Med. (1.75)
Kästle RX Racing Team	$250	200	177	2.1	66	Deep (.51)	43	Med./Firm/Med.	(7.0/66.6/9.7)	Med. (1.52)
Kazama Airflo Comp	$250	204	183	2.1	66	Medium (.46)	35	Soft/Med./Med.	(4.9/57.2/8.1)	Med. (1.41)
Kneissl White Star SL Professional	$245	205	185	2.2	66	Medium (.48)	36	Med./Med./Med.	(6.8/50.4/8.8)	Med. (1.39)
Olin Mark VI Slalom	$265	205	183	2.1	67	Medium (.49)	38	Med./Med./Soft	(6.2/59.2/5.4)	Med. (1.23)
Rossignol FP	$250	203	181	2.0	67	Medium (.45)	36	Med./Med./Med.	(7.6/50.6/8.7)	Med. (1.63)
Rossignol SM	$260	203	179	2.0	69	Medium (.47)	37	Firm/Med./Med.	(8.2/55.5/7.5)	Firm (2.48)
Spalding Squadra Corse SL	$295	201	179	2.1	68	Medium (.45)	42	Med./Firm/Med.	(6.9/70.3/7.8)	Firm (2.42)
Swallow Professor Graphite	$250	205	182	2.3	65	Deep (.55)	37	Med./Med./Med.	(7.6/53.4/7.7)	Soft (1.04)
The Racing Ski (TRS)	$285	203	177	1.8	69	Medium (.44)	39	Med./Med./Firm	(7.8/54.7/10.6)	Med. (1.68)
Völkl Explosiv R	$390	200	178	2.0	68	Medium (.44)	37	Med./Med./Med.	(7.5/58.7/9.3)	Firm (2.14)
Mean Values:				2.01	67	.46	37.1		7.1/55.0/8.2	1.55
Standard Deviations:				0.17	1.4	.03	3.7		0.9/ 6.6/1.4	0.5

HOW TO USE THE LAB DATA ON SKIS

Heading	Definition	Qualification	General Significance
CONTACT LENGTH	Length of ski touching a flat surface (the snow) with the camber depressed.	Contact length may vary for same advertised length. It is usually 22–23 centimeters shorter than the advertised lengths.	Indication of ski length felt by skier. Long skis are normally steady and stable; short skis are normally more maneuverable.
WEIGHT PER SKI	Weight of one ski without binding or appurtenances.		A light ski may require less effort to turn but may not be as quiet (damped) on hard snows.
WAIST WIDTH	Minimal width of ski in the binding area.		A narrow ski is usually quick from edge to edge; a wide ski provides more stability.
SIDE-CUT ANGLE	The degree of flare (the average angle the ski sidewall makes with the ski centerline).	*Shallow*: Low flare. *Medium*: Medium flare. *Deep*: High flare.	Quick-turning skis usually have deep side cuts; steady and high-speed skis have shallow side cuts.
OVERALL STIFFNESS	Resistance to bending when ski is supported at both ends and weighted in the center measured in Newton centimeters (N/cm).	Overall stiffness is an important and variable ski parameter. The higher the number, the stiffer is the ski.	Soft skis should be matched to light skiers, bumpy terrain, and slow speeds. Firm skis should be matched to heavy skiers, hard snows, and high speeds.
FLEX DISTRIBUTION	Resistance to bending of the shovel, middle, and heel ski sections, respectively, measured in Newton centimeters (N/cm).	*Soft*: Low resistance. *Medium**: Medium resistance. *Firm*: High resistance.	Easy-turning skis are usually soft at both ends. Skidding skis are usually softer in the middle than carving (giant slalom) ones.
TORSIONAL STIFFNESS	Resistance to twisting of the ski forebody measured in Newton-meter/degrees (Nm/deg.)	*Soft*: Low resistance. *Medium**: Medium resistance. *Firm*: High resistance.	Carving (giant slalom) skis are usually stiffer in torsion than skidding (slalom) skis. Recreational skis are usually soft in torsion.

* Medium values are those that fall within the range described by one standard deviation on either side of the mean value.
Reprinted with permission of *Skiing* magazine, October 1980.

SKI SPECIFICATIONS CHART

Manufacturer & Model	Length Tested (cm)	Pair Weight (kg)	Waist Width (mm)	Turn Index (m)	Flex Index (N/cm)	Flex Distribution			Torsion Index (Nm/deg.)	Price (Suggested Retail) $	Lengths Available (cm)	Ski Type	Skier Suitability
						Tip %	Center %	Tail %					
Atomic ARC Cup HV	200	3.69	66.8	199	43.5	04	90	06	1.09	215	180–205	Recreational racing	AR, TT
Blizzard Firebird Comp Pro	200	3.84	66.6	208	49.7	03	91	06	1.68	285	180–210	Racing	EX
Century 5.0	200	3.14	66.7	166	42.9	04	87	09	.81	335	190–205	Racing	EX, TT
Dynamic VR17 Equipe	204	4.18	68.9	216	40.5	04	89	07	1.45	290	172–207	Racing	EX
Elan RC-04	200	3.34	64.2	161	42.5	04	89	06	.89	280	175–210	Racing GS	EX
Fischer Target	205	4.44	67.6	195	44.2	04	90	07	1.14	210	180–210	Recreational racing	EX, AR
Hagan Flight	200	3.85	66.0	187	45.9	05	89	06	.88	190	175–200	Recreational	AR, TT
Hart HC Comp SL	200	3.79	66.7	177	46.0	07	84	09	1.46	260	175–205	Racing SL	EX, AR
Head SR 90	205	4.12	64.1	175	45.5	05	88	07	2.08	240	180–205	Racing SL	EX
Hexcel HDS-1 Splitail	205	3.77	67.2	185	45.0	05	88	08	1.86	325	190–210	Racing	EX
K2 810-FO Comp	205	4.46	66.6	187	43.9	04	91	05	1.82	275	180–210	Racing GS	EX
K2 710-FO Comp	200	3.88	65.7	176	44.9	04	88	08	2.02	250	175–207	Racing SL	EX, AR

Kästle												
RX Racing Team	200	4.02	66.4	177	50.1	04	89	07	1.58	250	180–205	Racing SL	EX
RX Performance Team	200	4.03	67.7	187	49.8	03	90	07	1.26	230	180–205	Recreational racing	EX, AR, TT
Kazama												
AirFlo Comp	207	4.42	66.3	196	44.5	03	90	07	1.83	250	188–207	Racing	EX
Kneissl												
White Star SL Pro	205	4.58	66.3	200	49.8	04	88	08	1.61	245	180–205	Racing SL	EX
Olin												
Mark VI SL	200	4.21	67.0	179	43.9	03	92	04	1.20	265	175–205	Racing SL	EX
Rossignol												
FP Comp	203	3.96	66.7	206	45.2	04	89	07	1.80	250	170–207	Racing SL	EX
Spalding												
Squadra Corse	205	4.58	68.7	240	46.7	03	91	06	2.42	295	180–223	Racing	EX
Swallow												
Professor Graphite	200	4.17	64.0	159	45.4	04	86	09	1.11	250	170–205	Recreational racing	EX, AR
The Ski												
TRS	203	3.82	69.0	203	38.7	04	88	08	1.89	275	170–207	Racing	EX
Völkl												
Explosiv R	200	3.99	68.5	203	42.5	04	89	07	1.94	360	175–210	Racing GS	AR, EX
Additional Skis (Tested in 1979)												
Dynastar												
Acryglass	207	4.26	69.5	216	52.8	07	85	09	2.92	270	170–210	Racing GS	EX
Elan												
RC-05	205	4.19	65.5	182	43.4	07	84	09	1.30	250	175–210	Racing SL	EX
Rossignol												
Sm Comp	200	3.91	67.8	181	45.9	06	85	08	2.27	260	170–210	Racing GS	EX, AR

Reprinted with permission of SKI, October 1980.

The following article by John Howe explains the aspects of ski performance and tells how to read SKI's specifications chart. It appeared in the October 1980 issue of SKI and is adapted from Chapter 2 of *Skiing Mechanics*, by John Howe (La Porte, Colo.: Poudre Publishing, 1982). It is reprinted by permission of the author.

There are many variables involved in ski design and construction—so many that a ski is a mysterious compromise between conflicting performance objectives. There are, of course, numerous ways we can measure ski characteristics; the properties listed in the table of ski specifications are just a few of the more important ones.

Longitudinal ski stiffness (flex index). The first element a ski designer considers is overall ski stiffness, or longitudinal bending stiffness. A ski too stiff for a light skier in moguls may still be too soft for a heavy skier trying to hold a precise, high-speed carved turn on ice. In general, soft flex results in a pressure distribution centered around the foot. Such a ski works well in moguls and easily flexes into a tight turn on a concave surface. Stiff flex results in more pressure at the ends of the ski. The ski is more stable at high speeds and does not change direction easily with foot-swiveling techniques.

Flex distribution. Stiffness is not evenly distributed throughout the length of the ski. Certain sections are inevitably firmer than others. A ski with a stiff forebody and softer tail will initiate turns quickly and tend to release at the tail, especially if the skier drives his weight forward. This is called oversteer. A ski with a soft shovel and stiff tail may be vague in starting turns and will tend to run straight as soon as the weight is pressed back toward the end of a turn. This is called understeer.

A ski with a firm midsection and soft ends (typical of a giant slalom flex distribution) absorbs terrain smoothly and carves long radius turns but may feel erratic in short radius turns because the midsection won't conform to the radius of the turn as easily as the tip and tail do. In other words, the ski won't flex into a smooth curve in a tight turn.

A ski with a soft midsection and relatively firm ends (typical of a slalom ski flex pattern) will carve round, tight turns and is stable at high speeds. If it's too stiff at the ends, however, the ski may feel edgy and erratic because the tip and tail will bite too suddenly.

Camber. In its relaxed, unflexed position, the ski is constructed in a graceful arch. This provides a small initial pressure against the snow at the ski's extremities, which in turn provides both sensitivity for turning and stability for straight running.

Camber and longitudinal stiffness are closely related and must be discussed together. A soft-flexing, high-camber ski works better in varied terrain and snow conditions. A firmer-flexing, low-cambered ski tracks more accurately and therefore lends itself better to high-speed skiing and longer-radius turns. Camber is typically measured with the ski sideways to a flat reference surface to eliminate the effect of the ski's own weight. Typical camber values are 5–15 millimeters per ski.

Torsional stiffness. Torsional stiffness is the ski's resistance to twisting. It's quite independent of overall flex. At first it would seem desirable to provide maximum torsional stiffness, to maximize edge bite throughout the ski's length. However, a ski must be able to release laterally from the snow as well as to hold on icy surfaces. If torsional stiffness is too high, the ski won't release smoothly and may be oversensitive to minor mistakes. Skis with higher torsional stiffness often work better on ice and for expert skiers; torsionally softer skis are smoother handling, more forgiving, and more manageable in soft snow.

Torsional stiffness is measured by clamping the ski in the center and applying a twist or torque at either end. Box construction skis and skis with an aluminum sandwich construction tend to be firmer in torsion than fiberglass sandwich skis. One way to soften the torsional stiffness of a ski is to add a layer or two of rubber. Skis with cracked edges tend to be stiffer in torsion since the ski has to be thicker to make up for the softer overall flex of the cracked steel edges, compared to that of continuous steel edges.

Ski geometry (turn index). The most important dimension of a ski, since it determines to a great extent how a ski will turn, is sidecut, the progressive curve built into the side of the ski, from wide shovel and tail to narrow waist. The radius of sidecut may vary between shovel and tail, but it typically varies from 3,000 inches to 1,800 inches. A high sidecut radius—a shallow sidecut, with a higher radius—means the ski tends to run straight and carve wide-radius turns. A low sidecut radius—a deeper sidecut—means the ski will turn much more quickly, but may be unstable at high speeds and may climb uphill on a traverse.

Ski width. Closely related to sidecut is the actual width of the ski. A narrow ski is easy to set on edge and feels more precise on hard surfaces. In soft snow, a very narrow ski lacks buoyancy. It's also easier to catch an edge or drag the side of a boot on a narrow ski. A wider ski floats better in powder, is easier to balance on and, because a wider ski requires more edging power to get it on edge, it feels more stable. Typical ski widths at the waist vary for adult skis from about 65 millimeters to around 72 millimeters.

Ski length. The two lengths to consider are the total (chord) length and the running surface length (the length of the ski's base actually in contact with the snow on smooth terrain). Some manufacturers continue to use the "developed" or material length—that is, the total length of all parts laid flat, before assembly.

A shorter ski requires less leverage to turn. The skier has a better chance of overpowering a shorter ski to correct course deviations. A shorter ski will also carve a tighter radius turn.

On the other hand, a long ski is more stable and less likely to be deflected from its straight-ahead or long-arc course.

The single most important decision to make in choosing a pair of skis is the length of the skis. The type of skiing you expect to do should be the deciding factor. Take into account the speed, terrain, snow conditions, and turn radius you like, plus your own strength and agility. If you expect to ski faster next season, move to a longer ski.

Damping. When a ski is flexed, it stores energy like a spring, and then, just like a spring, rebounds when the flexing force is released. If no outside resistance is present, the ski will continue to flex back and forth—that is, it will vibrate—until the original stored energy is dissipated.

There are two ways this energy can be dissipated: externally (against the snow and air), and internally (as structural fibers and other material parts of the ski move microscopically against each other). As long as the ski is used in soft snow and kept in contact with the snow, damping is not very important. However, when the snow is hard and icy, an undamped ski will bounce around excessively.

In a ski designed for fast skiing on icy, rutted surfaces—most racing skis, for instance—damping is extremely important. Damping can be increased through the addition of rubber shear layers, extra fiberglass, or by use of a foam core. Each of these techniques, however, has the effect of softening the ski's torsional stiffness, so the designer has to be very careful about the compromise he chooses to make.

Ski thickness is also related to damping. The primary purpose of increasing core or structural-layer thickness is to increase the ski's bending stiffness; however, by using more flexible materials and making the ski thicker a designer can cause the structural layers to move farther with each vibration, thereby absorbing more energy and reducing vibration faster. Finally, adding a cracked edge increases damping by eliminating the "tuning fork" effect of the continuous steel edge.

Skiing

• **ATOMIC ARC CUP HV** ($215) —Intended for racing and expert recreational use, the new Austrian-made Cup HV is said to be suitable for all conditions, especially ice. It has a two-part wood core, with wet-laminated fiberglass layers top and bottom. In the lab, our 200-centi- meter test model proved to be one of the lightest 200's tested, with a medium side cut and medium overall flex pattern. In flex distribution, the shovel, middle, and heel all tested medium, and in torsional stiffness, the forebody proved soft. Lengths: 180–205 centimeters.

SKI

• **ATOMIC ARC CUP HV**
  Vitronic core

New models from Atomic this season consist of a group of soft, quick-reacting bump-and-powder skis built with a new "Hy-Vitronic" or HV system. Atomic's Bob Park explains that the Austrian factory has designed a lightweight wood core of laminated poplar and beech, reinforced in the center section with an upper layer consisting of three laminations of tough ash. The ash, says Park, gives the ski better snap and greater strength. Major struc- tural loads are carried by fiberglass top and bottom layers. There are three HV models: The racing-length version, suitable for recreational racing and aggressive skiing in a variety of snow conditions, is the ARC Cup ($225, 180–205 cm). The midlength model is the MID Supreme ($185, 160–200 cm), a soft and lively mogul ski. Atomic's compact bump-ski is the ACS Leader ($160, 150–190 cm).

Skiing

• **ELAN RC-04** ($245)—Made in Yugoslavia, this is Elan's giant slalom ski for racers and "aggressive experts." Like the other Elan models, it has a wood core sandwiched between layers of fiberglass. Our 200-centimeter test ski showed a deep side cut and a narrow waist. In overall flex, it was among the softest in the racing group. The fore- body proved to be soft in torsion; in flex distribution, the shovel tested soft, the middle and heel medium. Lengths: 175–210 centimeters.

ELAN RC-05 ($250)—This slalom model is said to have the same construction used by Ingemar Stenmark. It was reviewed in last month's issue. Lengths: 175–210 centimeters.

SKI

• ELAN RC-04
Metal-reinforced

For the past three seasons Ingemar Stenmark, previously regarded as a slalom specialist, has absolutely dominated giant slalom racing at the World Cup level. At first he skied GS on his slalom skis. Then Elan designed and built a giant slalom ski to Stenmark's specifications. The RC-04 Stenmark used in winning the GS gold medal at Lake Placid was a fiberglass sandwich ski torsionally reinforced at the shovel and tail with sheets of aluminum.

According to Elan's Nick Schubert, a torsionally reinforced full-race RC-04 ($245, 175–210 cm) will be supplied to ski shops this season. The torsional reinforcement has been provided through the addition of extra layers of fiberglass. The all-fiberglass RC-05 ($250, 175–210 cm), Stenmark's medal-winning slalom ski, is back this season unchanged. New ski in the line is the RC-07 ($270, 210–223 cm) for downhill.

Skiing

• **K2 710-FO** ($250)—A new version of last year's 710 wood-core slalom ski, the 710-FO has a foam core wrapped with multiple layers of fiberglass. Below the core is an extra layer of bias-ply fiberglass that is said to give the ski more torsional stiffness without increasing overall stiffness. In the lab our 204-centimeter test ski showed a medium side cut and medium overall flex. In flex distribution, the shovel proved firm, the middle and heel medium. The forebody tested medium in torsion. Lengths: 175–207 centimeters.

K2 810-FO ($275)—This new GS racing ski from K2 replaces last year's 810. For a complete report on it, see the September issue. Lengths: 180–210 centimeters.

SKI

• K2 810FO/710FO
Foam core new

Introduced during the Lake Placid Olympics, K2's new FO Competition series helped Phil Mahre achieve a silver medal in slalom and the FIS Combined World Championship. FO stands for "foam," and the new racing skis differ from the old 710 and 810 Comps primarily in using foam instead of wood cores. The foam core is lighter and can therefore be made thicker, raising the ski's torsional stiffness. The

810FO ($275, 175–210 cm) uses thicker aluminum than its predecessor, along with two layers of pre-cured fiberglass, giving the new GS model higher torsional stiffness and better high-speed stability, especially on hard snow. The 710FO slalom ski ($250, 175–207 cm) is also stiffer torsionally than the wood-core version, deriving the additional beef from a new pre-cured bias-ply fiberglass layer and thicker core. The new ski is also softer in the shovel and firmer in the tail than the older model. Says product manager Tom Hamilton, "The ski now accelerates quicker, holds better and feels like a soft ski in the bumps."

Skiing

· **VOLKL EXPLOSIV R** ($390) —This German-made ski is said to be a racing-stock model similar to that used by World Cup champion Hanni Wenzel. Designed for GS racing and long-radius, high-speed turns, it has a wood core with torsion-box construction. Our 200-centimeter test model had a medium side cut and medium overall flex. In the torsion test, the forebody proved firm; in flex distribution, the shovel, middle, and heel all tested medium. Lengths: 175–215 centimeters.

SKI

· **VOLKL EXPLOSIV R**
  Hot for Hanni

When Hanni Wenzel won her two golds and a silver at Lake Placid, she was skiing on Volkl. The giant slalom model is the Explosiv R ($390, 175–215 cm). Like all Volkl skis, the Explosiv uses a fiberglass torsion-box construction and, like most giant slalom skis, incorporates two layers of aluminum for high-speed stability and torsional reinforcement. Volkl uses an expensive, super-slick racing base and polyurethane protective top edges on its racing skis. The German-made Explosiv R is built in relatively small quantities, and, according to the factory, the most recent racing experience is always taken into consideration when new skis are made.

HOW TO TEST SKIS

For all the intelligence the SKI and *Skiing* charts provide, the final decision must be yours. If you'll notice one thing from those charts and descriptions, no one's saying "Buy this ski" or "Don't buy that ski." The descriptions must, perforce, be vague, because no two people, even two very good skiers, will like the same ski. Even more important—as Doug Pfeiffer, former editor in chief of *Skiing* and more recently a contributing editor on SKI, has commented often—two pairs of the same mode, as in two K2/710s, for example, may vary as much as 10 percent or more in overall flex/torsion properties.

So you have to do the testing, make the decisions, and spend the money. Now, how do you do that? I wrote these guidelines for the 1980 pre-season issue of *Skier's Advocate*.

1. *Experience*. If you've generally liked Rossignol or K2 or Atomic in the past, that's probably a good place to start. Just don't be too quick to buy the first ski you can "live with," because you may find a better one with a little more investigation.

2. *Brochures*. When you cut through the marketing hype, each company's publication contains information of value. (Just remember that the people who write that stuff are the heirs of the sportscaster who calls any routine catch by an outfielder who doesn't fall down and hurt himself "a great play!!!!!"). The Austrians tend to write the cleanest copy, but you can find intelligence even amid the French and American prose as to the SL (Slalom), GS (Giant Slalom) and Recreational-Racing models. Ignore DH models completely unless you race Downhill.

3. SKI *and/or* Skiing *magazines*. Both do significant testing, both by static (machine) and on-snow methods, and the results, while not identical, are usually similar. The important items are the test charts. Once you find a ski or two you like (see below), compare its flex/torsion properties and ratios with those of other skis on the charts; those with similar numbers may well provide a similar ride.

4. *The telephone*. Virtually all brochures contain the phone number of that company's home office (some even have toll-free 800 numbers), and the home office has a listing for its representative in your area (as well as the ski shops that carry its line). Your local rep can tell you two things, what his company's lineup is, and

when his "demo van" will be at which ski areas. He can even offer a few hints as to which model he feels might be the best one for you to try first, but don't count on that: Giving advice isn't his business. Giving information is.

5. *Ski shops.* But only if you've known the shop, or the salesperson, for a while. Remember, of all the tools available, this is the only one with a vested interest in selling you a specific piece of equipment for a specific price at a specific time (right now!), and while you can find some very reliable and knowledgeable ski shops, you can also run into a hustler with a surplus of Brand X on his racks. Even the reliable shops will feel a greater responsibility to long-term "regular" customers. Also, any shop owner/salesman has a built-in bias based on his inventory: If he doesn't carry Dynastar he's not going to want to put you on an MV5.

To me, the hunt is as much fun as the kill. Maybe more. I enjoy trying different kinds of skis (and boots) because it forces me to develop a greater sensitivity to my own skiing and to get more in tune with myself. Besides, let's face it, there's nothing like a little one-upmanship at the bar as you compare all those top-of-line skis you've tried, offering casual comments like "that 710's as squirrelly as a skateboard" or "the Mark V is as dead as my old girl friend." Hopefully, one of your cohorts will like the 710 or Mark V and away you go.

Start out with one given: *You're right.* If you don't like a ski, it's no good—for you. Skis are very subjective, as are boots, and if for any reason one turns you off—you can't make it do your kind of thing—try something else. (One minor caveat there: Check to see how well it's been tuned. If it seems to be hooking, the edge may not have been "pulled back"—the shovel dulled—far enough. If it's skidding too much, the ski may have been pulled back too far. Check with the shop or demo van.) Ultimately you'll find a ski that turns when, where, and how you want it to—and from then on, the trick is to get it to do it better. If that ski (or one quite like it) has been run on the World Cup circuit, you've got a long way to go before you overski it.

Start with a second rule: *You've got to ski it before you buy it.* This won't provide a 100 percent guarantee; the demo ski you get from the van is apt to handle differently from the one you'll buy, if for no other reason than that it will have been tuned better (and certainly far more). The difference between van and rack skis from most Austrian companies will be less pronounced than from many American and French companies (in that order) because the Austrians tend to have the best quality control in the industry; but I can't guarantee even that. Flex patterns in one model may vary as much as 10 percent, and the larger the company the more the variance country by country. But most skiers won't notice a 5 percent difference, and even a 10 percent variation isn't significant provided the overall flex properties remain the same. (Most companies can assure that, at least.) Thus a good run on a ski from the van will give you a good idea of what to expect. (Ski-shop "demos" tend to be closer to off the rack, but they also tend not to be overly well tuned.)

And start with a third presumption: *Testing skis is fun*, and not only for the reasons mentioned above. It adds another dimension to the ski experience, provided you do it correctly. Here are a few tips on how to *test* the ski or skis you've selected after screening them as discussed earlier.

1. Take the first two runs of the day on your own skis. The first run is just a warmup to find out "where you're at" that day and what the snow and crowds are like. The second run is your first *test* run of the day, and the trail you pick (preferably an easy one) is the trail you'll use for all of your other second and third runs.

2. On that second run on your own skis, pick a good line that pushes you close to your maximum ability (and you can find that on many green-circle, and certainly blue-square, trails). Feed that run into your internal motion-picture camera—how often you turned, where, what the turn *felt* like—because you're going to try to repeat that run as close as exactly possible on your *second* test run on a new pair of skis. Work into that line both shortswing and wide-sweeping edged turns, even a few skids.

3. Put on the first pair of demos for the day. Find the easiest trail you can tolerate and just let the skis run free under you, adjusting your body position to find the point where they're comfortable. Make a few gentle turns. Do the tips meander? Does the tail wash out? Does the midbody grab, edge, or slide? Don't adjust your style to the ski; see how the ski adjusts to your style.

4. Take the second run on that ski on your test trail/line. You'll probably have to work a little harder to hold that line, because a new ski should be significantly better than your current one. But your style should be able to handle it.

5. Take your third run on that same test trail/line and copy that second run of the day identically—or take an even tougher, more

demanding line through it. If you can't do either comfortably, that ski is probably not for you.

6. If you can do either, move up to a more demanding trail and ski it as you would with your own skis on a first run down a fresh trail. If it works, if you're comfortable handling the greater speed/ quickness/solidity on alien terrain with your style, you're on target. Now take a bump run.

7. If you *really like that ski*, go back to the van (or area shop) and get that same model five centimeters long and repeat procedures 5 and 6. (This could be the most surprising, and often pleasant, experience of the day.)

8. Then, after you've determined which length you're most pleased with, go back to the van or shop and get *another* model in that length and do it again. This should give you a solid idea as to the variation within that line.

9. If you're displeased with the ski after procedure 4 or 5, ditch it and try another model in the racing line. Tell the rep in the van or the shop what you didn't like about it, and *don't let your ego get in the way*! Have no hesitation about saying "That ski didn't hold on ice, especially on long turns," even though 50,000 other skiers are making it work on that trail that day. The ski simply may not have been tuned well (*now*, he'll check!), or it may not be right for you. In any event, he'll have some clue to your ability and technique.

10. Repeat the process starting at number 3. Incidentally, keep alert to any change in the conditions on that trail as the day progresses; snowmaking trails in particular degenerate under traffic.

11. When you find the ski you're happiest with, check its flex/camber/ torsion characteristics on the SKI or *Skiing* chart and look for others with similar numbers/ratios. If the one you like is Austrian, pick one French and one American to try next. Call the reps or check the ski shops, pick up the demos, and run procedures 1 through 8 on both (preferably the same day).

Finally, you'll know something about the type of ski you like, the optimum length, and probably quite a bit about how you ski.

16

How to Tune Your Skis

Once you've bought a new pair of skis, your interest in and care of these carefully constructed instruments of fiberglass, metal, wood, and glue should not end. Like a good motorcycle or guitar, a ski needs to be taken care of. Even after your first day out on the slopes, skis should be inspected and possibly worked on. If you fail to look after your skis, you are easily able to lose 30 percent or more of the performance potential built into their design.

The single most common problem with skis is with the bottom running surface. When the ski base becomes concave or the steel edges ride above the running surface like two railroad tracks, the ski becomes very difficult to turn properly. It will be hard for you to initiate a turn on snow or you will get the feeling that the ski wants to keep turning . . . it's "hooky" or "grabby." The problem is particularly acute around the tip of the ski. And the higher the energy level of the ski, the more small flaws in the bottom surface will affect the way it performs on snow.

MAINTAINING AND REPAIRING SKIS

As the modern ski has become more sophisticated in its design and more highly tuned, it can undergo—like a high-performance racing car—significant

180

losses in performance quality if it is not maintained properly. A badly gouged running surface and railed edges can subtract seriously from the performance of a ski. With effort, time, and a small number of materials and simple tools, these faults can be corrected. The ski can be tuned up to its real performance capability. You can get the work done by a professional ski mechanic in a shop, but it will be expensive. And besides, if you ski a lot, maintenance of your skis should become a regular, frequent routine. Racers work on their skis almost daily. So, for economy and convenience, it is essential that you learn the "tricks of the trade" if you want to extract proper performance from your skis.

Smooth, flat ski bottoms not only slide faster on snow, but more important, they turn more easily. Filed flat and hot-waxed, ski-running surfaces slide forward, sideways, and track straight ahead unhindered by railed edges, deep gouges, or even minor scratches that can create resistance against turning and tracking.

Modern skis with soft polyethylene bases slide well over most kinds of snow with minimal waxing. However, these same soft bases are prone to scratching, especially during the fall months or at periods of bare cover when rocks and tree stumps crop out of the snow.

IMPORTANCE OF FLAT BOTTOMS

One of the most acute problems with skis, however, arises not out of external damage to the running surface but from bottom concavity in the ski itself. To determine if a running surface is concave in any area, raise the ski to eye level with a light source near the tail. Place a straightedge steel rule on the bottom surface, which is facing up. Sighting from the tip of the ski, run the straightedge along the bottom. Mark the sections where light shines through between the rule and the running surface. These sections are concave; that is, the middle or a part of the polyethylene surface is lower than at the side; or, more typically, the steel edges of the skis are raised above the level of the polyethylene.

To understand how a concave bottom or railed edges can hurt your enjoyment of skiing, imagine the "footprint" a concave ski leaves on packed snow. You'll see the deep penetration of the edges and only a light contact of the concave bottom on the snow. This means that in skiing you will ride on the edges of the skis. As noted in the previous chapter, the edges of the skis describe a very long curve, because the ski is narrow in the middle and flares out at the tip and the tail. Consequently, if you are riding on your edges as a

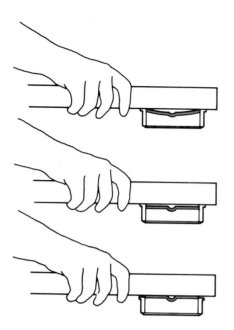

Using a straightedge steel rule, a skier can quickly determine any problem areas on the ski bottom, particularly near the tip. Top: Straightedge rule reveals a concave bottom that makes ski hooky and hard to turn. The ski also will be difficult to handle when the steel edges are railed (center). Bottom: A perfect ski bottom, steel edges and polyethylene running surface in perfect alignment.

The cure: Use a twelve-inch bastard mill file to remove edge steel and polyethylene material to make bottom perfectly flat.

result of bottom concavity, your skis, when weighted, will want to go off in different directions. They will feel hooky and grabby. In short, they become very temperamental creatures. Equally bad, you will experience difficulty in initiating turns unless you use a lot of up-unweighting (see page 269).

Characteristically, much bottom concavity is found near the tip of the ski. This is the part of the ski that most seriously affects performance; therefore it's critical that the running surface near the shovel be flat. With many new skis it is not. The final bottom grinding that ski undergo in the factory has a tendency to cause this fault. But concavity also can be caused by continued curing of the core of the ski after it has been made. In the 1972 ski season, for instance, it was estimated that as many as 70 percent of the new skis in shops suffered some bottom concavity, and it doesn't seem to have improved much by 1982.

Fortunately, the remedy for concave bottoms is neither radical nor difficult. All you need is a straightedge steel rule, a bastard mill file with diagonal teeth, and a short-bristle wire brush to clean the steel filings and plastic out of the teeth of the file. Put your ski, bottom up, in a wooden vise or set it on blocks on the workbench with the tail hard against the wall. To file, start at the shovel of the ski and progress toward the tail. Remember: The purpose is to make the ski bottom perfectly flat. You'll be removing some steel and, if concavity is marked, a certain amount of polyethylene material in order to bring the base to its lowest point.

Lay the file across the ski so that the handle end is in your right hand. The file should be slanted at about 45 degrees to the ski, your right hand being closest to the tip.

To prevent any rocking of the file as you work, hold the file in both hands with your thumbs on the ski's steel edges to guide it. This will ensure that the file is flat on the ski. Work the file down the length of the ski with short pushing strokes. As you pull it back to make a new push stroke, let the file glide on the ski with no pressure, but don't lift it off the ski. Turn the file over occasionally as you progress. Use the wire brush to clean debris out of the teeth. Lightly brush or dust off the filings on the surface of the ski.

Wherever the ski is slightly concave or railed, you will feel more resistance against your file. Concentrate on these locations. By the time you make your final pass down the ski, there will be little or no resistance to the file. Your ski has a nice flat bottom from edge to edge. As a final check, run your fingernail up and down the steel edges. Remove any burrs you detect by light file work.

You also can flat file your skis by propping the tip against the wall. The procedure in this case is to pull rather than push the file.

REPAIRING GOUGED BOTTOMS

Once your skis are in use, the plastic running surface is subject to a certain amount of scratching and gouging. The chances are that you won't notice the damaging effect of this scratching on your skis' performance because it is a gradual, cumulative affair. Only after you have patched the bottoms and hot-waxed the skis will you notice how much performance value you have been missing. The difference can be quite dramatic.

Again, a few simple tools will repair the damage. In essence, what you must do is fill in the gouges and deep scratches with fresh polyethylene material. This comes in the form of polyethylene candles that you can purchase in any ski shop, and they come in different colors to match the bottom of your skis.

To repair the bottom, stabilize the ski on blocks on a workbench or on the arms of an old chair in your basement. Use a pointed knife to dislodge wax and dirt from gouges in the ski bottom. Using the same knife, slice the polyethylene candle lengthwise into two strips. These narrow strips produce the best dripping for filler. Apply a match flame to the candle until it begins to turn. Working along the length of the ski, allow the drippings from the hot candle to fall into the gouges. Fill gouges with an excess of material.

After you have completed the filling process and extinguished the candle, use the sharp knife to remove the bulk of the excess filler from the surface of the ski. Finally, use a hardware-store steel scraper to produce a really smooth surface. Grasp the scraper in both hands and draw it along the surface of the ski. Scrape lightly over shallow gouges so as not to pull out filler material. It is very important that the scraper's edge be sharp and free of nicks. Use a file to keep the edge sharp and smooth.

Don't expect perfection. Some filler material will pull out and light scratches will still appear on the ski. A coat of wax will fill in areas where the filler refuses to bond.

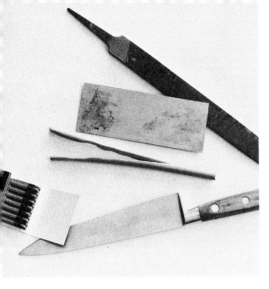

A simple group of tools used for bottom repairing of skis: sharp knife with a pointed tip; a fine steel scraper; a metal file to keep the scraper edge sharp; a P-tex candle that provides the polyethylene filler material for repairs, and matches to light the melting candle.

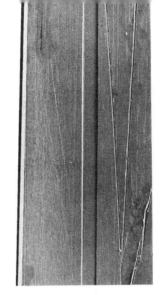

Before repairs, ski bottoms exhibit gouges and scratches received from rocks and other hard objects the ski encounters. Eliminating these marks can improve the turning performance of skis by as much as 30 percent.

Use pointed tip of the knife to dislodge wax and dirt from all gouges. Cleaning out holes in this way will create a better bond between the filler and the ski.

Cut the polyethylene candle lengthwise (left); a narrow strip produces the best dripping for filler. Apply match flame to candle until it begins to burn and drip (above). Extinguish after patching.

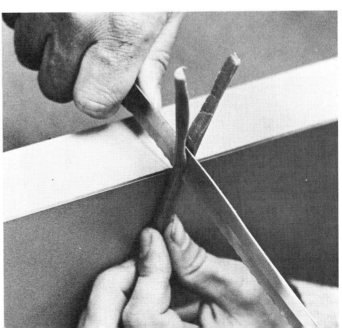

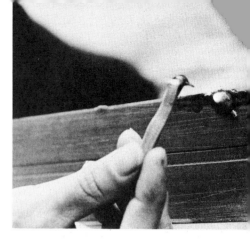

Overfill all gouges with drippings to create an excess of material above the ski's running surface (above). Don't worry about drops of polyethylene falling randomly on the running surface (right). Allow filler several minutes to cool.

A big blob of flaming polyethylene dripped onto the ski can burn a hole in the ski bottom (above). Quickly remove burning material from the ski.

Begin to remove the bulk of excess material using the sharp, pointed-tip knife over all patched areas (above). In lieu of the knife, a simple carpenter's plane easily shaves off excess filler.

Next, file the edge of the metal scraper sharp to remove the remaining filler material. Filing will also remove small irregularities in the scraper edge that might otherwise leave corresponding marks in the ski's running surface.

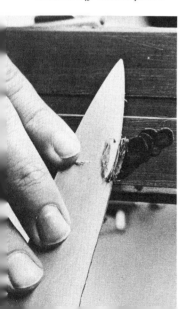

Shave filler smooth and flush to the ski bottom (left). Scrape lightly over shallow gouges at first so as not to pull out filler material. Don't expect perfection; some pulling out will usually occur from shallow grooves. A coat of wax will fill in areas where the filler refuses to bond. Using the metal scraper, go over the entire ski bottom. Below: Location of repaired gouges is still visible due to a difference in color between repair material and the original running surface. But the bottom is smooth and your skis are now ready to perform like new.

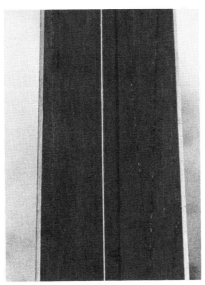
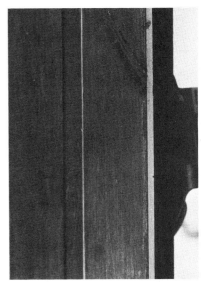

WAXING THE SKIS—WAX SELECTION

Although skis are designed to run well on the bare polyethylene (sometimes called P-Tex or Kofix) running surfaces, they will run and turn even better if hot waxed. As noted above, the wax will fill in minor scratches on the skis that impede turn initiation. The wax also helps to seal off tiny pores in the polyethylene base against moisture that might enter the core of the ski.

For a couple of dollars, you can get your skis hot waxed at most ski areas. But with a simple kit, you can perform the chore yourself the night before and get an early start in the morning, while saving yourself quite a bit of money over the course of a winter.

Snow temperature (not air temperature) and moisture content determine which wax or combination of waxes to use on a specific day. A typical wax kit includes green, blue, and red wax bars and white and yellow paraffin. Instructions will come with the kit. Generally speaking, use green when the snow is so cold and dry it squeaks when you walk on it. Use blue for regular

The basic ingredients needed to wax skis are shown at right: Five-inch-long steel scraper, file, table knife, one-and-a-half-inch brush with natural bristles, and a pot for melting wax. Bars of green, blue, red, white, and yellow paraffin will cover all conditions.

cold winter conditions, and red when the snow is warmer and holds enough moisture to form a snowball. When temperature and moisture content are borderline, mix a combination of blue and green or blue and red. To widen the temperature range of the wax, add a little white paraffin to green and blue waxes, or yellow paraffin to red.

There are two methods of hot waxing skis: the ironing method and the painting method. The finishing touches in both cases are the same.

To iron on wax, set the iron on medium heat. Press the edge of the wax bar against the heated iron, or two wax bars against it if you are mixing waxes half and half. Moving the iron from the front to the tail of the ski with the tip of the iron pointed down, allow the melting wax to run onto the ski in a small stream on each side of the groove. Next, use the flat surface of the hot iron to spread the two ridges of wax smoothly over the entire running surface of the ski. Keep the iron moving to prevent the wax from bubbling and to avoid excessive heating of the base of the ski.

In the painting method, you melt the bar(s) of wax in a pot. Using a one-and-a-half-inch paintbrush, apply the melted wax in steps along the running surface of the ski. Stroke in one direction only from tail to tip. Make the brush steps about twelve to eighteen inches in length. This method is particularly good if you're waxing for wet snow. The slight steps in the waxed surface will prevent the ski bottom from creating suction on the snow, which slows your speed. It is the method used by racers for long, high-speed downhill courses.

To finish the ski bottoms, use a metal scraper that has been carefully filed to be sharp and nickless so that it leaves no scratches in the waxed surface. Scrape from tip to tail. Scrape lightly, not deeply. Use a plastic or wood scraper to remove wax from the steel edges. Use a table knife to remove wax from the groove of the ski. Finally, to avoid marring the wax, carry your skis to the lift with newspaper or waxed paper between the skis at the tip and tail sections.

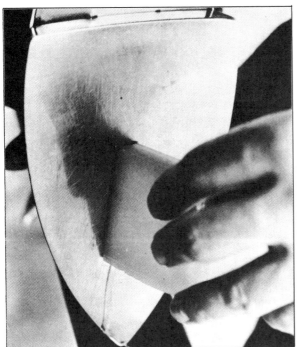

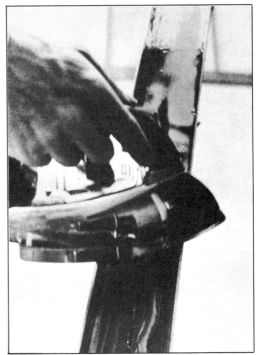

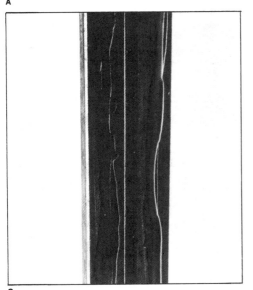

Ironing Method

A Lay skis flat and side by side suspended between two chairs. Set an iron on medium heat; be sure the iron cord is long enough to stretch the length of the skis. Press the edge of a bar of wax against the heated iron.

B Hold two wax bars against the iron if you are mixing wax colors half and half. Pointing the tip of the iron downward, allow wax to run onto the ski in a small stream from tip to tail and tail to tip on both sides of the grooves.

C Next, iron out the wax ridges to spread the wax smoothly over the entire running surface.

D Keep the iron moving to prevent wax from bubbling and to avoid heating up the ski base to the point where the polyethylene loses its bond to other materials in the ski. The ski's running surface covered by a layer of melted wax is now free of tiny nicks and scratches.

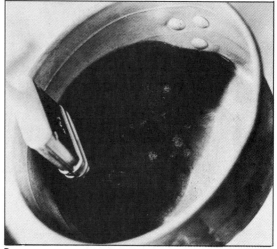

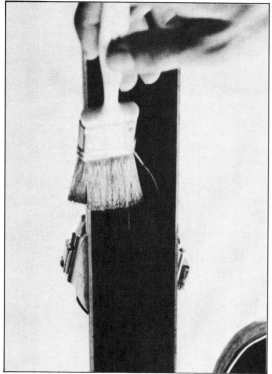

Painting Method

A *Melt one bar or a combination of waxes in a pot until gentle smoke rises or until wax runs in a steady stream from the brush.*

B *Don't allow the brush to burn or catch fire. Next, saturate the brush in wax and press it against the side of the pot to remove air bubbles.*

C *Beginning at the ski tail, hold the brush at a 45-degree angle toward the tip.*

D *And paint four or five twelve- to eighteen-inch-long brushstrokes toward the tip. Overlap each brushstroke to create steps, and paint only in one direction. In wet snow and long, high-speed downhills, steps prevent the ski bottom from creating suction on the snow, which slows the ski. Shorten brushstrokes to increase the number of steps when very wet snow conditions exist. Begin the last step or brushstroke at the ski tip about three inches behind the beginning of the groove. Paint the same length steps on both sides of the groove and on both skis.*

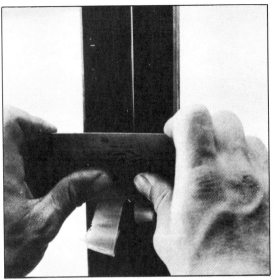

A

B

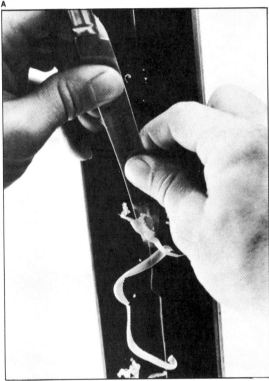

C

D

Finishing Touches

A   *Whether you paint or iron wax on your skis, use the metal scraper again to scrape the waxed surface to a smooth layer. Begin at the tip and scrape toward the tail using long strokes so as not to remove the steps. Scrape past a step before ending a stroke. Bending the scraper slightly will create a slightly concave base for better tracking, but don't scrape too deeply.*

B   *Also remove wax from ski edges with a plastic or wood scraper, not metal.*

C   *Use the table knife to remove wax from the groove.*

D   *Edges must always be filed prior to waxing because metal filings become ground into a wax surface. To avoid scratching and marring a smoothly waxed ski base when you carry your skis to the lifts, insert newspaper or waxed paper between skis at the tip and tail sections.*

SHARPENING STEEL EDGES

For a ski to perform satisfactorily on ice and hard snow, the edges must be sharp and free of nicks. Special racing skis use a relatively soft steel that can be filed very sharp and smooth, and they must be filed frequently. But most skis are made with hard steel that, while it cannot be sharpened as easily, offers the convenience of needing less frequent filing. In addition, the harder steel edges resist nicking from rocks better.

Most ski shops have machines to sharpen edges. But again, if you want to do the job well and save money, it's useful to know how to perform this chore yourself. Moreover, excessive machine filing of edges is not good because it removes too much material from the ski. Steel edges can only tolerate a certain amount of filing during the life of the ski.

The key tool for edge filing is a ten-inch Nicholson mill bastard file. Place the ski in a vise or against the wall. The position of the file on the ski is very important. The grooves in the file should run parallel to the steel edge so that

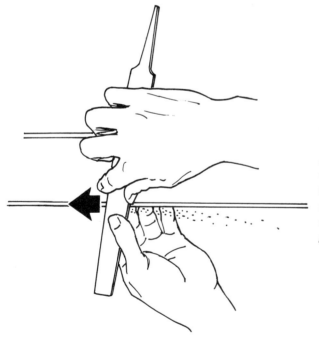

To sharpen edges, file must run along bottom of the ski as well as the side to create a perfectly square edge. Note that in filing the bottom side of the edges, the file is directed in such a way that the steel filings fall on the floor and do not accumulate on the bottom where they will scratch the relatively soft polyethylene running surface.

the microscopic lines formed on the edge run lengthwise down the ski, not diagonally across the edge so as to cause unnecessary friction on the snow. The file also should be held in such a way that the metal filings drop off the edge of the ski on to the floor, rather than onto the running surface of the ski, where they can be ground into the polyethylene base.

To file the side of the edge along the sidewall of the ski, hold the file at a 90-degree angle to the bottom of the ski so as to create a perfectly square edge. File from the tip and the tail toward the middle of the ski. To file underneath the binding, hold the file lengthwise.

If you take all of the steps outlined in this chapter to maintain your skis, you will be assured of enjoyable skiing. If you are serious about racing, anything less than this kind of care simply is inexcusable neglect. But even the recreational skier who has invested more than two hundred dollars in a pair of skis will extract full-performance potential only with periodic care and repair.

17

Bindings—the Safety Factor

Bindings initially were mechanical devices used only for fastening boots to skis. In the last few decades, however, their function has become far more sophisticated. They are now also the gadgets that stand between the skier and a broken leg, because nowadays they also release under sufficient stress.

As noted in Chapter 2 the popularization of skiing coincided with the invention of toe irons by Fritz Huitfeldt. Replacing the ancient cane bindings, toe irons provided crucial lateral control over the skis. Although they held the boot toes tight and allowed no release in a fall, they were nevertheless reasonably safe because speeds were relatively slow and because the arrangement was flexible enough—a lower, more supple boot was held in the toe iron by straps—to allow for some twisting in a fall.

All this began to change in the decade before World War II. Speeds became higher, hence precise control over the skis became more critical. The problem was solved by downpull bindings, which held the whole boot on the ski. The device by which it was accomplished was the cable—at that time aircraft control cable—which passed over the heel of the boot, through side hitches, and to a clamp, which tightened the cable. This worked admirably, but as the popularity of these bindings increased, so did the injury rate. Their release-retention capabilities were a joke—and a bad joke at that.

The first attempts to make a release binding go back to the days before World War I. However, the first such binding that had any substantial success was not marketed until 1939. It was invented by Hjalmar Hvam, and while it was imperfect it was good enough to get skiers thinking about the advantages of coming out of their skis in a bad spill.

Popularization of Hvam's binding was delayed by World War II, but starting in 1950 a number of bindings appeared featuring release mechanisms. Initially, these bindings were shunned by racers and faster skiers, who maintained that the bindings couldn't discriminate between a hard turn and a dangerous fall (what we now call elasticity or antishock). By a process of continuous refinement these prejudices were overcome, and today even the hottest Olympic racers use them. There is no longer any argument about their desirability, though controversy still continues over the merits of the various release mechanisms.

PRACTICAL SAFETY

Many attempts have been made to combine both functions perfectly in one binding, creating a device that will attach the skier to the skis as long as he or she wants but that will always release to prevent any leg sprain or fracture. Unfortunately, no such "perfect" binding has yet been made. No less an authority than Georges Salomon, inventor of the binding that takes his name and leads the world in popularity, has said that a perfectly safe binding probably will never be made. What is more important is that the skier can get practical safety from some very good bindings already available. To be perfectly realistic, this requires an attention to detail that modern consumers are often loath to accept as their responsibility.

An engineer who understands torque loads, friction, and inertia will be no safer than a layman if he or she ignores the common-sense use of bindings. A binding, like the amplifier in a stereo set, is a link or component in a system: An amplifier won't play music any more than a binding will ski by itself. The binding is a link between the ski and the boot; if the binding is mounted crookedly on the ski or if it doesn't fit correctly with the boot, then it won't function properly. Fortunately, *most* of this problem has been solved by the virtually automatic mounting jigs that each company supplies to ski shops, and by the training workshops they run.

THE MARKET TODAY

The designers and engineers may have come about as far as they can; the mousetraps *work*, and if the Stone Age methods of generating ski-injury statistics produce anything of accuracy (one whale of a big *IF*), the bindings people may have pushed the accident rate as far down as it can go. Current mythology—sorry, mathematical analysis—puts the serious-injury (fractures and major lacerations) figures at three per thousand skier days, which makes skiing not much riskier than tiddlywinks. Furthermore, injuries to legs have dropped significantly, and a far higher proportion of the damage is suffered by arms and shoulders, which means we're coming out of the bindings all right but either trying to break the fall with our arms (against everything we were taught playing football) or not rolling with the impact. Finally, the engineers keep telling us—perhaps a soupçon on the self-serving side—that most of the remaining leg injuries are caused by the fact that some falls don't generate enough torque (twisting force) to the foot and that therefore no binding could release.

Alas, being engineers, they don't realize the marketing implications of their remarks: If the current state of the art is so good, why do we need a next generation? If the top units on the market are producing far fewer than three injuries per thousand days (since the many old units still being used generate a higher ratio), can't we leave well enough alone?

Of course not. Not when the mousetrap business is as competitive and lucrative as it is.

The problem is this: Today's boot-ski combination and interaction put incredible stress on the binding. The skis are "high energy"; they vibrate and twang and twist and flex like a competition bow and a CB aerial. The boot soles have all the elasticity and flexibility of a brick, while the rigid sides have enough leverage and develop enough torque to move tall buildings at a single bound. So, as you blithely go bouncing down a wicked mogul field, leaning and edging and twisting and swiveling, the ski is changing shape a zillion times a second and the boot isn't changing at all. All that lengthening/shortening between heel and toe as the ski shifts from flex to counterflex must be absorbed by the binding—fore-aft elasticity via forward pressure in the heel—while the constant high-speed jarring must be absorbed by the antishock mechanism in the toe, which must "decide" whether to return your boot to center or eject it. (Much of the purpose of the electronic binding we'll discuss later is to make the "decision" process more sophisticated. As the telephone company and postal service have become.)

The last generation of bindings—such as the 555/444—just couldn't do that quickly enough. It didn't have to: The skis weren't that lively and many of the boots still had some elasticity. A 555 or 444 in good condition is perfectly adequate for some skis even today—but *not* for a high-performance racing or "super-sport" skis and *not* for a Lange XLR or XLS and its companion competitors.

How serious is this problem? One shop I know in New Hampshire made a good sale in the spring of 1980, $400 worth of new skis and boots, and if you're aware of how bad that season was in New England, you'd appreciate how much that shop needed the bread. But the customer balked at buying new bindings, feeling his old Dovres were still OK, and the shop refused to mount the old bindings. "I even offered to sell him any new bindings he wanted at my *invoice* price"—zero profit to the dealer—"and not charge for the mounting. He wouldn't go along. I gave him back his money." Many area shops simply refuse to adjust old bindings because of liability-insurance problems (does that tell you something?), although a few shops will mount old bindings only if you sign a release to the effect that you had been warned but persisted.

Alas, not all retailers are that ethical. Some will make a tentative pitch, meet resistance, and decide to take the profit on the skis or boots, mount and test the unit under static conditions, and pray that if you smash yourself up you won't realize the inherent ski- or boot-compatibility problem caused the crash.

But buying and properly setting the right binding aren't enough. As you can easily understand, any binding undergoing that constant high-speed jiggling is going to work loose; the old days of setting a binding in November and ignoring it until the following November are gone. I check mine every five days of skiing, but I'm in the minority. One February my son and I were at Pat's Peak, New Hampshire, where the Ski Patrol had set up a testing station; we wandered over about 2:00 P.M. "You know," the patrolman said after the checkup, "you two are only the third and fourth people all day whose bindings were set correctly."

Now, let's talk about buying bindings and how to make intelligent decisions.

• All five major companies—Geze, Look, Marker, Salomon, and Tyrolia, in alphabetical order—produce acceptably efficient models in at least their top two units. Both Burt and Spademan make highly effective plate bindings, but I don't think even the best possible plate could work as well for a competent intermediate skier as even a moderately efficient step-in or rotamat.

• The models the five majors produce are variations of the now-traditional step-in heel-and-toe system. The toe is either a pincer (see page 199) or a single-pivot; in all models except the expensive ($225) Geze SE3 the toe ejects only to the side, although virtually all new top-of-the-line models today make some accommodation for reaction to upward pressure at the toe, at least to the point where the torque needed to release the toe is decreased. The heels on the step-ins only eject upward, though the Tyrolia also has a diagonal fail-safe to assist lateral release at the toe. Marker and Look also make rotamat heels, discussed later.

• The differences in prices among the top-line units are all but non-existent: about $140–150 for the racing unit, $130–140 for the recreational top-end, about $110–120 for the second line. This price should include the brake. The most you can look for in a discount is 10 percent, and those are hard to come by unless you're getting last season's models (which work). If you're buying skis and bindings, or boots and bindings, the retailer should mount the bindings without charge.

• Brakes are mandatory; the leash (formerly, ha ha, the "safety strap") is lethal. Brakes are a spring-loaded pair of arms that drop down when pressure (your weight) is released in an ejection; they grip the snow and don't move, which means that they won't hit either you or any other skier. They should be mounted under the heel, since the upward thrust by the spring could interfere with the release from the toe. Look has compromised and put it under the sole, which seems to work all right. You have to add a looong leash for deep-powder skiing to prevent loss, but otherwise the brakes work fine by themselves.

• The second line of bindings—for example, the 637 or 280D—is more than adequate for 90 percent of American skiers. However, if you're in the top 10 percent—be honest with yourself: Are you expert or advanced, do you weigh 160 pounds or more, and do you ski at least twenty-five days a year? Then opt for the racing rather than the top recreational (e.g., 380R rather than 380D, 737E rather than 737). The only major difference, generally, is that the racing unit uses a heavier spring, which could be dangerous if you're at the light end of the weight scale (take the other binding) but otherwise will give you a longer consistency of release.

• Philosophically, I prefer the pincer toe (Geze, Marker, Tyrolia) to the single-pivot (Look, Salomon). Pragmatically, I've seen no functional difference, nor do the test charts reveal any. Today's single-pivots are very sophisticated.

• Although Look and Marker these days also make step-in heels, their real strengths and traditions are locked into the rotamat, where the heel can pivot around on the ski to absorb some of the shock without ejection. Most World Cup racers still prefer this system to the step-in—these days you also can step into a Look rotamat quite easily—but for most skiers the rotamat

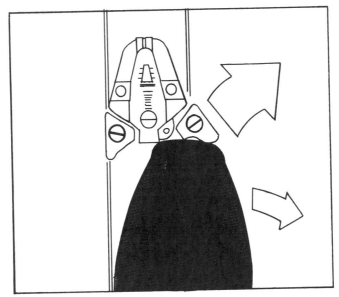

In the pincer toe binding above (based on the Geze Model), only the right wing (large arrow) *moves to allow the boot to eject to the right* (small arrow); *the rest of the binding remains stationary. In the single-pivot* (below), *the whole toepiece swings to the right at the same time—a more massive movement.*

Rotamat (or turntable) heel revolves to absorb shock. Other types, called step-ins, only release upward.

isn't quite as convenient. My son rates his Look 77C rotamat (just discontinued) dead even with the Tyrolia 260D step-in (ditto); I lean to step-ins, period. These days, they both work, but I remain unconvinced that the Marker and Look step-ins work as well as their rotamats or, for that matter, as well as the other step-ins, but that could just be me.

• Virtually all problems of boot-binding compatibility have been eliminated under the pending ASTM (American Society of Testing and Measurement) code. BUT this may not apply to older boots or even to some of the lower-priced, lesser-known new models. Double-check.

• Check for ease of voluntary release by putting the shop's mounted "demo board" on the floor and working it the way you're supposed to. If the binding seems to be a pain or unnecessarily cumbersome in the shop, imagine how it will feel on the slopes when you are manipulating the poles with gloves or mittens on.

• Listen to what your favorite ski-shop owner tells you. He knows which binding(s) he's happiest and most comfortable with. (He also knows which he has the most of in inventory, but no system is perfect.)

THE ELECTRONIC BINDING

By the middle of the eighties, the point of the spearhead of a "new generation" of bindings will appear in the form of an "electronic binding," a series of battery-controlled black boxes that will monitor and control the release-retention "decision." Marker, leading this assault, had prototypes being tested on slope as early as the 1980–81 season and had a larger number of hand-built units in action during 1981–82. However, anyone familiar with the problems of shifting from hand built to mass produced should be a tad cautious about being the first on the lift line to own one when they appear, under present marketing schedules, for the 1983–84 season. Even something as essentially derivative (evolutionary) as the Salomon 727—and no one has more experience in the bindings business than Salomon—had a few minor bugs in its forward-pressure mechanism when it first appeared in 1978, which generated one of those great off-the-record quotes the following spring: "We had no problem but we fixed it for 1979."

So, caveat: Electronic will probably supersede mechanical decision making at some point, simply because it has in so many other sectors. But both Salomon and Tyrolia are approaching this cautiously, focusing more on designing a new mechanical generation for better boot-binding compatibility, with Tyrolia and Look also refining toe-piece sensitivity.

QUESTIONS TO ASK THE SHOP

How can you be sure a shop will mount your bindings properly? Thanks to major improvements by manufacturers in training and certifying shop personnel, this is far less serious a problem than it was a few decades ago. Now you can be assured that the shop employs a skilled, experienced ski mechanic—and more than ever, don't buy bindings at an outlet that doesn't offer certified mounting service. The good shops now have mounting "jigs" for all major bindings that all but assure perfect mounting.

To ascertain the quality of service you're likely to get, even assuming expertise, here are some questions that you can ask the shop.

Can I bring in my present bindings to have the release setting checked? The shop that says "no" is exhibiting apathy or disdain that is likely to carry over into the rest of the service it offers.

Do you use a mechanical device to set binding adjustment? Yes, all good shops use a device that is carefully calibrated to react to the new, universal standards.

How often should I have my bindings checked? At least two or three times a season, preferably every five days you ski. Alas, most skiers still check their bindings less than once a year. This amounts to negligence by the consumer.

What kind of preventive maintenance do you recommend for bindings? Any good shop will lubricate with a variety of silicone sprays designed for this purpose. Check for dirt and grime on moving parts and on the contact area between boot sole and binding.

Is it advisable to mix a toe unit of one manufacturer with a heel unit of another? No. No. No. And again, No!!

If I buy new boots, will I need new bindings? If the binding is more than five years old, the shop should answer "yes." Vastly improved step-ins, together with the stiffer boots of today, make replacement advisable. If your present bindings are satisfactory, the shop should be able to tell you whether your new boots are compatible with the binding design—although this problem, common in the seventies, has virtually vanished under the new ASTM rules.

What kind of retention device do you recommend? Use brakes except in deep powder, when an extra-long leash is preferred. In normal skiing the old "safety straps" are lethal.

Can I see your mounting operation? This can be a nuisance to a shop at busy times, but some retailers like to show off their repair shops. Score higher marks for shops that operate their own repair facilities.

Do you keep a record of the adjustment on the bindings after they're sold and have left the shop? Score high marks for the shop that takes the trouble to keep records. It's the sign of a safety-conscious retailer.

If your inquiries lead to getting good vibes from a shop, then put your confidence in the sales representative. He'll help you select a good binding, and the shop will mount it competently for you. The rest is up to you. For the binding to continue to contribute to your safety during its lifetime, you must maintain it by cleaning and lubrication and see that its release adjustment is checked periodically.

CHECK OUT BINDING INSTALLATION

Unfortunately, not all bindings are installed correctly. Many things can go wrong in the process of mounting. Here are some of the flaws to look for.

One of the more common problems occurs when the binding installer drills a screw hole completely through the ski (especially common with thin skis like Atomic). In this case, he'll try to patch it with P-Tex as close as possible to the color of the ski bottom. A good patch job will make the ski as good as new. With a bad patch job, the filler may come out, leaving the inside core of the ski open to moisture and corrosion. You can spot a patch by examining the ski bottom directly beneath the binding. Usually it's outlined as if a piece of bubble gum had been stuck on and smoothed out.

Running a close second as a binding installer's nightmare is drilling the wrong-size holes or using the wrong-size screws to mount the binding. If the screws are too big for the holes (or the holes too small for the screws), the binding will be raised slightly from the ski's surface, even though the screws appear tight. This is because the screw is forcing material out of the hole and therefore is preventing a flush, flat mounting. A binding mounted in this way may move up and down on the ski and vary widely in release tension.

If the screws are too small (or the holes too big), they will seem "stripped." That is, the screws will still turn when they should be tight. Use a screwdriver to check. Applying a moderate amount of pressure, you should not be able to turn the screws, or they should turn only slightly.

To fix holes that are too large, the repairman will drop a plastic plug into the hole, center punch it, and drive the screw in. It will appear to be in tight, but it may not be. And if all the screws were put in this way, your binding would be in danger of pulling right off the ski.

The ski world used to be full of discussions about the exact point where a binding should be mounted on the ski. The "midpoint" is the correct answer, but there were even arguments about what constitutes the midpoint of the ski. Today, most major skis come with the top surface or sidewall already marked for binding position. Boots now are similarly marked. A good shop usually will know where to mount the bindings by matching the arrows. No more arguments.

As a final check before you leave the shop, put on your boots, get into the bindings, and ask the sales representative or serviceman to instruct you in how to get in and out of the binding and how to adjust its release mechanism. Be sure to ask also for a copy of the binding manufacturer's manual, which will contain detailed instructions on the product and how it should be maintained and adjusted.

MAINTAINING YOUR BINDINGS

Assuming that you, your boots, and your skis have emerged satisfactorily from the buying and mounting phase, you now have good equipment properly mounted and adjusted. You have skied for a few days with delight and relative safety. As with most mechanical things you must now consider minimum maintenance. Bindings don't require oil changes, grease jobs, or sparkplug gapping, but they are subjected to all sorts of contaminants and environmental changes. Your skis, with bindings attached, generally ride on the roof of your car, not in it, and are subjected to road dirt, rain, sleet, and salt if you don't use bindings covers (as you should). So it is only reasonable to expect them to need cleaning occasionally.

The internal parts of the bindings are usually well lubricated with a silicone grease and are fairly well protected. The external parts, however, should be wiped clean and sprayed with a silicone lubricant, available in aerosol cans. This will provide a protective coating against pitting corrosion. Release your bindings a few times occasionally to help redistribute the grease. This is a good idea after a long drive in freezing wet weather to be sure that they haven't frozen up.

Squirting oil into the bindings may only dilute the special greases used and do more harm than good. Avoid it. If you feel that internal lubrication is needed, see your qualified ski shop. Keep your antifriction pad clean and wipe your boot sole clean when getting into your skis. If your pad falls off, replace it. If it gets chewed up, replace it.

SWITCHING SKIS RIGHT AND LEFT

Since most of the wear on your skis occurs on the inside edges—the ones you pressure most in turning—you can extend the life of a pair of skis by switching left and right skis, like rotating the tires on your car. To do this, however, you must be sure your bindings are compatible with the switched boots. While today's boot-binding compatibility shifts easily with new units, this will become a problem as they age.

18

Poles and Accessories

Unlike skis, boots, and bindings, poles are very simple devices—but getting a pair with the right length and swing weight is important in modern ski technique.

When skiing was in its prelift stage, poles were primarily used for walking and climbing. As uphill transportation became widespread, they were relegated to a secondary position on the equipment list. In the period just before World War II, they reached their low point—literally. They had shrunk to the point where they were only waist high, and some experts actually considered them a dangerous nuisance.

This trend rapidly reversed immediately after the war with the popular acceptance of parallel techniques. Poles were found to be useful in establishing timing and rhythm and almost indispensable in aiding the beginning parallel skier to eliminate the stem. Yet oddly, there was little development in ski-pole design until 1959, when a lightweight aluminum alloy pole was marketed by Edward Scott of Sun Valley, Idaho. While 50 percent more expensive than any pole then in existence, it had such obvious advantages of balance, weight, and strength that it quickly revolutionized ski-pole construction throughout the world. Now all poles incorporate Scott's design features.

Although good pole design is elementary, numerous refinements can improve on the basic product. Since the pole plant is the "trigger" to the parallel turn, you must be able to plant the pole as quickly as possible; the pole

205

should therefore be as light as possible without sacrificing necessary strength. For this reason, the good poles are made of highly tempered aluminum alloy.

As important as mere weight is the "feel" or "swing weight." In order to swing easily, the pole should be lighter at the tip. This is accomplished by tapering the pole downward and moving the balance point as close to the grip as possible. A well-balanced pole has its balance point in the upper three-eighths of its length.

The other essential elements of a pole are grip, strap, and basket. The grip is usually made of molded neoprene. Some grips are contoured to fit the hand and fingers to prevent the hand from slipping down the pole. Straps are usually made of leather and are adjustable, but more and more models are using strapless "breakaway" grips for safety. The baskets are made of plastic or rubber to prevent the pole from plunging through the snow's surface. In addition, most aluminum poles have a separate steel tip bonded to the end of the shaft, since even the hardest aluminum alloys wear rather rapidly. Today's tips are increasingly hollowed rather than spear tipped, again for safety.

FITTING POLES

The length of poles tends to vary slightly from year to year depending on the technique variation in vogue. Currently, if you hold the pole upside down and your forearm is parallel to the floor with your hand on the basket, the length is good. When in doubt, go short. Too long a pole throws you backward.

POLE MAINTENANCE

Poles need little maintenance. Most of what goes wrong with poles cannot be prevented or repaired. Corrosion, though, is merely unsightly and can be prevented by washing the metal. The life of the leather straps can be extended with an occasional treatment of saddle soap.

Even the best poles can be broken, either by falling on them or by cutting them with the edges of the skis. The latter is far more frequently the case, particularly with aluminum poles. When the edge of the ski rubs against an aluminum pole, it leaves a small nick. If this happens often enough, the pole is weakened at that point and eventually snaps. One way to reduce edge damage on poles is to wrap two or three layers of cellophane tape around the pole for about six inches up from the basket. The tape doesn't last long and won't

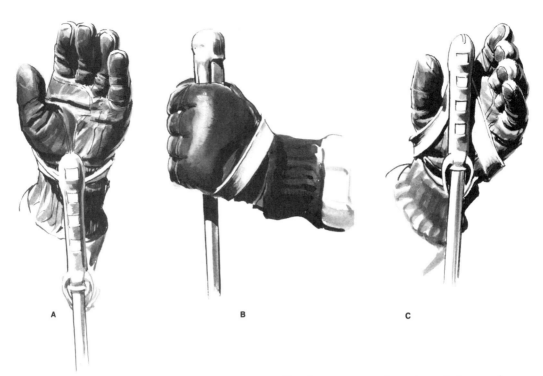

A   B   C

Correct gripping of pole if you use a strap: Hand enters strap loop from below and grips handle.

prevent the heavier cuts from penetrating to the metal, but it avoids a great deal of the wear and tear.

Poles occasionally bend. If the bend is not too severe it is best to leave it alone, since straightening the pole only weakens it. The life of a straightened shaft is limited, and it is a good idea to have a replacement close at hand.

ACCESSORIES

In addition to skis, boots, bindings, and poles, the well-equipped skier needs a number of accessories. Goggles with interchangeable lenses are essential to safe skiing. Because the glare on a sunny day is abnormally brilliant, the eyes should be protected by dark lenses. When the sky is overcast the light is flat, making it difficult to see bumps and to judge the steepness of the slope; yellow lenses improve the contrast somewhat and make it possible to distinguish variable terrain. The choice between goggles and sunglasses is a matter of individual choice for most adults; all children and any adult whose eyes tend to water when exposed to wind should use goggles, which offer more protection. However, goggles are more awkward and fog more easily. If you wear contact lenses, the type that covers the entire eye is preferable. These lenses are expensive and difficult to fit (some people can't wear them at all), but they are more practical than the iris type of contact lens, which not only offers less protection but also can be jarred loose easily in a fall with virtually no hope of recovery. Today's "soft lenses" are a good choice.

No skier should be without a small wax kit. Although most skis will glide easily under average conditions, waxing not only improves the skis' performance under all conditions but also makes them track better and offers a certain amount of protection against wear and minor scratches.

For carrying wax and other small items, a belt bag is a useful accessory. Included in the contents should be suntan lotion, waterproof matches, a few Band-aids, a small screwdriver, and a pair of pliers, with sufficient padding to prevent damage to you and the contents if you fall.

Theft remains a problem at most ski areas. A cable lock enables you to secure your skis and poles to a rack when you enter the base lodge to eat, rest, or warm up. If you don't have a lock, use the coin-operated locking rack provided at most areas. Also be sure you keep the serial number of your skis in your wallet. If your skis are stolen, they may be traced later by the police.

A ski bag is particularly useful if you're traveling by bus or plane. It comes with a shoulder sling for easy carrying and will protect your skis and poles from being scratched when piled with other luggage and subjected to rough handling. Bags range from $10 to over $50 in price. A big bag can even hold two pairs of skis as well as boots or items that can be stuffed into the bag.

19

Clothing

Few people know how to dress properly for playing in snow and cold weather in general. The challenge is to keep warm, dry, and mobile, and the great enemy is bulk. "We try to educate people to the value of proper layering, using *thin* layers of high-quality clothing, because that's the only effective way to keep warm," explains Gail Sweeney of Norm's Ski Shop in Keene, New Hampshire. "We're getting through, finally."

This is probably the one universal article of agreement among the experts. Professionals who'll argue with each other just for the sheer joy of dissent all agree on this point: Layering—a series of intertied, overlapping sets of thin apparel—is everything, provided it is held together by the greatest advance in ski equipment since the step-in binding and the steel edge—the bib overall. To complement the bibs, get the matching/contrasting parka. It will probably cost less than buying the pieces individually. I've tried both routes, and unless you're trying to make do with a cheap parka—an unwise decision in the *long* run—you always seem to spend more piecemeal.

As with all things in this less-than-perfect world, some items in even the best of lines are more equal to the task than others. If you spend much below $125 for a matching overall-parka suit you're sacrificing something important —the materials and workmanship. Most of the companies offer high- and low-end models, and you can't tell them apart at a glance. Two separate decisions must be made: one on the insulation, the other on the surface fabric. To weigh this intelligently, you should know what's best and why.

On the insulation, down may be out. Even before the Great Duck Scandal of a few years ago (when the goose feathers developed a high canard content), some of the new synthetic fibers were beginning to render nature's premier insulator obsolete. Polarguard really supplied the coup de goose; it's lighter, better integrated, thinner, dries faster (in both the air and machine), lasts longer, and costs less than down. It's also nonallergenic.

Against this, down's main advantage is that it produces that aggressively nonfashionable look I've always associated with the Boston skier and the backpacking/environmental crowd who'd rather freeze than look pretty. Down is bulky and *looks* warm and has that "head" advantage of being *natural*. Personally, I've often wondered exactly why plucking the bellies of geese (and ducks and chickens) is better for the ecosystem than making synthetics; but maybe the preservationists have a point.

However, looked at strictly from the vantage point of durability, practicality, and warmth (ignoring fashion completely), the *good* polyesters have the edge. The compacted polyesters, needlepunch and Thermoslim, will hold in body heat, Gail says, and with proper layering underneath will be just as warm as the high-loft polyesters with less layering. For men, most authorities feel, Polarguard is about the best compromise: It has the advantage of looking and feeling warm. Women prefer the less bulky Thermoslim, equally warm and more expensive. Some of the inexpensive fiberfills just don't seem to hold up as well on repeated washing-drying cycles, and their initial price advantage often proves, in the long run, to be uneconomical. For those who have heard a rumor that Polarguard was being discontinued, fear not—that has been allayed.

In picking the outer shell, remember that no fabric used in skiwear is waterproof. Nor, frankly, should it be, because a waterproof fabric doesn't breathe. However, several of the nylon-based fabrics are water-resistant (the treatment has to be renewed after several washings) and quite durable. The two most popular nylon fabrics are Antron and Taffeta, with the former costing a bit more because it's softer, drapes better for a more fashionable look, and offers a nicer sheen. (Some cotton-polyester shells aren't as water-resistant but are tougher, Gail says, especially some of the antigliss.)

If you opt for anything else, Gail feels, you're being pennywise and pound-foolish, because the other nylon shells don't hold up well under heavy use or repeated washings and lose their water repellency quickly. If you couple this with a cheap fiberfill, you've got a jacket and bib that, after a few weeks of wear, *might* afford some warmth on a fairly pleasant spring day.

Finally, make sure the cuffs are tight and long enough or narrow enough to tuck into the mittens with no wrist exposed.

Skiers do not stay warm by parka-and-bib alone. Equally important are good hats, mittens, socks, long johns, turtlenecks, sweaters (or shirts), dickeys, and goggles. Let's take them in order of importance.

HATS

Wool is better than even the best of the Orlons, provided you're not allergic to wool. With either, look for a tight weave; those fashionable soft-weave-with-pompom hats are a no-no, especially in the East, Midwest, and northern Rockies, where it does get cold and damp. On the West Coast and through the southern Rockies you can probably survive with a lighter hat, although the humidity on the coast can offset the relatively warmer temperatures. With any hat, look for a double-layer cuff around the ears.

MITTENS

Gloves should really be used only when you need the superior flexibility of a glove for racing. Mittens are warmer and far more durable, and if you size them properly you can add a thin wool liner for those really cold days.

The best mittens are made of Polarguard fill and leather covers, but many of us hate to spend $25 to $50 for something we all lose with amazing ease and frequency. You can shave maybe $5 with a nylon rather than a leather cover (this is okay), and still another $5 if you opt for a padded foam lining (this isn't). In those cold and damp regions of the East and North, don't drop below the nylon/Polarguard level. Down mittens are not a good idea because they retain water.

Under no conditions should you use those cheap plastic or woven-wool or Orlon ("nets") mittens.

SOCKS

The authorities are beginning to split into two camps here, with the majority still favoring the two-sock theory. I agree with the growing minority view that because of the improvements in ski boots one good pair of thin wool or wool-and-Dacron socks is enough. That's all I use, and I have no complaints even on cold days.

If you do use two pairs of socks, put one pair inside the other before you put them on; otherwise, putting the second one on pulls the first too tight and cramps the toes.

Don't use tights or leotards, because the fabric is wrong for the feet: It doesn't absorb and dispel dampness, as wool (or even cotton) does. My wife used tights for years and always complained of cold feet (literally as well as figuratively) when mine were quite warm. Three years ago we bought the same model Lange boot (always among the warmest), yet the same pattern existed until Gail Sweeney informed her she'd never be warm with tights. Gail proved to be accurate.

LONG JOHNS

This is a mandatory layer for most people with most bibs, but it can be formal long johns, jeans, even pajamas, or union jacks. The one advantage of springing for higher-priced LJs is that the cuffs around the ankles hold up better; cheaper ones get too loose and wrinkle at just the place where you clamp the boots: sheer hell. Jeans are okay because you can pull them up above that juncture, but they get bulky under bibs. Overall, I prefer to spend the extra dollars for good LJs, especially since they survive well.

Incidentally, if you get hung up on this kind of thing, I prefer wearing socks *over* rather than under LJs—at least until the cuffs on the LJs loosen enough to pull them over the socks. As long as the cuffs stay tight, pull socks over them, which makes it easier to change the socks when they get wet.

TURTLENECKS

This is another mandatory layer. Cotton is by far the best initially, with its warm-and-dry qualities, but it shrinks mighty soon in the washing machine. The best compromise is a cotton-and-polyester blend. A good turtleneck can run $10 or more, but again, it endures. One thing to watch for is that the neck be long enough to allow at least one fold, preferably two, but that it not be too tight when folded.

SWEATERS AND SHIRTS

This is a key layer. I prefer a good flannel or chamois shirt to a comparable-quality sweater. Good shirts are warm and thin, allowing good mobility; they have pockets inside the zippered parka (invaluable); they can be unbuttoned easily to insert a dickey (or "neck-gaiter"); and priced for quality and warmth, they're cheaper than sweaters (unless you opt for wool rather than cotton, which is unnecessary although I do it). Whether you decide on a sweater or a shirt, make sure the garment has a tight weave, is thin and reasonably large, and is machine washable.

DICKEYS (OR NECK-GAITERS)

Although sent by Ullr to protect us from some of our follies, a wool (superior) or Orlon dickey isn't a perfect answer to all problems of wind and cold unless you're attentive. It's among the better forms of protection for your face, especially when riding a chair lift, and it rolls down as an auxiliary turtleneck. To use it properly, you roll it up to where it overlaps the hat at the ears and covers the tip of the nose, after which you clamp the goggles over the opening to create a (nearly) perfect seal. The problem is that you have to breathe, which tends to make the dickey wet; if you simply rotate it you can expose another area of skin to the damp material, which then increases the chances of frostbite. What you must do is continue to reroll the dickey so that the damp places are kept away from the skin, which can be tricky. In any event, a wool dickey is far superior to that hat that pulls down into a face mask, which guarantees that you'll have a damp spot right in front of your nose and mouth around the openings.

One important warning: Do not use long scarves. Otherwise responsible people often recommend them, but I equate a scarf with a hangman's noose on most lifts.

THE SEQUENCE

Putting it all together so it holds is the final challenge. The best sequence I've found is: undershirt, briefs, turtleneck, long johns/socks, shirt or sweater, bib overalls, parka, hat, goggles, and mittens (have you ever tried to put on a hat or goggles with mittens on?). The dickey is a last-minute optional choice, depending on weather.

Paying for all this, of course, is the initial challenge. I've computed that it costs about $200 to clothe an adult for skiing the first year. Once you're past that first year, though, you can begin to alternate some of the purchases. Obviously, you can spend a lot more than $200, but you don't have to.

Four stages of ski dress: first a suit of thermal underwear, then a cotton turtleneck, next a flat-knit sweater or shirt, and finally a ski suit.

You can, of course, allocate part of the cost to outfitting yourself generally for winter. Turtlenecks, shirts, sweaters, and hats are certainly good items to use all winter long. However, let's not fool ourselves: Outfitting yourself for skiing isn't cheap, and trying to do it cheaply is the falsest of economies. The last thing you want to be is an uncomfortable, cold, and miserable skier.

THE AUXILIARIES

After-ski boots speak for themselves, especially if you want the during-ski boots to last. The purpose of an après-boot is to get from house to lodge (and back) without getting your socks wet or wearing out your ski boots. The boots should be lined, waterproof, high (about three inches higher than the deepest puddle), and ugly (so no one steals them). The best models are made from that rubberized gunk, although you have to make sure the socks don't get damp from perspiration, and are sold by most army-navy stores. Ignore fashion.

Knapsacks are Ullr's gift to the skier, especially if you buy the proper one. A good knapsack should have *at least* two pockets, one big enough for the boots and the other for the stuff you'd like to keep dry. Finally, the knapsack should have another strap you can put around your stomach so it won't fall off. Zippers on the small pocket(s) are a good idea (or else everything falls out), and the main (boot) pocket should have both a drawstring and a cover flap with another tiable string or buckle to give you an even-money chance of getting to the lodge and back again with both boots.

After-ski boots are a popular extra item of clothing.

20

Winter Driving and
the Skier's Car

I once figured out I spend damn near as much time driving as skiing in a typical weekend—an average of ten hours and occasionally a lot more. Yet, since driving is not per se part of the "ski experience," most otherwise complete tomes have tended to ignore the proper preparation of a car and how to select equipment for it, while lavishing excruciating detail on the same problems for ski hardware. So let's see if we can do something useful to eliminate eons of neglect.

I've done a pretty fair chunk of writing about autos, and I might as well admit it straight out: I'm an aftermarket junkie. I actually read the monthly Whitney catalog cover to cover, subscribe to one of the car magazines, and read others occasionally. I regularly consort with speed-shop operators and can maintain an intelligent dialogue with good mechanics; I have the shop manual for my car and, in extremis, can even do some of the work myself. I drive 30,000–40,000 miles a year, at least 15,000 of that with snow underfoot; so although I haven't had a number painted on my door in years, I'm not quite an amateur either.

Over the past several winters (and in detail during 1982) I also tested the two most popular four-wheel-drive (4WD) vehicles, the Subaru and the Eagle, comparing them against each other (see pages 223–25 for the report) as well as against my own traditional rear-wheel-drive (RWD) Mustang and a few of the highly touted front-wheel-drives (FWD). And yes, I can tell them all apart quite easily.

217

This chapter focuses mostly on buying, maintaining, and modifying a car; yet by far the single *most* important factor in survival is how you drive a car, because—as in skiing—you must select equipment that complements your technique, and you must constantly try to improve your technique to make maximum use of your equipment. So let's begin with technique.

IT'S ALL IN THE TOUCH

So here I am, whipping down I-91 with a cigarette in one hand, the cassette mike in the other, and a chocolate milkshake between my thighs, dictating this draft on safe winter-driving techniques. Every so often, I move from the cleared right lane to the snow-covered left (Vermont hasn't quite got the hang of plowing highways), pass, and cut back again, making the uncountable little adjustments without missing a word. A wise guy, right? Bad driving, yes?

Not really. The problems and perils of winter driving have been vastly exaggerated. Sure, the next hundred feet may be your last, but that can happen anywhere, anytime, even on the driest of warm spring days, so why sweat it? A better idea is to relax and enjoy it, regard it as another challenge to be faced and skill to be mastered. Panic and tension, not the road and snow, are the real enemies; and if this sounds like another commercial for inner/centered skiing, well, believe this: It's all the same. Your reflexes and subconscious know more about driving than your conscious mind does; so just cool it and let the seat of your pants, your hands, and your feet do the work.

Much like skiing again, good winter driving is a function of mileage. You have to condition those reflexes and understand how handling a car differs on snow and ice from more normal conditions. Not so difficult, really; do things earlier and more slowly. Get rid of preconceptions; skidding is not an ultimate evil unless you can't control it, and you can brake and accelerate and steer just as in real life. Different timing? Sure. But even in July you don't drive a country road the way you drive an interstate or a city street. All driving conditions differ, and winter just offers a few more interesting variations. Let's look at the general rules.

1. *Don't panic; don't drive tensely.* If you take nothing from this chapter but this, I've done most of my job. Relax. You'll get there.
2. *Learn to anticipate.* Go into turns earlier and come out earlier; *use* the skid rather than fight it, and after a while it becomes fun. Brake earlier and more gently, because even four studded tires plus chains won't stop a car as quickly on snow as regular rubber will on a dry

road. Start your pass earlier, accelerate more gently, and adjust for the additional passing room you'll need.

3.   *Learn how to read terrain and conditions.* Hard-packed snow is different from ice is different from slush is different from loose, deep snow. Your car reacts to these changes the same way your skis do, so position your car differently on all of them. *Feel* it in your steering wheel and the seat of your pants. Ice is the killer; the others are easily manageable—and even ice can be lived with gently, subtly, delicately. Equally important, learn to anticipate drifts and ice by looking for open blowing snowfields, and back off before you hit that stretch. Winding back road? Sit a little closer to the right side, even on left curves, than you usually do, because the snowplows often miss the center line. See a dark wet spot ahead at night? Assume it's ice, not water, and hit it straight on if possible; if not, anticipate a skid and get ready to correct.

4.   *Know the outside temperature.* A road that is reasonably safe at zero or 10 degrees above becomes tricky at 20, dangerous at 30 . . . and the road you drove easily during the day at 40 degrees becomes lethal at night. The trick here is that you don't skid on ice, you skid on a thin film of water the heat from your tires generates from the ice or packed snow, and the closer the temperature is to 32 degrees Fahrenheit, the easier it is for your tires to melt the ice. Different tires do different things under different conditions, as we'll discuss later, but nothing performs brilliantly at 30 degrees.

5.   *Learn your car.* No two cars of the same model, much less different types of car, perform identically on snow and ice. Variations in tires, suspension wear, load (number of people, amount of luggage), ski racks, and overall condition create unique personalities for each vehicle that can alter skidding, steering, acceleration, and braking patterns. Go out in a parking lot and learn yours. At the same time, learn what your gauges (which we'll discuss later) are trying to tell you about how well your car is performing.

6.   *Learn to live with your car's and your driving abilities.* Don't get into a macho head on winter driving. When that battered Porsche comes blasting past you, don't accept the challenge; the car may be better and the driver more experienced or attuned.

7.   *Learn when to quit.* A few times every winter, driving in any locality becomes overly difficult, especially during a major storm. Wait till it's over and the roads are cleared. Remember, tomorrow does come, and six months later you'll hardly remember taking that extra day.

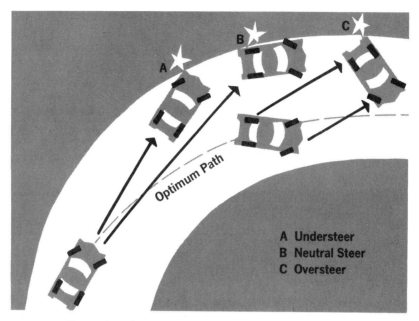

Examples of steering-wheel handling on ice in a turn.

The more astute among you will have noticed that much of the "technique" is linked to the proper use of equipment. The fact is that the two are inseparable. Sure, I've pushed some of the worst slick-rubbered, light-assed Rentmobiles through whiteouts on Rocky Mountain passes and survived. I once took one particularly obnoxious piece of junk up the Big Sky and Red Lodge access roads in Montana and, believe it, those are two of the worst drives in the country. In 1980 I took a rented Pinto (ugh) into Snowbasin and Little Cottonwood Canyon in Utah! But a poor car made it a sweat all the way; who needs that when, with a little planning and a few dollars, you can transform virtually *any* car into a solid performer all winter long?

I think the logical sequence in this analysis is picking a car, picking tires, maintaining the car, and modifying the car. This is by no means their relative order of importance, however—tires and maintenance far outstrip the other two, with the choice of car a very distant last—but at least it creates a flow. So let's start there.

THE PERFECT CAR FOR WINTER

Late one February as I watched a foot of new snow bury the parking lot at Okemo, a woman came up to me and asked, "What kind of a car do you recommend? You ski writers should know what can handle this kind of mess."

"Snowmobile or Thiokol," I muttered, just hoping I could *find* the white Subaru I was testing (see my review, page 223), much less drive it out of that 4:00 P.M. quagmire. "Or just as good," I added, "a four-wheel-drive truck with a high-low transfer case; big, fat tires with an open tread; three feet of road clearance; and a pipeline to Ullr."

"But what will I do with that monster the rest of the year?" she wailed—and there she had it. Most of us drive people cars, not camouflaged trucks, and how esoteric can we be in describing the "perfect winter-driving vehicle"? Most people need a car to live with twelve months a year for three to five years and that, from time to time, can get you to and from a ski area under adverse conditions.

Anything will go if you have the touch, as we discussed, but some are more equal to the task than others. What makes this true is *not* the type of car, no matter how jingoistic these front-wheel-drive types may be; a well-set-up rear-wheel drive can do just as well if you put the pieces together properly. Each type of car has different handling characteristics, but there are more important considerations.

• *Engine Size: Is Bigger Better?* Sadly, yes, because these days it would be nice to push the small engines. However, that's all too often what you *will* have to do, because a harsh winter kicks the hell out of cars. Small engines feel it more: Each cylinder has to do more work. In addition, the larger electrical system that usually accompanies a larger engine can absorb more use of accessories before it starts sputtering, and when you have fog lights, front and rear defrosters, wipers, radar detectors, and the CB working, you are putting a mean strain on the whole system.

• *Engine Type: Gas or Diesel?* No issue here. Diesels just can't hack it in the cold, cold ground; not even the new ones. On a mean day you'll need fifteen minutes to warm it up enough to *start*, and sometimes the fuel literally turns to jelly. No way!

• *Transmissions: Manual or Automatic?* Despite my eon-long preference for a four-speed manual, the issue is not one-sided. The manual offers more control in crisis, but the automatic is more dependable these days (an unpleasant reversal of a prior trend). Most clutches, especially German and

Japanese, blow out at 40,000–50,000 miles, and a manual gearbox will freeze before an automatic. Against this, though, the manual gives you selection of gears, which, combined with that art form known as "feathering" the clutch, lets you come out of deep snow or off ice much more easily.

• *Batteries: Will it Turn the Engine Over?* We've all been so oversold on the "lifetime service-free warranty" aspects of the new batteries that we forget to look for the single most important feature: cranking power. Most new cars offer more than the minimum, which is amperage equal to engine size. (For example, the Ford V–6 I drive has 171 cubic inches of displacement [CID], and the minimum battery for it would be 171 amps.) For heavy-duty driving in Ski Country, with its −40 degree start-ups and high use of accessories, look for at least 100 percent more amperage. Also, make sure the "reserve power"—how long the battery can keep your accessories running without the alternator—is at least three hours. All these numbers are displayed clearly, these days, on the battery.

• *Gauges: Are They Really Necessary?* Yes. This is no macho affectation, and if your car doesn't have them, add them. Oil pressure, more than water temperature, tells you when your car is ready to drive; a tachometer warns you about wheel spin and torque; and the amperage dial warns you about electrical overloads *before* you blow out (The red lights, alas, tell you these things *after* they happen.) A vacuum gauge tells you if your engine is properly tuned.

Basically, *cars* come in three types: FWDs, RWDs, and the all-but-vanishing rear-engine/rear-wheel drives (REDs). Which of these types is best? No such thing. I've always had a grudging respect for the REDs—but never enough to buy one. Between the FWD and RWD I see no major differences.

Admittedly, the FWD people make a good case, but before you buy it completely go out and try a few. Its fans insist you don't have to worry about the inability to pull an FWD out of a skid because "it doesn't skid," but I can tell you firsthand that that's a lot of yellow snow because I've skidded in them. "Then you must have applied the brakes," one FWD champion challenged. "Yes," I admitted, "I tend to do that when I want a car to stop." "Well," he sneered, "what did you expect?"

A good FWD can do some things—braking, steering, *initial* traction—better than a good RWD under *normal* driving conditions. But in a *crisis*, a well-set-up RWD will pull you out of a skid easily, let you stand on the brakes hard (inadvisable though this usually is), and execute a maximum-evasion slalom more surely—even though an RWD will reach that crisis level earlier. Also, it's very hard to use a controlled-skid technique with an FWD, whereas an RWD is designed for it. FWD fans will note, however, that FWDs need to use it less. So? It's your money.

Still another fiction seems to be edging into the "factual" realm in recent years—namely, that a small car is better on snow and ice than a big one. Bull. Without delving into the esoterics of low versus high polarity, the truth is that a well-balanced large car, once it gets rolling, can do wondrous things that small cars have to struggle to achieve. Patriotism, gas miserliness, overall fun, and control are good reasons to buy small cars; snow handling isn't. I happen to like how a smaller, 100-inch wheelbase performs, but I'm not going to insist it does a better job in snow than a monster wagon.

When racing driver R. David Sheff and I were coauthoring the then-definitive winter-driving article in SKI about a decade ago, we really got hung up over 4WDs and Saabs and the like until in one blinding flash, we realized we were both using good ol' RWDs; and when we surveyed the rest of the SKI staff, we realized we were far from alone. So I called Dave's racing nemesis of that time, Chuck Gibson (then as now a power in USSA as well), and was more amused when, instead of mentioning some arcane mid-engine low-polarity whizbanger, he said, "I have this great station wagon . . ." And not to belabor the point, we all got where we were going.

So instead of getting overly hung up on the best possible winter car, buy what you like and, if you have to, modify it for winter.

Still, two 4WD machines that look like cars have earned a fair quantity of ink these past few years (three, if you include the new Audi Quattro at a mere $35,000), so perhaps the Subaru and the Eagle earn a bit more than glancing reference. At least I felt so, so I got both companies to lend me the smaller of their two models, the hatchback and the SX4. I had driven the larger stationwagon variations in 1979 and 1980, respectively, and was curious to see if the smaller models could handle a family of four. That answer is simple: NO. If you have two or three kids or another couple with whom you ski frequently, get the full-sized model.

Let me tell you right off the bat that I have more than my share of jingoism and really wanted to prefer the AMC Eagle to the Subaru, much as I keep hoping that K2 or Olin will finally develop a world-leading ski, or at least one ready to challenge the Austrians' top models. The results, I'm afraid, were not "buy American," which I can somewhat justify emotionally by saying that, well, Subaru does support the U.S. Ski Team and other major racing ventures here. However, on a strictly automotive scorecard, here goes.

The Eagle is a tough car, more rugged than the Subaru. Its high clearance allows it to plow over or through huge mounds of snow that could give a Subaru some trouble. Its added weight and tire size make it stronger battling "set-up" snow, where you have to tangle with the deep ruts and tracks of cars that have preceded you before the snowplows have arrived. The Eagle is also superior in the traditional American comfort categories of heater, defroster, and headlights.

Further, one of the car's major weaknesses that I found—an instability on slick roads above thirty-five mph—could probably have been cured had the company listened when I requested winter tires; instead, they insisted that year-round radials (see page 227), the Goodyear Eagle GT, would do as well. They were wrong, of course, but I ascribe some of that sudden "lightness" to the tires, not to anything inherent in the car. (They did, however, tacitly agree to one of my earlier points: I had requested the four-cylinder engine; they gave me the six-cylinder.)

Finally, the Eagle's engine and five-speed transmission were faultless, but the instrumentation, mostly an afterthought add-on, was less than reliable.

In contrast, the Subaru merely got the job done well in all categories with subtle understatement. The engine is nowhere near as powerful, and the gearbox isn't quite as positive (it could also use a fifth gear!). And lord knows the ground clearance isn't anywhere near as majestic, but in its defense I never met anything the Subaru didn't get over or through comfortably—often without resorting to 4WD, by the way—and it was a bit more relaxed over passages of ice (not the Eagle's forte), and at higher speeds on snow; but then, it did have winter tires (Bridgestone M & S). Its instrumentation is vastly superior —it has one of the best dashboard layouts of any car—and its rear visibility, while far from great, was better than the Eagle's.

Neither car's seats are anything to write paeans to ("pains" was more often the appropriate word), and I'd replace the driver's seat with a Recaro were I to buy either of the larger models. The Subaru also had more legroom in back for the kids, and the carrying space in the small Subaru was far more functional than in the small-model Eagle. So much for the traditional criteria, which at this point seem far more even than my results really suggested.

Where Subaru won the war was in the 4WD: no comparison, on two fronts:

· You needed 4WD more often, more quickly, in the Eagle; in its two-wheel mode (RWD) it was marginal on snow and ice, especially with those tires. In contrast, the Subaru was quite solid and dependable in its two-wheel mode (FWD) much longer.

• You can't shift quickly into 4WD with the Eagle, and you're not always certain that you've locked in. The Subaru shifts from 2- to 4WD to 4WD low range with a flick of the lever while you're driving (make sure your wheels are pointed straight ahead), while the Eagle has to be parked, a lever on the dashboard moved, the car backed up a few feet, and then driven away in 4WD. (Once, in fact, I got into trouble with the Eagle because backing up was the problem!) The Subaru dashboard tells you when you're in 4WD with a signal light; the Eagle's doesn't.

In addition, Subaru's gas mileage—I averaged 24 to 27 on the highways and back roads over 3,000 miles—was far better than the Eagle's, 17 to 19 over 6,800 miles.

Oddly, I wasn't nearly as uncomfortable in several categories with the original full-time 4WD, full-size Eagle wagon. That's its proper design mode for several technical reasons, and that's the one you should buy if you feel its added ruggedness, power, and mass are what you want or need and you're willing to pay the extra $3,000-plus (and gas) over the full-size Subaru wagon. I'd be prone to buy the Subaru, replace the seat and headlights, and live with it, even though I occasionally felt slightly more secure with the Eagle.

ONLY THE TIRES TOUCH THE ROAD

Face it, no matter how good your car is, only its tires touch the road. Pretty obvious, no? But let's drive it home: Nothing, but nothing, is more crucial to survival on winter roads than the right set of snow tires.

Making that selection, though, is confusing—not difficult, understand, but confusing. More misleading ad claims and half-truth folklore have been spun about this winter-tire business than anything in autodom save the EPA mileage claims. I've heard otherwise intelligent people *insist* that (1) two snow tires are all you need, (2) you must use radials, (3) you must use steel-belted radials, (4) you don't need studs anymore, (5) the best thing to do is slap on the biggest, fattest, widest tires you can squeeze, jack, or pound under your rear fenders, (6) year-round radials have rendered the traditional snow tire obsolete, and (7) chains make it unnecessary to mount snow tires.

The problem is that every one of those statements is partly true. And partly false. To me, each is mostly false, but I do a lot of winter driving. The relative degree of truth varies with the mileage and terrain you drive and is vastly affected by the annual snowfall you face. But before we get into that analysis, let's start with a few basic rules.

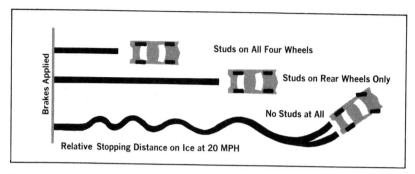

Relative stopping distance of cars on ice with and without studded tires.

• *Four Are Better Than Two.* Yes, a couple of snows on the rear will improve handling over year-round tires—but not enough. Different tires have conflicting "slip angles"—the rate at which they turn compared with how the car is pointed—and too much of a difference creates dangerous under- or oversteer, which, under stress, can produce unplanned skids. Studs on the rear only make this problem worse. For safest handling, mount four of the same snow tires.

• *Radials Do the Job Best.* (If you received bias plies on your car, ask your dealer if you can use radials.) The radial combination of stiffer tread area and more flexible sideways vis-à-vis bias plies was designed, it seems, with winter in mind. The result is to keep the tread more solidly on the road with more of the sway taken up by the sidewall. But I've also used bias plies quite safely in the past.

• *Studs Are Better Than "Contact" Tires*—under some conditions. As I mentioned earlier, tires don't skid on ice, they skid on a thin film of water generated by the heat of your tires passing over ice—and this is no niggling distinction. The closer the outside temperature is to freezing, the more readily your tires generate water from ice. At −10, almost *any* tire is safe; at zero, an unstudded regular snow tire starts to slide; at 20 above, most of the new "contact" (or studless, if you prefer) snow tires lose adhesion; above 35, almost any tire is safe. Studs are the only configuration, aside from chains, that have consistently excellent traction in that critical 20-to-35-degree range. But it's not all one-sided. These new contact tires are much safer on rain-slick or dry highways, are fine in deep snow, and—very important—are legal in those northern midwestern states that have outlawed studs. But they're about 30 percent more expensive than studded tires, and only a few of them to date—Semperit, Uniroyal-Europe, and Pirelli, according to my experience and sources—are really first-rate. Personally, I prefer these studless tires; but I don't knock studs.

 • *And a No, No, No on Year-Round Radials.* Yes, first-line year-round radials can survive in minimal-snowfall regions during their first winter, assuming you got the car no earlier than the late fall. I never changed the excellent Pirellis that came with my new Capri in January 1976, and they did fine; but a year's tread wear changed that radically for the 1976–77 winter, and I had to go back to winter tires. Also, the winter of 1975–76 was fairly light on snowfall in the Northeast, and the year-round Pirellis I got had a zigzag winterlike tread configuration; friends who got the typical American parallel-groove tread pattern didn't fare so well, especially in heavy snow. But the new Michelin TRX I got with my Mustang in November 1979 were terrible the first year—and it didn't even snow much. It's an overall "maybe" situation at best if you're urban-based and a no-no if you live or spend much time in snow country.

 • *Chains Are for Panic Only.* Sure, chains are terrific—especially when you have to put them on and take them off late at night at −20 degrees. Pheh. They belong in the crisis category reserved for flares, shovels, and first-aid kits: something to carry which, with luck, you'll never have to use. Not only don't I remember the last time I *mounted* a set of chains, I don't remember the last time I *carried* any except, courtesy of Hertz, in the trunk of some rental. And I've never had to use chains even *then!*

Overall? I've grown fond of these new studless/contact tires and spent the winter of 1978 testing the lowest-priced of the top three, the Semperit M229. I logged 15,000 miles with them, and on only one day they failed in crisis: Like a tyro, I parked nose down against a fence in a snow-covered icy parking lot and then wondered why I couldn't back up the hill.

LESS BOUNCE TO THE OUNCE, OR MAYBE MORE?

As many of you have heard, tires are connected to a car by a wild jumble of gizmos known cumulatively as the suspension system. Automotive engineers positively freak out with innovations, variations, permutations, and combinations designed to produce both a firmer and a more comfortable ride—but the two things, alas, are about as complementary as pollution controls and energy conservation. I love reading the auto magazines' desperate efforts to try to make this madness sound sane.

Stripped of the technosis, a suspension system essentially has four parts: springs (to keep the car up), shocks (to hold the car down), torsion or anti-sway bars (to prevent side-to-side swaying and/or body roll), and ball joints (to keep the whole package together). No one is inherently the most important, but new shocks will usually produce the most immediately noticeable improvement in handling. This is especially true if you upgrade, rather than simply replace, the original equipment.

Most original-equipment shocks aren't very good even brand-new because they're designed more for comfort than for performance. This usually means the car jounces and wallows when it should hang tough. A top-line replacement shock eliminates that slopover by increasing the "damping" effect—yes, just as in skis—on the springs: when springs go up, shocks hold them down (and vice versa). To a limited degree, good shocks will also reduce the roll on a turn and the nosedive on braking (although this is not their primary role) and will alter steering response by reducing spring-induced sway. The result is a tighter, stiffer car—which is an obvious gain—but for winter driving this can also produce a few secondary problems if it's overdone.

The problem with a *soft* shock in the rear is that it doesn't eliminate the spring bounce fast enough, and if you hit two or three good bumps in a row you create sympathetic vibrations that can roll or swing you off the road (especially if you're turning at the same time). A *stiff* shock absorbs that spring bounce with one fast *wrummb*, which can rap you off the road if it happens on ice. For this reason I prefer one of the adjustable rear shocks—Gabriel (my choice) or Koni—which lets me run very stiff from spring through fall; then I reset it slightly softer for winter. (For the handy, it's roughly a half-hour job to readjust the setting.)

You'll get some dispute here, but I don't feel you have to use the same shocks front and rear or replace all four at the same time. But it is *mandatory* to mount the same shocks at the same time on the same axle.

LORD, I CAN SEE AGAIN

A renowned fast-ball pitcher once noted, "They cain't hit what they cain't see." Unfortunately, the rule of the road is rather reversed—and aside from tire/suspension/electrical selections, I can't think of a modification more designed for safety and well-being than upgrading your lights, if for no other reason than that the tension that builds up from prolonged poor visibility wears you down and reduces your response time.

The basic problem here is that, unlike shocks or tires, the headlights that came with your car were obsolete before they were installed—and the only thing they illuminate is the old maxim "Ya gets what ya pays fer." That standard sealed beam retails for $5 to $8 a pair; good quartz-iodine (Q-I) of the type you should use goes for roughly $40 to $70 the pair. Some new cars come with Q-I's.

Recent auto-design changes have made the original-equipment situation even worse. The old 7-inch sealed beams—one big round eye on each side—were merely diffuse; the new quad setups—two on each side, either 6-by-4 rectangles or 5¾ circles—are actually dangerous.

Fortunately, technology follows need (as anyone who buys skis and boots is well aware), and a whole new generation of superb lights has been whelped these past few years: the Q-I H4 headlights, and the Q-I H2 or H3 auxiliaries.

The old H1 Q-I's, which many of us suffered with, had several problems: They drew too much power and occasionally shorted out or blew a fuse, and they didn't work on the high-beam switch; both have now been solved by the H4. However, their quasi-legality remains murky, especially if you face state-run inspections every year when you must put the old beams back in, pass, then restore the Q-I's. If your state uses the garage-or-dealer system . . . well, you can solve that, can't you? These lights are not exactly legal—although DOT thinks they are—just frowned on by the red-tape types.

Auxiliaries—essentially for people who don't want to mess with head-lights—come in two types, fog lights and driving lights. The latter function to augment the high beams and are quite helpful on dark back-country roads if you haven't shifted to Q-I H4 headlights; if you have, don't bother with driving lights. "Fogs," if mounted properly *below* the bumper, throw a short, flat, wide beam directly in front of the car, picking up the lane markers far enough ahead to keep you on the road despite fog or blizzard. However, the prisms on the better H4 headlights throw the same type of beam, albeit not quite so well, and so I'd suggest checking out the headlights before you invest the same $40 (wholesale, or at a good speed shop) for first-line fog lights. And yes, amber lenses do the job better than clear lenses, which may be the major fog-light advantage over the top H4's—but fogs do draw a lot of power and must be wired separately, especially with 16-amp foreign-car wiring.

Currently, the best auxiliaries are produced by Carello, Cibie, Hella, and Marchal, although some of the cheaper, secondary-brand fogs aren't too bad.

No major functional difference exists between H2 and H3 bulbs, no matter what you hear.

MAINTENANCE, THE ONLY WAY TO GO

Well, by now we've picked you a good car and fine tires, tightened up the suspension, and improved your visibility—and otherwise shown some restraint by ignoring all those peripheral goodies we car nuts really dig. We've even mentioned a few of the basic driving techniques to move you, and your machine, with some élan. And you know what? It'll all be for naught if you don't take care of your machine. Just like tuning your skis.

Underscoring that, the most cogent comment about winter preventive maintenance was offered by a salesman at a speed shop I use frequently: "Anything that seems shaky in summer will break down in winter. Any job you've delayed doing in the fall you'd better get done before the winter really hits." So let's get specific.

• Especially vulnerable are the *ignition and electrical systems*, which really take abuse in winter; this is even more critical in foreign cars with their 16-amp wiring. Pay careful attention to your starter motor, alternator, coil, distributor, spark plugs, and fan belt—and if anything seems even remotely worn, replace it *now*, in the convenience of your repair shop or home garage. (It beats doing it at 2:00 A.M. on a back road in Vermont—and that's chilled firsthand experience talking.)

There's also something *you* can do to help by modifying your driving habits: Turn off *all* your accessories—heater, defrosters (especially rear!), auxiliary and headlights, wipers, radio, and so on—*before* you turn off the engine. Sure, the new ignition turns them off for you—but the load you put on the systems when you restart the car with everything still on is brutal. If you have an amperage-voltage gauge (and you should), don't turn on any accessory until the needle is back to zero after start-up; then add the next one when the needle again returns to zero, and so on. Take the extra two minutes.

• Equally vulnerable, although often ignored, are *the tires and the suspension system*. Tires especially take a beating because the heat-cold extremes they encounter are vicious. Make sure your valves and caps are airtight, and check your air pressure every time you buy gas. The *minimum* pressure you want is the amount stamped on the outside of the tire—and to hell with what the car manual tells you. Why minimum? First of all, that pressure applies only in the morning or at the end of a day of skiing—cold measurement—after the car has been standing awhile. As soon as it runs even a mile or two, the pressure increases; after half an hour of sustained running, you can figure another two to four pounds of pressure! In addition, I like to run tires about two pounds over the pressure recommended at cold measurement. And forget that business of running tires underinflated for better traction: All it will do is blow the tire off the rim. (If you're dug into very deep snow, yes, drop the pressure—but get it back up at the first station you see.)

In suspension—aside from the problems we've already discussed—the biggest threat is not getting the shocks warmed up. The best ones, those we discussed, work on intricate gas or oil-and-gas mixtures, and these compress in the cold just like engine oil. Hit a pothole or frost heave hard the first few miles and you can snap the piston or break the seal—or, as I learned years ago, pop the shock mounts right off the car. ('Twas a most interesting day of driving.)

• Less vulnerable these days—because of superior additives and formulas—is the *oil system*. The trick here is to get the best of the new oils and filters, and one rule applies: Use the best grade of 10-40W (the newer 20-50W is better only for summer) that your favorite company makes.

Even the best oil needs a little time to wake up. Heat from the waterline engine heater will keep the oil from freezing into a lump, but it still needs a few minutes to reach running speeds.

• Highly susceptible to cold is the *gas line* (including the carburetor) —especially to rapid drops in temperature and to high humidity, and especially if you use unleaded gas. (Don't we all!) Add a can of *gas* additives (such as STP) at the beginning of every trip, plus a can of dry gas—if it feels as though it's going to be a mean, wet night—before you go to bed. (If you have to add it in the morning or after skiing, put a few drops into the carb also and give it five minutes to work before you try to start again.)

Equally important is learning how to read your gas gauge in winter, especially in conjunction with your trip odometer (if you don't have one, add one). Mileage varies from tankful to tankful more dramatically in winter than in summer, and gas condenses more abruptly after stopping. Thus, your gauge may register more gasoline than you have, which can be a tad annoying the following morning when you're empty. Learn to calibrate tank markings with odometer readings—reset to zero at every fill-up—so that by the time the clock hits the half mark you'll know how many more miles you really have left before tap-out.

AND FINALLY, ALL THAT EXTRA JUNK

When I first started hitting the North Country in the bleak of winter years ago, I used to carry a small auto-parts shop in my trunk and a mechanic in my back seat. But I've finally weeded it down to the essentials—until of course, I find I left the wrong thing home. However:

1. An AAA card with two dimes Scotch-taped to it and the most current national or regional directory. Yes, I write nasty letters to the AAA now and then, but mostly they get the job done.
2. A spare fan belt (especially since it's one job you can do yourself) and the appropriate socket wrench.
3. One can each of Hot Shot (quick engine-starter gunk) and dry gas —you hope just as security blankets.
4. Jump cables. Get good ones, not the cheapie specials, which you'll melt out. Remember: You can only jump smaller engines, and jump from bigger ones.
5. A squeegee and a flapjack flipper. A succession of those garbage $1.98 brush-and-scraper doohickies having been rendered hors de combat, I finally settled on a window-washer rubber squeegee to remove the snow and a heavy spatula to handle the ice. It works so well I usually don't even bother to use a liquid de-icer first.
6. Lock de-icer—except that as you've probably discovered, it's always locked *inside* the car when you're outside.
7. All the stuff you should carry year-round but probably don't: flares, flashlight, fuses, first-aid kits (small variety)—and a good shop manual for your car, especially if it's anything but a Ford or a Chevy.

SKI RACKS

Regardless of the type of car you have, it should be equipped with a ski rack. Ski racks can be purchased at prices ranging from about $15 for a single Volkswagen carrier to $75 for a six-pair, locking rack.

Skis carried inside the car not only can damage the interior, but they can be dangerous in the event of a hard stop, even hurtling through the windshield. However, there's nothing wrong with keeping them inside a wagon or hatchback, if they fit comfortably.

There are two basic types of racks: those that fasten to the roof and those that attach to the trunk. The roof type is more convenient, if the design of your car allows it, and it is better for the skis. But it will cut your gas mileage by as much as 10 percent.

Always carry skis in a roof-top rack with the tips pointed up and back.

Buy a locking rack—one that not only locks your skis on but also locks the rack to the car.

PART FOUR

LEARNING TO SKI

A class at the Waterville Valley ski school.

Introduction

So you want to learn how to ski or to ski better? You want to know which are the best areas and schools for this purpose?

Well, good luck. No matter how positive the writers in SKI and *Skiing* often sound, let me tell you honestly that we're still trying to sort out the vast improvements that descended on the Professional Ski Instructors of America (PSIA) establishment in the latter half of the seventies, complementing—and often confusing—what had seemed "final breakthroughs" in the early seventies. However, one thing was (fairly) certain: The not-so-good-old-days of "final forms" have finally departed, routed by a broad-front attack of new theories. But while all of the new theories work better, it's often tough to decide which of them works the best—and for whom.

Today's skier at any level of ability is better than his counterpart of a decade ago: more controlled, more efficient, more aggressive; faster, stronger, quicker. Why? The equipment is better and the grooming is better and the instruction is better, and those are unassailable facts. They are also totally interrelated facts, because today's teaching/learning methods might not work so well with wooden skis and leather boots and low-energy bindings on unmanicured trails. Nothing evolves in a vacuum.

Instruction has changed so quickly and completely that it's often hard to realize that as recently as the late sixties we were still tied to final-form, tight-parallel turns. It wasn't until Jean-Claude Killy and the whole French racing team, plus Rossignol and its running mates, blew the ski-world apart in the 1968 Olympics that we realized the new times, they were a-coming. Seemingly within weeks *avalement* became *the* word on the slopes—and even though its popularity was short-lived (thank Ullr) it blew apart forever the Austrian-dominated contortions of the Modified American Technique (MAT). (We'll return to avalement later.)

About that same time, give or take a season or two, a pair of innovators were finally catching public fancy with a new method of teaching beginners by using shorter skis: Clif Taylor with Graduated Length Method (GLM), Walter Foeger with Natur Technik. The underlying theory of both was that by beginning on teenie-weenie skis—roughly three to four feet long—a novice could ignore those convoluted snowplow/stem/christie movements (discussed in Chapter 24) and work immediately into some form of a parallel turn, increasing ski length rather than changing technique as he or she improved. This developed a whole new technique of foot swiveling rather than up-unweighting to initiate a turn, which found a strange echo in the foot-swiveling, down-unweighting *avalement*. In time, however, some of the more astute instructors realized that the wedge (as the snowplow was renamed) and stem had validity. Since the short-ski approach otherwise proved generally effective, it evolved into the Accelerated Teaching Method (ATM) currently popular at many leading resorts: short*er* (but rarely three-foot) skis, introduction to the wedge, and a rapid progression up in length and technique.

Then came the biggest breakthrough of all: the development of the "carved turn" as the essence of all levels of ski learning, coupled with the realization that fear, not technical (or "skills") deficiencies, was the great barrier to skiing well. And these doctrines—ATM plus the "carved turn" and a focus on overcoming fear—define the current idiom of ski instruction.

What also evolved—a more important factor in changing instruction than we often give it credit for—was American skiing. Toward the end of the sixties, American ski-resort owners stopped feeling like second-class citizens in the world of skiing; in time, so did the instructors. Even before the American Demonstration Team swept to the world title at the Interski competition among instructors in the late seventies, the younger members of the instruction fraternity in the United States felt they were at least the equals of their European counterparts and, furthermore, better understood the American psyche. That old Germanic whip-cracking teaching method bombed in Colorado and California (and wasn't doing so well even in Europhilic New England); Americans, the PSIA young Turks felt, had to be chivied and kidded and pampered into learning. Americans also have this unconscionable (by European standards) belief that they're supposed to be having *fun* while all this is going on and that both the process and the end are supposed to produce *something that's good for you.* Suffering to acquire skills that are their own reward hasn't sold well with the American soul since Jonathan Edwards was reunited with John Calvin.

This produced some interesting results. Max Dercum, one of the most creative ski-school directors in the United States (as well as developer and promoter of the Keystone Ski Resort), used to boast not about the mountain's (admittedly limited) expert terrain but rather about Schoolmarm, possibly the best novice train in the nation, which wends its way from the tippytop to the bottom. "In three days," he often said, accurately, "I can take a fifty-year-old beginner safely and comfortably off the top of this mountain." Nor is Keystone unique: Show me an American ski area with high volume, and I'll show you an area with a good novice or low-intermediate trail off the summit. (The exceptions are few.) The reason for this is simple: American skiers not only want fun, they want their money's worth: If they're paying the same $15 to $25 for a lift ticket as the good skiers are, they damned well better be able to ski as much vertical.

In addition, that shift to corporate ownership of ski resorts we discussed earlier (Part Two) began to produce a Harvard Business School outlook for ski schools: They were supposed to be profit subcenters, not merely "service" facilities. The gold that a ski-school director had to produce was coin of the realm, not a medal from the Lauberhorn, and PSIA became less and less the last resting place for down-and-out racers. Many instructors who rose to prominence during the seventies were self-imposed refugees from public-school teaching gigs rather than from the World Cup circuit, and they often had master's degrees in instructional theory. (Typical are Tom Montemagni and Bob Kunkel, of Mount Snow, Vermont, and Copper Mountain, Colorado, respectively, who created the popular SKIwee children's program in 1978–1979.)

Equally important was the interest in Oriental philosophy and martial arts so prevalent in the sixties and seventies among collegians, who have the sad but inevitable habit of becoming money-making adults a few years later. This disposition to the awareness/kinesthetic/intuitive school of athletic performance first gave rise to the awesome popularity of Tim Gallwey's *Inner Game of Tennis* and then, one way or another, to a whole series of "head-trip" ski-instruction programs for good skiers: Inner Skiing, Centered Skiing (see the interview with Martin Marnett beginning on page 309), Superlearning,

Woman's Way, and workshops and seminars of all sizes, types, philosophies, and prices (mostly high). What started bluntly as a method to extract sizable sums of money from good skiers who otherwise would boycott ski school as if it were Iranian caviar had an amazing by-product: It worked!

Finally, as Sugarbush's ski-school director Sigi Grottendorfer comments in his interview, beginning on page 302, recreational skiers had a major improvement in what they could do foisted on them by staggering innovations in top-line racing skis (as discussed in Part Three). This breakthrough exploded out of the Innsbruck Olympics of 1976; the new skis winning medals were soft enough for any good recreational skier to handle. This meant that henceforth not only racers or high-end experts could make the "carved turn" but that a high-intermediate or advanced skier also could. Thus instructional theory had to moderate to accommodate this potential. (It did, quickly.) Further, inevitably, the new ski technology began its descent down the line into the "sport" models, which meant that virtually any skier above tyro could get hardware that could carve a turn; again, theory had to moderate.

Today, teaching/learning theory works on the concept that anyone can learn to make a carved turn.

"The carved turn." One big problem with all educational theories is that they have to have shibboleths. No sooner did the establishment deride the "final-form tight-parallel" turn of Stein Eriksen's day than they replaced it with the "carved turn." A few, like Grottendorfer and Marnett of Sugarbush and Mort Lund of Superlearning, believe that the skidded turn ("christie" in earlier times) not only has its place but must remain paramount until a skier becomes credibly good, at least high-intermediate. (Lund, in fact, feels that even very good skiers need and use the skidded turn on very steep, narrow trails. Doug Pfeiffer, one of the top ski-instruction writers in the country, feels that few skiers will ever master a true carved turn.) But most instructors, and ski schools, jumped on the carved turn as if it were the Anointed Successor to the Final-Form Tight-Parallel: a classic case of overreaction because it's always easier to learn dogma than true teaching skills.

Now, what is the "carved turn"? In theory, it means that every centimeter of the inside edge of the turning ski passes over the same imaginary dot on the snow—like a knife cutting through butter, if you need an image. In contrast, in a skidded turn the tails turn faster than the tips, producing an arc such as a windshield wiper does. A carved turn is faster, quicker, and far more efficient—and a lot more dangerous.

Why? Because in a true carved turn—a racing turn—you come out of it faster than you went into it, and if you link carved turns properly you're soon flying down that trail. By putting the ski on its edge you reduce resistance and minimize body movement—when you get really good you can turn primarily with ankles and knees and let centrifugal force and gravity do the rest—and you don't have to be a physicist or an engineer to realize what that does. In contrast, a skidded turn reduces your speed and demands much more movement and change of body position; in a sense, you're jumping rather than skating from turn to turn, and you're far more apt to find yourself perpendicular to the fall line rather than constantly and sharply diagonal to it.

So why teach the "carved turn" from day one? Because it's easy to teach and easy to learn (passably), and it's the way everyone wants to look when he's on skis. Also—based on early GLM results—most skiers intuitively shift into a skidded turn and wedge when they get into trouble, especially if they've mastered the basic skills, so why spend much time teaching them? Especially if it's inefficient?

As "carved turn" became the shibboleth, "skills" demarked the Talmud. The dictionary distinctions between "technique"—the watchword of the earlier final-form progression—and "skills" are quite minimal, but the shift from one to the other in usage marks a change in focus. "Technique" refers to the earlier gradations—changes in body positions and actions as you move from snowplow to wedeln—while "skills" refers to the concept of using the same movements, actions, and positions for all levels of ability. We discuss them in depth in Chapter 27.

Earlier, we mentioned, and casually glossed over, the concept of fear. We also touched briefly on the Oriental philosophy/martial-arts concepts. Let's expand on them now.

Assuming you've mastered "skills" well enough to survive in "D"-level class—high intermediate—you've got enough skill to ski virtually any trail in the country. The main reason you can't ski Widowmaker is because you're scared spitless looking down that @#$%er and your skills abandon you. You tighten up, your reaction times slow down, you don't hit your turn where you want to, and every turn is worse than the one before. Disaster.

Don't think you're unique. There probably aren't a thousand skiers in the world who don't hit their panic point on some combination of steepness/narrowness/snow condition. Roxy Rothafel, one of the great ski broadcasters and a former ski-school director, tells of one day when one of the famous forerunners of freestyle, a superb skier by any standards, blew apart when he hit blue ice on an intermediate trail at Gunstock, New Hampshire, overlooking frozen Lake Winnipesaukee. It happens—and lord knows, another lesson in skills isn't about to solve the problem.

The only way to counter fear is to develop a *belief* that you "can do it." This isn't a rational process because fear isn't rational (although its causes well may be). It's an intuitive sense: If you look down a trail and say "I can do it," you believe it and you turn the problem of making the turns over to the quicker-reacting, nonlogical side of the brain and you *do* it. But you must develop a faith in your motor reflexes and sensations. You must accept firmly that the logical thought processes are too slow at thirty miles an hour. Alas, you must work very hard to develop this acceptance because it runs counter to everything we ever learned in college and law school and all those Kant-inspired critiques of pure reason.

How do you do this? I don't think there's any "best" method or philosophy; what works best for you is best. I found that the Oriental martial-arts concepts that form the basis of the Sugarbush Workshop for Centered Skiing worked well for me, but in my own mind I've never decided if it was the approach itself or the instructional talent of Marnett, Grottendorfer, and Denise McCluggage that "made it happen." I'm not sure it matters.

Just what is the inner/centered theory? I assume everyone reading this knows what the *other* theory is: You stand up on a slope, freezing your rear off, while some instructor tells you where your knee and hand simply *must* be. Basically, an oversimplification, inner/centered allows—even forces—*you* to find out where your knee and hand must be. To *feel* it, not to understand it. And rather than try to paraphrase this anymore, let me pick up part of an article I did after I spent a week at Sugarbush a number of years ago:

> For most of us, "centeredness" is an alien concept, a word which in western civilization immediately connotes ego-centrism, self-centeredness, arrogance. We are a rational people, an intellectually dominated and mind-oriented people, and if we cannot grasp something on a level nearing pure logic we cannot do it. The intuitive, the videotape (rather than the script) of the mind, is suspect. Kant's "pure reason" is the shibboleth of higher education, and if you cannot reduce a problem to a thin, perfect line of thought, one note in perfect tune, you don't have the solution and you flunk the course.
>
> And this screws up our skiing. . . .
>
> Most ski lessons I have taken in recent years have done little to correct [my] multi-faults; some, in fact, have served only to engrave them deeper on the printing plate of the mind. They've attacked the symptoms, either one at a time (momentarily helpful) or as a gang (useless), but until I descended upon Sugarbush, hang-ups and habits intact, no one had ever keyed on the cause.
>
> And Sugarbush attacked it on *all* levels, like a Swedish health clinic pounding on some rich fat lady: they assault the mind and belabor the

body, then flip videotapes of your shattered performance at you; then ski school director Sigi Grottendorfer turns his three instructors loose on you again for another ego battering. . . .

Yet by Friday morning, an awesome amount of work had been done. Improvement achieved. Panic allayed into apprehension. And most of all . . . a significant breakthrough into feeling. Sensation. Intuition. . . .

Grottendorfer—plus three instructors and a video cameraman on full-time assignment to the program—attacks the problem on a technical level: upper-body position, pole-plant, initiation sequence, things like that. Yet he doesn't stop there; rather, each part works on that basic idea of getting "centered" not only on the ski but also in the turn. A fluid thing, that. A sense of balance, a sense of movement, a sense of . . . person.

[Denise] McCluggage [in the daily breakfast workshop] comes at that same result from the other direction, working on another level, challenging not the hips but the head, the intuitive, non-verbal, Coney Island of the Mind, breaking that separation of mind and body and creating a flow, a unity. It had nothing/everything to do with skiing, as such; it was directed at creating a sense of your own core, moving the "control" from the head and shoulders down to the general area of the bellybutton . . . at least, that's how I read it. McCluggage did the job of imparting in five days a sense that takes years to master fully (or which, in conundrum, can never be mastered). . . .

Talking about "centered" on another level . . . Sugarbush stresses body position in this program. . . . They have this interesting display showing O. J. Simpson about to juke a linebacker into yesterday and his position is exactly what they want you to do on skis: he is "centered" . . . lower body slanting waist-down into the center of the action, weight on the outside foot. But these guys already *know*; they were born able to make an early weight transfer. And you think you have to tell Muhammad Ali about hand position? Or Jimmy Connors to keep his knees flexed, not bent? These guys are . . . athletes, the best there are, but what the hell do they have to do with you and me?

According to McCluggage and Grottendorfer, more than you think.

Denise: "Visual perception gets an overwhelming preponderance of attention. Our eyes are peeled. We look sharp—*soften your eyes*. Close them. Massage them gently, then open them softly. Allow images to reach them. Trust your other receptors too. . . . 'Look' from your center . . . don't channel everything through your thinking center. Let movement speak to movement. As an instructor demonstrates a movement, watch with soft eyes letting his action find its correspondence directly in you. Imitate from the 'feel' of it. Avoid verbalizing. Just do."

Make sense? Possibly not, yet. That's okay, we have a ton of pages to go, and then we'll return to it in Marnett's interview.

21

The Best Way to Learn

Skiing is surprisingly easy to learn. Reasonable competence can be reached with about five lessons from a good instructor. Expert skiing—meaning efficient skiing with speed on all types of terrain and snow conditions—can take several months or several years to learn, depending on how much you ski and how dedicated you are.

What prevents many people from even giving skiing a try—though they'd like to—is the attitude expressed in the frequently uttered phrase, "I can't do that," *that* meaning a graceful run down a steep, exciting expert trail. Naturally *that* can't be done right away, nor can a half-gainer off the diving board or driving a golf ball 250 yards.

For some unexplained reason, nonskiers seem to feel that expert skiers were born with skis already on their feet. Actually, there is a logical, relatively simple progression of steps that can make anyone an expert—in time and at almost any age. Naturally, it is easier to learn when you are young (children being the best and fastest learners), but there are expert skiers at almost every age, including the late seventies. The national 70-Plus Club has almost 1,000 members, and a turnout of eighty racers at the annual Lloyd Lambert Day at Hunter Mountain, New York, is quite common.

Perhaps the most important single piece of advice for any skier or would-be skier is to *relax*. It is a constant theme, not only during the learning process but also when skiing on your own. If as a finished skier you have one of those

Ski-school class on a snowy summit in Vermont.

days when nothing seems to go right, the chances are that you have become tense and are not allowing your muscles to do what comes naturally. (We'll expand on this theme later.)

In learning, be particularly wary of well-intentioned friends who would like to teach you how to ski. They may be excellent skiers, but they have long forgotten what it was like to be a beginner; they don't know any of the hundreds of tricks instructors use to get people to ski correctly; and, although they don't say so, they are actually very anxious themselves to be off and skiing on steep trails and slopes.

Ski school, of course, is the answer. But before you report to the ski-school meeting place, do yourself, your fellow students, and your instructor a big favor by arriving prepared. One of the best ways to get prepared is to attend a Sunday night orientation session, if your school offers one (and most of the better schools do). The program includes familiarization with equipment and how to use it—and will often fit your boots and skis—plus some of the beginning maneuvers, a few light exercises, and a movie on skiing. The dry-land ski school is not a substitute for snow ski school, but it will help you progress faster once you are on snow because you will be familiar with the language of the instructor and what he is trying to accomplish.

It should be stressed that ski school is not only for the learning skier. If you find yourself in unfamiliar terrain and snow conditions, a lesson is the easiest way of becoming familiar with the area.

Ski-school procedure is simple and practical, and more or less standard at most resorts. You register for a lesson at a desk in the base lodge. One advantage of entering ski school at areas that have long lift lines is that your class can go directly to the head of the line without waiting. Most group lessons run for ninety minutes. At the designated time, students assemble at the ski-school meeting place, where they are classified by the way they make a turn. Today, by focusing on your skills, a shape-up director can place you quickly and accurately in a class.

Private lessons—that is, lessons where you have the instructor to yourself, or at most share him with one or two others of your own choosing—have much to be said for them, particularly if you are easily embarrassed. Aside from the additional expense, however, the beginning skier is not really in a position to get full benefit from such a lesson. He will probably find that too much physical effort is required. Even in a class of half a dozen or so, he usually finds himself getting more work than he can handle.

Experienced skiers are in a better position to benefit from a private lesson. If you want to work on certain phases of technique or to shed an undesirable skiing habit, a private lesson (or a workshop) may be a quick answer to your problem.

By taking the mysticism out of ski teaching, instructors are imparting competence and confidence to all types of people, including many who may have labeled themselves mediocre athletes. In fact, many previous "failures" have found their skills in other sports improved as they became skiers.

22

Conditioning and Warm-up

One of the best ways to speed up the learning process and, at the same time, to enjoy the sport is to be in adequate physical condition. Not only is the sport more enjoyable when you are in shape, but your chance of injury is substantially reduced. There is a considerable body of evidence to support this statement. For instance, a Westchester, New York, ski club averaged five thousand skiing days a year for eleven years with no fractures and only two mild sprains. During this time preski conditioning was practiced. When this program was abandoned, three fractures occurred within a year.

Strength, to be sure, is of some importance in skiing, but as Dr. Hans Kraus, a New York specialist in physical medicine and a member of the President's Physical Fitness Council, points out, it is muscular flexibility as much as strength that protects the skier from injury. There is an old saying in skiing that the best safety bindings are well-conditioned muscles. (There's a newer saying, that there are no "safety bindings" at all.) Oddly, today's vastly improved bindings demand even greater upper-body conditioning to absorb the impact after the bindings release.

Willy Schaeffler, the former coach of the U.S. national ski team, puts it another way: "Don't get in condition for skiing. Get in condition for living!" It is Schaeffler's contention that there is no need for dull, laborious "living-room" fitness programs in October if you hike, swim, water ski, row, fence, or play handball in summer or take a brisk half-hour walk every day when these aren't possible. It should be recognized that muscles *must work* to stay in shape. It does not matter whether this work is in the form of play or calisthenics. Its rewards are more than worthwhile: better skiing and a strong sense of well-being.

5BX PLAN FOR SKIERS

Dr. William Orban, author of the Royal Canadian Air Force *5BX Plan for Physical Fitness*, developed an effective series of special exercises for skiers in SKI Magazine, and they are demonstrated in the following pages. Here is what he has to say about this program:

> To help skiers of any age achieve proper conditioning, I have designed a program of four basic exercises in three series—beginner, intermediate, and advanced. In addition, there is a bonus exercise. The five exercises have been selected for their contribution to the conditioning of the muscles and joints which play an important role in skiing.
>
> The first exercise is a mobilizing exercise designed to produce a greater range of movement in the ankles, knees and spinal column of a rotational nature.
>
> Exercise two will develop the abdominal muscles which are used in the trunk and hip rotation so essential for certain maneuvers in skiing.
>
> Exercise three is primarily for the development of lower and upper back muscles on which there is an additional demand in the skiing posture. Exercise three, particularly in the advanced series, will also improve the strength of the upper arm muscles needed for pole action.
>
> Exercise four is the key exercise for strengthening the lower muscles of the limbs used in skiing as well as for strengthening the knee and ankle joints which are so prone to injury. The exercise also provides practice in dynamic balance if hands are kept on hips and an attempt is made to exercise by jumps on a designated mark on the floor.
>
> Exercise five lays particular emphasis on strengthening the lower leg.
>
> My exercises are designed to improve physical condition without soreness or stiffness in a minimum length of time when regularly performed. The exercises may be performed by men or women of any age with maximum benefit as long as the directions for performing them are carefully and accurately followed. If you have any previous history which makes you feel uncertain about following the 5BX program, you should first obtain your physician's approval before starting.
>
> Physical conditioning will enable you to engage in skiing for more hours per day, more days a week and more years in a lifetime. It will also contribute to the prevention of injuries. Many injuries, particularly of the

sprain variety, can be attributed to poor physical condition. Lack of strength in the muscles involved in skiing and lack of strength and mobility in the joints, particularly in the knees and ankles, contribute to the incidence of injuries. Furthermore, lack of organic or muscular endurance increases the onset of fatigue, frequently cited as a prime cause of injuries among weekend skiers.

The principles of progression and overload have been completely utilized in the program. Progression enables the development of physical condition from a very low level to a very high level by increasing the rate at which each exercise is regularly and gradually performed. Each exercise, while remaining basically the same, increases in intensity (and difficulty because of increased resistance) as you graduate from series to series.

It is important, therefore, when you undertake the exercises—regardless of your present physical condition—that you start with the first level of the beginner series in order to prevent discomfort. No matter how physically fit you may feel, you are courting trouble with muscle soreness if you undertake a new exercise without specifically conditioning your muscles for it. So perform the allotted number of exercises in the unit of time given for that exercise. This means that if five repetitions of an exercise are suggested for one minute, they should be evenly spaced so as to take the full one minute.

BEGINNERS SERIES: Number one exercise, five repetitions per minute for the first five days, then add three repetitions per day for five more days. Exercise number two, five repetitions per minute for first five days, add three per day for next five days. Exercise number three, five repetitions per minute for the first five days, then add three per day for the next five days. Exercise number four, twenty-five repetitions per two minutes, then add five per day for next five days.

INTERMEDIATE SERIES: Exercise number one, ten repetitions per minute for five days, add two per day for ten days. Exercise number two, ten repetitions per minute for first five days, add two per day for two weeks. Exercise number three, ten repetitions per minute for first five days, then add two per day for ten days. Exercise number four, thirty repetitions per two minutes for first five days, add seven per day for ten days.

ADVANCED SERIES: Exercise number one, ten repetitions per minute for first five days, add one per day for thirty days. Exercise number two, ten repetitions per minute for first five days, then add one per day for thirty days. Exercise number three, ten repetitions per minute for first five days, then add one per day for thirty days. Exercise number four, thirty per two minutes for five days, then add five per day for thirty days.

EXERCISE ONE

BEGINNER: Starting position is with feet parallel and flat on floor about shoulder width apart, hands clasped behind head, elbows back. To perform the exercise turn the upper trunk slowly toward the left, twisting as far as possible without losing balance and without moving the feet. Slowly return to starting position, then twist to the right as far as possible allowing the hips and thighs to follow trunk without moving feet. Returning to starting position completes one repetition. This movement should be slow and performed without any jerking action.

INTERMEDIATE: The starting position is the same as exercise one of the beginner's series except that the arms are held horizontal and at shoulder height to the trunk. Exercise is also performed in the same manner except that when the rotation is made, the head is turned to follow the arm which is moved backward. The arm should be pushed as far back as possible without moving the feet. The rotation should be in a twist from the ankles and hips. One rotation with each arm completes one repetition.

EXERCISE TWO

BEGINNER: Starting position is lying on back, feet straight together with arms stretched to the side, palms flat on floor. The exercise is performed by lifting left and right leg alternately across the body so that the raised foot comes directly above the hand. The other foot and hand maintain contact with the floor during this movement. The second movement of the exercise is raising the left foot to a position over the right hand and returning to the starting position.

INTERMEDIATE: Starting position is the same as the beginner's series. The first movement of this exercise is raising both legs simultaneously so that the left knee is almost directly over the right shoulder. The legs then are returned to the starting position. The second movement of the exercise is raising the legs simultaneously so that the right knee is vertically above the left shoulder before returning to the starting position. These two movements complete one repetition of the exercise.

EXERCISE THREE

BEGINNER: Starting position is lying flat on the back with arms by sides and hands flat on floor. The exercise is performed by lifting the buttocks just high enough to clear the floor. The complete length of the arms, shoulders, head and heels maintain contact with the floor during the entire exercise.

INTERMEDIATE: Starting position for this exercise is lying on the back, arms by sides, hands flat on the floor as in exercise two of the beginner's series. Now move the feet close to the buttocks by bending the knee. The buttocks should be on the floor and the feet flat before the exercise is performed. The exercise is performed by raising the buttocks and forcing the hips upward as high as possible. Feet should remain flat; the head, shoulders and the entire length of the arm should maintain contact with the floor during the entire performance. Each time the hips are raised is one repetition.

ADVANCED: Starting position of this exercise is similar to the beginner's except that the arms are held across the chest with the upper arm horizontal from the shoulder. The exercise is performed by swinging the left arm backwards to rotate the upper trunk, the hips, knee and ankles as far as possible without moving the initial placement of the feet. The first movement is completed by returning to the starting position and bending the arm. The second movement of the exercise is the flinging of the right arm backwards, rotating the trunk and hips to the right and backwards as far as possible. One repetition is completed when the initial starting position is assumed after the second movement.

ADVANCED: Starting position is the same as the beginner's series. Exercise is performed by raising both legs together, then lowering them to touch floor just beyond the fingertip before returning to starting position. The second movement of the exercise is performed by repeating first movement but touching floor to the right. The completion of these two movements is one repetition of the exercise.

ADVANCED: Starting position is the same as in exercise three of the intermediate series. The exercise is performed by raising the buttocks and the shoulders off the floor forcing the hips and chest upwards as high as possible. Force for the movement is applied at the elbows, the back of head and the feet. Only the feet, lower arm and back of head should be in contact with the floor when hips are raised. One repetition is completed when buttocks are lowered to the starting position.

EXERCISE FOUR

BEGINNER: Starting position is feet wide astride with hands on hips. The exercise is performed by alternately jumping from one foot to the other to the outside of two imaginary parallel lines which are a leg-length apart. Cause your entire weight to shift from one foot to the other as you jump from side to side across the parallel line. Each time the foot touches the floor completes one repetition.

INTERMEDIATE: Starting position is hands on hips, feet together. Exercise is performed by jumping from side to side while keeping the knees and feet together. The distance of the jumps should be between one-and-one-half to two foot-lengths apart. Both feet should come in full contact with the floor each time.

ADVANCED: Starting position is the same as exercise five for the intermediate series. It is performed by jumping from side to side, keeping and landing on both feet together. Distance should not be less than three foot-lengths apart. Each jump is one repetition.

Exercises *(continued)*

BONUS EXERCISE FIVE

STARTING POSITION of a bonus exercise for the ladies but from which men can receive benefit as well. Place hands flat on the wall or immovable object about chest high, then move feet backward until heels are just making contact with the floor.

EXECUTION is performed by raising both heels together as high as possible before lowering them to the starting position. Raising and lowering of the heels constitutes one repetition.

> BONUS: Because of high-heel shoes and the subsequent shortening of the Achilles' tendon, an exercise to produce an adequate mobility in the ankle joint is recommended for women. However, men can gain benefits from this exercise too because it does help to mobilize the ankle joints as well as increase the strength of the muscles of the lower leg. The schedule for this exercise should be as follows: two repetitions the first five days, about five seconds apart and increasing one repetition per day for the next forty-five days till the completion of the training schedule. The exercise may be performed as rapidly as desirable after the first five days but up till that time the five-second interval should be maintained.

Time units are established for individuals twenty years or younger. Anyone over twenty years of age should add one second for every year on to the time allotted. For example, if an individual is forty years old, she should add forty seconds to the time allotted to each exercise. Women, in addition to this age factor, should add another fifteen seconds to the time allotted for each exercise. This means that if a woman is forty years old, she should add forty plus fifteen, or fifty-five seconds to each exercise time unit.

In addition to the basic exercises, you should endeavor to strengthen arm and shoulder muscles by practicing regular pushups. To improve heart and lungs, I would heartily recommend a program of running, starting with a quarter mile (one large city block) and working up to the mile distance. Hiking in hill country also benefits both legs and wind.

For best results with the 5BX program, follow directions carefully. Perform exercises gradually, remembering never to give in to the temptation to skip parts of the schedule or to accelerate repetitions.

WARM-UPS

Much of your conditioning effort will be negated if you fail to warm up either before your first run on a warm day or before every run on a chilly day. Usually a few kneebends and body twists are sufficient. The important thing is that you should feel loose before starting down the trail.

Even if you have taken a few warm-up exercises, ski the first few runs cautiously. When muscles are chilled it takes considerable effort to warm them up, and you should avoid jarring stops or extreme maneuvers. A series of snowplow turns, which involve more body and leg motion, are better than schusses or long traverses, which usually require the body to be held in one position. Or—the method I prefer—you can take one or two runs on a very easy slope to accomplish the same result more pleasantly and efficiently. Both theories work.

Another way to warm up is to sidestep and herringbone uphill until you feel yourself getting warm.

If normal warm-up exercises won't do the trick, by all means go inside to thaw out. If you ski with cold legs, you won't enjoy it very much, and you'll be needlessly risking injury as well.

Start your conditioning program now, warm up, stay loose. It pays off in good health and good skiing.

23

First Steps

In the company of experienced skiers, the beginner may feel somewhat less than heroic. Yet, as he moves from one maneuver to the next and becomes master of his skis, no temporary feeling of inferiority can squelch his sense of accomplishment.

One of the achievements of modern skiing is the way it has reduced and simplified the learning process to a minimum. But what remains is important and stays important, even if the skier should reach international racing ranks: Even the best skiers have occasion to use the snowplow and the stem turn.

From the very start, a cardinal law of skiing becomes clear: Improperly or sloppily executed maneuvers end in falls, either immediately or when the skier gets on more difficult terrain. Even when it doesn't lead to a fall, faulty technique will soon tire a skier, particularly if he is skiing at high altitude. In skiing there is no way to fudge without paying a penalty in one form or another.

At some risk of being repetitious, we would like to repeat again: *Relax*. The beginner, especially the adult beginner, has a natural fear of sliding down a slope uncontrolled. Yet he must not let this feeling—which is not fully justified if he is in ski school—get the best of him. Tense muscles have a mind of their own, and the very thing the skier tries to avoid actually happens. This is one of the reasons for this chapter—to prepare you for what is coming.

TERMINOLOGY

One of the major difficulties that hampers progress is a confusion of terms. Uphill, downhill, inside, and outside have a disconcerting way of changing as the turn is made, and sometimes it is hard to tell which is which, particularly on certain types of terrain. A skier who has a clear grasp of terminology, who is not puzzled by terms a ski instructor will use, can learn much faster than one who has to have an explanation. A good way to practice and appreciate these terms is to get on a small slope at home and spell them out to yourself from the following explanations. Many of today's top instructors will also use imagery to reduce or eliminate the confusion.

Uphill, Downhill; or Outside, Inside

The ski, edge, pole, arm, leg, and shoulder closest to the top of the hill, regardless of the angle of the skis to the hill, are *uphill*, or *outside*. Conversely, the ski, edge, pole, arm, leg, and shoulder closest to the bottom of the hill are *downhill*, or *inside*. The confusion arises on two counts. When a skier makes a turn so that he faces in the opposite direction, everything that was uphill before becomes downhill and vice versa. When he comes straight down the hill and goes into a traverse or a turn, he must determine beforehand which will be the uphill and downhill side of the body.

Once a turn is started, it is customary to refer to the equipment and parts of the body furthest away from the center of the turn as the outside and those closest to the center of the turn as the inside. Thus, in a turn to the right, the right ski is the inside ski; in a turn to the left, it is the outside ski.

"Inside" and "outside" references to edges should not be confused with the inside-outside terminology used in a turn. The inside edges are those on the big-toe side of the foot, the outside edges those on the little-toe side. This is constant, *regardless* of the location of the skis in relation to the hill. To put it another way, the inside edge is the turning edge.

Fall Line

The fall line, as one instructor puts it, "is the fastest route between you and the bottom of the hill." By technical definition, it is the fastest and most direct way down. Therefore, if you want to pick up speed, you must get into the fall line. If you want to cut down on speed you must ski at some angle to it. This is known as a . . .

Traverse

When a skier makes a deliberate move to cross the fall line and slow down, he is traversing. In traversing, the edges are the critical elements.

Edges

Any time the skis are not flat on the snow, they are on their edges. The "bite" of the edge is determined by its angle to the snow. The edges are the key to modern skiing, and any exercise or maneuver involving them should be practiced diligently. It will pay large dividends.

Method, Technique, Skills, Style, and Teaching Devices

This is a source of much confusion and the cause of many semantic difficulties. There are frequent references to new skills when in fact the subject is only a new teaching device or a new style. Unfortunately, ski instruction doesn't follow dictionary definitions too closely, mainly because the origins of much of the language of ski technique are to be found in French or German texts, and many of the translations frequently leave a great deal to be desired.

For all practical purposes, *system*, *method*, *technique*, and *skills* mean the same thing, that is, a complete approach to skiing from the most elementary to the most advanced steps. The important thing is not to confuse skills with style. *Style* is the individual interpretation of a skill. Physiological differences, physical condition, and personal idiosyncrasies all may account for a difference in style without invalidating the fundamental skill.

It is also important not to confuse style or skills with *teaching devices*. In order to get across a certain point of technique, the instructor will have numerous teaching devices and exercises. Finding that one explanation doesn't penetrate, he may use a different approach to reach the same objective. This does not mean that he is teaching a different skill. The end result will be the same. (Thus, the shift to imagery.)

WALKING AND GLIDING

The difficulty the beginner encounters in walking on skis is that the skis are intentionally slippery. To overcome this slipperiness on the level, the skier makes use of his poles and edges.

Paul Valar demonstrates simple walking on skis. Right ski and left ski are alternately weighted.

Walking on skis involves a step somewhat shorter than the one used in normal walking. Again, there is a pronounced shift of weight, from the ski to be moved forward to the ski remaining in place. This weight shift momentarily "sets" the ski, enabling the skier to push off on his step. The skier also makes use of his poles. The pole and arm opposite the forward-moving leg move forward as the leg is moved forward and the pole planted in the snow. This enables the skier to pull against the pole in the first part of the stride and to brace against it when he brings the other leg forward.

If the skier is walking up a slight incline, he can prevent backslip by more bracing against the pole and by slightly edging his skis.

A more vigorous form of walking is gliding. Each gliding step is preceded by the skier going into a slight crouch. As he takes his forward step he rises out of his crouch and propels himself forward and upward, using the pole as an aid. The skis are then allowed to glide for a distance before the next step is taken.

FALLING AND GETTING UP

All skiers fall, even the best of them. In skiing it is not considered a disgrace. You will soon learn to recognize an impending fall. Try if possible to stay on your feet, but when it becomes inevitable relax and enjoy it. Try to fall backward and to one side, using your seat as a shock absorber.

To get up, simply swing your skis across the slope so that they are at a 90-degree angle to the fall line. Then tuck your legs under your hips and

get up. If this is too difficult, use both poles, pushing them into the snow near your hips. Then, with one hand around the handles and the other around the poles near the basket, push down hard and get on your feet. (Actually, standing up on skis is as easy as falling down. What makes getting up "tough" is that you don't want to.)

Traverse side step is a combination of sidestepping and walking diagonally up the hill. It is the most common way of climbing on skis.

THE SIDE STEP

The skier soon reaches a point where he no longer can walk up a hill. Backslip becomes too pronounced, and tiring as well. The side step is the simplest way to go uphill.

In the side step the skis are placed directly across the fall line and edged enough to prevent them from sliding downhill. The skier then moves the uphill ski uphill for about a foot and then draws the downhill ski alongside it. This is repeated until the desired altitude is gained.

If the slope is very steep, the skier can support himself with his poles. However, care should be taken not to rely on the poles to the point where they substitute for positive weight shift. The weight-shift rule applies in side-stepping particularly. There must be no weight on the ski to be moved. (Note: It can also be used effectively to get *down* a steep or awkward slope.)

TRAVERSE SIDE STEP

In climbing longer distances you will soon find the side step excessively tiring. To reduce both the effort and the tedium of climbing, the traverse or diagonal side step will prove somewhat easier.

The traversing side step combines walking and sidestepping. Instead of going straight uphill, the skier walks across the slope, gaining altitude by moving the skis uphill slightly as well as ahead. The skis are edged at all times.

A frequent error in this approach to climbing is to move the ski up the hill too much for comfortable walking. The uphill motion of the ski is usually less than in the straight uphill side step.

The purpose of the traverse side step is to gain both attitude and distance. The angle of the climb to the fall line of the slope is governed both by the destination to be reached and the steepness of the slope. If the slope is very steep, it may be necessary to make several traverses before the destination is reached (turning at the edges, of course).

STRAIGHT RUNNING

Straight running or schussing may seem simple enough, but it is important to practice it to learn correct body position. In addition, it is an excellent confidence exercise because it gives the skier a feeling for his skis.

In straight running, the skis slide straight down the fall line. There is nothing for the beginner to fear. The slope he will practice on in ski school will be gentle and with sufficient run-out so that he can come to a stop safely.

In straight running the skis are flat on the snow, close together (but not touching) and with the weight distributed equally on both of them. The body should be in a forward leaning position, perpendicular (90 degrees) to the angle of decline.

It is important to assume the correct body position. The best way to do this is to lean the entire body slightly forward from the ankles. Then flex the knees and hips. Do not lean forward by bending from the waist.

Once you are sliding downhill, stay loose. Do not freeze into a position. Raise and lower your body. Let your legs absorb the shock of the bumps. Develop independent leg action. Rock back and forth slightly on your skis. These motions will relax you and give you a feeling for your skis.

THE SNOWPLOW (OR WEDGE)

The snowplow, while mainly a beginner's tool, is often used by even expert skiers because it is the only way to slow down on skis without changing direction. However, it should be considered more than a brake. Through it the beginner learns the basic elements of edge control, which are so vital to advanced skiing.

To get into a snowplow, you can either start from the standing position, pushing off with your poles, or you can get into it from a straight running

Jerry Muth of Copper Mountain demonstrates correct snowplow form.

position. The tails are displaced into a V at equal angles from the fall line. The tips are together, and the surface of the skis are at right angles to the lower legs. This means that the skis are edged.

From a running position you get into a snowplow by pushing the tails apart with a gentle, brushing motion, being careful not to overedge by pressing the knees together. If you want to slow down more, do not use your edges for this purpose. Instead press the tails further out.

The slowing action from a snowplow does not come immediately, and it will take a few yards for the braking action to take effect. So anticipate your need to slow down. A good exercise for getting a feeling of what a snowplow can do is to move from a straight running position into a snowplow and back into a straight running position several times when going down a slope. (This is often how good young skiers handle easy trails.)

In the herringbone, the pole opposite the step supports the skier.

HERRINGBONE

The herringbone is a slightly faster means of walking straight up the hill than the side step, provided the hill is not too steep. The skis are formed into a V with the tails of the skis forming the point of the V (in essence, a reverse snowplow). The skis are put on the inside edges. Weight is shifted to one ski, and backslip is prevented by bracing against the opposite pole. The unweighted ski is then moved forward and the process repeated.

In the herringbone the points of the poles should not be ahead of the skier's boots. If the pole is too far forward, particularly on steeper hills, it will require a rearrangement of the pole before the next stride is taken. This breaks the rhythm of the herringbone stride.

THE KICKTURN

The kickturn is a means of making a 180-degree change in direction from a standstill. The turn starts with a complete shift of weight to the uphill ski. Then the downhill ski is kicked up high enough so that the ski rests on its tail. From there it is swung around so that its tip faces the tail of the uphill ski. Then, in one motion, the uphill ski is brought around and moved alongside the other ski.

Care should be taken to see that the poles are in the right position so that they are out of the way of the skis swinging around and that they provide proper support when the skis are facing in opposite directions. After the leg is kicked up, the support of the body should come from the uphill pole, and the downhill pole should be placed above the skis either before or as the downhill ski is swung around.

Timidity and lack of vigor are the major problems in executing the kickturn. To get the ski on its tail, the leg should be swung up briskly and the rest of the action should follow quickly.

Combined with traverses, the kickturn is an extremely useful maneuver. The skier who finds himself atop a slope he hesitates to negotiate in the usual way (whatever that is) can use the two to make a safe descent.

A kickturn executed in stationary position. Left to right: *The ski is swung back, lifted and placed on its tail, twisted around 180 degrees, and remaining ski is swung around alongside.*

24

Learning to Turn

The thrill of skiing is speed, or more accurately the knowledge that you can control the speed at which you want to descend the hill. To master speed, you must know how to turn the skis. You must also be able to maneuver around trees and rocks, around other skiers, and, if you're a racer, around the flags. Finally, the turn in skiing becomes an end in itself. Few experiences in skiing are as satisfying as turning through a field of virgin powder and stopping at the bottom to contemplate your tracks.

Much of the controversy for much of the past decade over learning to ski has centered around whether or not the pupil should start out immediately by swiveling short skis with feet parallel or learn to control speed first with steered turns and longer skis in a V shape (wedge or snowplow). In 1966, SKI Magazine labeled the short-ski approach GLM (Graduated Length Method) to describe a system whereby the pupil graduates to longer and longer lengths of skis as he or she improves. Today the GLM system has begun to fade in popularity, merging into the other approach, ATM (Accelerated Teaching Method), which starts you out on slightly longer short skis and more traditional methods, including a focus on different body positions.

In theory, according to current PSIA doctrine, the aim of every recreational skier is to ski efficiently and *carve* turns with no skid in them. In practice, this doesn't always work out because most people don't ski often enough to learn how to carve. This clash is inherent in current ski learning. Obviously, whatever PSIA decrees as new is best; yet the fact may be otherwise for the vast number of occasional skiers. The old may, in fact, be better than the new for *you*, and in any event it may be quite important to learn both. Mort Lund, my long-time associate on SKI Magazine and the creator of the Superlearning program at Stratton, feels that skiers should learn how to skid as well as carve turns, especially on steep terrain. I've found it useful to resort to now-unpopular shortswing (pretty, tight, skidding turns in the fall line), stem, even wedge techniques when, for one reason or another, I'm in trouble.

Also the carved turn puts a lot of stress on your lower body—far more than the older skidded, tight-parallel turn does—and after a serious spill left me a bit battered, Dr. Milton Wolf of Mount Snow suggested strongly that I might wish to bring my skis back under me again ("The way God intended them to be"), rather than working with the popular "lateral displacement" of the carved turn, at least until I healed.

Thus, for the balance of this section, I'll try to focus on both theories of learning: the older, tried-and-true as the main text, contrasted with the new carved concepts. Even for the serious skier, some knowledge of both is useful.

TRAVERSING

Although linked, carved turns don't really involve traverses, it is a good technique to know when you want to cross the fall line and slow down. In order not to slide down the hill when traversing across it, you must be able to make the uphill edges of the skis bite into the snow. This is accomplished by pressing the knees and ankles into the hill, with the uphill ski leading slightly. As the need to edge increases (for instance, on ice), you will notice that your hips also tip toward the hill, while your upper torso and shoulders will tip down the hill. (This is called angulation.) The sensation of leaning out over the skis is uncomfortable at first for most beginners. Just as the fledgling rock climber wants to hug the cliff for security, so the novice skier wants to stay close to the hill. But it is the antithesis of sound technique. If you lean your whole body into the hill, your skis will slide out from under you. Rather, you must roll the knees and ankles into the hill, distribute more of your weight on the downhill ski, and ride on your edges in the traverse; all of which requires some tipping of the upper body down the slope.

Learning to traverse accomplishes the first principle of skiing: how to apply the edges of the skis to the snow to stop, control speed, and hold a line.

Jerry Muth traverses across the hill. Because of the gentle slope here, his upper body needs to be tipped only slightly downhill to enable him to weight his skis on their uphill edges. Notice his excellent hand position, increasingly critical in the carved turn.

across the hill. It also is important to know how to release the edges of the skis from the snow . . . to let the skis slide and skid when you need to.

SIDESLIPPING AND THE SKIDDED TURN

To experience the feeling of edging and sideslipping, stand with skis across the hill. From the standing traverse position, straighten up slightly and relax the knees and ankles. The pressure of your uphill edges on the snow will be released, and the skis will slide downhill. To stop, simply press the knees and ankles into the hill again to put your skis on edge again.

Applying and releasing the edges—that is what a great deal of ski technique is all about. Your first rudimentary turns require some mastery of

Othmar Schneider demonstrates edging (front) *and sideslipping* (rear) *of skis.*

Skis as they are edged, sideslipped (center), and edged again. This is a basic maneuver every skier must learn.

both. In order to link up traverses into a continuous run down the hill, you must make a change of direction or turn. The skis are swung around in a new direction and a new traverse. It is a change from one set of edges to another. So that the change is not too abrupt and likely to upset your balance, some skidding of the skis is necessary between edge changes. Skidding is like side-slipping: It is the ability to release the pressure of the edges on the snow. From an edged traverse, the skis are pivoted in a new direction and allowed to skid before you gradually apply the edges in a new traverse in the opposite direction. It is called a skidded turn. Many excellent skiers use it on very steep slopes, even though the carving-minded authorities frown on it.

At this point, it is useful to understand some theory about the ski turn. While there are many ways to turn, one of two fundamental principles usually is at work. In the *steered turn*, the skier applies weight to the inside edge of the outside ski of the turn. Because the ski is built with the edge in a slight curve

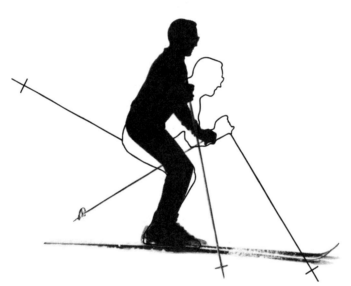

Ernie McCulloch demonstrates up-unweighting. In preparatory motion (line figure), *he sinks at the knees. Then he extends* (solid figure) *and attains maximum un-weighting at the top of the up-motion. Unweighting reduces pressure of the skis on the snow, allowing them to respond to turning forces; it's useful when skiing heavy, deep snow.*

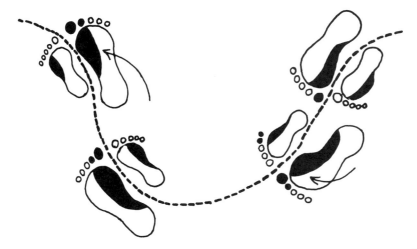

Illustration of pressures felt by a skier in his feet as he makes a turn. At top: The pressure shifts from the inside of the downhill foot, which is edging the ski, to the uphill foot, which starts the new turn. As the radius of the turn increases (lower figure), *pressure increases on the inside of the downhill foot as it applies edge pressure. Then, again, pressure shifts to the uphill or outside foot to start the next turn.*

from tip to tail, it will automatically turn, assuming your body position doesn't thwart it. The skier simply is utilizing the turning properties of the ski itself. Snowplow and stem turns are steered turns, as are carved turns.

The other fundamental kind of turn is a *weighted turn*. This is not now considered a good skill, but it can be useful for skiing heavy, deep snow. The principle at work here is that the skis resist changing direction unless the skier removes their pressure on the snow by unweighting them. The skier can unweight upward or by dropping his body suddenly to ease the pressure of the skis on the snow. To test the efficacy of this method, stand on a bathroom scale. Now drop your body quickly by bending the knees; as you do so, you will see the needle on the bathroom scale drop suddenly, also indicating a brief moment of relative weightlessness. Unweighting reduces the resistance of the snow to the skis turning. Usually the change of direction accomplished by unweighting and swiveling the skis is only partial. The rest of the turn is accomplished on the edges or curved sides of the skis.

DIRECT PARALLEL GLM

Perhaps the most obvious way to reduce the resistance of the skis to turning on snow—both in terms of the length of the sides lying against the snow and in terms of the swing weight of the ski that must be hefted around by the skier's legs—is simply to shorten the length of the ski used by the beginner. This is what the short teaching ski is all about. It enables the novice skier to start swiveling his skis around almost from the beginning and to get up earlier on the lifts and the mountain where the action and fun are. Not surprisingly, ski schools began to introduce short-ski or graduated-length teaching (GLM) in the late 1960s and early 1970s experienced an immediate boost in business. And for reasons no one has yet identified, this method began to wane in the late 1970s.

To a beginning skier endowed with a modicum of coordination and athletic ability, the advantages of the direct parallel approach is that you can start skiing in the same basic manner as your ultimate goal: that is, to turn with skis and feet parallel. (This is echoed, albeit differently, in teaching the carved turn from Day One.) You can begin with a crude parallel turn and refine it gradually as you progress. Direct parallel GLM starts the novice out on skis from three to four feet in length, usually without poles at first. Turning starts with a simple twisting of the feet. For balance, the feet are kept about six inches or so apart, in what is known as a wide-track stance. As you progress, you will want to move faster. In this case, the very short skis become somewhat unstable. So after one or two days, you move on to longer skis, continuing to practice a kind of sloppy, skidded, windshield-wiper turn with a wide-track stance. By the end of a five-day learn-to-ski week, the student can be on six-foot skis or whatever length he purchases for his own permanent use. But many people who have no intention of skiing beyond speeds of around twelve miles an hour will be content to stay on a five-foot ski.

ATM

For several years after GLM was introduced in 1966, most large ski schools—and the instructor associations—in North America and Europe resisted the trend to teaching with short skis. The resistance was partly ideological: an acceptance of the tried-and-true, traditional methods. It was also partly economic. Starting up a GLM ski school frequently required a substantial

Karl Pfeiffer demonstrates beginning parallel turn on three-foot skis. In this GLM direct-parallel approach to learning, the novice moves to longer skis as he grows more proficient. Skiing without poles at the very beginning, the skier uses his extended arms for balance.

investment in different lengths of rental skis, all mounted with rental bindings. There is also more administration involved in arranging the shift of large classes from one length ski to another. But as the advantages of short-ski teaching became apparent, more and more ski schools took it up. Quite simply, many of them found that it was easier for beginners to learn the basic and traditional stem and weighted, wide-track turns on five-foot or 150-centimeter skis. The Professional Ski Instructors of America later refined this approach into what it called ATM, or the Accelerated Teaching Method (as we noted earlier).

While the stem, V, or wedge position has been traditional to ski teaching since the 1930s, one of the immediate benefits of learning on five-foot skis is that far less time is spent on this method of controlling the skis in a descent. But because it is basic to sound control, the wedge or partial stem is not totally bypassed in ATM.

From a wedge position on five-foot skis, feet apart, the novice quickly learns another important principle of turning: the use of independent foot action for stability and quick reaction to terrain change under the skis. This movement has become increasingly important in the latest theory. From the downhill ski, the skier steps onto the outside ski of the turn and uses it to change direction down the hill. It is the kind of turn that youngsters make almost instinctively when they are learning to ski. A quick push off the downhill ski is then brought alongside the outside ski to complete the turn. When the dean of Austrian ski instruction, Prof. Stefan Kruckenhauser, first publicized this turn in 1968, he bolstered his argument with hundreds of feet of slow-motion film of youngsters turning. Racers use this turn also.

TRADITIONAL STEERED TURNS

The historical method of learning to turn starts with the snowplow described in the previous chapter. The ski tips are together in front, and the skier spreads his legs to put the skis in a V position on the snow. In so doing, the wobbly beginner sets up a solid triangular base under himself. As confidence and progress increase, the V or stem diminishes and is eventually eliminated in parallel skiing—until it reappears in racing!

Begin by assuming the snowplow position. To execute the **snowplow turn,** shift your weight onto the ski that will become the outside ski of the turn. The skis will then turn in the direction in which the weighted ski is pointed. Keep the knees bent and press the knee of the turning ski in to put the ski on its edge. (In the carved turn, this is called "leading with the knee.")

Independence of leg action is essential to every skier. This youngster exhibits it in a totally natural way without instruction, as he is compelled to turn around poles. This natural wide-track turn is quite similar to a racing turn and, thus, to a carved turn.

The **stem turn** is used initially by beginners to link one traverse to another in a continuous turn-traverse-turn descent of the hill. From the traverse with feet parallel, fan the uphill ski out to form a V. Now apply weight to the uphill ski by tilting the upper body out over the ski. Your skis will turn down and across the hill into a new traverse. When you reach the traverse position, bring the skis together again parallel. The traverse should be in a comfortable, relaxed manner—skis separated by about six inches, the uphill shoulder, hip, and ski leading the way slightly. (This is similar to the expert/racer "step turn.")

Jerry Muth demonstrates a snowplow turn in which the skis are steered by the legs. To turn, he leans over the outside ski and puts it on edge. The application of his weight on the edged ski and pointing the knee in the direction of the turn cause the ski to change direction. (Mentally move the inside ski close to and roughly parallel to the turning ski, especially in the third and fourth positions, and you've got a basic carved turn.)

The next step on the way to parallel is the **uphill christie** or simple christie across the hill. This is not a turn to link you from one traverse to another but, rather, the completion phase of the first parallel turn you will experience. Other versions of this turn are called the "hockey stop" (because it resembles a quick stop on skates) and the "natural turn."

A simple "hockey stop" turn. Skier has descended the fall line and hopped the skis across the hill to come to a stop. Notice how the twisting of his legs and skis across the fall line causes his upper body to twist in the opposite direction so that he is facing downhill. This results in a sharp bite of the edges on the snow. (The position shown here is a more extreme one than is usually favored.)

From a simple traverse with skis parallel, drop the knees and push the tails of the skis downhill. The skis will christie uphill and come to a stop. If you do this while the tips are still pointing down the fall line, you've got a very good skidded turn in the steep, and they link well with step turns.

The hockey stop or natural turn should be practiced on a very gentle slope. Start out in a steep traverse or straight down the fall line of the hill. From a knees-bent stance, hop up slightly to unweight, and as you do so pivot the skis across the hill to turn. When you come to a stop, you will notice that your upper body is facing partially downhill to compensate for the twisting of your feet in the opposite direction.

25

The Many Turns of Skiing

Progress from being an intermediate skier capable of making rudimentary parallel turns to becoming a proficient master of technique is a function of time, practice, and good instruction. The following chapters are designed as a useful reference and guide for the serious, proficient skier who is interested in becoming better.

At one time, it was believed that learning to ski was accomplished in certain steps that led up to a rigid, final form of the turn. Much of this kind of thinking now has gone by the boards. It has given way to a more pragmatic approach: namely, that there is a variety of ways to turn a pair of skis. These techniques can be appreciated for their simple athletic or aesthetic value or for their value in mastering certain snow and terrain conditions. Several of the basic ways to turn or change direction will be described in this chapter. Quite obviously, on the way to learning these turns, the skier will commit errors or fall into bad habits. Several of the more important faults are detected in Chapter 26.

The fundamental goal of every proficient skier is to be able to master the terrain and snow so that he or she can get down almost any mountain. That's what Chapter 26 is all about. Whether it's steep, bumpy, or bowl-shaped, covered with deep powder, ice, wet snow, or wind-packed slab, the hill should be capable of being mastered by the good skier. And that means mastery of technique and the many turns of skiing.

277

PARALLEL TURN WITH EDGESET

A skier who has reached the ability of skiing with skis parallel is prepared to practice parallel turns. In fact, the basic body movements for this turn were described in the previous chapter.

To execute the parallel turn with edgeset, start across the hill in a traverse. To prepare for the turn, make the skis turn very slightly uphill. This is a counterrotationary movement in preparation for the turn; in turning uphill, the skis go on edge (edgeset or platform) while the upper body rotates in the other direction to face slightly downhill, anticipating the direction of the coming turn. This preparatory edgeset is executed by sinking the knees. (You do the same thing to initiate the step turn, page 287.)

To make the turn itself, straighten up the knees, first planting the pole downhill and forward. The straightening of your knees, following the force of the edgeset, will produce a very pronounced unweighting—virtually a hop— of the skis. At this moment of unweighting, roll onto the inside edge of the uphill ski by leading downhill with knee and hip, turning the ski to complete the turn.

Parallel turn with edgeset.

A SMOOTH PARALLEL TURN

A skier who has mastered the edgeset turn will want to progress to a smoother, more fluid style of turn, unpunctuated by the rather bumpy, up-and-down motion created by the edgeset with its rather wide lateral displacement of the skis. The accompanying illustration shows how this is done. The skier enters the turn in the same manner as before. He flexes his knees while turning his skis a few degrees uphill. He is then on the edges of his skis and begins to straighten his legs, using the pole plant to time the weight change and to assist balance. How is the upward bounce from the edgeset suppressed? At the split second you feel the skis lighten from unweighting, push the feet four to eight inches forward and in the direction of the turn. This action, characterized by a slight sitting back attitude on the skis, will keep you in contact with the snow. The tails of the skis have slid slightly uphill (note that they slide, that they're not abruptly displaced), and you incline slightly to the inside of the turn. As the radius of the turn increases, feel the pressure increase on the outside turning ski. The bending arc of the ski causes it to turn. This is a useful turn for difficult snow conditions, but it's slow and somewhat awkward to use in a linked sequence and has waned in popularity.

A smooth parallel turn in which the up motion of the edgeset is suppressed by a deep flexing of the knees. Feet are pushed forward into the turn.

ANTICIPATION (SOMETIMES CALLED INITIATION)

Both of the turns described above make use of the principle of anticipation. To understand what anticipation is, try this experiment. Hold a piece of spring wire at both ends. Twist one end, while holding the other steady. You are now illustrating what happens at the moment of the edgeset. The upper body is twisted, anticipating the direction of the oncoming turn, but your feet—the other end of the wire—resist turning because the skis are solidly planted in the snow as a result of the edgeset. To continue the analogy, release your fingers (unweighting) from the fixed end of the spring wire. It turns rapidly in the direction of the original turn (the twisting of your body in anticipation). You don't have to plan doing this; the pole plant (see page 290) is usually enough.

Turn with anticipation.

AVALEMENT

Boiled down to its simplest form, all skiing is simply a series of controlled changes of direction down the hill. The key word here is *controlled*. And the key to control is to keep the skis in contact with the snow. That's what avalement is all about. It is a French word that means "swallowing." The skier swallows up the bumpy action of unweighting or bumps by a folding and unfolding action of the legs, which act as shock absorbers. In this way, his skis stay in contact with the snow and the upper body rides in a smooth, short, and efficient line down the hill.

An example of an avalement turn off a bump is shown in the accompanying photo sequence. As the skier reaches the bump, his legs fold up so that

Turn with avalement.

he appears to sit back for an instant. This leg retraction swallows up or controls the up-unweighting effect of the bump. The skis are not thrown wildly in the air but remain in contact with the down side of the bump to carve out the turn. The feet are pushed forward in the direction of the turn. This technique does tend to produce skidded, swiveled turns rather than a true carve and can be tiring in a long, linked sequence. But it still works on occasion and is a good auxiliary weapon to have in your arsenal.

ROTATION TURN

The essence of this turn is to use a rotational movement of the upper body to power the change of direction. The power of rotation is transmitted to the legs by blocking it with the hips. That is to say, the abdominal muscles contract and act as a clutch between the upper body and the legs, transferring the

Rotation turn.

rotary power to the feet and skis. One pitfall to avoid here is overrotation. The skier who overrotates the shoulders at the beginning of the turn without transferring the rotation to the legs will end by using up all of the rotary power before the turn is complete.

Rotation is still a practical turn for all kinds of deep snow, and it's the best for the wet-and-heavy. Best of all, when executed by a good skier, it is an elegant, fluid turn that imparts a wonderful feeling to the whole body.

COUNTERROTATION; WEDELN

This kind of turn became popular in the 1950s. To explain the principle at work, ski-instruction experts used the analogy of a man standing on a piano stool. If he twists his feet in one direction, his shoulders rotate the other way, or vice versa. This reverse shoulder, or counterrotation, principle became the

Turn using counterrotation. (Vastly exaggerated here for effect, it's essential to most carved turns.)

Hop in fall line:
short swing or wedeln.

basis for explaining the Austrian wedeln or tail-wagging—a series of short turns down the fall line in which the shoulders are reversed from the direction of the turn or, in more modified form, provide an anchor for the feet to twist under the body.

Because counterrotation turns only work easily where the skis meet little or no resistance from the snow, they are desirable in all kinds of turns that involve extreme unweighting or airborne skiing or on hard, even icy trails. This makes it a good turn for a quick, tight series of turns with edgesets (short swings) down a steep slope and a bouncy, up-and-down flight through the bumps. It's also used for quick-punch turns in slalom or tight maneuvers in bumps. If you want to see extreme counterrotation sometime, watch a racer making a recovery turn.

DOUBLE-POLE RUADE

This is a turn that has been around a long time in skiing, but it still has its uses. Ruade literally means "horse kick." Planting both poles, the skier stays forward over his skis and kicks the tails from side to side, like a horse kicking his heels. It's a practical turn to get down a very steep slope under complete control or to get through a narrow, uninviting gully. It's also handy for getting through heavy, difficult snow such as slab crust and extra-heavy "mashed potatoes."

PURE CARVED TURN

The idea of every good skier is to carve a precisely arced turn without any wasteful skidding of the skis. As explained previously, the beginning parallel

Tracks in the snow show examples of carved (at left) *and skidded turns. Pepi Stiegler demonstrates a typical skidded or windshield-wiper turn. The goal of expert skiers is to carve turns precisely. (Note the extreme overangulation, the skis glued together—and the lovely counterrotation and hand position.)*

Corky Fowler carves a turn. For hard-snow conditions, his hands would be much lower to hold a carve and his skis farther apart.

skier starts by making a kind of sloppy, windshield-wiper turn, with a lot of skidding around of the tails. As the skier becomes progressively better, he learns to carve the turn on the edges of the skis, gradually reducing the amount of skidding. The ultimate carved turn is one that takes optimum advantage of the curved side camber of the ski.

Like the boomerang, the ski is a delicately designed instrument made to turn. The boomerang's medium is air; the ski's is snow. Put a ski on its edge on snow, apply increasing pressure at its waist to increase its arc of curvature, take it up to a high enough speed, and it will virtually make the turn for you. In the carved turn shown here, the skier simply tips his skis on to their edges by a direct knee and ankle action to make the turn. This is high-speed skiing brought to the final, irreducible limit of efficiency.

The carved turn, as demonstrated by Swiss racer Josef Odermatt.

THE STEP TURN

This is a turn developed especially for giant slalom racing where the aim is to go in as short a line as possible from one gate to the next without losing speed. It is a good turn for nonracers as well and increasingly important in modern technique. It not only will help you regain a higher line of traverse across the hill, but it also teaches you how to step off the downhill ski and "go outside"— that is, get on the outside ski early in the turn and make it carve on the snow. In the sequence shown here, the skier has already left his traverse across the hill. He is pushing off the downhill ski, which, in itself, helps to maintain his speed, as opposed to an uphill christie, which would slow him down. Finally, he steps on to the uphill ski, puts it on edge, and starts to carve the turn—as we suggested earlier and will detail later.

The step turn.

4

5

6

26

Detecting and Correcting Faults

Whenever bad habits appear, return to ski school. An experienced instructor can watch you ski down the hill and, through observation of your body in different parts of the turn, be able to point out what you are doing wrong. A number of ski schools have a video camera positioned at the bottom of the practice hill. It records your descent, and you can immediately watch a replay of yourself skiing. While watching this instant replay, the instructor can analyze any faults and then go up on the hill with you to show the correct way to ski.

POLE PLANT

One of the most common faults in skiing is incorrect planting of the pole or failure to plant the pole at all. The main purpose of the pole plant is to establish good body position and to trigger the timing of the turn. The correct position for a pole plant depends on how close you're skiing to the fall line and how narrow or wide your turns are. If the pole is planted too far behind, the skier will fall backward. Planting the basket of the pole too far forward (up near the tips of the skis) will result in improper edging because of faulty body position and will act to block the oncoming turn. Failure to make any pole plant at all results in inadequate preparation for the turn: failure to set edges, failure to trigger other body actions timed to the turn, and results usually in a need to throw the hips and outside shoulder around to make the turn.

Dixi Nohl exhibits correct angle of pole plant, using flexing of knees to plant (in a wide, GS-type turn).

A correct pole plant establishes the correct body position: knees pressed into the hill, upper body tipping down the hill, weight forward, body coiled and anticipating the coming direction of the turn. It also insists that your hands remain forward and low, or your body position disintegrates.

FEET COMFORTABLY APART

A good rule of thumb in establishing a correct stance for skiing is to think of your feet establishing a vertical line to your hips. In this manner your skis will be three to six inches apart and will provide a solid base for balanced skiing. Feet held tightly together provides too narrow a stance and leaves the skier unprepared to recover when the skis hit small irregularities in the terrain. Skis too far apart (usually a problem of skiers who are unable to emerge from the

Example of incorrect pole plant. By swinging his pole way forward to plant it near the tip, the skier has surrendered his good body position that enabled him to traverse and make his edges bite. As a result, the lower ski slides out in an unwanted stem.

stem phases of skiing) results in easily caught edges and an inability to execute smoothly linked turns. Learn to ski with your feet just comfortably apart. In this way, you will come to learn independent foot action and how to move from the downhill ski onto the outside turning ski.

BEND AND FLEX THE KNEES

Correct body stance starts with the knees. To get body weight forward, bend at the knees. The upper body should be fairly upright; you should have the sensation that the weight of your upper body is riding smoothly on the frame of your pelvis and that your knees are acting as shock absorbers as you glide across the snow. In other words, "flex" the knees, don't just bend them. Proper edging of the skis is accomplished by pressing the knees forward and into the hill. When you do this, you should feel the upper body tilt slightly down the mountain. One of the most common faults of all skiers is leaning the upper body up the hill. It is impossible to edge the skis effectively in this position.

This skier has allowed his hips and upper body to cross way outside the arc of the turn made by the skis. As a result, his lower ski slips downhill.

LOOK AHEAD

Don't make the mistake of looking at the tips of your skis when you are moving. The correct head position is erect and looking ahead. The good skier is aware of bumps, icy patches, changes of terrain, and other skiers and obstacles ahead. The distance you should be looking ahead is a function of the speed at which you are skiing.

HAND POSITION

One of the best ways to check for faults in a skier is to look at his hands. If the hands are not forward, it is usually a sign that the skier is too far back on his skis. If the downhill hand is too high or too far forward, the skier usually has too much weight on the uphill ski. Correctly speaking, the hands should lead the body in skiing. As you cross the hill, the uphill ski, uphill knee, hip, and shoulder should be slightly ahead. For this reason, it is a good idea to lead with the uphill hand as well. Ski with both hands forward, but with the uphill hand leading slightly. The downhill hand should be slightly lower than the uphill hand, indicating that the upper body is tilted somewhat out over the hill so that the skis edge properly. This position is known as angulation.

OVERTURNING, CATCHING EDGES

Watch a poor skier attempting to make a series of linked turns down the hill. Chances are that by the fourth or fifth turn, he is overturning his hips and the downhill hand and shoulder are swung way forward. The result is that the tail of the lower ski slips away downhill in a stem. The skier cannot edge. The lesson here is that turning the hips can help turn the skis, but the hips should not cross outside the turning arc made by the skis.

Sometimes you will have the feeling that your skis want to keep turning, that they are hooking uphill. This may be the result of bottom concavity on the skis. (See Chapter 16 for remedy.) Also, if you have a tendency to catch edges in the snow frequently, you may need to cant under your boots.

Billy Kidd gives examples of bad (left) and good hand position leading to incorrect and correct body position in a traverse. (His good, low hand position shows that he learned to ski in the East, and he currently emphasizes it in his racing camp at Steamboat Springs.)

EASIER TO TURN ONE WAY THAN THE OTHER

Everyone tends to have a strong side that is more developed in coordination. Right-handed skiers, for instance, find it easier to turn to the left, which requires pivoting on the right leg. There is only one remedy for improving your turns in the other direction: practice. Repeat the successful motions of your strong-sided turn on the weak side.

27

The Development of Skills

Avalement, or "compression," as it was occasionally called, was the final phase of the history of "technique." This tended to refer to a series of "correct body positions" (or "final forms") that changed as your ability improved. Beginning in the mid-seventies, as we've noted, the PSIA began to move toward the development of "skills," a series of maneuvers that transcended body positions and remained constant as you moved up the ability ladder.

What the skills approach does is to break the skiing action into basic components of (a) edging or edge control, (b) pressure control, and (c) steering. Properly done, these three skills are taught as the basis for all levels of skiing, classes "A" through "F," and to explain all maneuvers, from basic wedge to advanced short-swing, racing, and freestyle. The strength of the skills approach is that it develops an "awareness"—I'm beginning to hate that word—of how a ski feels when you make it do the job it was designed to do. You don't analyze it to death; you feel it and you do it. Instructors deeply into the Inner/Centered game ask, in effect, do you think about how you walk? No, you just do it. How do you turn a ski efficiently? You make it carve. How do you make a ski carve? You just do it. How do you know when you're doing it right? When it doesn't skid. How much angulation? Not too much or too little. How much is that? Well, how do you walk?

All skills-approach drills are designed to create this feeling of knowing when you're doing it right. The closer a skier is to the age when he learned

295

to walk, the easier this feeling is to instill. A two-year-old can learn how to feel how to ski as naturally as he learned how to feel how to walk. It will be harder for a six-year-old beginner, harder still for a teenager, and almost impossible for an adult novice. Yet at the other end of the scale, an advanced recreational skier of any age who has logged high mileage and developed a sense of confidence in his ability to make skis work can be lured into trying to reach the little-child ski-as-you-walk state of near-intuitive reaction, especially when he's told that achieving this state of grace will push him into true expert status. (We all need some of that.)

Another problem that prevents an adult beginner from accepting this childlike state is something called expectation levels. The adult (and older teenager) wants to get on that lift as soon as possible and begin to ape his fellow adults high on the hill, and if he's delayed by doing easy drills at ground zero for too long he begins to feel cheated; the lessons, as they say, become "counterproductive."

What are these skills: edging, pressure, and steering?

EDGING

When I started skiing in the late 1960s, I asked the instructor after that first exhausting hour-plus, what's the essence of skiing? What makes it happen? "The edges," he said. In the hundreds upon hundreds of days I've spent skiing since, I've never forgotten it. I also haven't mastered it, except on rare days and runs and turns.

We all know what the edge looks like: It's that inset sliver of tempered steel, preferably sharp and clean, that borders the black or clear P-Tex bottom. The edges, in the words of the SKIwee children's instruction program preamble and syllabus, are like the "claws of a cat"—a lovely image, especially for children—and when they are extended they grip, or hang onto, the snow and the side of the mountain.

However, when they're retracted, the edges let you slide smoothly down the mountain on top of the snow (assuming your ski bottoms are tuned). Thus, if you like a Zen-type approach, an edge is present even when it's absent: They're extended when you traverse, turn, or climb, and retracted when you run straight.

But you don't extend the edges as if they were an on-off light switch; rather, you adjust them as if they were a rheostat. What controls that rheostat is the amount of angulation at knees, hips, and waist and, as you get better, ankles and shoulders and even the head. That rheostat is a subtle switch, and all skills-approach drills key on developing this rheostat.

Beginning instruction starts with simply walking around, first off skis, then on them; then it moves quickly to shuffling along. The initial sequences first develop the flat-ski sensation (retracted-edge) by having the beginner make short, straight runs down onto a flat or slightly uphill run-out; this stops him without his needing any skills. The next sequences key on developing the extended-edge sensation as the skiers climb (herringbone and/or side step), then use a wedge, first to stop, then to turn. At this point the drills begin to overlap with those to develop pressure control.

PRESSURE CONTROL

A very bright writer named Denise McCluggage commented that the great problem in illustrating a book or article about skiing (or tai chi, tennis, or any movement sport) is that a picture stops the movement at an artificial position, interrupts the flow, and creates the false illusion of a "proper position." Movement, flow, balance, and change are everything; static positions are nothing. Drills that focus on pressure control develop this sense of flow and change.

A ski, as we've mentioned, is a sensitive machine with many different properties; furthermore, different skis work differently. What distinguishes the true expert from the rest of us is his ability to get on an alien ski and, with a few adjustments in pressure, know how that ski will perform under a wide range of conditions. Children can also adjust quickly, although they can't explain why and how.

The reason is sophistication or instinct in pressure control. This breaks into two subskills: position and weight.

Position

Virtually every ski is marked with a midpoint under the ball of the foot that dictates where the bindings are mounted, and now that boots have that same notch (or should), the guesswork has vanished. A difference of even half an inch or a centimeter fore-aft in boot position on a 200-centimeter ski can change how that ski turns. However, that presumes that the center of your balance is over that notch and that you're applying pressure downward directly over that center point. If you are, you have the full length of that ski pressed into the snow. Too far forward you lose the tails. Too far back you lose the tips. This fore-aft pressure is another rheostat, because as you're skiing you may want to unweight the tips or tails at different points in a turn or to adapt for different conditions and angles of decline.,

Pressure is also applied from side to side to extend the claws. The combination of fore-aft and side-to-side is part of pressure control, and the same movements apply equally to the most rudimentary wedge turn and the most advanced racing turn. The more you press forward and incline to one side, the sharper that turning ski bites and the more aggressively you turn. This reaches its peak when you lift the nonturning ski and focus all your centrifugal force on the inside edge of the turning ski, but it's equally at play when you apply maybe 5 percent more angulation to the turning ski in a beginner's wedge.

Pressure control, especially combined with body position and initiation —how you start to turn—is where today's top instructors focus much of their thinking and imagery. "Pressure control is enhanced by standing against the ski rather than on it," Tom Montemagni says, echoing a statement instructor-writer and U.S. Demonstration Team member Stu Campbell had made earlier in SKI. "This is what happened to you [meaning me] when that instructor [Martin Marnett of Sugarbush] told you to 'throw your hips down the hill.' You're getting your body away from your skis," (extreme angulation and early initiation) "which will cause a higher [degree of] edge sooner in the turn. This is a real thrust move, and kids without lots and lots of mileage don't go for it very readily. But once they feel the results they never go back to just standing on their skis." Sure, it's a rather esoteric concept, but to get that young "E" or "F" class skier to execute and to feel that maneuver comfortably means he should have been playing with its basic sensation as early as "A" class. (Why mention "young"? Because Dr. Milton Wolf warned me against doing too much of that kind of thing.)

Weight

Known at an earlier time as "unweighting." Proper pressure control these days also involves learning "independent leg action," which means that you're using both legs all the time and doing different things with each. This is not a simple concept, especially if you were schooled in the Austrian technique. Look at it this way: Assuming you have the proper length/camber of skis, they are perfectly flat on the snow when your weight is distributed equally between the two. The moment you apply more weight pressure on the turning ski, you counterflex it and allow the other ski to flex upward. This means the two skis are turning at different rates in different arcs, which strongly suggests you get a little distance between them or else the tips may cross. (This becomes most apparent in powder.) By shifting and standing on the previously nonturning ski and stepping off the turning ski, you change direction (assuming you also lean the other way). You've released the weight pressure on one ski and applied it to the other. You get a little natural "unweighting" as you step from ski to ski as the previously counterflexed ski rebounds into its normal flex-camber position, just as a bow does.

The skills approach spends a lot of time in the early lessons teaching the proper positions and sensations so that the skier can develop both aspects of pressure control. A major problem children have—adults also, but not to the same degree—is a tendency to sit back on their heels in a knock-kneed posture, putting the skis on edge but not applying pressure to the tips that, like front brakes in a car, do most of the stopping. There's nothing wrong with a knock-kneed position in a wedge provided the skier is also applying forward pressure.

Can you turn without using pressure control? Sure. You can jump around a turn, which is essentially what you did in the up-unweighting MAT theory; you can kick your heels around the turn in a skid, the essence of GLM, or you can simply muscle your way through by swinging your shoulders and arms and hips and like that, which is how most intermediates turn and which is what Sugarbush finally broke me of to a large degree. Almost all skiers use a combination of the four methods—jump, heel-thrust, muscling, and pressure control—depending on the instant challenge, but the fine skiers rely mostly on pressure control with a small residue of jumping and/or heel-thrusting and only rarely a touch of muscle (except in crud or heavy powder). The higher the reliance on pressure control, the better the skier.

STEERING OR CHANGING DIRECTION

Dave Sanctuary, who wrote the kids' manual for Copper, prefers the word "steering"; SKIwee uses "changing direction." Neither is supposed to be synonymous with "turning," which involves using all three skills at the same time.

The best image I've heard to describe "steering"—and everyone uses it with kids—is: "Pretend your knees are the headlights on a car. They have to point in the direction the car is turning." Basically, the skill you're trying to develop is pushing and leaning the knee forward and into the direction you're turning—or, as Martin Marnett describes it, letting the knee lead the turn.

One problem area in "steering" I don't feel the "skills" people have solved—so far as imagery and description are concerned—involves the feet. To a person, the instructors oppose a heel thrust and favor a foot swivel in making a turn. It sounds good and a thrust is a no-no—except that as I watched my own feet doing both maneuvers with skis on, I saw no discernible difference in what actually happens. (You can see a difference in soft snow using just your boots.) Further, if your skis are close together and you want to fall into a wedge, you better thrust your heels apart because if you just swivel off the balls of your feet, you're going to cross your tips; somehow, I do not believe this is a pattern anyone wishes to foster unless he enjoys watching people mash their noses in the snow. This is an area that remains to be defined and redefined.

What they're really saying is that good skiers "ski off the balls of their feet," the point where you would swivel. This is more of a mental set than a true physical difference: It gets the skier thinking about standing upright on the balls of his feet rather than sinking back on his heels. Just thinking about your heels in skiing is self-defeating, and a good instructor at Pat's Peak told me that when you're sinking backwards, "Push onto your big toe." Same idea.

That pretty well covers the basics of the skills approach. Each has a series of subskills involving initiation and sequence and balance and leverage, different theories of pressure to adapt to different types of terrain and snow conditions and the like. Best of all, these skills now carry forward from that first trembling effort at skiing through those first trembling efforts at one of the increasingly popular adult-racing camps. The old system could never do that.

28

The Carved Turn and the "Head Trip"

How much of the "carved turn" is mythology and how much reality? It's hard to say. The authorities and experts will debate this endlessly, and sometimes you wonder if it really makes any difference. Virtually all turns, even those executed by World Cup racers, have a bit of skid in them, and the chances of a recreational skier making a series of perfectly linked carved turns are infinitesimally low. So why belabor it? Because it's the right way to ski, that's why.

The closer a skier comes to making a carved turn the better his control and the greater his fun. Just making the effort increases pleasure, fosters sensitivity to equipment and terrain, and expands perception of what you're doing out there. And the closer you come to mastering it, the more the skills and "awareness" refine your other experiences: Even driving a car becomes easier. Yet you won't achieve perfection—which itself is good, since it keeps the goal in the future, where goals belong.

Still, one of the more fascinating facets of the evolution of "skills and the carved turn" is the realization that the major limitation is mental and emotional rather than physical: You *can* make a carved turn. So why don't you? Because you can't. Why can't you? Perhaps it's an excess of fear (everyone has some); possibly you can't put the pieces together because you react logically when you have to react intuitively. Either way, the mind impedes the body and you don't carve your turns.

How to solve this? Beginning in the mid-seventies, several different groups began examining the problem. Tim Gallwey came at it early with "Inner Game of Tennis," and together with Bob Kriegel and Mort Lund evolved "Inner Skiing." Denise McCluggage, a famous automotive and ski writer and devotee of the Oriental martial arts, got together with Sigi Grottendorfer up at Sugarbush, Vermont, and evolved "Centered Skiing." These remain the dominant strains as more of these workshops evolve—yet oddly, despite the greater initial fame of "Inner," "Centered" seems to have set the pace for the future with its insistence that physical skills are as important as the mental/emotional awareness and that, further, the two must be integrated. Lund underscored this by splitting from "Inner" and developing his own "Superlearning" program at Stratton, Vermont, which is similar to "Centered" although the mental/emotional exercises aren't quite so rooted in Oriental philosophy. Elissa Slanger is on the same track with "Woman's Way," which plays a different circuit every year. And frankly, it's the only way to go.

How does this work? McCluggage, before she left Vermont for New Mexico, wrote an excellent book called *The Centered Skier*; Gallwey and Kriegel produced two books, *Inner Skiing* and the *Inner Game of Tennis*, which aren't quite as good but are still worth reading. However, for a shorter version, I've interviewed both Grottendorfer—who runs the ski schools and ski shops at Sugarbush and at Portillo, Chile—and Martin Marnett, who runs the Centered Skiing Workshop under Sigi's overall direction. That isn't to say Sigi and Martin are the best instructors in the country, but I haven't met anyone who's any better (although several others are as good). These interviews follow.

Incidentally, I've included an illustration (page 304) of one of Ingemar Stenmark's classic carved turns, from the Major and Larsson *World Cup Ski Technique*—but in deference to the inherent theory of Centered Skiing, I haven't included a caption.

AN INTERVIEW WITH SIGI GROTTENDORFER

Berry: How has ski instruction changed the past ten years?

Grottendorfer: It hasn't changed that much technically; it's just been simplified. People work the whole year, they have a complicated business, they have nothing but problems; when they're on vacation they don't want to hear complicated rules that just confuse them more. They get discouraged. So we boil it down to the basics. A complete beginner is a complete beginner, and you only work so many exercises with him and get him to a snowplow turn. You don't get him to perfect that exercise. Years ago that was the typical Austrian technique, where I came from. If you made snowplow turns, they had to be absolutely perfect before you could go any further. That's a waste of time because they're never going to use it again. So I said, listen, I mean this is crazy. As soon as we feel that they are ready for the next maneuver, we'll come up to the next thing. We keep them interested constantly. The person never gets bored, and the person always feels like, oh, it makes sense, it cooks, I finally understand it.

Berry: Currently, modern teaching is based on the carved or racing turn. Do you feel that most skiers can learn how to handle the carved turn?

Grottendorfer: Yes. It depends on what speed they're skiing. If they're very slow making skidding turns, then it does not make sense to get them into a carved turn because when you start carving a turn you must have a much more delicate balance on skis. There is nothing more difficult in skiing than making a very narrow carved turn. Personally, I think they're wrong out west when they say you don't have to carve a turn in powder snow because even in soft snow the more you carve the more you have the skis under control. You can't improve skiing anymore after a certain level if you don't start carving because there is no traction.

Berry: When would you actually start on the carved turn?

Grottendorfer: When the people already have some speed and feel comfortable on skis. They have to be more aware of where they're going and what they're doing. That's also when the equipment comes in; it's very important when you carve that you have sharp edges and a good pair of boots. As long as you skid the turn and slide all over the place it doesn't make any difference if the edges are sharp or if you ski over some rocks. But if good skiers ski over obstacles and ruin their edges and then try to do what the instructor told them to do, they can't do it because every time they push the knees in and try to get the ski on the edge, *whoosh*, the skis are gone.

Berry: Is most of modern ski-teaching technique tied to what skis can do?

Grottendorfer: Absolutely. Short skis are fantastic for a complete beginner. As long as you don't have any speed, the shorter the ski the easier it is to maneuver, to turn, and that's all the person is interested in. But when people start to pick up speed, all of a sudden the ski starts to swim and they feel very uncomfortable and say, "oh, something is wrong, it doesn't work right."

From *World Cup Ski Technique*, by James Major and Olle Larsson. Copyright © Editions Buchheim, Fribourg, Switzerland. Used by permission.

That's when the person needs a longer ski. This is a delicate thing because it's stupid for a skier to carry ten extra centimeters if he never skis that fast. On the other hand, if he's ten centimeters too short and he still wants to improve, he's going to stop at that level and just never get any better. So the length of ski is important.

Berry: How about the model? Do you feel that the average recreational skiers could use an SM or the old ST [Two of Rossignol's racing skis]?

Grottendorfer: Yes. Sometimes I suggest they should *not* buy that ski because that ski is built better, has more durability and more response, and is more expensive than they need. An intermediate skier may stay at that level for a couple of years; so he shouldn't spend the extra $100 because he won't be able to tell the difference between the racer and a lower model. But the racing ski isn't going to hurt him. He can ski it.

Berry: How did this change occur?

Grottendorfer: Years ago a racing ski or a good ski used to be a stiff ski. Those wooden slalom skis we had when we raced were so stiff you could hardly turn them. Now it's almost the opposite because the top racer has the softest ski. Unfortunately, the companies can't make the ski that soft in the normal production line because people will bend them. But a good racing ski is not stiff anymore. It's just as soft as anything else.

Berry: How does modern teaching technique use this new softer ski?

Grottendorfer: A simpler explanation is that a softer ski is easier to maneuver. You probably remember [in the old days] when we made parallel turns by jumping around, lifting the tails, and getting *up* because there was no other way to get those tails around. Now, with a soft ski, you can leave it on the ground and push those tails out. Also, we don't use heel thrust anymore but actually bring the tips down into the fall line—I think you remember that from Centered Skiing? We do that now with the beginning parallel skiers. It doesn't make any difference then how steep the terrain is; he's making the turn because the tips are going down rather than the tails coming up. [In the old days] the rule was: the steeper the terrain the harder it was to get those tails around—and some people who weigh over 200 pounds just can't do that all day long. Now you see skiers out there who have been skiing for a week or two who can turn those skis back and forth nicely. Also, when the skis are softer they're a little more forgiving of errors.

Berry: When I first started skiing in the late sixties, we moved up in class based on final form. You learned a wedge, then a stem turn and a stem christie. Now you're teaching skills rather than form. What skills are you now teaching, and what's the technical word for them?

Grottendorfer: It's not like it was even five years ago, when just the word *snowplow* turned everybody off skiing. In my whole teaching system I just add things on, not take things off. [In the old days] you started with one thing, and the following week you said no, the skier must unlearn all this and start something else. Now what we do is this: As soon as they make snowplow turns, they also begin to make traverses with the skis parallel, opening up a little into the wedge to get into the fall line and then bringing the skis parallel again with a finishing turn into the hill. This is called a basic turn, which years ago was called a stem christie. After the basic turn we go into parallel skiing. (Just to keep the communication between the instructors clear, we still have a beginning parallel, parallel, and advanced parallel at Sugarbush.) But we try to get the people onto different terrain before moving them into a new exercise.

Berry: You mentioned having skiers "drop the tips into the fall line." How do you actually teach that?

Grottendorfer: When we show that the first time, we put the skier on a small mogul so that the skis are weighted only underneath the bindings and he can pivot the skis back and forth. He needs a little pressure by the toes [to swivel] the balls of his feet and guide the skis into the fall line. Just to get the feel of pushing down slightly and naturally. If he can do it standing still he can definitely do it skiing, because when you move it's easier.

Berry: When do you start teaching them how to *feel* the edge?

Grottendorfer: Beginning parallel. Almost any exercise should be started with a turn into the hill. If I watched a skier for the first time, all he has to do is go straight down the fall line and make a turn into the hill and I can tell pretty much how he skis. If he skids the skis around, it means he's pushing the tails out and sliding. Up to this point, he probably has most of the weight evenly distributed on both skis; he may have a *little* more on the outside ski. But as soon as we have him get the ski on its edge, he has to move the knees or the hips—the center of the body—to the inside of the turn. At that moment you have to transfer the weight onto the outside ski; if you do that with the weight on both skis, you automatically put more weight on the inside ski and you fall into the hill. So the first thing you do is a few exercises in transferring the weight onto that outside ski. Then, while you have the weight out there, you show him how to move the knee into the direction where he wants to go.

It's a sensation almost like a first-time straight run down the hill, as if the skis are trying to run away under you. Because all of a sudden the ski is on its edge: The skis are moving in a forward rather than a sideward direction, and people have to be more precise. The first time skiers get that sensation they're hooked on it because it produces a lot of control; after a while you feel great. And if you hit an icy spot here and there, it's no big deal; if you have sharp edges you go over it without even feeling it. In time, you start carving *before* the fall line, although you'll need more speed and a little more experience on skis to do it properly.

Berry: How do you get people to learn how to *feel* what a ski is doing? How do you impart the sensitivity to know when a ski is on edge, how far on edge it should be, and what the ski is doing compared with how it was designed?

Grottendorfer: That's the most difficult part of this whole thing. An instructor only can *tell* the pupil what to do; that's where a racer becomes a good racer. [An Ingemar] Stenmark *feels* that he is one-tenth of an inch too much in or out, and he can make the correction right there. That's total awareness. But usually you have a person in front of you who's thirty-five years of age who's never thought of awareness, of looking, of "how am I standing? what am I doing? how do I sit down?" It's a waste of time to tell him, "Now, feel what those skis do." You've got to educate him; that's where Centered Skiing works best because you have the full week, and after five days those people might not be aware *all the time*, but they know they missed something there. A lot of people never have that. Then we have to give them certain exercises when they're standing on skis: How are you standing now? Where is your weight, on your heels or on your toes? And they say, "Oh yeah, I never noticed that." Do you think your knees are bent right now or are they straight? Where do you think your arms were? If he doesn't know, then it's no good to tell him what to do. He has to be aware of it so that he can do it himself. But if he doesn't start out with the basics he'll never get there.

Berry: Are you bringing that down into the first, beginner class?

Grottendorfer: Yes, right away. We call it the general skiing position: knees slightly bent, arms forward, the body right over the heels, weight evenly distributed over the skis. After the first few runs we ask, "Are you aware of where everything is? Do you feel the snow? Here it's a little slippery; the ice is a little faster. Do you feel those things?" We do that right at the beginning. We usually don't have problems with those people. It's the person who's skied for twenty years and never thought about anything where it's more complicated. If you do it the first day, you don't have to worry about it anymore.

Berry: How do you teach them to see terrain?

Grottendorfer: We also do that right from the first day. When they look down, the first thing everybody wants to see is their ski tips. So the first thing you say is, "Look straight at me, forget everything down there. Look a little farther ahead." Terrain is so important if you use it correctly. That's why when people follow right behind the instructor, they always do better because the instructor uses the right terrain on which to turn. And you're teaching this. You say, "Now, there's a little bump down there; as soon as you get to the top, start turning there because it's much easier." The next time you let him turn just ahead of it, and he'll notice the difference. Now he knows that if he turns before that bump it's harder than when he does it right on top. And that you can do from the very first day. Those are things that make the whole lesson less boring because the guy always has something to do; he always has to think about something without making things complicated. This is entirely up to the instructor. A good instructor can do those types of things.

Berry: Do you see any major changes in ski teaching coming up in the next five years?

Grottendorfer: I really don't know. I doubt it. There are no major changes in equipment due; they're fooling around with boots, but I don't think it's going to be major.

AN INTERVIEW WITH MARTIN MARNETT

Berry: How do "Centered" concepts work into regular teaching?

Marnett: Skiing technique becomes very simple to explain if you focus on the "center." You might not introduce a person to the Oriental concept as such, but you'd introduce it to him in the first run in a wedge. If the person is a bit crooked, you say, "Let your zipper stay in the middle."

Berry: By "center" you mean what?

Marnett: The point in your body located below your navel inside the body. The center of mass.

Berry: How would you make [a beginning class] aware of "center" on its first day out?

Marnett: I might not do any specific exercises to get them into "the center," but in giving them a description I would focus on that point. For example, if someone fell down and was having trouble getting up, I might explain it as simply allowing for this part of your body—touching them or showing them my center—to come up to *here*, because when you get up from the ground you pick up your center to the level where you're standing. Very often just that phrase, just showing him that you're going to lift that part of you, is all he needs.

Berry: At what point do you get into the Oriental concept?

Marnett: In the Centered Skiing Workshop. I avoid doing it with regular ski-weekers. When people come to take Centered Skiing and pay almost $300, you know they're ready. But in a regular ski week, if I say, "Okay, we're going to allow for our *chi* to flow downward to the edge of the ski and for our center to fall inside the turn," some guy from New York, who may be the most linear-minded person in the world, is apt to say, "I don't need this California-style (expletive)." I may present Centered concepts to anybody, but I wouldn't tell them its origins lie in the martial arts or Oriental philosophy.

Berry: How can you do that?

Marnett: If I can do some breathing exercises with you on the slopes, you'll probably realize you're holding your breath. Therefore, we'll work in something where you'll allow yourself to breathe and you'll ski better. I don't have to get into the Oriental involvement of breathing.

Berry: How is Centered Skiing as an advanced skiing workshop different from a regular five-day ski week?

Marnett: The basic *foundation* of Centered Skiing is this: Learning is seeing the picture more whole. Because of all the time we have with the people in the workshop, we can bombard them with that visual image. Plus the tactile feeling: What does it *feel* like to ski? This is why we're using the metaphor; the metaphor *conveys* to a much greater extent than technical description what skiing feels like. Rather than talking about making a snowplow turn, you can tell a skier to put the skis into a V position and to imagine there's a tube of toothpaste under one foot and that the ski must expel the toothpaste out of the tube slowly. Then the knee will bend; angulation will probably occur, but we don't have to mention it. All we have to talk about is the toothpaste: Crush the toothpaste and you're going to have the pressure, that edge is going to curve, the edge will run in the snow, and you've got a turn.

Berry: How does a workshop differ from a ski week technically?

Marnett: When I do a regular ski week, I give them about 15 percent of a workshop. Mainly because of time. A regular ski week is only two hours a day. Sometimes I have to give people a lesson that I know isn't very good, but we're in business and I give them what they want. Some guy comes to me with a "What am I doing wrong, coach?" attitude. I can't go out and work for an hour on breathing, which may be the thing that he wants or needs the most.

Berry: What are the main things a ski-weeker isn't getting?

Marnett: The video; the morning [head] sessions; the *Tai Chi* exercises; the movement exercises. Plus something that people underestimate: We now have five instructors for maybe twenty people. Thus the students hear the same thing in different ways from five different instructors. We've eliminated the [ski week] chances of your not getting the message simply because you only heard one instructor explain it. And since Sigi [Grottendorfer] is added to the sessions for the video critique, that's actually six instructors talking about the same thing in different ways. The skier has to respond well to one of us.

Berry: What are they talking about?

Marnett: Modern ski technique. The efficient use of the ski as a tool to make a turn. Maybe we could almost call it the calligraphy of skiing.

Berry: What is a carved turn?

Marnett: A carved turn is one made with a minimum of sideslipping, one where the ski is going forward. We present the techniques as a perfect carved turn in the workshop; and skiers, depending on their ability, grasp it at their own level. This is important. All the people teaching Centered Skiing know how to let the student be free enough to learn, which overcomes one of the biggest faults of teaching anything at any level: Most teachers try to push— and therefore meet resistance—when they should let the student go. People will learn if you let them go; it's the process of learning, the process of doing the thing, that's important. And everybody who's teaching the workshop knows that, and we're getting better at it all the time.

Berry: You've got nine two-and-one-half hour classes on snow. What do you do in them?

Marnett: The first session focuses on awareness. I often make a joke that the title of this lesson is "What the heck are you doing?" We present some aspects of the technique, but we really don't focus or push it on the people at all. By that point, in the morning exercises before we start skiing, we've "burned our expectations" and we've "emptied the cup," those excellent Zen exercises. Sometimes I opt to go back and "empty the cup" and "burn the expectations" again on Tuesday, Wednesday, or Thursday, or maybe all three days.

The afternoon session on Monday focuses on pole plants. We're very cautious with this because in a lot of techniques the instructors have forgotten about the *flow*, that skiing is motion. Very often, for people who've been *lessoned* a lot, this is a dramatic change, this idea of the peripheral motion of planting the pole. They've been taught to make one turn at a time. In *exercises* you can do that, but in *skiing* you really can't. That afternoon, too, we start to tune into energy blocks.

On Tuesday morning we really bomb them with the technique: initiation and transition, the way your center moves to the inside of the turn, how pushing against one ski would cause your center to move in. That's the morning session, aided by video. The afternoon session—carving—returns to initiation and transition but is related to a bigger sense of carving.

Wednesday morning focuses on terrain awareness, and now we introduce a lot of the Oriental concepts, the concept of self and flow, *Tai Chi*, yin-yang, all of those things. We tell the skier that the point where the skier ends and the terrain begins is nonexistent—that you are the terrain at that point.

Berry: How do you teach that?

Marnett: By having the student realize—by looking at the terrain, by watching us ski, and watching the bumps—that we have that *flow* through the terrain and, therefore, that he can choose to operate against and fight with it but that once you've joined up—the vision becomes very important here—you're using your eyes like a camera. The image, the energy, come in through the eyes, flow down through the body, and in a sense out through the feet. And what is sent out through the feet is what connects you to the earth. We teach the concept of soft eyes—looking at the cup, first looking *hard* and then looking *soft*—which tunes people into the idea that the eyes can accept the O. J. Simpson move, loosening the muscles in the neck. Because those muscles have a direct relationship to the eyes and to the leg muscles, the suspension system, the yielding. Most people get on skis and their concept is that they have to do something. Whereas to a great extent—for example, skiing bumps on Wednesday afternoon—it's not so much what you do as what you *don't* do. There is a violent action that you make, but then there's a complete letting go.

We're also running gates now, and again we focus on the eyes. The mode of the eyes is almost as if you got hit on the head with a two-by-four and at the point right before you're going to fall asleep you *see*: You look at nothing but see everything. Especially in the race course, that's so important because if you look at the poles you've had it; you don't know where you're going. If you look at pictures of Ingemar Stenmark, watch the expression on his face: Everybody else's teeth are gritted, you can see the tension in the neck and whatnot; but Stenmark looks as if he's dumbfounded. That's why one difference between Stenmark and the other skiers is that he goes inside the turn farther than anybody else. And therefore he can unite with the forces to get the inclination that nobody else gets. And he does it mainly because of his relaxed, alert mode.

Berry: How do you feel the group dynamic works into Centered Skiing?

Marnett: I learn more and more about letting the energy of the entire group go rather than feeling we have to control it and direct it. We have certain lessons that let the skiers interact. People are learning how to ski, and they get excited about it. The group dynamics catch on: Someone gets excited and he may come up with a description, a metaphor that's better than any of ours, and in turn someone else learns a bit better and it's contagious. Even if there's somebody who's completely negative, they either get caught up by the enthusiasm of the others or feel, by Wednesday or Thursday, that everybody else is having a good time and they're being the jerk. Then they get involved in the whole thing.

Berry: How has video changed your teaching technique?

Marnett: We don't focus on what people are doing wrong. People get negative if you give them a lot of negative input. But when they *see* how they look, we don't have to say quite as much about their technique or make error correction. When we know the video is there, we know they're going to see it. People are generally going to be more critical of their technique than we are. Very often we have to say, "It's not so bad. Look at it again."

Berry: Why do you pin up photos of racers?

Marnett: You have to study the best skiers. In Portillo, when we watch the national teams train, we can't tell the nationality because they're all doing the same thing.

Berry: What?

Marnett: Using the ski to make a turn. They're pressing against the outside ski, and by doing so they cause their center to start moving to the inside of the turn. The transition to the next turn is made before the turn simply by pressing down and against what at that point will be the uphill or inside ski. As I stretch *that* leg, it is going to force my center down the fall line, which is the line inside the turn. But it's all coming from that pushing with and against the snow (or ski), rather than from any action by the body, because when you start to talk about the position you start to block energy.

Berry: How many people coming through your ski school can learn this? Have the physical strength and the physical conditioning to handle it?

Marnett: Just about everybody, unless someone is really a wreck.

29

How to Ski Varied Terrain, Snow

While a great deal of ski teaching focuses on the mechanics of turning on smooth, packed slopes, that is only the beginning for the truly accomplished skier. The final goal is to be able to get down any mountain regardless of the snow or the difficulty of the terrain. This chapter therefore deals with the specific problems posed by different kinds of snow and terrain conditions.

OFF THE FALL LINE

Most ski slopes are designed to go straight down the fall line of the mountain. But there are many sections of trails where the terrain crosses the fall line. In effect, you are skiing on a sloping side hill. The problem here is that you must prolong your turn in one direction while shortening it in another.

Open Stance Sideslip

One advantage of a side hill is that it is an ideal place to perfect the forward sideslip. With ski tips pointed up into the slope, place your feet four to eight inches apart, with the uphill ski about a boot length ahead. To start, push off with your poles keeping both baskets uphill from the skis. Bend the knees and ankles, and let your skis slide down and forward at the same angle of drift as the slope. You can keep moving continuously along a sidehill in this position.

Breaking through "crud." Note the powerful rotation. It may not be pretty, but it works.

Open stance sideslip.

Rolling Sideslip

Begin by doing the open stance sideslip just described. When you have gained speed, press your knees forward and into the hill to edge the skis. Your skis will turn uphill. As you slow down, raise your body and lean back slightly to put some weight on the tails of your skis. This will cause the tips to drift downhill. Let them run until you feel you are moving fast enough; then push your knees forward and into the hill again, thrusting the tails downhill. You will start turning uphill into the slope again. Repeat it in a rhythmic motion as you move along the side hill.

Bank Turn Against Slope

Good skiers can do this one. Pick up speed along the trail and turn gradually up into the side hill. With enough speed, you should be able to bank the skis against the hill, lean inside the turn, and come around like a racing car on a steeply banked curve. When you end the turn, your skis will be headed straight down the fall line to the opposite side of the trail. Keep picking up speed and gradually turn the skis up into the side hill again. Then repeat the banked turn.

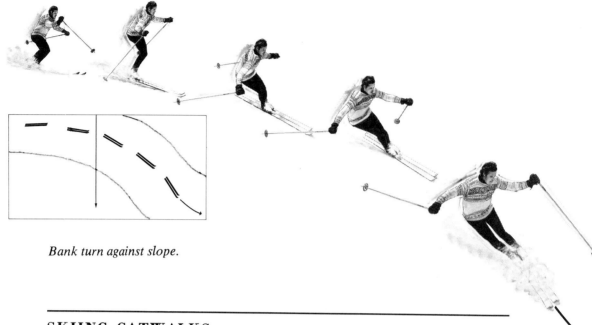

Bank turn against slope.

SKIING CATWALKS

A catwalk is a narrow, frequently steep trail shaped like a gunbarrel cut in half lengthwise. The high banks on each side of the trail can make it difficult to ski. One way, for beginning skiers, is to ski down one side of the catwalk. Let one ski run straight along the crest of the side bank while the other ski does the plowing in the trough to check rate of speed.

Plowing one ski at the edge of a catwalk.

Garland Sidewinder

In this maneuver simply stay at the side of the trail skiing along the bank. Turn the skis up into the side of the catwalk to check speed; allow the tips to run downhill to regain speed. This foot-on, foot-off-the-accelerator approach enables you to control your speed all the way down the catwalk.

Midway Wedeln

Here is the common expert approach to skiing catwalks. Simply stay in the middle of the trough, making very quick, very tightly linked parallel turns. Use

Garland sidewinder.

Wedeling down the middle of a troughed trail. (You can eliminate the extreme un-weighting-and-hopping to get the same effect.)

Heavy edgeset turn on steep slope.

sharp edgesets to control speed. The trick of wedeling is to keep the skis following the line of the catwalk. If they cut across the slope too much, the banked sides will grab the tips and pull you off line. (A smoother shortswing will work just as well.)

STEEP SLOPES

Stationary Kickturn

A beginner or unconfident skier who finds him or herself on a slope that seems too steep for comfort probably should not try to ski it directly. Instead, make a series of carefully checked, forward sideslipping traverses back and forth across the hill. When you reach the side of the hill, make a simple kickturn in position to reverse direction. For the very cautious skier, another approach is simply to sidestep down the steepest sections.

Heavy Edgeset Turns

The clue to this turn on steep slopes is an exaggerated planting of the pole straight down the hill and almost at right angles to the skier's body. (Return to the comments on pole plants, page 290.) The result of such a pole plant is deep flexing of the legs, vigorous angulation of the upper body and, consequently, strong edging of the skis to check speed on even the steepest slope. The stronger the edgeset and the more you turn the skis up the hill, the slower your descent. Following the powerful edgeset, you will experience equally powerful unweighting. Use this momentary unweighting of the skis to swing them quickly across the fall line into a new edgeset turn. (This is when and how the pros use a skidded turn.)

BUMPS

The first thing to know about skiing bumps or moguls is to use the flexing of your knees to remain stable as you move over the up-and-down terrain. In between the bumps, legs are extended or straight. Then as the skis ride up the side of the bump, retract your legs like shock absorbers. Think of your head as riding smoothly in a straight line while your feet and knees flex and extend underneath you. (Note: There are a zillion theories about how to ski bumps. The best method is having teenaged knees.)

Skiing through the bumps. Knees flex, head attempts to move along a straight line.

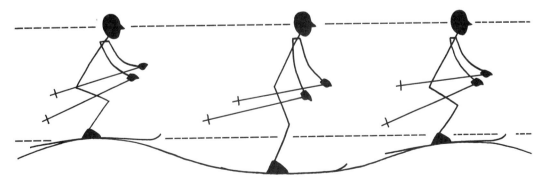

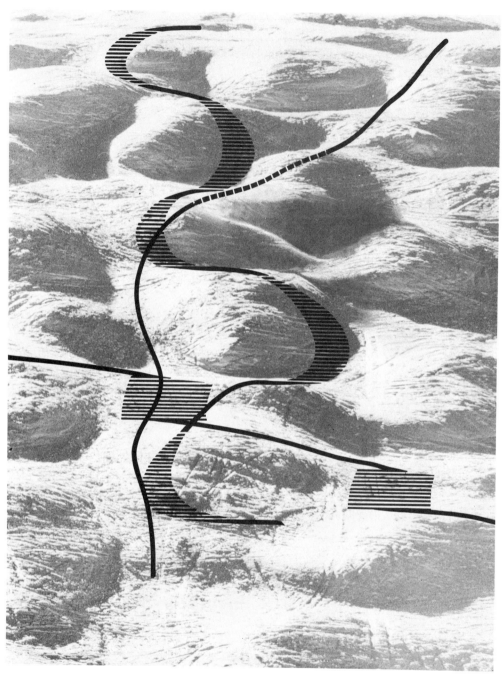

Skiing through the bumps. Examples of paths followed by a beginner (traverse and sideslip), intermediate (turn at top of bump, skidded turn on downside of bump), expert (skiing through the troughs, with aerial jump off bump top). (For fun, pick two other routes, staying off the peaks and on the snow. A hint: Try both sides.)

Skidded Turns

If you're an accomplished intermediate to advanced skier, this is the usually prescribed turn for getting through a field of moguls. Ski toward the mogul. As you reach its top, flex the knees (down-unweight) and swivel the skis into the new turn. Skid or forward-sideslip on the down side of the bump, then head to the side of the top of the next bump. Look ahead and mark mentally the line you will take through the bumps.

Through the Troughs

A good skier should be able to wend his or her way through the bumps like a slalom skier through the flags, not always having to cross the tops of the moguls like the intermediate. Pick your line to ski between the moguls—that is, in the troughs. When you pick up too much speed, check it with an edgeset on the flat top of the bump. Then keep moving through the troughs.

ICY CONDITIONS

The two keys to successful skiing on ice are a set of sharp edges and quiet, technical skiing to keep the edges in contact with the ice.

Traverse with Angulation

It is important to apply as much force to the inside edge of the downhill ski as you can if you want to get a firm bite on the ice. The skier at left, below, is attempting to edge his downhill ski simply by pressing in his knee. This angles

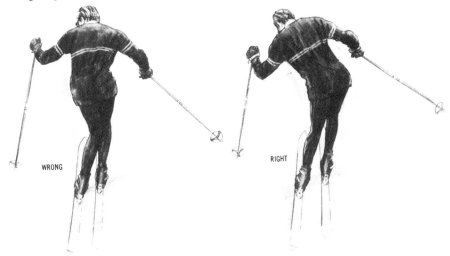

Wrong (left) *and right examples of how to traverse on ice with edge bite (although skier at right is overangulating).*

the ski, but it does not apply weight to it. To weight the ski, tip the upper body down the hill. Notice in the illustration how this applies the body's center of gravity on a line directly over the inside edge of the downhill ski.

Even with proper edging, you may find it difficult or impossible to hold on glare or blue ice. In this case, simply allow the skis to forward-sideslip over the patch of ice until you reach some snow. Another theory is to make quick on-off turns, even steep turns, and stay as close to the fall line as steepness and nerve allow.

Suppress Up and Down Action

In turning on ice, the best way to stay in control is to maintain constant ski-snow contact. Throwing your body around and jamming the edges will not necessarily keep you in control. Rather suppress any vigorous up-and-down motion. Get the weight on the outside-turning ski early, and use angulation to obtain edge bite. (As you may sense, this is the beginning of the move away from unweighting and into carving.)

DEEP POWDER

Skiing in deep snow is quite different from skiing on packed slopes, and you should start with a few cardinal rules. The first is that the way to achieve successful powder skiing is primarily psychological. If you can convince yourself that turning in the deep stuff is as easy in practice as the simple theory of it, half the battle is won. Then remember two things: Sit back slightly so that the tips of the skis plane out of the snow; and keep your weight evenly distributed over both skis (quite the opposite of the technique for ice discussed above).

Skiing in deep powder. Many experts ski light powder without such extreme contortions—more like they ski packed snow.

Deep powder skiing in Park City, Utah.

Some instructors, however, feel that you can use an Eastern-based ski-to-ski shift in powder much as you can on ice. Still others dispute the need to "sit back," and prefer to keep as evenly balanced fore–aft as they do on hardpack. In short, there doesn't seem to be as much of a consensus today on the "proper way to ski powder" as there is for hardpack, which may mean, in the final choice, that you should do what feels best. But start off using the first technique mentioned here, then adapt it to your own style and for your own comfort.

In starting to ski a field of deep powder, begin by pointing the skis directly down the fall line. Practice up-and-down motions to get the feel of how far back you should sit on the skis to feel them plane. Turn the skis, but not abruptly. Simply feel the pressure of the snow built up against the bottoms. Then sit back farther and extend your legs, pushing them in the direction of the new turn. Don't ski across the hill. Keep the skis moving in a snakelike path down the fall line. Soon you will feel a gentle, rhythmical up-and-down motion as your skis build pressure against the deep snow, unweight, and turn.

SOFT, HEAVY SNOW

The principle here is much the same as with deep powder, with one exception. In heavy snow the action of unweighting the skis may have to be much more pronounced. It may even require a hop (and a shift to pronounced rotation) if the snow is exceptionally heavy. Otherwise, ski as you would in any deep snow. Use shorter skis if they're available to you. The skis should be soft in flex. Don't dive the tips into the deep stuff, but keep your weight back slightly. And try to maintain fairly even distribution of your body weight over both skis. For extra-heavy snow, use the ruade turn described in Chapter 25.

30

Ski Safety and Courtesy

Safety is usually something you think about after an accident. Until then, an injury is something that happens to other skiers.

Skiing is not the safest of sports and, let's be honest, part of its appeal is in its risks. In our super-tame, super-safe civilization, the taking of physical risks can be a distinct relief. The man-against-nature struggle is a test of nerves, of courage, and it would hardly be a struggle if there were no physical danger involved.

It is not the purpose of this chapter to preach caution—say, to tell you not to ski slopes over your head. Such advice is silly, first because it must be ignored if you are to make progress in the sport and second because most skiers are only too well aware of the risks. Indeed the problem of most beginners is overfearful caution.

Rather than suggest you avoid all danger, the purpose of this chapter is to make you aware of it so that you can recognize it when you see it. You should be able to look it in the eye, so to speak, and make your own decision whether to challenge it directly or avoid it.

Simply because there is danger, however, does not mean that you must get hurt beyond an occasional bruise. Because you live with danger does not mean that you have to lose to it. Many skiers, including some who have courted the extreme dangers of the top international racing trails, have never had a serious injury. Why? Because they are in top physical condition, have the best equipment (including the best release bindings properly adjusted), and possess athletic skill and judgment. If they lack any of these, they are not very good racers. To the extent that the recreational skier lacks them, he is less safe on the slopes.

The best means of avoiding injury is to be in good condition, as we discussed earlier. Although sheer physical strength is helpful, it is not critically important. What is important about good condition is that it provide flexibility, mobility, and sensitivity to conditions underfoot. Good physical condition enables you to sense impending difficulty more quickly and to make adjustments.

It makes similar good sense to learn to ski properly in a good ski school. Injuries in ski school are minuscule compared with the injuries incurred in free skiing. This is because the instructor knows what he is doing and selects instructional approaches and terrain with safety in mind. But equally important is the fact that in class you are always concentrating on what you are doing. If you carry the habit of concentration over into your free skiing, your chances of injury are greatly reduced.

Statistically, the snowplowing and stem-turning skier is the best candidate for the ski patrol toboggan (another reason for using the newer learning systems). The reasons are not difficult to divine. Beginning skiers are a great deal less skilled and experienced—they're clumsy—but, more important, the very nature of the stemmed turn invites injury in the event of a fall or entanglement. In the typical beginner-accident situation, the skier gets the feeling that he is going too fast. He tries to check his speed by desperately sticking out his skis in a rough stem. The tips cross and he falls, actually quite slowly. At this point his bindings should release *if properly adjusted*, but they may not. (This is the toughest problem for the bindings designers to solve: the slow, twisting fall that produces low torque.) In that case, the position of the skier is such that the weight of the body holds the foot firmly on the snow while the body continues to rotate above the leg—to such an extent that either a sprain or a fracture is entirely possible. Of course, the possibility of such an accident is compounded if the skier is on a slope beyond his real capability.

There are many ways to reduce the injury potential of this typical situation.

• Good bindings, properly adjusted, will release before the twist turns into a sprain or fracture.

• Ski-school training, with emphasis on learning to fall, is excellent insurance.

• Good physical condition will protect muscles and tendons, even though the fall is a bad one.

Ski patrol in action at Aspen, Colorado.

But above all, what the skier needs in the beginning stages is patience. As the beginner makes the transition to intermediate, he should be carefully on guard against seeking the thrills of more difficult skiing. During this stage the emphasis must be on correct execution. (Of course, it never really happens that way.)

Short of senseless schussbooming, speed in itself is not the problem; judgment concerning it is. A slope is not like a tilted billiard table but consists of an infinite variety of angles, pitches, bumps, rolls, side hills, and snow conditions. Light, wind, snow, and other skiers are responsible for constant change—even from run to run. The skier who takes a trail for granted, or runs it without being constantly alert, is asking for trouble.

One of the best ways to avoid trouble is to keep looking far ahead. In looking at a slope the skier should think in terms of two or three turns beyond the one he is making. This prevents him from being surprised. He can adjust his speed, change his direction or come to a stop in the event of a hazard.

The experienced skier's difficulties usually begin when either snow conditions or some error in execution separate the skis. The proper procedure is to unweight the straying ski and replace it in its parallel position. In a turn the situation is somewhat different: If the straying ski is the outside ski, it means you haven't enough weight on it and that you are at least partially riding the inside ski. The answer to this problem is to increase the weight on the turning ski.

The caught edge is the major cause of twisting falls, the type that produce injuries. The problem is failure to maintain proper edge control. But what can be done about it once an edge has caught? Generally speaking, not much—because it happens too fast. But if your body twist can be untwisted, if you can turn back toward the ski tips, the chances of a twisting fall and resulting damage are minimal.

Falls are not the only source of injuries. Poles have a way of snagging in brush or branches when skiing near trees. A wrenched and dislocated shoulder can result unless the skier takes precaution by taking the pole straps off his wrist. People find an amazing number of ways to jab themselves and others with poles, though the new breakaway grips are an excellent solution. Heel units have a disconcerting way of mashing thumbs, and edges can cut fingers and slash through expensive stretch pants and into shins, though brakes reduce this problem. And there is always the possibility of frostbite, just one of the many reasons why you should never ski alone. Your companion can always spot the oncome of frostbite by the grayish white appearance of the affected area, usually the tip of the nose or the ears.

COURTESY

General courtesy, which strongly implies awareness of others, not only promotes ski safety but also enjoyment of the sport by yourself and others. There are some helpful rules to follow:

• Join the end of the lift line and keep your place. It's not only polite and orderly, but it also prevents needless damage to equipment and possible cuts and bruises as a result of the confusion.

   • Avoid stepping on the back of the skis of the skier in front of you as you would avoid stepping on his feet. You may not hurt him physically, but you won't do his skis any good.

   • If you are alone in a busy line, double up with someone early by yelling "single." A last-minute rush to join a single can lead to accidents. When sharing a chair with a safety bar that lowers, make sure that you each know when the bar is coming down, or mashed fingers may result. On a T-bar, don't ride with someone a great deal taller or shorter than you.

   • Treat lifts with respect. Horsing around on a lift may cause the cable to derail, endangering you and the other riders. On T-bars and platterpulls, keep your skis in the tracks and avoid the temptation to run some kind of uphill slalom. On rope tows, release the rope gradually so as not to jerk it when getting off at the top.

EASIEST

Green means easiest slopes or trails at an area.

MORE DIFFICULT

Blue means more difficult.

MOST DIFFICULT

Black means most difficult.

CAUTION

This red-and-black sign means trail is closed to all skiers except authorized area personnel.

This red-and-yellow sign tells skiers to exercise extreme caution in handling a section of trail.

CLOSED

• Move out of the unloading area swiftly when getting off a lift. Contain yourself and look at the view, adjust bindings and goggles, at a safe distance.

• Ski where you belong and in control. If you are trying something more difficult than anything you've done so far, wait until the coast is clear and keep checking that it is. There is nothing more dangerous than the basher, who, unable to turn or stop, knocks down skiers like bowling pins.

• Ski defensively. The skier in front of you has the right of way since he hasn't got eyes in the back of his head. Call out if you are passing on the right ("On your right") or on the left.

• If you stop on the way down, do so only at the side of the hill where you will be out of the way of other skiers. If, for some reason, you have to walk down, walk at the extreme edge of the trail.

• Do not jump or turn full tilt into blind areas or blind corners. Use someone as a spotter if you plan to jump. Check your speed when entering a new trail.

• Fill your sitzmark, the hole you make when you fall in softer snow. A hole is like a bear trap to the skier that follows.

• Respect flags and trail markers put up by the area, its ski school, and its patrol (see illustrations). They are there to tell you something. Learn the meaning of degree-of-difficulty trail markers and their limitations. They vary widely from area to area.

• Put your skis and poles in the racks provided for them instead of leaning them against the nearest building where others can trip on them and gash themselves if they fall. Be really safe and lock them.

• Be generally considerate, particularly of skiers not as adept as you. Many trails for better skiers terminate on the beginner's slope. Make allowances for this. Stop for those who seem to be in trouble. Be helpful. You may make a friend.

THE SKI PATROL/INJURIES

Despite having taken all the necessary precautions, there may come a time when either you or one of your companions is injured sufficiently to require the help of the ski patrol. If you have been wondering what those folks with rust-colored parkas and crosses on their backs do other than ski and go to the head of the lift line, you are about to find out.

The members of the National Ski Patrol System are rightly called the "Good Samaritans of the Slopes." Actually, they do a great deal more than rescue the fallen. They also do their bit in accident prevention—filling holes, smoothing out ruts, flagging soft or bare spots—which is a never-ending chore at busy ski areas.

Most members of the ski patrol are volunteers, although larger areas also employ crews of professionals so that there is always someone at the area who is competent to deal with injuries. Whether volunteer or professional, he or she goes through a rigorous training course and then must keep current with regular brush-up courses. They have earned their right to wear parkas. Unless you are a doctor, it is best to leave injuries to them.

In the event of injury to a companion or someone you come upon, avoid panic at all costs. With the exception of avalanches, ski injuries are usually not fatal providing you keep your head.

By all means summon help, but before you rush off, do several things first.

1. Determine the damage without moving the skier.
2. If it can be done without discomfort, take off the skier's skis. Stick the skis, crossed fashion, into the snow about twenty feet above the injured skier to warn others of the accident.
3. Keep the injured party as warm as possible to minimize the effects of shock.
4. Stay with him if at all possible, or get someone else to stay with him while you summon help. If you are asked to summon help, don't let the injured skier down. In either event, make certain of the location so that you can direct the patrol as precisely as possible. If you are not sure, fix a prominent landmark and stay alert for location indicators.
5. Get back to the injured party as quickly as possible. For one reason or another, it may take a little while for the patrol to arrive.

After the patrol arrives, let them do their job without any assistance, unless it is specifically requested. If it is a friend, you will want to know where they are taking him and where his equipment will be stored.

AVALANCHES

A much more serious matter than trail injuries, because of the fatal danger, are avalanches. Any reasonably steep slope can avalanche if conditions are right, though some are more subject to avalanches than others. The problem of

Avalanche "busting," in this case by means of a 75mm shell, is resorted to when a huge accumulation of snow on a hilltop presents a serious hazard to skiers in the immediate area.

avalanches need not be of overwhelming concern within a ski area provided that you observe avalanche precautions and warning signs.

However, if you are skiing in the West and Europe, it is the better part of valor to approach any untracked slope with caution. There are hundreds of avalanches in these regions every season. Those that bring death do so because of factors not easily predicted even by experienced mountaineers.

There are two principal types of avalanche: loose snow and slab. Loose snow has little internal cohesion and tends to move as a formless mass, the slide growing in size as it descends. Slab avalanches, on the other hand, are characterized by internal cohesion—a large area of hard snow begins to slide at once from a well-defined fracture line across the slope. Frequently caused by wind drifting, which often gives the snow a dull, chalky color, the slab avalanche constitutes a great winter slide hazard because of its unpredictability.

Elaborate avalanche-prevention techniques are common at major ski resorts. Artillery mortars and explosives are often used deliberately to trigger avalanches, clearing and subsequently making the terrain safe for skiers.

Steep gullies and open, treeless slopes are natural avalanche paths; ridges, outcrops, and terraces are natural barriers. Other things being equal, a convex-shaped slope is more dangerous than a concave profile. But both can avalanche.

Avalanche danger is high during and after heavy winter storms. It usually declines as snow settles and stabilizes. But cold weather does not readily allow stabilization.

Underlying snow conditions have an important bearing on avalanche danger. Deep snow smooths out irregularities and promotes sliding. Smooth surfaces, such as rain or sun crust, also make good sliding bases. Rough, firm snow, on the other hand, offers a good anchorage for subsequent layers. Wet-snow avalanches occur when rain or melting water lubricates and weakens snow layers that already are somewhat unstable.

When Avalanche Conditions Exist

Never travel alone.

Pick the route carefully. The safest route is along the top by way of the ridge. The next safest route is along the valley floor *under* the avalanche. Most avalanches occur on slopes of 30 to 45 degrees.

Beware of lee areas, especially convex profiles beneath a cornice.

Never expose more than one member of the party at a time to avalanche danger. The other members should watch the person crossing so they can plot his probable course in case a slide is started.

Don't assume a slope is safe just because the first few crossed safely.

Don't camp or stop under an avalanche path. Prolonged exposure is always risky.

If you must cross an avalanche slope, remove wrist loops of your ski poles. Unhitch Arlberg or safety straps from your skis so you won't be tied to them in a slide.

Close up your clothing, don hat and mittens, and raise your parka hood. If buried in the snow, your chances of survival are much better if snow doesn't get inside your clothes to cause chill.

Wear a brightly colored avalanche cord if one is available. Tie one end to your belt and let it trail out behind you. If you bring down a slide, the cord has a good chance of floating to the surface.

If You Are Caught in an Avalanche

Call out so other members of your party can observe your course in case you are buried.

Discard skis, poles, rucksack.

Try to stay on the surface by swimming. Attempt to work to one side of the moving snow. In a large or fast-moving avalanche, such efforts will probably be of little avail, but they may save your life in a smaller one.

If swimming doesn't help, cover your face with your hands. This will keep snow out of your nose and mouth, and you will have a chance to clear a breathing space if you are buried. Avalanche snow often becomes very hard as soon as it stops moving, and your arms may be pinned when the snow halts.

If you are buried, try to avoid panic. Many avalanche victims have been recovered dead, apparently uninjured and after only a few minutes of burial. The only explanation doctors can offer is that they were actually frightened to death.

In soft snow you may be able to dig yourself out or at least make room to breathe. Try to keep your sense of direction; actually you might be digging *down* under the impression that it's the way out.

What to Do If Your Companions Are Caught

Don't panic. The lives of your buried companions may depend on what you do in the next hour. Check for further slide danger. Pick a safe escape route in case of a retreat.

Mark the point on the avalanche path where the victim was last seen as he was carried down by the snow. This will narrow the area of search.

Search quickly. If there are only two or three survivors, they must make a quick but careful search of the avalanche before going for help. One man should then be left at the accident scene to continue the search and guide the rescue party. The chances of a buried victim being recovered alive diminish rapidly after two hours.

Search the surface *below* the last seen point for evidence of the victim or clues to his location. Mark the location of any pieces of his equipment you find—these may provide additional indicators of the path taken by the flowing snow.

Begin probing. If the initial search fails, probe with the heel of your ski, an inverted ski pole, or a collapsible probe *below* the last-seen point. Trees, ledges, benches, or other terrain features that have caught the snow are likely places.

Send for help. If there are several survivors, send only two. The remaining survivors can search for the victim in the meantime.

If you must go for help, travel carefully, avoiding further avalanche or injuries from skiing too fast.

The victim's chance of survival depends on your getting through. Mark your route, especially if fresh snow is falling, so you can find your way back. Try to avoid complete exhaustion. The rescue party normally will expect you to guide them back to the accident scene.

If the victim is found, apply first-aid treatment immediately for suffocation and shock. Free nose and mouth of snow, and administer mouth-to-mouth artificial respiration if necessary. Clean snow from inside clothing, and place the victim in a sleeping bag with head downhill.

It cannot be overstressed that safety in skiing is not a matter of timidity but calm common sense. The skier who is oblivious to danger isn't courageous; he is stupid.

To the roar of the happy Aspen crowd, Phil and Steve Mahre, first and third in the 1981 Subaru World Cup Giant Slalom, announce to the world that American ski racers have arrived. In 1982, they finished first and third in the overall World Cup.

PART FIVE

SKI COMPETITION

The U.S. Women's Ski Team, 1982 Nations Cup winners, at Waterville Valley in March 1982 for the World Cup races. They are standing in front of a snow sculpture of the World Cup. Left to right: *Abbi Fisher, Christin Cooper, Tamara McKinney, Heidi Preuss, Cindy Nelson, and Karen Lancaster.* Not shown: *Holly Flanders.*

Introduction

Late in January of 1982, I had an opportunity in St. Anton to see just how well the United States has done in major-league, World Cup ski racing during the past two years. I happened to be in Austria for a travel-related article at the same time the U.S. Ski Team was training for the upcoming World Championships (a biennial one-week orgy akin to the Olympics, as distinct from the season-long Cup competition), and whenever I wore my SKI Magazine uniform, thus identifying myself as an American, foreigners of all types congratulated me on behalf of our team. Even more impressive was the fact that the only significant poster hanging in the Arlberg Tourist Office window in St. Anton featured Phil Mahre, who'd just won the overall Cup title for the second straight year. The Austrians were giving Phil top billing even over their own Franz Klammer, the great 1976 Olympic downhiller who, after a few seasons of decline, was making one of the most incredible comebacks not only in the history of skiing but, frankly, of all sports—akin, say, to Muhammad Ali winning back the heavyweight title in 1985.

Nor was the admiration just for Phil and twin brother Steve, the other American male who scored against the Europeans. Equally praised was the U.S. Women's Team, in which a far larger number of competitors were proving able to win events against Europe's best in all three disciplines: downhill (DH), slalom (SL), and giant slalom (GS): Tamara McKinney, 1981 World Cup winner in GS, returning to form after an early-season injury; Cindy

341

Nelson, the perennial three-discipline racer who refuses to age; Chris Cooper and Holly Flanders, relative newcomers showing real power in SL/GS and DH respectively; and young depth behind them like Heidi Preuss, who'd stunned everyone at the Olympics of 1980. A few Europeans admitted that the U.S. Women's Team is probably no more than a year away from becoming the best in the world, which actually proved pessimistic. The U.S. women won the Nations Cup that season, albeit not by much.

But not the men. For the women, in fact, the emergence is more a reemergence: Many times in the long history of international ski racing the Americans have been among the best of the women's teams, stretching back into the prewar period and peaking in the mid- to late 1960s under then-Coach Bob Beattie with such stars as the Cochran sisters, Kiki Cutter, and the irrepressible Susie Chaffee (known more recently as "Susie Chapstick"). But the American Men's Team has never been a powerhouse, despite occasional flashes, in the postwar era, by such as Buddy Werner, Billy Kidd, Spider Sabich, Tom Corcoran, Jimmie Heuga, and Tyler Palmer. Don't misunderstand, none of them, not even the durable and perennial Kidd or the legendary Werner, ever really approached the international number one status of Phil Mahre, despite Billy's combined Gold Medal at the World Championships in 1970, but individually they were respected. Respectable. But the Men's Team has always lacked depth, consistency of performance, and a true presence. It's worse than ever, in fact: Today, the Men's Team is Phil Mahre and Steve Mahre, who finished fourth in the Cup in 1981 and third in 1982, and if you were to examine it closely the Men's Team really doesn't even include them because they tend to go their own way, do their own thing, train independently (often jointly with Sweden's renowned Ingemar Stenmark, for the latter half of the seventies the world's best racer), and coach each other. For some inane reason their offers to help coach some of the younger American men have been spurned.

So the United States has the best racer in the world, another man in the top three, and a group of women who have the respect of the world of ski racing. All things considered, for a racing program that was virtually bankrupt as recently as the 1980 Olympics at Lake Placid, New York—only one silver medal (Phil Mahre's) for a $2-million investment in the team that year, which makes Bunker Hunt's commodities play seem successful by comparison—the recovery is impressive.

The situation in Canada is, on its face, even stranger. Aside from the Soviet Union, the United States is, after all, the largest nation involved in alpine ski racing (and the Russians are rather an Ivan-come-lately to downhill despite impressive performances for two decades in cross-country), and therefore it should be a real power—more, in fact, than it usually is. But Canada is far smaller (albeit larger than Austria, Sweden, and Switzerland), and therefore its perennial inability to produce a powerful team isn't surprising. As with the United States, a few women have shown occasional flashes of brilliance, but, until recently, the men have failed to distinguish themselves.

What has happened recently, however, is interesting. A few years ago the Canadians essentially abandoned their international effort in SL and GS (aside from minor-league competition on the North American Trophy Series, known as the Nor-Am circuit, against U.S. skiers) and focused totally on DH. The result has been nothing short of amazing: Steve Podborski and Ken Read, leaders of the "Kamikazes," are the equal of Franz Klammer, Switzerland's Peter Mueller, and Austria's Heini Weirather. Canada also took a major step forward in the Equality of the Sexes when Gerry Sorensen won a distaff World Cup DH early in 1982.

When the powder had finally settled on the 1981–82 season, Phil Mahre had won four World Cup titles: Overall, Combined, SL, and GS. Podborski won the World Cup DH title for a clean sweep for North American men. U.S. women won the Nations Cup, with four in the top seed overall. Flanders finished second in DH, Cooper third in SL, McKinney fourth in GS, and Nelson fourth in Combined. Steve Mahre finished third in SL and won a gold in GS at the World Championships, at which Cooper won two silvers and a bronze.

So the North Americans are a force to reckon with on the World Cup circuit—all the more so since the overwhelming majority of the races are held in Europe, which puts the Western Hemisphere's athletes at a wicked disadvantage. Just as important, the Mahres, Podborski, and Read are among the world's most feared and respected competitors, and the American women may be on their way to becoming the best in history. Switzerland and Austria probably have too much depth in both sexes to yield the overall Nation's Cup to the United States until the American men start listening to Phil and Steve, but there is no longer any question: North American ski racers are very, very good. As my Austrian hosts kept telling me.

Yet what makes this amazing is that the 1970s were a decade of enduring disappointment for American ski racers on the international circuit, until Phil Mahre simply became the best ski racer not only in American history but on the entire World Cup circuit. By now everyone reading this should know the Phil Mahre Story, which often seems to have been written by John R. Tunis:

Phil Mahre carves a deep turn on his way to winning the 1981 World Cup.

a shattering fracture of the ankle at the pre-Olympics at Lake Placid in 1979, prematurely ending his first serious thrust for the overall individual World Cup title; a flashing recovery on the same course during the Olympics in 1980 to win a silver medal, yielding only to his long-time super-Swede nemesis, Ingemar Stenmark; a come-from-behind last-race-of-the-season explosion to wrest the overall World Cup title from Stenmark in 1981, while brother Steve finished fourth; and then blowing everyone away, including Stenmark, right from the opening gun in 1982, virtually locking the Cup win before Christmas vacation. Steve was one of only two people to beat him early that season. And Stenmark, who for three years had played Bjorn Borg to Phil's Jimmy Connors, began the long slide toward ultimate retirement. Phil Mahre, it appears, is about to join such luminaries as Jean-Claude Killy, Karl Schranz, Gustavo Thoeni, and Stenmark among what sportswriters call "all-time greats," and he has already relegated such American stars as Kidd, Sabich, Buddy Werner, and possibly even Dick Durrance to the second level.

The problem with the men's team remains perplexing. Throughout the seventies, it's true, many abandoned the team in favor of joining Bob Beattie's professional racing circuit—often before they reached their peaks. This drain started with Kidd after he won the combined Gold medal at Val Gardena, Italy, in 1970 (that same year he became the first pro champion as well); continued with Sabich the following year (he won the next two pro titles); Hank Kashiwa soon after the 1972 Olympics (he was pro champ in 1975), along with the Palmer brothers (Tyler gave Killy fits during his exciting "comeback" year of 1973); and ended, more recently, with such as Lonnie Vanatta, Richie Woodworth, and Cary Adgate. What was perplexing wasn't the decision to quit the team—quick money, after all, has its lure—but rather the fact that these racers, often barely also-rans on the World Cup circuit, were able to compete equally against Europe's best on the pro tour.

This pattern—the failure of talented skiers to stay with or score on the World Cup—doesn't seem to have changed, even though the pro circuit died in one moment of blinding arrogance in California in 1981, discussed later. Top young men, such as Pete Patterson, who during and immediately after his fifth-place finish in the 1980 Olympics looked like the Great U.S. Hope in downhill, continued to "retire" from the team that summer and fall, even without the lure of the big bucks.

What makes resolution of this situation increasingly important is the resurgence of interest in the early 1980s in racing at the junior levels. Whether this is an enduring trend or simply a short-term reaction to Phil Mahre's brilliance—much like the quick swell of interest in chess in America after

Bobby Fischer won the world title—obviously remains to be seen (you have to be more cautious in books than in magazine articles), but either way many junior coaches worry about what will happen to the best of their charges.

This has led to open enmity between the official U.S. Ski Team hierarchy of coaches and the junior coaches, who tend to owe their allegiance strictly to the ski areas or clubs that employ them. Some junior coaches have all but ruled the ski team talent scouts off their hills and away from their young racers, whom they literally hide, while such authorities as Warren Witherell have become, in his words, "the loyal opposition, although the team omits the 'loyal.' "

As Witherell, who runs the famed Burke Mountain (Vermont) Academy, and the top area junior coaches see it, the biggest problem the young racers in America face is "burn-out": They get picked for the team's "ladder"—a progressively narrowing pyramid that climaxes with selection to the World Cup team—while they are far too young and can't break into it if they start racing or peak at an older age. (The marvelous paradox is that the Mahres began racing at the rather elderly age of twelve and might not qualify for that ladder today!)

One reason Witherell thinks this hasn't seemed to affect the Women's Team as profoundly is that girls reach puberty earlier. Another is that fewer nine- and ten-year-old girls than boys sign up for the junior racing programs. A third is that fewer girls *race*, period, and thus a later-blooming star has a better chance of being seen.

A possible beneficiary of this evolving pattern—more young racers, angry junior coaches, and an extremely youth-oriented U.S. talent-hunting staff—could be the reemergence of collegiate ski racing as an alternate route to selection for the U.S. Ski Team squad that competes on the World Cup circuit.

But overall, as is so often the case, the situation has remained unchanged in international racing: The U.S. women are a recognized powerhouse, as they've been seemingly forever, and the U.S. men are a third-rate force relying on outstanding performances from a few talented athletes. Perennially, the U.S. team has been somewhere between third and sixth in the Nations Cup (see chart on pages 364–65), and that pattern didn't change in 1981 or 1982. We were just a closer third.

One of the saddest stories of the past decade in skiing concerned freestyle, or hotdogging as it was called initially. The sport exploded as quickly as a triple-reverse gainer and ended almost as suddenly with a fiscal head plant: The Short Happy Life of Freestyle.

Freestyle/hotdogging, as it evolved at the end of the sixties, was a fun happening, luring some of the far-out snowflakes off the cornices and headwalls (and occasionally out of the opium dens) to do their Moebius Flips for real bread. It attracted gymnasts and acrobats and ice-skaters and kids with the fastest knees in the universe and somehow, in barely a twinkle, a trio of highly entertaining "disciplines"—if something this melange evolved can be so described—involving ballet (figure skating on skis), moguls (just as it reads) and aerials (jumps and flips). Around it grew a new skiing subculture and jargon and, inevitably, a new class of hero: Airborne Eddie Ferguson and Wayne Wong and Genia Fuller and the Post twins, very few of whom even knew (or cared) that such "greats" as Stein Eriksen and Tom Leroy had predated their best moves by a decade. Everything was young and hip and new and like-wow-do-it/go-for-it—and lord how the money rolled in. For a short time.

Perhaps its own inception demanded extinction; racing, after all, is a long-established discipline with but one criterion: You win if you run through the gates faster than anyone else. But how do you decide "best" in an inherently undisciplined "discipline"? When the only criterion is to do something new/exciting/dynamic/unlike-anything-that-went-before? A score of "right-on" is hard to codify and quantify, but if the purses (growing rapidly) were to be divided along the Traditional American lines of win/place/show/also-ran ... how? Some method of scoring the unscorable had to be evolved, and when this happened the unbridled spontaneity that was hotdogging/freestyle's great strength vanished. Inevitably, the "rules" that had evolved over the eons in figure skating and platform diving were adapted to the uniqueness of snow-on-an-inclined plane, because that was the only route the organizers could find. And the joy began to wane.

Even more lethal to the sport's future were the rapidly emerging/merging/vanishing groups of competing organizers. Even more than the women's racing circuit, the freestylers lacked a scrambling, tough professional to run the show. The minor schisms and problems that Beattie smoothed over among the men racers erupted into full-fledged guerrilla warfare among the freestylers; sponsors and networks never knew with whom to negotiate (or that the "executive director" could produce the show), and they finally just gave up. Without the money, the firm schedule, the ability to establish a "tradition"—as Steamboat and Hunter, for instance, did with Beattie's circuit —the joyous Freestyle Carnivals at Snowbird and Waterville Valley and Heavenly Valley and Stowe faded. Finally, like spectators as a great fire is brought to its end, the wild-bunch crowds filtered away. Exit, crying.

Will freestyle reappear from its own ashes? Perhaps. We may hope. It never disappeared—merely went "underground"—on the amateur circuit, where a new generation of teenagers is comfortable with the skatinglike discipline of ballet, the prohibitions against the more deadly aerials, and the efforts to define a "best" way to mash moguls. Maybe all that freestyle needed—needs—is time to digest the disasters of the past and reemerge as a true American innovation in the world of skiing, possibly to be included on the schedule of the 1984 and 1988 Winter Olympics. Or possibly to grow as a professional touring show, as Alan Schoenberger has put together.

But even if it does, it will never be what it was: a pure and joyous expression of the freedom and wildness of blowing out on a snow-covered mountain. Many of its new skills have filtered into ski-school classes at the advanced and expert levels—mostly from ballet and mogul maneuvers—to improve "edge awareness"; but never again will we see the incredibly spontaneous expression of the late sixties and early seventies in such great movies as *Ski the Outer Limits* and *Moebius Flip*.

Or will we?

31

The Fun of Racing

Have you ever been skiing on top of a hill and suggested to a friend that you race to the bottom? And when it was all over, there was probably a lot of good-natured joshing and debate why you won or lost—the equipment you were using, the quality of your technique, and your choice of line down the mountain. It was all great fun, and, surprisingly, the next time you skied, you found yourself skiing just a bit better.

Simply because you have raced a friend down the mountain, you hardly consider yourself a competitor. Yet, essentially, that is what you are. Virtually every racer, no matter how impressive his or her reputation, starts this same way. If you enjoy competition, skiing can provide it, no matter how seriously you want to take it or how old you are.

When racing first started before the turn of the century, it was very similar to what you and your friend were doing. A group of competitors got together on top of the mountain, and at a signal all took off at once and headed for the designated finish line. There were no prepared tracks, no flags to mark the course, and, for all practical purposes, no rules. The first man to arrive was the winner. These mass starts were known as *geschmozzle* starts because of the mixups after the starting signals. This kind of racing was colorful, exciting, but, as speeds increased, dangerous. To decrease the danger, racers were started individually and each racer's run was timed. This is the method for competition today. There are a few competitions in which more than one racer starts at a time. One of the most exciting is a dual slalom in which two racers descend parallel courses. Another is the cross-country relay where the first runners of each team start together, leading to some interesting jockeying where the track narrows.

The original races were pure tests of speed over open alpine terrain. It was very daredevilish (the British were remarkably good at it), but it did little for skiing skill as such. To emphasize the necessity for skill and judgment in maneuvering, Sir Arnold Lunn invented slalom competition, which was originally supposed to simulate skiing through the woods and around obstacles. Sir Arnold utilized the two-pole gate, a series of which were set in various combinations on a hill. Skiing around poles was not new in itself, but the two-pole gates were a distinct innovation since they could be set in such a way as to trap the skier who did not use sound judgment.

As downhills became faster, they too became more closely controlled. Today, while still a test of speed, they no longer offer an option of course down the mountain. The course is preselected and carefully prepared, and where speed may become excessive control gates are placed in such a way as

A geschmozzle *race, 1935. The simultaneous start of racers down the mountain was a popular form of competition in the thirties, but it led to many high-speed collisions.*

to slow the racer down. Furthermore, because of the speeds possible in downhill, the courses no longer plunge down what is necessarily the steepest part of the mountain. Rather, the emphasis is on challenging terrain with such problems as bumps, rolls, sudden drop-offs, and accuracy of line. No matter what the levels of competition, downhill is not a sport for the faint of heart.

Giant slalom was originally developed just before World War II as a compromise event between downhill and slalom. Since that time, however, it has gained a distinct character of its own. Where downhill follows the fall line as closely as is practical within the limits of safety, and where slalom puts the emphasis on turning, giant slalom is essentially a test of traversing at high speed. The turn that follows the traverse should put the racer in such a position that he can traverse at high speed to the next gate. Although there are gates in giant slalom, they are not put together in combinations. Thus, at lower levels of competition, giant slaloms are the easiest to set and the easiest to run. Only as the competitive level rises does the event require special skills.

For many years now, the most common and enjoyable form of racing for recreational skiers has been the area standard race. Generally, this is an open-gated giant slalom course usually set on a fairly gradual hill that a good intermediate skier can handle without difficulty or fear. The idea is to go down the course in a given time to win a gold, silver, or bronze medal. Since snow conditions vary from day to day, making speed a variable, the time for the day is set by a pacesetter, usually a racer attached to the area's ski school. He runs down the course first and sets the time or standard for the day.

While standard races have been prevalent at ski areas in North America and Europe since the 1930s, it is only in recent years that the results of races at different ski areas have been made comparable. The idea of a race with national standards of ability got its start in a limited way in France with the Chamois races. But for a nation whose skiing origins trace back to the downhill racers of the 1860s in the gold fields of California (and a decade later in the Rockies), American recreational skiing during the 1950s and 1960s boom proved to be surprisingly noncompetitive—aside, that is, from the inherent battle between man and mountain. For the most part, the skier who created the current "industry" showed little interest in "running bamboo" —challenging a race course—until suddenly, as the 1970s ran their course, that began to change.

Middle-aged skiers rediscovered the joys of racing.

THE GREAT NASTAR/EQUITABLE BOOM

The initial thrust into this movement dates back to the late 1960s when SKI Magazine's editor, John Fry, and the U.S. Ski Team's soon-to-be-departing coach, Bob Beattie, put together a program called NASTAR (NAtional STAndard Race). The concept was essentially simple: If a system could be designed properly, a racer at Mount Snow, for instance, could compete directly with a racer at Vail. Initially, the execution proved more difficult. How can you be sure that the courses are sufficiently the same, or that snow conditions don't change it too much, or that philosophies at different resorts aren't too disparate? In time, this problem was solved via a complex system of regional and national pace-setting trials: Each area designates one or two employees who first race against each other to set a pecking order (*handicap*) and then forerun each race at their areas to set the base time (*par*), which, when computed against their national handicap, tells you what your actual time down the course means against that of the best racer in the country (*zero handicap*). Actually, it's simpler than it sounds, and while it does assume a consistency of performance by each forerunner that probably doesn't happen, by and large it works.

It works so well, in fact, that currently more than 100 of the nation's ski

---

TIPS FOR SETTING SLALOM

1. Don't set gates too tight. 12–15 feet for open gates, 10–15 feet for closed gates is sufficient.
2. Set gates to maintain smooth, flowing run. Don't set sharp corners that will break rhythm.
3. Allow natural checkpoints or gate combinations to hold down speed.
4. Utilize terrain to require variation in technique and permit alternate lines of approach to gates.
5. Set gates to test total technique, keeping in mind the skier's ability. Slalom is a test of ability, not endurance.

TIPS FOR RUNNING SLALOM

1. Strive for precision, not speed, at first.
2. Climb the course from the finish up to the start. Memorize the tricky sections and the sequence in which they come.
4. Try to brush the inside pole of the gate with your thigh and knee, not your shoulder.
5. Check equipment meticulously before the start. Stay in control. A missed gate means disqualification and no result at all.

OPEN GATE   CLOSED GATE

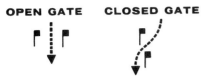

Open and closed gates are twelve-and-one-half feet wide for competitive slalom, can be wider for recreational use.

HAIRPIN   FLUSH

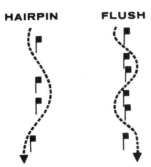

Hairpin consists of two successive closed gates; third gate makes it a flush. Neither should be set so tightly that rhythm is broken, but both should require proper technique.

ELBOW

Elbow is made up of a closed gate followed by an open gate set off to one side. As in all combinations, approach depends on the location and type of the next set of gates.

H- OR SEELOS FLUSH

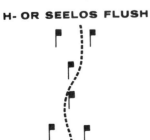

The H- or Seelos flush is a three-gate combination. Slalom gates can always be entered from either direction; choice is with the racer and is determined by position and figures that follow.

A thirty-five-second slalom recommended for intermediates. Note that it is made up of all basic gate combinations, including a trap in the lower section.

A participant in a NASTAR race held at Copper Mountain.

areas are cranking more than 100,000 runs—not racers; that number is harder to glean—every season.

The rewards are gold, silver, and bronze medals, based on how quickly you come down the course compared with that forerunner, computed for his handicap. If you come within a certain percentage of what the nation's fastest racer would have achieved on that course, you get one of those medals. For this privilege you pay anywhere from $2.50 to $5 (areas have some latitude), which will cover one or two runs (ditto).

In addition, to see how well all this really works, some years back NASTAR created national finals in which the top two racers in each region, sex, and age group compete head to head at one area, all expenses paid.

That's the basic system.

Inevitably, Americans being Americans, the system began to take on new dimensions. A few years back a new version emerged called Super-NASTAR (I would have preferred NASTAR II or Son of NASTAR), for which much more difficult courses were set—slalom rather than giant slalom —on far more demanding terrain, and only medal winners from NASTAR could enter. In addition, more recently, the format was expanded to include Family NASTAR, where any tandem—father-son, husband-wife—could compete in a different set of races with still another national finals to look forward to. This, however, was simply a response by NASTAR to the Equitable Family Challenge, which has also gained popularity quickly.

So today, many people are, in fact, running bamboo.

But it goes deeper than that and has some serious implications apart from the little medals: The trend is adding all manner of opportunities for the resorts to make some extra money and for skiers to improve their skills. These are called clinics.

What happened, and it was inevitable, is the skiers racing NASTAR wanted, as we say, to grab an edge, to get a few tips from some people who knew how to get out of the starting gate faster or to pick a better "line" through the gates or to ride a ski properly. Since the ski areas already had someone on the ski-school payroll who by definition knew something about all of this—the pacesetter or forerunner—they said, "Why don't you take a small class out an hour or two before the races, for a few dollars extra, and see what happens? Maybe we'll even let you use the video machinery." Several areas, small as well as big, found this to be a quite profitable venture, and in time the clinics expanded from one or two hours to a three-day workshop and, by the early eighties, into five-day racing-class ski weeks.

Their popularity, though, was something of a surprise to those of us who are paid to know "what's happening." Frankly, my convincing SKI to let me do an article about these new camps for the 1982–83 season was accompanied with fingers, toes, and eyes crossed as I headed to the first-scheduled workshop, two weeks before Christmas 1981 at Waterville Valley. It was run by Steve Lathrop, with help from such other former Ski Team members as Ron Biedermann and Viki Fleckenstein. I hoped that a program so early in the season would draw fifteen to twenty people. It drew more than fifty, a number that held all season long as the tour traveled from resort to resort.

Nor was Lathrop's program unique. Billy Kidd put together an effective workshop at Steamboat Springs, split between learn-to-race and serious-racer classes, while Otto Tschudi cranked into high gear at Winter Park. Mammoth, which had been involved in this concept earlier than most, cranked up its big guns. And across the nation, areas and resorts that had previously reserved racing programs for juniors began to study the possibility of expanding them to include adults as well. Within another few years they'll be as common as stem-christie classes—and a lot more profitable for skier and area operator.

Why? Because the American skier market is maturing. The days of every season seeing millions of new skiers are gone, and the higher the cost of skiing rises the more the industry will see only the hardened veterans, the addicts, and the price-wise remain. Skiing, no matter what the drumbeaters say, has become very expensive to learn and to enter, but it can still be reasonably priced if you know how to beat the costs.

Thus, today's skiers, by dint of that experience, have become quite competent. They know how to ski. They may not be able to tangle tip to tip with Phil Mahre or the Post sisters, but they can sure as hell get down the hill. They can turn both ways with both boards under control. They can vary technique between ice and slush. Their only fear, in fact, is that they might get bored after too many years of competency, especially since—in most cases—traditional ski-school lessons have not caught up with this situation, the grooming has become too good, and the equipment is too easy to master.

Recreational racing provides the next level of challenge: time. To improve time you have to improve skills that are often all too adequate for most mountain-skiing situations, and you have to learn to understand, to feel, how your equipment works best. This, in turn, will improve how you ski the mountain as well as how you run gates. It is, perhaps, that simple.

32

Learning from the Top Racers

What distinguishes the good or the competent racer from the great one? A high level of courage, a powerful determination to win, and a great deal of natural skiing ability, of course. But beyond these, a winning performance at the international level requires the extra effort for that lost foot when it seems a mile, a passion for detail, a highly refined knowledge of all aspects of the sport, sound judgment, and, above all, a frame of mind that former Canadian Coach Dave Jacobs calls "mental buoyancy." The latter is probably the most difficult to achieve. The racer must arrive at the starting gate with a certain amount of tension to enable him to perform at his highest level, but too much or too little will reduce his effectiveness.

Racers are well aware of this tension. They think of ways to "psyche" their opponents, trying to make them feel overconfident or somewhat less than adequate. Psyching is accomplished by gentle persuasion through tone of voice, careful manipulation of equipment, waxing, and clothing, and by behavior on and off the course. One of the classic instances of psyching occurred in 1965 at the Three-Nation Team Meet at Vail. The meet was important, but it had been grossly overbilled as a final demonstration of the United States' arrival as a ski super-power. The Austrians and French, whatever they may have felt about it, treated the meet with utmost casualness, and the overanxious Americans were thoroughly deflated. To demonstrate their casual attitude, the French on the last day turned up with baseball caps

French slalom ace Patrick Russel, the first to use extreme high-backed boots, sits back as he flies through the flags in the 1970 FIS World Championship slalom at Val Gardena, Italy.

turned backward, umpire style, instead of the usual headgear. The Europeans thereupon cleaned up, and the Americans never really recovered for the rest of the season.

You can only psyche an opponent if he is your equal, and to be his equal may take a good deal of work. Ski racing has developed to a point where as many as a dozen racers are within a second of the winner's time. A few hundredths of a second might separate first and second place, although Phil Mahre or Ingemar Stenmark are capable, a few times in a season, of blowing the others away by more than a second.

One would be tempted to describe the winning margin as luck were it not for the fact that certain racers win all season long by just such margins. For example, it was a well-known fact that crouching cuts wind resistance and results in greater speed. But it wasn't until 1960, when the French refined the position and developed exercises to enable the racers to hold it longer, that the differences became noticeable. To the unpracticed eyes, the French downhill racers were not doing anything especially different from the other downhillers. But their early start in developing the so-called egg position at a time when downhill courses were in a state of flux enabled them to dominate downhill for two years. This "domination" averaged about half a second a race.

Racers are constantly looking for such refinements, for ways to cut a few inches off a turn through a gate, to reduce the braking effects of turning, or to get into a faster line. Instructive in this respect is the development of giant slalom. Until the late fifties, giant slalom was approached much like slalom. That is, racers thought of the event as a series of turns. Then came the big change. The Swiss in particular approached GS as a series of traverses linked by turns. They headed straight for the gate, scrambled around it, and headed for the next gate. The turns were rough, but the racers more than made up for lost speed in the traverses. They stepped their turns, stepping uphill to start them, and on completion stepping uphill again to get a steeper line to the next gate. The modern giant slalom turn actually commits what used to be a cardinal sin in skiing, getting on the uphill ski in the final phase of the turn. Instead of finishing on the downhill ski, the racer drives forward and over his uphill ski, which, of course, has the higher line. In this way he saves a split second, which previously was spent on a lower line prior to the step up.

There is no denying that equipment plays a major role in such small but important differences of performance. It isn't merely that skis have become faster through refinements of design but that they have also become easier to control and to turn. Metal and plastic skis give almost instantaneous edge set and edge release along the entire length of the ski. The racer takes advantage of this characteristic—in fact, the turn that finishes on the uphill ski would be impossible without it. (Thus, the *beginning* of modern ski technique.)

Where next? It's hard to say. Currently, the styles evolved by Phil and Steve Mahre and Ingemar Stenmark, as different as they are, result as much from their work with K2 and Elan respectively in designing and refining skis as in their physical dedication and skills: none of them could do what they do using the skis of a decade earlier.

However, one result is clear: As Sigi Grottendorfer comments (see page 306), today's recreational skier can use today's racing skis, while a decade ago he couldn't have *flexed*, much less *turned* a pair. So in that respect the progress has been infinite.

Dick Durrance, one of the first great American racers, skiing at Alta in 1939.

33

Great Races, Great Skiers

Ski competition on an international scale is about as old as skiing itself—that is, skiing as a recognized sport. Almost from its very beginnings, skiing has had international participation, particularly in the alpine events. The young Hannes Schneider, one of the most spectacular competitors of his day, used to cross over into Switzerland regularly to participate is races there. Downhill, of course, was his forte, but he also jumped and raced cross-country. (Schneider later developed Mt. Cranmore, New Hampshire.)

Even before Schneider's time, ski competition had an international flavor. The first ski competitions in central Europe invariably featured Norwegian students as well as local talent. The British, who had no skiing of their own to speak of, were regular competitors in alpine races and, until the mid-1930s were among the world's best. And Scandinavian-born jumpers and cross-country racers were invariably the favorites at American meets in the early days and dominated early downhill races in California's High Sierra in the 1860s.

The oldest premier event in skiing is the Holmenkollen, held in Oslo, Norway. It started in 1892 and had foreign participation as early as 1909, the year before the first meeting of the International Ski Congress. The events at the Holmenkollen have evolved as the sport developed. However, although alpine events were added in 1948, the emphasis is still on jumping and cross-country. In those years when there are no Winter Olympics or FIS

World Championships, the winners at the Holmenkollen are usually considered the best jumpers and cross-country racers in the world.

While ski competition was always international to some extent, the sport did not command major public interest until well after World War I, actually not until 1924 when jumping and cross-country racing were incorporated in the first Winter Olympic Games at Chamonix, France. That was also the year the International Ski Congress decided that skiing needed an international governing body. The result was the Federation Internationale de Ski, which to this day makes the rules for the sport, compiles seeding lists, selects the sites for World Championships, and, through its officials, approves race courses and jumping hills for international competition.

OLYMPIC CHAMPIONS IN ALPINE SKI RACING

MEN	1948	1952	1956	1960
Slalom	1. E. Reinalter—Switz. 2. J. Couttet—Fra. 3. H. Oreiller—Fra.	1. O. Schneider—Aus. 2. S. Eriksen—Nor. 3. G. Berge—Nor.	1. T. Sailer—Aus. 2. C. Igaya—Jap. 3. S. Sollander—Swe.	1. E. Hinterseer—Aus. 2. M. Leitner—Aus. 3. C. Bozon—Fra.
Giant slalom	NOT HELD	1. S. Eriksen—Nor. 2. C. Pravda—Aus. 3. T. Spiess—Aus.	1. T. Sailer—Aus. 2. A. Molterer—Aus. 3. W. Schuster—Aus.	1. R. Staub—Switz. 2. P. Stiegler—Aus. 3. E. Hinterseer—Aus.
Downhill	1. H. Oreiller—Fra. 2. F. Gabl—Aus. 3. K. Molitor—Switz. R. Olinger—Switz.	1. Z. Colo—Ita. 2. O. Schneider—Aus. 3. C. Pravda—Aus.	1. T. Sailer—Aus. 2. R. Fellay—Switz. 3. A. Molterer—Aus.	1. J. Vuarnet—Fra. 2. H.P. Lanig—Ger. 3. G. Périllat—Fra.
WOMEN				
Slalom	1. G. Frazer—U.S. 2. A. Meyer—Switz. 3. E. Mahringer—Aus.	1. A. Mead Lawrence—U.S. 2. O. Reichert—Ger. 3. A. Buchner—Ger.	1. R. Colliard—Switz. 2. R. Schöpf—Aus. 3. E. Sidorova—Sov.	1. A. Heggtveit—Can. 2. B. Snite—U.S. 3. B. Henneberger—Ger.
Giant slalom	NOT HELD	1. A. Mead Lawrence—U.S. 2. D. Rom—Aus. 3. A. Buchner—Ger.	1. O. Reichert—Ger. 2. J. Frandl—Aus. 3. D. Hochleitner—Aus.	1. Y. Ruegg—Switz. 2. P. Pitou—U.S. 3. C. Chenal-Minuzzo—Ita.
Downhill	1. H. Schlunegger—Switz. 2. T. Beiser—Aus. 3. R. Hammerer—Aus.	1. T. Beiser-Jochum—Aus. 2. A. Buchner—Ger. 3. G. Minuzzo—Ita.	1. M. Berthod—Switz. 2. F. Dänzer—Switz. 3. L. Wheeler—Can.	1. H. Biebl—Ger. 2. P. Pitou—U.S. 3. T. Hecher—Aus.

The 1936 Winter Olympics at Garmisch-Partenkirchen marked the first time that the alpine events were incorporated in the Olympic games. Franz Pfnur of Munich dominated the combined event that year.

1964	1968	1972	1976	1980
1. P. Stiegler—Aus.	1. J.-C. Killy—Fra.	1. F. F. Ochoa—Spa.	1. P. Gross—Ita.	1. I. Stenmark—Swe.
2. W. Kidd—U.S.	2. H. Huber—Aus.	2. G. Thoeni—Ita.	2. G. Thoeni—Ita.	2. P. Mahre—U.S.
3. J. Heuga—U.S.	3. A. Matt—Aus.	3. R. Thoeni—Ita.	3. W. Frommelt—Licht.	3. J. Luethy—Switz.
1. F. Bonlieu—Fra.	1. J.-C. Killy—Fra.	1. G. Thoeni—Ita.	1. H. Hemmi—Switz.	1. I. Stenmark—Swe.
2. K. Schranz—Aus.	2. W. Favre—Switz.	2. E. Bruggmann—Switz.	2. E. Good—Switz.	2. A. Wenzel—Licht.
3. P. Stiegler—Aus.	3. H. Messner—Aus.	3. W. Nattle—Switz.	3. I. Stenmark—Swe.	3. H. Enn—Aus.
1. Egon Zimmerman—Aus.	1. J.-C. Killy—Fra.	1. B. Russi—Switz.	1. F. Klammer—Aus.	1. L. Stock—Aus.
2. L. Lacroix—Fra.	2. G. Périllat—Fra.	2. R. Collombin—Switz.	2. B. Russi—Switz.	2. P. Wirnsberger—Aus.
3. W. Bartels—Ger.	3. J.-D. Daetwyler—Switz.	3. H. Messner—Switz.	3. H. Plank—Ita.	3. S. Podborski—Can.
1. C. Goitschel—Fra.	1. M. Goitschel—Fra.	1. B. Cochran—U.S.	1. R. Mittermaier—W. Ger.	1. H. Wenzel—Licht.
2. M. Goitschel—Fra.	2. N. Greene—Can.	2. D. Debernard—Fra.	2. C. Giordani—Ita.	2. C. Kinshofer—W. Ger.
3. J. Saubert—U.S.	3. A. Famose—Fra.	3. F. Staurer—Fra.	3. H. Wenzel—Licht.	3. E. Hess—Switz.
1. M. Goitschel—Fra.	1. N. Greene—Can.	1. M.-T. Nadig—Switz.	1. K. Kreimer—Can.	1. H. Wenzel—Licht.
2. C. Goitschel—Fra.	2. A. Famose—Fra.	2. A. Moser-Proell—Aus.	2. R. Mittermaier—W. Ger.	2. I. Epple—W. Ger.
3. J. Saubert—U.S.	3. F. Bochatay—Switz.	3. W. Drexel—Aus.	3. D. Debernand—Fra.	3. P. Pelin—Fra.
1. C. Haas—Aus.	1. O. Pall—Aus.	1. M.-T. Nadig—Switz.	1. R. Mittermaier—W. Ger.	1. A. Moser-Proell—Aus.
2. Edith Zimmerman—Aus.	2. I. Mir—Fra.	2. A. Moser-Proell—Aus.	2. B. Totschniz—Aus.	2. H. Wenzel—Licht.
3. T. Hecher—Aus.	3. C. Haas—Aus.	3. S. Corrock—U.S.	3. C. Nelson—U.S.	3. M. T. Nadig—Switz.

It is indicative of the state of alpine racing in 1924 that the FIS first refused to recognize downhill and the (then infant) slalom. It was not until 1928 that the group tentatively recognized the Ski Club of Great Britain rules for alpine races and not until 1932 that it sanctioned such races officially. As a result, alpine events were not incorporated into the Olympic program until 1936.

Starting in 1925, the FIS organized so-called FIS Races on an annual basis, at first only in jumping and cross-country, and beginning in 1931 for downhill and slalom. Although the winners of these races were called world champions, the title was not officially sanctioned until 1936 when the name of the races was changed to FIS World Championships. Except in the Olympic years of 1924, 1928, and 1932, they were held annually until 1939. Since World War II, World Championships have been held only in even-numbered years.

The Olympics, the most important sports spectacle in the world, bring winners the greatest international renown. And the World Championships, while confined exclusively to skiing, run a close second.

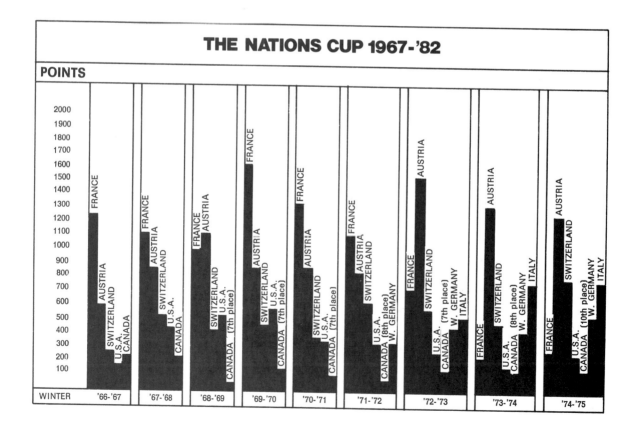

WORLD AND NATIONS CUPS

On a year-to-year basis, however, the results watched most closely by ski racing cognoscenti are the individual performances in the World Cup competition and the team results in the Nations Cup. The World Cup, conceived in 1966 by the French ski journalist Serge Lang, is fashioned after the Grand Prix of car racing. A specified number of races are selected before the winter season starts to count toward the World Cup. A World Cup season lasts about four months, from November to March. It is a genuine international circuit, perhaps the most far-flung in all of sports, spanning the whole northern hemisphere of the world to include Alpine Europe, North America, Scandinavia, Yugoslavia, and Japan. Almost as tough on the racers as the competition is the amount of travel to get from one World Cup event to another. Yet a racer can ill afford to miss a race, particularly the classics like the Arlberg Kandahar, the Hahnenkamm in Kitzbuehel, Austria, the Lauberhorn in Wengen, Switzerland, and the great races in France.

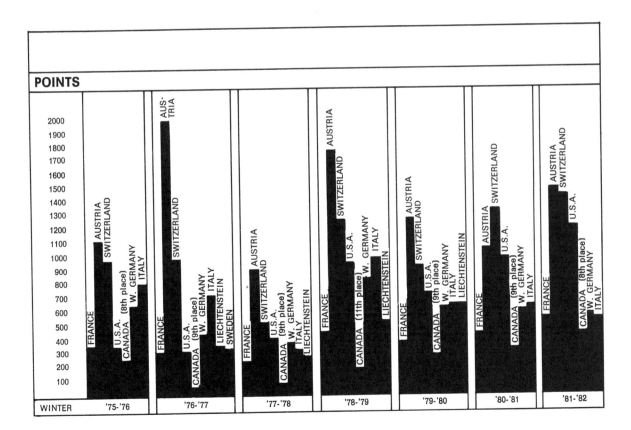

A racer who does well picks up a certain number of points in a World Cup designated race. The emphasis is on winning, with the highest points going for first, second, and third places. As the winter progresses, the racers accumulate points. Sometimes the fight to win the World Cup goes down to the very last race of the season. In 1967 Nancy Greene of Canada won the women's World Cup over Marielle Goitschel of France by a margin of only .007 of a second in the final race, a slalom, held at Jackson Hole, Wyoming. On other occasions, though, such as in 1967 when Jean-Claude Killy won the Cup, he was so far ahead at midseason that victory almost never was in doubt. (When the same situation developed in the late seventies, the FIS changed the scoring rules to minimize Ingemar Stenmark's dominance and make sure one of the Alpine Nations' skiers would have a better chance for the overall title. The chief beneficiary proved to be Phil Mahre of the United States, in 1981, although he won it all outright, and early, in 1982.)

Interesting from another point of view are the annual results of the Nations Cup based on the totals of all the World Cup points won by the racers of each national team. These national results are watched closely by all of the coaching staffs and by the national ski associations and ski manufacturers whose supplier "pools" finance the expensive training, travel, and equipment needed to participate on the World Cup circuit. The Nations Cup results, subdivided into men's and women's team results for each country, are a kind of Dow-Jones index of the rising and falling fortunes of the Alpine ski nations of the world. They indicate whether the money and training lavished on the development of the country's ski racers are paying off. Coaching staffs are bullish when Nations Cup point totals rise over several seasons. Uneasy lies the head of a coach, however, if his team's Nations Cup results start sliding downhill. As might be expected, the French and the Austrians have tended to dominate World and Nations Cup results. But starting in the 1970s, the Swiss and Italian men's teams have presented a distinct threat to the French and Austrian dominance (especially since the French disintegrated following an inane "night of the long knives" in the mid-seventies when virtually all of their first-line skiers and coaches were cut from the team, and have faded in major international competition to a second-class power).

PRO RACING

Professional ski racing, in which prize money is awarded for winning positions, has been predominantly an American affair. In 1969 Bob Beattie quit

Bob Beattie interviewing France's Henri Duvillard.

the U.S. Ski Team and began to turn his energies to developing the International Ski Racers Association, a well-financed pro circuit. Beattie had excellent connections in the television industry, which started to pay off. He found cigarette, automobile, and ski-equipment companies that would put up purses of $10,000 and more for his events (these soared to $50,000 and up before the tour died in 1981). He persuaded ski-equipment companies to finance "factory teams" of racers on his circuit.

But Beattie got his biggest shot in the arm when American racers (rather than European ex-greats with names unfamiliar to U.S. fans) began to win the pro races regularly. In 1970 Billy Kidd of Vermont and the University of Colorado won the FIS World Combined title at Val Gardena and became a hero to the American ski public. Kidd promptly retired from the FIS racing circuit, joined Beattie's pro-racing group, and gave it instant fame by winning the pro title the same year. When Spider Sabich joined the following year (after a classic blowup with Willy Schaeffler, at that time coach of the U.S. Ski Team) and displaced Billy, popularity grew even faster. Spider repeated as champ until, in 1973, the great Jean-Claude Killy came out of retirement and whupped him. (This story is told quite well in a book Killy wrote with Al Greenberg, editor of *Skiing*, called *Comeback*.) Not too many years

Spider Sabich, twice world professional skiing champion.

later, Spider's ensuing decline on the racing circuit ended when singer Claudine Longet accidentally shot and killed him, according to the courts in Aspen.

Killy's tenure as pro champ pretty much ended American skiers' short dominance of world pro skiing. The popular Hank Kashiwa—another good-but-not-great amateur U.S. ski racer—did outscramble Henri Duvillard in 1975 and had a shot at repeating until he blew his knee apart the following season. The competent but colorless Duvillard won the title in 1976 and 1977 and retired; a totally unknown Austrian "amateur," Andre Arnold, won for the next four years, until the tour folded in 1982.

Exactly why the tour folded is hard to explain to laymen. For some reason, the top racers decided that the course was too hazardous, on the last

Hank Kashiwa (above) *was pro champion in 1975, and Henri Duvillard* (right) *reigned in 1976 and 1977.*

Four-time pro champion Andre Arnold of Austria.

day of the season at Mammoth Mountain, California, and refused to race (even though the women's tour, same course on the same day, did race). That itself mightn't have been serious, but they also refused to allow the other racers to run the course, by blocking the starting gate. This, in turn, gave Bob Beattie whatever reason he needed to end his involvement with the circuit, and all efforts to find a "new Beattie" came to nothing. The heart of the pro tour died, although a few races were held in 1981–82.

However, on the theory that need finds a way, a series of smaller pro tours —three regional events sponsored by Peugeot, for smaller purses—evolved during the season, often with more interest, excitement, and involvement by the racers, who suddenly learned the hard way that the world could live without their derring-do a lot more easily than they could live without racing.

Emerging several years after the men's pro circuit was its women's counterpart, copying Beattie's side-by-side, head-to-head format but never quite getting the hang of the sponsorship business—which is what pro racing is all about—until 1980–81 tour director Jill Wing had a real shot at making it big: One of Europe's truly great women racers, Lise-Marie Morerod, agreed to join. Wing had already lured a few top American women off the U.S. team right after Lake Placid—Viki Fleckenstein and Jamie Kurlander in particular—who gave the two reigning women, Jocelyne Perillat and Toril Forland, fits during the 1981 season. The 1982 season moved the women up to the type of parity in skiing they have in tennis, and, in fact, their tour became the only surviving national ski tour in the United States, with the same four battling for first. Forland won.

Another noteworthy development is that pro racers no longer are inferior to the top "amateurs" on the World Cup circuit. The reason is not necessarily that they have become better athletes but rather that they have created a new kind of ski competition with its own rules, strategy, and psychology. Traditional alpine ski competition, as it has developed since the 1930s, is predominantly a race of the individual against the clock. In involves sixty-five-gate slaloms set on icy *steilhangs*, marathon two-run giant slaloms, and tough, two-mile downhills at speeds of up to eighty miles an hour. In contrast, pro competition has become a half-day series of short sprints down the fall line with jumps thrown in for spectator and TV excitement. Two racers start simultaneously out of the starting gate and race down two parallel courses to the bottom. The head-to-head competition entails more psyching of the opponent and the ability to know when to pour it on. Racing is done by elimination. The winner of a heat goes on to meet the winner of another heat, until finally the competition boils down to the last two competitors. And while a run may last only thirty-five seconds, a racer may have taken a dozen runs or more before he can win. The result is that while a pro racer may have no chance of beating an Olympic medal winner in giant slalom against the clock, he may easily trounce the Olympic champion in the pro format of dual slalom, head-to-head racing. As they say, it's a whole different ball game.

GOLDEN NAMES FROM THE PAST

Probably one of the most dramatic competitors of the mid-thirties was Birger Ruud, the most successful of three brothers who were Norway's top ski family for a decade. Birger was not only an outstanding jumper, but to this day he is the only competitor who has won Olympic gold medals in both Nordic and alpine disciplines. This unusual feat took place in the 1936 Olympics, when he won the downhill over highly touted German, French, and Austrian racers and then went on to win the jumping.

The racing hero of the mid-thirties was Anton (Toni) Seelos, who revolutionized slalom technique by skiing parallel and with rotation. Seelos was so far ahead of his time that slalom victories of his by ten seconds or more were not at all unusual. Because of his superiority in this event, the rules were rigged in such a way that he could not (always) also win the combined—in figuring combined, downhill was worth about one-third more than the slalom. Still, Seelos kept winning until he turned pro to coach the French team.

The female counterpart of Seelos was Christel Cranz, who won the World Championship in 1934, 1935, 1937, 1938, and 1939 and the Arlberg-Kandahar in 1937. She also won the alpine combined medal at the 1936 Olympics. No woman racer since has performed as consistently and successfully.

In the last three years before World War II, the great races were dominated by two men—Emile Allais and Rudolf Rominger. It wasn't merely that they took eight World Championship titles between them; they were also important as pioneers of great new alpine techniques. Allais was one of the innovators of the French rotational technique; Rominger was the only skier of

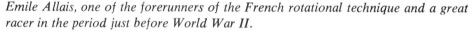

Emile Allais, one of the forerunners of the French rotational technique and a great racer in the period just before World War II.

his day who was complete master of the counterrotational system. Of the two, Allais was the more famous. It took almost twenty years for history to prove that Rominger was an extraordinarily skilled and analytical technician.

In the years before World War II, the United States could not boast of any world champions or Olympic medal winners. Except for the women, who campaigned annually in Europe, American skiers were too isolated from world developments in the sport. Nevertheless, as the decade came to a close, America could boast of a small group of racers who might have been the equal of the Europeans had not the war prevented the U.S. team selected for the 1940 FIS World Championships from going to Europe.

The first great American racers were Dick Durrance, Clarita Heath, and Marion McKean. Durrance, who spent several years in Germany as a boy, had a distinctive style and unlimited courage. He might well have been a medalist in 1936 had he not been penalized five seconds for straddling a gate in the slalom. The manager of the team failed to protest this penalty, and Dick had to settle for eleventh. He was later to distinguish himself by winning the Harriman Cup three times against many of his Olympic rivals.

By 1937 American women had made rapid strides under the managership of Alice Kiaer. Clarita Heath and Sis McKean could be counted on to finish in the top ten in any European race they entered. Miss Heath was fourth in the World Championship downhill, and in the Arlberg-Kandahar Miss McKean was fourth in downhill, fourth in slalom and fourth in the combined. The following year, Miss McKean was sixth in the World Championship downhill and eighth in the combined.

Meanwhile, back home, other talent was coming along. Gordon Wren and Barney McLean were two youngsters of exceptional ability. A Norwegian-born jumper, Torger Tokle, who was subsequently killed while serving in the Tenth Mountain Division in Italy, was breaking every American record in the book. And a pigtailed girl by the name of Gretchen Kunigk, who had never been outside the United States, was beating the European-seasoned American girls with disconcerting regularity.

It can only be guessed what American skiers might have done in the forties had it not been for the war, but there are clues. At the 1948 Olympics, Gretchen Fraser won a gold medal in the special slalom and a silver medal in the combined (an Olympic event no longer held officially, although Phil Mahre won FIS gold at Lake Placid). Gordon Wren, who switched to the Nordic events at the last moment, was second in combined jumping (which carried no medal) and fifth in the special jumping. Considering the state of skiing at the end of the thirties, American racers might have developed to the point where they could have been considered among the best in the world. It is unfortunate that the proposition was never put to a proper test.

The discontinuance of international competition from 1940 until 1947 did not affect the Americans alone. James Couttet, who was a mere seventeen when he won his first World Championship downhill title in 1938, really should have been one of the sport's superstars. Even after the war, he won three A-K's, but the Olympic gold medals that could well have been his escaped him by frustratingly small margins. Karl Molitor was a six-time winner of the Lauberhorn, but by the time international competition resumed he had passed his peak. The war also cut short the racing careers of Willy Walch, Edi Rominger, and many others of great promise.

When ski competition resumed after World War II, it was an entirely different sport. Competition gained in intensity; technique was refined and improved over and over again; coaching and training became major factors; and equipment made extreme high speeds possible. With one or two exceptions, the new heroes of the Olympics, the World Championships, the A-K's, and the Hahnenkamms were products of systems whose only objective was to turn out championship skiers, no matter the cost.

Mrs. Gretchen Fraser of Vancouver, Washington, the first U.S. competitor to win a ski medal in the Winter Olympics.

Gordon Wren, one of the top American racers of the prewar era.

Zeno Colo was probably the last of the old school of racers. He trained, all right, but an occasional cigarette and glass of wine before the start were not out of order. Colo defied almost every racing convention. At all times he enjoyed himself, which didn't prevent him from winning the 1950 downhill and giant slalom World Championship titles in Aspen and from taking the A-K in 1949 and 1951 from more dedicated competitors. There was no mistaking when Colo was in town for a race.

Witnesses to the 1950 World Championships were aware that the old order was changing and that soon a new generation of racers would take over. The harbingers of this change were Christian Pravda and Othmar Schneider of Austria and Stein Eriksen of Norway. Of the three, Eriksen was by far the most dramatic. His technique, while not as polished then as today, had certain distinctive characteristics obvious to the galleries. Eriksen did not disappoint them. In the 1952 Olympics he won the giant slalom, and at the 1954 FIS he took the slalom, giant slalom, and combined. If ever a racer was made to heroic proportions, Eriksen was it. Blond haired, blue eyed and relatively tall for a racer, he is one of the few competitors who has been able to capitalize on his racing successes in a big way.

Andrea Mead Lawrence at Cortina. "Andy" won two gold medals in 1952 Olympics.

Othmar Schneider, one of the finest slalom skiers of the modern era.

Othmar Schneider, while not as spectacularly successful as Eriksen, was and remains one of the most influential racers in the world. He was really the first modern counterrotational technician and won a gold medal in slalom at the 1952 Games. More important has been his subsequent role as teacher, both to recreational skiers and racers.

Christian Pravda was in many respects his equal. With good right he was called "The Old Fox." A master technician with edge control a particular forte, he became a consistent winner on the professional racing circuit even as he approached the age of forty. His amateur moment of glory came in 1954, when he became world downhill champion.

It took some time for Americans to appreciate these three men, for they had a champion of their own—Andrea Mead Lawrence. Andy had made the 1948 Olympic team at the age of fifteen, then the FIS team for 1950. But it wasn't until a year later that she came into her own. She won the 1951 A-K downhill, the first American to have won this event, and only a momentary disqualifying lapse in the slalom prevented her from taking the combined. The following year, at the 1952 Olympics at Oslo, she won gold medals in slalom and giant slalom.

The next few years were to prove frustrating to American skiers, and nearly every other skier in the world. It was the era of Toni Sailer and Anderl Molterer. When the chips were really down, one of these two could be counted on to produce victories for Austria. And when they didn't win, there was always a youngster named Karl Schranz, who won at the Arlberg-Kandahar with clocklike regularity. Out of ten A-K's between 1953 and 1962, Molterer won three times and Schranz four times, a record that will be hard to equal with ski competition growing more intense all the time.

But the man with "it" was Toni Sailer, one of the greatest pressure skiers of all time. Essentially a downhiller, he nevertheless could produce in slalom and giant slalom, which is exactly what he did in the 1956 Games.

During the Sailer era, American racers had more cause to be frustrated than most other racers. In Bill Beck, Brookie Dodge, Ralph Miller, Buddy Werner, and Tom Corcoran, the United States had racers potentially the equal of any in the world. Unfortunately, there was no program to develop these racers to their ultimate potential. Still, they were a remarkable lot. Beck was fifth twice in downhill, in the 1952 Olympics and the 1954 FIS. Dodge came tantalizingly close to a medal in the 1956 Olympic slalom, and Corcoran, despite the fact that he was deep in the second seeding, came within four-tenths of a second of an Olympic medal in the 1960 giant slalom.

Christian Pravda, "The Old Fox."

Toni Sailer winning the Slalom at Cortina in the 1956 Winter Olympics.

Buddy Werner, before Phil Mahre perhaps the greatest American skier of the modern era.

But the best of them all in that era, and probably in all eras until Phil Mahre arrived, was Buddy Werner. He startled the world at the tender age of seventeen by beating the world's best in winning the Holmenkollen downhill just before the 1954 FIS. But even then he was haunted by bad luck. A training injury put him off the team. Year after year he returned to Europe to do battle with the world's best, until he was one of the world's best. In 1959 he was the world's best downhiller and also strong in slalom and giant slalom. But bad luck struck again shortly before the 1960 Olympics when an ankle fracture put him out of the Games. He was at a point in his development where a medal was as certain as a medal can be in ski racing.

If Werner was bitter or discouraged, he didn't let on. He gave his all for four more years. Shortly after his retirement from racing in 1964, the bad luck that haunted him through his racing career struck for the last time. He was killed in an avalanche in Europe during the filming of a ski movie.

If medals proved to be elusive to the North American men, they were far from that for the women. Since Olympic and FIS World Championship competition resumed after World War II, Americans and Canadians have failed only twice to bring home medals—in 1950 and in 1956. After 1956, Lucille Wheeler of Canada stunned the world by winning the downhill and

Billy Kidd (left) *and Jimmie Heuga at the 1964 Olympics after capturing the silver and bronze medals in slalom.*

At the 1960 Olympics, Penny Pitou won two silver medals.

the giant slalom in the 1958 FIS. In 1960 it was another Canadian, Ann Heggtveit, who captured a gold medal in slalom at the Squaw Valley Olympics. America's Penny Pitou and Betsy Snite completed the rout of the European women with silver medals in downhill, giant slalom, and slalom.

But 1960 was also notable for the great French renaissance. Using metal skis for the first time in international competition and with the egg position, the French swept to victory in almost every downhill in 1960 and 1961. In the Olympics, the hero was Jean Vuarnet, a journeyman racer from whom little had been expected. Yet there was justice in his surprise victory. He, along with the French ski theoretician Georges Joubert, were primarily responsible for developing the egg position that carried the French to victory.

The Olympics at Innsbruck in 1964 brought the long-awaited breakthrough for the American men, and they waited until almost the last day to secure it. After Jean Saubert had won bronze and silver medals against the impressive Goitschel sisters in the slalom and giant slalom, Billy Kidd and Jimmie Heuga came through for silver and bronze in the slalom on tremendous second runs. Kidd lapsed in 1965 against the French and Austrians, but was the toast of Europe in January 1966, with impressive slalom and giant slalom victories over Austria's Schranz and France's Killy.

As in all sports at the championship level, once a racer has mastered the basic skills, then psychology and meticulous attention to technical detail tend to become the dominant factors in winning. Billy Kidd was a classic example of this principle. Raised in Stowe, Vermont, he was never an outstanding athlete. During most of his years of international racing, he was hampered by ankle and back injuries. Despite these liabilities, he was one of the top-ranked all-around alpine ski racers in the world from 1964 to 1970. How did he do it? By a tremendous theoretical understanding of turning on skis and where to make time on a course, by the ability to psych himself up for a race, and by exhaustive analysis of his equipment and how it must be prepared for competition. It all paid off for him in 1970 when his placings in slalom, giant slalom, and downhill won the gold medal in the combined of the World Alpine Championship at Val Gardena, Italy. It was the first World Championship gold medal in skiing ever won by an American man (Steve Mahre's 1982 win was the second). After winning the first U.S. pro championship and losing the second to Spider Sabich, Billy retired and built himself a nice business and an industry presence as Steamboat Springs' leading skier-celebrity (a job he does with style and élan) and as a consultant to several equipment companies, notably Hart and Salomon. He now runs an excellent racing program at Steamboat.

KILLY AND THE FRENCH

While ski racing is very much a competition of individuals, it also is true that a strong competitor with the ability to win consistently can pull the rest of his team along with him. That, plus the superb leadership of coach Honoré Bonnet, was pretty much the history of the French ski team from 1965 starting with the incredible string of victories chalked up by Jean-Claude Killy. Along with Austria's Toni Sailer, Killy is a superstar of skiing. His record of success may never be repeated (especially since Stenmark has refused to ski downhill and Phil Mahre doesn't yet excel at it). Virtually raised on skis in the French resort town of Val d'Isère (where his father still runs an inn), Killy was a marvelously relaxed athlete, a technician, and a master of the psychology of ski racing. He left the care of his equipment to another former French racer, Michel Arpin, so that he could devote himself entirely to preparing for victory. He and the rest of the French team steamrollered the Austrians so effectively that their racing empire did not recover until 1973. Killy won the 1967 World Cup with the maximum number of realizable points, a feat never since duplicated. In his most famous appearance in the

Jean-Claude Killy, after four years out of competition, turned pro in 1972 and wrested the 1973 championship away from America's Sabich.

United States in 1967, at Cannon Mountain, New Hampshire, he won all three events in the North American championships—downhill, slalom, and giant slalom—in a single World Cup meet.

Killy's greatest glory was reserved for the Winter Olympics of 1968 in his homeland of France, at Grenoble. Killy started by winning gold in the downhill over teammate Guy Perillat. The reason he won was really not understood until afterward. Then it became known that Killy had been working for more than a year to perfect a new kind of start. In the Killy start, he built up his arm muscles so that he could project his upper body forward and down the course before his feet broke through the starting wand to set the clock running. It was enough to win the downhill by a mere 8/100ths of a second. The next men's event at the 1968 Olympics was the two-run giant slalom, and Killy won it almost effortlessly. Only one hurdle now stood between Killy and the duplication of Toni Sailer's triple gold victory in the 1956 Olympics: the slalom on the final day of the Winter Games. And some

Karl Schranz of Austria making his second disputed run in the controversial, fogbound slalom race of the 1968 Olympics. He was later disqualified, and Jean-Claude Killy of France won his third gold medal.

Nancy Greene of Canada, Olympic gold medal winner in 1968, twice winner of the World Cup.

day it was. The fog on the slalom hill was so bad that racers could barely see two gates ahead. Killy enjoyed the fastest first run, but there were a dozen racers within .06 of a second behind him before the second run started. In that run Killy was at a disadvantage in that he went first and so every other racer could take a shot at his time. Killy's archrival of many winters, Austria's Karl Schranz, started down the fogbound slalom but spun out of the course at the 21st gate claiming that a course policeman had crossed his path. He returned to the top, took another second run, and wound up with a time a half-second faster than Killy. Later, however, the race jury ruled that Schranz had genuinely missed a gate in his initial second run and was disqualified. Killy, who had resigned himself to second-place silver, was now the gold medal winner in slalom and winner of all three golds in the alpine races of the 1968

Winter Olympics. It assured him worldwide fame. In a curious way, it also assured notoriety for Schranz. Four years later, just before the 1972 Winter Olympics at Sapporo, Japan, IOC president Avery Brundage expelled Schranz from the Games. Austrians were enraged by what they strongly felt to be the second unjust treatment of Schranz in as many Olympics: first the Killy affair, then Brundage. Two hundred thousand strong, they lined the streets of Vienna in February 1972, to welcome the disbarred Schranz home. It was the biggest crowd in the modern history of Austria, exceeding even the throngs who met Hitler after the Anschluss.

The Olympics of 1968 lent fame to the greatest skier in Canadian history, Nancy Greene. She won a gold medal in the giant slalom, a silver in the slalom, and the title of FIS Combined women's champion. Later in the winter, Nancy went on to win her second World Cup.

The 1968 Winter Games were a disappointment to the American women who traditionally have always fielded a stronger team than the men. In the 1972 Olympics in Japan, however, petite Barbara Ann Cochran recouped the loss. Barbara Ann is a member of a remarkable family of Vermont skiers

Barbara Cochran poling to victory in the Olympic slalom.

Marie Therese Nadig of Switzer-land won two gold medals at Sapporo.

coached so successfully by their father, Mickey Cochran, that one brother and three sisters have been members of the U.S. Ski Team. In the Sapporo slalom, the last women's race of the 1972 Winter Games, Barbara Ann beat off an onslaught by the entire French women's team to win the gold medal. It was the first Olympic gold won by an American ski racer since Andrea Mead in 1952. (Alas, it proved to be the last for the U.S.: Phil Mahre took a silver in 1980 and Cindy Nelson a bronze in 1976 in downhill. The Canadians did better: a gold in giant slalom by Kathy Kreiner in 1976 and a downhill bronze in 1980 by Steve Podborski.)

SCHUSSING THE HEADWALL

Victory in the great races is usually essential for a racer to be ranked among the great. But sometimes—not often—a man's legend is bigger than his records. Such a racer was Toni Matt.

Toni was a good racer, no question about that. He won the Harriman Cup in 1939, the U.S. Nationals in 1949, and several other important races. But this is not what he is remembered for.

In 1939 he stood atop Mount Washington for the third and, as it turned out, the last running of the American Inferno, a four-mile downhill with a vertical drop of over 4,000 feet. Part of the course was across the frighteningly steep Headwall of Tuckerman's Ravine. There were no control gates on the Headwall. The race organizers assumed that the racer who treasured his life would throw in a couple of turns to check his speed as all other racers had done in previous runnings.

What prompted Matt to take the Headwall straight is the subject of numerous stories. Toni himself claims that he intended to take it straight.

Tuckerman's Ravine, 1939: Toni Matt's final check turn near the lip of the Head-wall.

Witnesses to the race claim that he lost control momentarily as he went over the lip of the Headwall and by the time he regained it he was heading straight down. There is still another version—that he checked as he came to the lone control gate on the lip, looked down the Headwall, and took the plunge.

Strangely enough, Matt's schuss received no attention to speak of at the time. Newspaper accounts of the race and an article in the *Ski Annual* of the following fall merely state that Matt won the race in record time. Perhaps because of this oversight, the story bounced around among skiers of how Toni Matt schussed the Headwall. It soon became a fixture of skier conversation, lovingly passed on from skier to skier until it became the greatest deed in American skiing history.

And maybe it was. No one has done it since.

34

Freestyle and Hotdog Skiing

Layback, Outrigger, Kickout, Worm Turn, Charleston, Daffy, Royal (Reuel) Christie, 360, Double Gainer, Moebius Flip . . . such is the arcane jargon of the hotdog or freestyle skier. While some of the early forms of way-out skiing came to America via such European skiers as Stein Eriksen (Mambo and flips) and Arthur Furrer (crossover, Charleston, and Royal Christie), the hotdog movement has become primarily an achievement of young American skiers.

Hotdog skiing actually breaks down into three different disciplines, although frequently they are mixed together. In pure acrobatic skiing, the hotdogger takes to the air. A specially constructed jump, with or without a kicker, enables the skier to become airborne, performing such stunts as long geländesprungs (gelandeys), tip-drop gelandeys, split and double-split gelandeys, back flips (single, double, and triple), and more. A second discipline is ballet, freestyle skiing on an open slope. The skier is scored chiefly for the elegance and technical excellence with which he performs royal christies, outriggers, laybacks, crossovers, and so on. A third discipline is pure hotdogging. It is done on a steep, heavily moguled slope at high speed. The fastest, most fluid, and most imaginative (in terms of terrain use) run down the slope is considered the best.

It would be impossible in a single chapter of this book to show all of the many hotdog stunts and how they are done. More are being invented every winter. The following are a few.

MAMBO

This is a fun turn to be executed on smooth slopes. It combines anticipation with counterrotation and angulation and requires a fine feel for the edges.

Start by running in the fall line. The skier sinks and as he or she rises rotates as far as possible in the direction of the turn. When the skis begin to turn out of the fall line, the skier counterrotates but continues to press in with knees and keep the skis turning. When the skier is overrotated in the other direction, he or she unweights and allows the skis finally to turn. As the new turn begins, the skier overrotates in the other direction but keeps the skis turning the opposite way. Change of direction in mambo always occurs when the skier is overrotated in relation to the next turn.

Stein Eriksen demonstrates a mambo turn across the fall line.

My skis point in the fall line.

I am running in the fall line.   *I sink, prepared to rise.*   *I rise, start to twist.*

Skis in fall line, hips twist.

My shoulder, hip, arm stop.

My skis turn out of fall line.

I reverse, hand back.

I reverse, hand is way back.

I overrotate.

My arm, shoulder, hip block.

Blocking turns skis.

I continue reversing.

I sink, prepare for next turn.

My reverse continues.

I hold turn into fall line.

The crossed-ski turn.

Art Furrer does the Charleston. The exercise is designed to get the skier used to balancing on one ski. Choose a gentle hill. Start down the fall line and, without shifting the central position of the body between the skis, jump rhythmically from one ski to the other; at the same time swing the tail of the unweighted ski out so that it forms an angle to the ski in the snow. The pole on the unweighted side may be used to help the maneuver. The quicker the change can be made, the better. The skier coming down the slopes should look as if he's kicking up his heels in the Charleston dance step.

CROSSED SKI TURN

Originated by acrobat Art Furrer, this stunt involves turning on the outside ski while lifting the inside ski and twisting it at right angles over the outside ski. The turn is made with strong angulation and the inside shoulder leading the turn.

CHARLESTON

Choose a gentle hill. Start down the fall line. Now jump rhythmically from one ski to the other, swinging the tail of the ski out to the side. Keep the upper body steady. The quicker it's done, the more it looks like a dancer doing the Charleston.

THE KICK OUT

The kick out is a basic hotdog trick that teaches the skier how to turn on the inside ski. As such it is the basis of a number of other hotdog stunts like the royal christie. To do the kick out, start in a traverse. To turn, balance all your weight on the inside ski and bank to turn; at the same time, lift the outside ski completely off the snow, pointing the tip to the outside. If you can lift the outside ski all the way in the air, it's a royal christie.

OUTRIGGER

The name of this turn derives from the pontoon used on the side of a sailing canoe to stabilize it. And that's just what the skier's outside leg does in this turn. From a traverse, step the downhill ski in the direction you want to go. As you squat on your skis, extend the outside leg to the outrigger position. Return to an upright traverse, and then repeat turn in the other direction.

Basic to any hotdogger's bag of tricks is the kick-out. From this stunt, which teaches the hotdogger skiing on the inside ski, the skier goes into royal and flying royal christies (see box above), and other difficult inside ski maneuvers. Shown in these pictures is a flying kick-out. To give any acrobatic skiing trick the "flying" title, the hotdogger uses a bump to toss himself into the air and completes all the necessary preparatory body movements and edge changes while airborne. But let's go back to basics and build the straight kick-out from a traverse. As you start the turn, step onto the downhill ski (the inside ski as you execute the turn) and lift the outside one completely off the snow. Lean back and to the inside to keep your balance. If you remember to keep your weight slightly behind your boot to plane the turning ski, you shouldn't have any trouble with this stunt. If you do have problems, drag your inside pole on the snow behind you to let yourself "feel" how far you have actually leaned to the inside.

The kick-out, by Bob Theobald (former exhibition ski school director)

Bob Theobald executes an outrigger.

Tom Leroy does the kangaroo.

KANGAROO

Here is avalement at its most extreme. The idea is to look for a very tall, sharp bump—maybe three feet high. As your skis go up the side of the bump, make no attempt to stay over them but rather let them get way ahead as you sit back on the tails. The pole is planted to the side, and you come almost to a standstill on top of the bump. At the same time, twist your arms and torso downhill and pivot the skis to turn. When you are in an extreme reverse position, the skis come down the side of the bump and the turn, also called the slow dog noodle, is completed.

A perfect Daffy is performed by Henry Palmer, a member of Camelback's Free-style Team.

Genia Fuller, a top American freestyle skier.

The following article by Doug Pfeiffer, reprinted with permission from SKI Magazine's September 1980 issue, is a good summation of where we are now with freestyle skiing.

FREESTYLE: LOW PROFILE, HIGH ANTICS
by Doug Pfeiffer

The best-kept secrets aren't always meant to be either kept or secret.

Ever hear of Bob Howard (25, Reno, Nev.), Jan Bucher (22, Salt Lake City, Utah) or Hilary Engisch (22, Williston, Vt.)? Or that Greg Athans and Stephanie Sloan won SKI Magazine's World Freestyle championship awards?

Last season, on the professional World Cup of Freestyle circuit, Howard repeated his previous year's achievement of winning in each of five ballet events held in Europe, Canada and the U.S. to become men's ballet world champion. Bucher (pronounced *Boo*-er) duplicated Howard's winning ways last year to become the women's world champion. And Engisch bombed her way through the meanest of the world's moguls to an undefeated season.

Perhaps you didn't even know there was a World Cup of Freestyle, let alone any pro freestyle events in the U.S. last season. Word just hasn't seemed to get around that there were at least two additional pro "B" circuits, and nearly 100 amateur events, including an international meet in Chamonix, France, plus a Canadian-American team challenge.

If you knew nothing about all this, don't be upset. There's enough "upset" in the ranks of the U.S. professionals to deplete the world's reserves of crying towels. The upset is due partly to a constantly diminishing interest in the sport by commercial sponsors, ski areas and the ski media, with each feeding on the disinterest of the other.

The upset is also due to a doggedly determined push by Canadian ex-freestyler Johnny Johnston to do away with the pro circuits and establish a strong worldwide amateur movement sanctioned by the International Ski Federation (FIS). Johnston hopes that the International Olympic Committee might recognize FIS freestyle in time to include it in the 1984 Winter Games—or, at least, in the 1984 curricula of events.

That's fine for Europe and Canada, but where does it leave the U.S. pros? In other countries where sports are recognized as a viable political tool and an opiate of the people, ski team "amateurs" receive salaries euphemistically disguised as "broken time payments." So do our U.S. Ski Team members, except that these monies are raised by private donations whereas other countries use government funds raised by lotteries. In Europe and Canada, where these systems are well entrenched and operative, a national freestyle team can readily be absorbed into the scheme of things and nurtured to Olympian perfection. But what about the U.S.?

For a moment, pity the U.S. pro freestyler. Until now, he and she depended upon prize monies and victory schedules from equipment sponsors for their livelihood. In amateur events, there are no cash awards—at least no publicly acknowledged ones. A national ski team pool takes in all monies and reapportions them to all team members, in relative proportion to their level of achievement. Currently, there is no freestyle team pool in the U.S., and precious little money or time to set up one within the jurisdiction of the near bankrupt U.S. Ski Association, which is now fighting for political and financial survival.

A further hangup—the FIS says it will grant amnesty to all current pros, allowing them to compete on equal terms with amateurs. "Big Deal!" say the pros, knowing that once you've received money for any type of sports competition, the IOC will not let you play in their Games (as happened to ski racer Karl Schranz at the 1972 Olympics) or will threaten to take away your medals (as they did to Jean-Claude Killy after the 1968 Winter Games).

If the IOC should object to amnesty, which it almost certainly will, the FIS has an answer. Even if the pros can't take part in the Olympics, then at least they can take part in FIS events as "B license" competitors (which Ingemar Stenmark did after the Olympics) which allows them to arrange their own financial deals.

Another hangup: The tight little clique which manages the amateur freestyle events in the U.S. has already appointed a U.S. Freestyle Team, based on results of the Amateur National Championships held at Sugarloaf, Me., last April. Of course there are no pros on this team. However, the pros have been promised the rights to "ingress" into the ranks of the team during an early-season competition. As good as the amateurs are, there are at least 15 to 25 pros who can outski them walking away.

"It's not an easy situation for the pros," says Scott Brooksbank, one of the world's great freestylers and the man who almost single-handedly put together the World Cup pro circuit and kept it going. "I'm retiring from competition this year, and from organizational politics. But I feel for my fellow pros. Even though we've taken steps to prevent injuries and we now can get insurance, have had three events in Pennsylvania's Poconos and TV coverage from NBC and CBS and have had spectator crowds of at least 20,000, we simply haven't had exposure from the print media. And so sponsors have lost interest, and there aren't any in sight for the coming years. So, where can the U.S. pro turn?"

If freestylers—pro and am—suffered a low media profile, there was nothing down about their stunts, particularly in the air. Whistler Mountain, British Columbia, was the site of the final World Cup Event last season. Seven competitors turned triple back somersaults, with several of them adding difficulty to the feat by including two full twists. Obviously, the pros are highly trained, very skilled athletes.

So too are the ballet skiers. At Whistler, champions Howard and Bucher put on such a razzle-dazzle of fancy footwork and gymnastic prowess that the pros of five years ago would not have believed their eyes. Remember such exotica as the killer kick, the outrigger, the worm turn, the Polish doughnut? Those stunts are now considered so basic—if considered at all—that no one talks about or does them.

The early freestyle events were less a competition than an orgy of spontaneous athletic creativity. Most of that excitement and spirit has now gone from the game, but not all of it. During the Whistler mogul event, an impish spirit of rebellion still survived. Quebecker Dominic Laroche apparently couldn't resist the temptation of a straight schuss down the mogul field, which was covered with almost two feet of fresh fluff. He posted fastest time of the day but earned no points for turns or air time. Austrian Siggi Innauer, who completed a fast helicopter, earned first place.

Too bad the vanity rampant in our world is such that someone must be judged "best." As in world figure skating, the top five or six competitors are so good that who is better than the others is merely a matter of opinion. The skiing performances of freestylers have become so good, the competitors should all be appreciated as athletic artists.

Among the super athlete-artists of last season, Canadians Greg Athans and Stephanie Sloan were judged season-long best. Athans, after several years of almost making it, finally topped Montrealer John Eaves. Last year Eaves ended up in fifth place Grand Prix standings. Ahead of him were Brooksbank (fourth), Rick Bowie (third), and Frank Beddor III (second).

Of note was the performance of Frank Beddor III. Despite a broken leg which kept Beddor out of the Labatt's-sponsored finals at Whistler, he hung on to second place in overall aerial standings.

The amateurs: International events

While prospects for pros are clouded for the coming season, the amateurs' future is clear indeed. Amateurs, of course, are delighted with the FIS recognition given to the sport of freestyle. About 3,000 card-carrying members of the USSA compete just as often as snow and scheduled conditions permit— which wasn't all that frequent last season. Nonetheless, Sugarloaf, Me., was host to the final event last April, when 122 freestylers arrived for the competition. The surprise winner of these national championships was a strong 14-year-old from Minnesota, Eric Sampson, who placed first in aerials (upright only), fourth in the moguls event, and 34th in ballet.

Overall best among women was senior-class skier Joan McWilliams from Dover, N.H. She earned her crown with a first in moguls, fourth in ballet, and 13th in aerials.

The U.S. National Freestyle Team was chosen after this Sugarloaf event—12 men and 11 women—to represent the U.S. in FIS-sanctioned events this season. Will any pros be among their ranks, or will ex-pros supplant them all? Only the politics of freestyle will bring the answer, presumably before the season's first swirl of snowflakes.

APPENDICES

GUIDE TO 400 SKI AREAS IN THE UNITED STATES AND CANADA

NAME OF AREA	ADDRESS	GONDOLA/ TRAM	CHAIR	SURFACE	TOW	VERTICAL RISE (IN FEET)	BASE ELEV. (IN FEET)	ADV.	INTER.	BEGINNER	PERCENT- AGE OF AREA COVERED BY SNOW- MAKING	OTHER FACILITIES*
ALABAMA Cloudmont	Mentone 35984				3	150	1650		50	50	100	NS, GLM, ATM, lodging
ALASKA Alyeska	Girdwood 99587		5		1	2800	200	open bowls				NS, ATM, XC, lodging
Arctic Valley	Anchorage 99701		2	1	3	1400	2500	15	65	20		GLM; open weekends and holidays
Eaglecrest	Juneau 99801		2	1		1400	1200	30	40	30		NS, ATM, XC
ARIZONA Arizona Snow Bowl	P.O. Box 158, Flagstaff 86001		2	1	2	2300	9500	36	25	39		GLM, ATM, XC
Sunrise	Box 1237, Whiteriver 85941		3	2	1	1632	9300	25	45	30	yes	NS, N, GLM, ATM, Nastar
CALIFORNIA Alpine Meadows	Box AM, Tahoe City 95730		10	3		1700	6970	40	35	25	80	N, GLM, XC (trails only), Nastar, lodging
Badger Pass	Yosemite National Park 95389		4	1	1	900	7200	20	50	30		N, GLM, Nastar, lodging
Bear Valley (Mt. Reba)	Box 38, Bear Valley 95223		9			2100	6400	25	50	25		GLM, ATM, Nastar
Boreal	Box 39, Truckee 95734		9			600	7200	20	60	20	yes	NS, ATM, lodging
Dodge Ridge	Pine Crest 95335		6		3	1000	6600	20	60	20		N, GLM, ATM, Nastar, Skiwee
Donner Ski Ranch	Box 66, Norden 95724		4	2		800	7035	33	33	33		XC, lodging
Heavenly Valley	Box AT, So. Lake Tahoe 95705	1	16	3	6	3500 CAL 6550 4000 NEV 6100		25	50	25	70 acres	Nastar, lodging

Area	Address											Other Facilities
Homewood	Box 165, Homewood 95718		3		2	1650	6230	30	50	20		ATM, lodging
Holiday Hill	Hwy. 2, Wrightwood		4	1	1	1590	6580	40	30	30	75	NS, GLM, ATM
June Mtn.	June Lake 93529		8	5	1	2562	7650	25	45	30	40 acres	GLM, lodging
Kirkwood	Kirkwood 95646		8	1		2000	7800	25	50	25		N, ATM, XC, Nastar, lodging
Mammoth Mt.	Box 24, Mammoth Lakes 93546	2	21	4		3100	7953	30	40	30		ATM, Nastar, lodging
Mt. Baldy	Box 567, Mt. Baldy		4			2100	6500	mostly int.; some adv.				GLM, ATM
North Star-At-Tahoe	Box 129, Truckee 95734		8			2200	6400	17	50	33	25 acres	GLM, ATM, XC, Nastar, lodging, Skiwee
Sierra Ski Ranch	Twin Bridges P.O. 95735		8			1585	7282	30	50	20		GLM, ATM
Snow Summit	Box 77, Big Bear Lake 92315		8		1	1200	7000	30	50	20	95	NS, ATM, XC (trails only), lodging
Snow Valley	Box 8, Running Springs		12			1141	6700	30	40	30	50	NS, ATM
Squaw Valley	Box 2007, Olympic Valley 95730	2	21	3		2700	6200	30	40	30		NS, ATM, XC, Nastar, lodging
Sugar Bowl	Norden 95724	1	8			1500	6883	50	30	20		NS, ATM, XC (rental at area, trails nearby), lodging
Tahoe Ski Bowl	#305, Homewood 95718		2	1	2	1630	6250	20	40	40	yes	ATM
COLORADO Keystone/A-Basin**	Box 267, Dillon 80435		5			1670	10,780	40	50	10		GLM
Aspen Highlands	Box T, Aspen 81611		8	4		3800	8000	30	40	30	10	N, GLM and advanced Long Ski, Nastar, lodging
Aspen Mt.	Box 1248, Aspen 81611		7			3300	7912	75	25		155 acres	GLM, Nastar, lodging

*OTHER FACILITIES. Abbreviations are as follows:
   NS—illuminated night skiing.
   N—nursery for small children at the area.
   GLM—ski school offers Graduated Length Method of instruction and GLM equipment rental.
   ATM—ski school offers American Teaching Method (CTM in Canada) of instruction.
   XC—area maintains cross-country trails for touring and also either rents cross-country equipment or offers instruction, or has both.
   Nastar—Nastar races (Molstar in Canada) held regularly.
   lodging—lodging is available within walking distance of lifts (i.e., requires no car or public transport to get from lodge to hill).
   Skiwee—SKI Magazine's special children's program taught at the area.
   All areas are open daily unless otherwise noted.

** Arapahoe-Basin is part of Keystone Resort; free shuttle bus between the two.

COLORADO (cont.)

NAME OF AREA	ADDRESS	GONDOLA/TRAM	CHAIR	SURFACE	TOW	VERTICAL RISE (IN FEET)	BASE ELEV. (IN FEET)	ADV.	INTER.	BEGINNER	PERCENTAGE OF AREA COVERED BY SNOW-MAKING	OTHER FACILITIES
Beaver Creek	Box 7, Vail 81657		6			3280	8100	40	35	25	yes	ATM, lodging
Berthoud Pass	Idaho Springs 80452		1	1	1	993	11,022	20	40	40		GLM, ATM, lodging
Buttermilk	Box 1248, Aspen 81611		5	1	1	2000	7868	19	32	49	20	GLM, ATM, Nastar, lodging
Breckenridge	Box 1058, Breckenridge 80424		11	2		2213	9630	25	45	30	85 acres	N, GLM, XC, Nastar, lodging
Broadmoor	Colorado Springs 80901		1		1	600	6200	20	20	60	100	NS, GLM, ATM
Copper Mt.	Copper Mtn. 80443		12	1	1	2450	9600	15 (10 expert)	50	25	13	N, ATM, XC, Nastar, lodging, Skiwee
Crested Butte	Box 528, Crested Butte 81224		7	1		2150	9100	27	38	35	30	N, ATM, XC, Nastar, lodging
Eldora Ski Area	Box 438, Nederland 80466		5	1		1100	9400	20	64	16	60	NS, N, ATM, XC, lodging
Geneva Basin	Grant		2	2		1250	10,500	30	45	25	40	N, GLM
Hidden Valley	Box 1020, Estes Park 80517		2	4		2000	9400	40	30	30	yes	N, GLM, ATM
Keystone	Box 38, Dillon 80435		9	1		2340	9300	15	65	20	80	N, GLM, XC, lodging
Loveland	Box 455, Georgetown 80444		6	2		1430	10,800	25	50	25	120 acres	N, ATM
Monarch	Garfield 81227		4			1000	11,000	28	52	20		ATM, Nastar
Powderhorn	Grand Junction 81501		2	1		1600	8200	27 (expert)	56	17		GLM, ATM, XC (trails), lodging
Purgatory	Box 666, Durango		5	2		1600	8950	25	50	25		N, ATM, lodging
Ski Cooper	Leadville 80461		1	2		1200	10,500	10	50	40		ATM; open Wed.-Sun. and daily 12/16–1/10 and 3/17–4/11

	Address					Vertical	Elevation				Area	Facilities
Snowmass	Snowmass, Aspen 81654	1	13			3600	8208	23	67	10	160 acres	N, GLM (rentals in village), Nastar, lodging
Steamboat	Box 1178, Steamboat Springs 80477		13		2	3600	6900	28	49	23		NS, N, GLM, XC, Nastar, lodging
Sunlight	Box 1061, Glenwood Springs 81601		2	1		1800	8050	18	58	24		N, ATM, lodging
Telluride	Box 307, Telluride 81435		6			3105	8735	35	50	15	30 acres	N, ATM, XC (trails at area, rental in town), Nastar, lodging
Vail	Box 7, Vail 81657	1	16	1		3050	8200	30	40	30	14	N, ATM, XC, Nastar, lodging
Winter Park	Box 36, Winter Park 80482	1	13			2125	9000	37	39	24	20	N, GLM, ATM, Nastar, lodging, Skiwee
CONNECTICUT												
Mohawk Mt.	Cornwall 06753		4	1	2	640	960	40	40	20	75	GLM, ATM, XC
Mt. Southington	396 Mt. Vernon Rd., Southington 06489		2	4	1	425	100	20	50	30	85	NS, N, ATM, Nastar
Powder Ridge	Powder Hill Rd., Middlefield 06455		4		1	540	450	20	50	30	75	NS, N, GLM, XC, lodging
Ski Sundown	Ratlum Rd., New Hartford 06057		3	1		550	500	20	60	20	33 acres	NS, GLM
GEORGIA												
Sky Valley	Dillard 30537		1		1	250	2000	2 slopes			yes	NS
IDAHO												
Bear Gulch	St. Anthony 83445		1	1		1240		6 slopes, 1 trail				GLM
Bogus Basin	731 No. 15th, Boise 83702		6		4	1800	5800	36	43	21		NS, N, GLM, ATM, XC, lodging
Brundage Mt.	Box 1062, McCall 83638		2	1	1	1600	6000	bowl and 2 trails beg. and int.				ATM
North–South	Emida 83828		1		2	450	3350					NS, ATM, XC
Pebble Creek (formerly Skyline)	Pocatello 83201		2	2		2000	6600	20 runs				ATM, Nastar
Pomerelle	Albion 83311		2	1		1000	8000	16 slopes and trails				NS, GLM, ATM, XC
Schweitzer Basin	Box 815, Sandpoint 83864		7	1	1	2000	4400	30	50	20	20	N, ATM, lodging

NAME OF AREA	ADDRESS	GONDOLA/TRAM	CHAIR	SURFACE	TOW	VERTICAL RISE (IN FEET)	BASE ELEV. (IN FEET)	ADV.	INTER.	BEGINNER	PERCENTAGE OF AREA COVERED BY SNOW-MAKING	OTHER FACILITIES
IDAHO (*cont.*) Soldier Mt.	Box 354, Fairfield 83327		2	1	2	1400	5800	36 runs			yes	GLM, ATM, XC
Sun Valley (Baldy, Dollar, Elkhorn)	Sun Valley 83353		16			3400	5750	25	50	25		N, GLM, XC, Nastar
ILLINOIS Buffalo Park	Box 177, Algonquin 60102				6	200		4 slopes			100	NS, GLM, ATM
Chestnut Mt.	Blackjack Rd., Galena 61036		2		6	465	1200	13 runs			95	NS, N, ATM, lodging
Four Lakes Village	5650 Lakeside St., Lisle 60532				6	130			80	20	100	NS, ATM
Holiday Park	Ingleside 60041		1		5	200	650	beg. and int.			100	NS, GLM, ATM
INDIANA Pines	Rt. 7, Box 36 Valparaiso 46383		1		6	170		7 slopes, 1 trail			yes	NS, GLM, ATM, XC
Ski Starlite	Clarksville 47130		4	4		500	504	24	65	11	100	NS, ATM
IOWA Fun Valley	Montezuma 50171			3	5	240		5 slopes			yes	NS, GLM
Holiday Mt.	Box 102, Estherville 51334			2	2	190	1300	5 slopes			100	NS, GLM, ATM, XC
Sundown	Dubuque 52001		3		3	475	584	10	70	20	100	NS, ATM
MAINE Camden Snow Bowl	Camden 04843		1	2		900	100	10	80	10	40	NS, N, ATM, XC; open Wed. only
Evergreen	Stoneham 04231		3			1040	600	40	40	20	50	NS, ATM, XC, lodging
Lost Valley	Lost Valley Rd., Auburn 04210		2	1	1	249		30	30	40	90	NS, N, ATM, XC

							12 miles of trails and slopes				
Mt. Abram	Locke Mills 04255		1	3	1030	465	20	40	40		ATM, XC
Pleasant Mt.	R.F.D. 1, Bridgton 04009		3	3	1250	650	40	28	32		ATM, XC, lodging
Saddleback	Box 430, Rangeley 04970		2	3	1800	2500	30	40	30	4.3 miles	N, ATM, XC, lodging
Sugarloaf Mt.	Kingfield 04947	1	5	5	2600	1637	25	50	25	40	N, ATM, XC, Nastar, lodging
Sunday River	Box 601, Bethel 04217		2	2	1630	980	25	50	25	50	N, GLM, ATM, Nastar, lodging
MARYLAND Braddock Hts.	Braddock Hts. 21714		1	2	250	900	3 slopes, 4 trails			100	NS, GLM, lodging
Wisp	Oakland 21550		2	1	610	2470	20	55	25	45	NS, N, GLM, lodging
MASSACHUSETTS Berkshire East	S. River Road, Charlemont 01339		4	2	1180	540	40	40	20	yes	NS, N, GLM, XC, Nastar
Berkshire Snow Basin	West Cummington 01265		3	3	550	1175	8 trails, 3 slopes				ATM, lodging; open weekends and vacation weeks
Blue Hill	4001 Washington St., Milton 01286		1	2	300	100	7 slopes			90	NS, Nastar
Boston Hill	Rt. 114, N. Andover 01845		1	3	340	100	7 slopes			yes	NS, ATM, XC
Bousquet	Pittsfield 01201		2	2	750	1125	20	50	30	75	NS, N, GLM, ATM
Brodie Mt.	U.S. Rt. 7, New Ashford 01237		4	2	1250	1450	200 acres			80	NS, N, ATM, lodging
Butternut Basin	3 Mile Hill, Gt. Barrington 01230		6	1	1000	800	25	60	15	90	N, GLM, XC, Skiwee
Groton Hills	Groton 01450		1	5	150		10 slopes			yes	NS, XC
Jiminy Peak	Hancock 01237		4	1	1200	1300	40	30	30	75	NS, N, ATM, lodging
Mt. Tom	Rt. 5, Holyoke 01040		3	3	680	700	10	60	30	100	NS, N, GLM
Nashoba Valley	Westford 01886		2	1	240	200	30	50	20	90	NS, ATM
Ward Hill	Shrewsbury 01545		1	2	200	200	5 slopes			yes	NS, N, GLM
Mt. Watatic	Tr. 119, Ashby 01431		1	2	550	1250	30	60	10	40	NS, GLM, ATM, XC
Otis Ridge	Otis 01253		3	5	375	1250	30	45	25	80	N, ATM, XC, lodging
MICHIGAN Alpine Valley	6775 East Highland, Milford 48042		9	16	250	910	30	40	30	100	NS, GLM, ATM, Nastar, lodging

MICHIGAN (*cont.*)

NAME OF AREA	ADDRESS	GONDOLA/ TRAM	CHAIR	SURFACE	TOW	VERTICAL RISE (IN FEET)	BASE ELEV. (IN FEET)	ADV.	INTER.	BEGINNER	PERCENTAGE OF AREA COVERED BY SNOW-MAKING	OTHER FACILITIES
Big Powderhorn	Box 136, Bessemer 49911		6			600	1218	20	65	15		NS, GLM, ATM, lodging
Boyne Highlands	Harbor Springs 49740		7		2	515	775	35	35	30	90	N, GLM, XC, Nastar, lodging
Boyne Mt.	Boyne Mt. Lodge, Boyne Falls 49713		8		3	460	720	40	40	20	90	N, GLM, XC, Nastar, lodging
Caberlae Ski Resort	Cadillac 49601		2	6	14	280-350	740	20	50	30	50	NS, ATM, XC, Nastar, lodging
Cannonsburg	Cannonsburg 49317		3	2	10	250		15	60	25	100	NS, N, ATM, Nastar
Cliffs Ridge	County Rd. 553, Marquette 49855		1	2	2	600	1200	25	50	25	80	GLM, ATM, XC
Crystal Mountain	Thompsonville 49683		3		2	375	757	30	45	25	95	NS, N, GLM, ATM, XC, lodging
Indianhead Mt.	Wakefield 49968		4	3		638	1297	25	50	25	85	N, GLM, ATM, XC, Nastar, lodging
Mt. Brighton	4141 Bauer Rd., Brighton 48116		6		9	230	1100	25	45	30	100	NS, GLM, ATM, Nastar
Mt. Maria	Spruce 48762		1		3	285		5 slopes			70	NS, GLM, ATM, lodging
Nub's Nob	Rt. 2, Harbor Springs 49740		5	1	1	425	915	30	40	30	70	NS, GLM, XC, Nastar, lodging
Pine Mt.	Pine Mt. Rd., Rt. 2, Iron Mt. 49801		3	1	1	400	1400	20	60	20	100	N, GLM, ATM, XC
Schuss Mt.	Mancelona 49659		3	1	1	400	742	35	40	25	100	N, GLM, ATM, XC, Nastar, lodging
Ski Brule/Ski Homestead	Rt. 3, Iron River 49935		3	1	1	419	1440	30	40	30	90	ATM, XC, Nastar, lodging
Skyline	Rt. 1, Box 328, Grayling 49738		1		10	210	1305	11 slopes				NS, ATM
Sugar Loaf	Route 1, Cedar 49621		5	1		610	772	35	45	20	80	N, ATM, XC, Nastar, lodging

Resort	Address										Facilities
Thunder Mt.	Boyne Country, Boyne Falls 49173	2		2	410	900	25	50	25	yes	GLM, XC; open weekends, daily Christmas through New Year's
Timberlee	Traverse City 49684	2	1	2	385		20	40	40	100	NS, XC, lodging
Timber Ridge	Kalamazoo 49001	2	1	7	240		12 runs			100	NS, GLM, ATM
Tyrolean Resort	R.R. 1, Box 203, Gaylord 49735	1	1	2	270						NS, XC, lodging
MINNESOTA											
Afton Alps	Hastings R.R. 4 (15 miles E. of St. Paul) 55033	18	4	2	330		20	60	20	100	NS, GLM
Buck Hill	15400 Buck Hill Rd., Burnsville 55378	4	1	3	325	919	15	45	40	100	NS, GLM, Nastar
Eagle Mt.	Grey Eagle 56336		1	5	200		10 runs, 3 trails			75	NS, GLM, XC, lodging
Hyland Hills	Bloomington 55420	1	2	4	175		10	30	60	100	NS, ATM, XC
Lutsen	Lutsen 55612	3	2	3	635	1000	18 runs			65	N, XC, lodging
Powder Ridge	Kimball 55353	2	2	3	310		9 runs			yes	NS, GLM, ATM
Quadna Mt.	Hill City 55748	1	2	2	325		14 runs			25	N, GLM, XC
Spirit Mt.	Duluth 55806	5		1	610	710	25	50	25	100	NS, N, GLM, ATM, XC, Nastar, lodging
Sugar Hill	Box 369, Grand Rapids 55744	2	3	4	400	1350	30	50	20	90	NS, N, GLM, ATM, XC, lodging
Welch Village	Welch 55089	5	2	2	350	725	19	50	31	100	NS, N, GLM, ATM, Nastar, lodging
Wild Mountain	Taylors Falls 55084	3		2	300	813	30	40	30	90	NS, GLM, ATM, XC
MONTANA											
Big Mountain	Box 1215, Whitefish 59937	5	1	1	2130	4750	20	55	25		NS, N, ATM, XC, lodging
Big Sky	Box 1, Big Sky 59716	4		1	2300	7500	25	50	25	yes	N, GLM, XC, lodging
Bridger Bowl	Box 846, Bozeman 59715	5	1	2	2000	6100	30	45	25		ATM, XC, lodging
Marshall	Rt. 4, Missoula 59801	1	2	2	1500	4000	7 slopes				NS, N, ATM, XC
Montana Snow Bowl	Missoula 59801	1	2	1	2600	5000	bowl skiing				GLM, ATM
Red Lodge Mt.	Drawer R, Red Lodge 59068	4		4	2016	7400	25	60	15	yes	GLM, Nastar

409

NAME OF AREA	ADDRESS	TRAM/ GONDOLA	CHAIR	SURFACE	TOW	VERTICAL RISE (IN FEET)	BASE ELEV. (IN FEET)	ADV.	INTER.	BEGINNER	PERCENTAGE OF AREA COVERED BY SNOW-MAKING	OTHER FACILITIES
NEVADA												
Mt. Rose	Box 2406, Reno 89505		3	2		1400	8200	15	40	45	20	GLM, ATM, lodging
Ski Incline	Box 824, Incline Village 89450		7			900	6700	40	40	20	80	ATM
Slide Mt.	Box 2748, Reno 89502		3	1	1	1450	8250	16 runs			15	NS, GLM
NEW HAMP-SHIRE												
Attitash	Bartlett 03812		4			1550	600	25	50	25	75	N, GLM, ATM, XC, Nastar, lodging
Black Mt.	Jackson 03846		1	3	1	1100	1200	14 trails			15	N, GLM, ATM, XC, lodging
Bobcat Mt.*	Rt. 47, Bennington 03442											
Bretton Woods	Bretton Woods 03575		2	1		1100	2000	22	45	33	35	NS, N, ATM, XC, lodging
Cannon Mt.	Franconia 03580	1	3	3	1	2146	2000	25	45	30	30	N, ATM, XC, Nastar
Crotched Mt.	Box 222, Francistown 03043		3	3	1	900	1352	25 slopes			yes	NS, N, XC, lodging
Gunstock	Box 336, Laconia 02346		3	3		1400	900	25	50	25	86 acres	N, GLM, ATM, XC
Highland	Bear Hill Rd., Northfield			2	1	700	800	2 slopes			yes	NS, N, Nastar
King Ridge	RFD, New London 03257	2	5			800	1000	17	28	55		N, Nastar
Loon Mt.	Kancomangus Hwy., Lincoln 03251	1	5			1850	900	20	60	20	80	N, ATM, XC, Nastar, lodging
Mt. Cranmore	North Conway 03860	2	3	1		1500	500	20	60	20	50	ATM, XC, Nastar

* NOTE: Bobcat and Crotched have merged.

Resort	Address										Acreage	Features
Mt. Sunapee	Mt. Sunapee State Park 03772	5	2		1	1500	1300	15 runs			75	N, XC; open weekends
Pat's Peak	Rt. 114, Henniker 03242	3	3			710	690	24	39	37		N, ATM, XC, Nastar, lodging
Ragged Mt.	Danbury 03230	1	1		1	1125	1100	12 slopes and trails				GLM, ATM, lodging; open weekends and holiday weeks
Temple Mt.	Peterborough 03458	2	2		3	550	1486	3 slopes, 9 trails				GLM, ATM, XC; open weekends and school vacations
Tenney Mt.	Box 11, Plymouth 03264	2	1		1	1400	750	2 slopes				NS, GLM, XC
Tuckerman Ravine	Appalachian Mt. Club, Pinkham Notch	(climb)				4300 (max.)					planned for '82 season	
Waterville Vy.	Waterville Vy. 03223	6	2		2	2020	1815	30	40	30	115 acres	N, GLM, ATM, XC, Nastar, Skiwee
Wildcat Mt.	Rte. 16, Jackson 03846	3	1	1		2100	1950	35	45	20	80	N, ATM, Nastar, Skiwee
Balsams Wilderness	Dixville Notch 03576	1	2			1000	1700		65			N, ATM, Nastar
NEW JERSEY												
Campgaw	17 Fyke Road Mahwah 07430	2	1			270	450	open slope and trail			60	NS
Craigmeur	1175 Green Pond Rd., Newfoundland 07435	1	1		2	250	1050	4 slopes			100	NS, N, ATM, XC
Hidden Valley	Vernon 07462	2				620	780	4 trails			100	NS, ATM; private club weekends and holidays—open to public all other times
Ski-Mt.	Branch Ave., Pine Hill 08021	1	1		3	237		3 slopes			95	NS, N, GLM
Vernon Valley/Great Gorge	McAfee 07428	15				1033	440	30	45	25	100	NS, N, ATM, XC, lodging
NEW MEXICO												
Angel Fire	Eagle Nest 87718	6				2180	8500	18	47	35	15	GLM, ATM, Nastar, lodging
Red River	Box 303, Red River 87558	4			2	1524	8750	25	40	35	25	GLM, Nastar

NEW MEXICO (cont.)

NAME OF AREA	ADDRESS	GONDOLA/ TRAM	CHAIR	SURFACE	TOW	VERTICAL RISE (IN FEET)	BASE ELEV. (IN FEET)	ADV.	INTER.	BEGINNER	PERCENTAGE OF AREA COVERED BY SNOW-MAKING	OTHER FACILITIES
NEW MEXICO (cont.)												
Sandia Peak	#10 Tramway Loop, N.E., Albuquerque 87101	1	3	3		1700	8600	10	75	15		ATM, Nastar
Santa Fe Basin	Box 2287, Santa Fe 87501		2	3	1	1650	10,350	40	40	20	20	GLM
Sierra Blanca	Box 220, Ruidoso 88345	1	5		1	1700	9700	20 (+20 expert)	40	20	5	ATM, Nastar
Sipapu	Box 29, Vadito 87579			3		800	8200					GLM, lodging
Taos Ski Vy.	Taos 87575		6	2		2612	9207	12 (+51 expert)	13	24	2	N, Nastar, lodging
NEW YORK												
Belleayre	Pine Hill 12465		4	3		1265	2125	17	59	24	24	N, ATM, XC
Big Birch	Box 418, Rt. 22, Patterson 12563		2	1	2	500	820	30	30	40	100	NS, GLM
Big Tupper	Box 820, Tupper Lake 12986		3	1	1	1152	2000	10	30	60	20	NS, GLM, ATM, XC
Big Vanilla	Woodridge 12789		3	4	2	500	1000	19 slopes		60	yes	NS, N, GLM, XC, lodging
Bluemont	Box 5, Yorkshire 14173		1	2	2	800	1300	5 slopes		30	30	NS, ATM
Bristol Mt.	RD. 3, Canandaigua 14424		4		2	1100	1000	20	50	30	95	NS, N, ATM, Nastar
Catamount	Hillsdale 12529		3	3		1000	1000	20	40	40	85	NS, N, ATM, Nastar, lodging
Cortina Valley	Haines Falls 12436		2		2	625	1925	20	60	20	90	NS, GLM, ATM, lodging
Gore Mt.	No. Creek 12853	1	5	2		2100	1500	30	50	20		N, GLM, ATM, XC

Area	Address										Facilities
Greek Peak	RD 2, Cortland 13045	5	3		900	1200	35	43	22	80	NS, N, GLM, ATM, XC, Nastar, lodging
Grossinger Ski Valley	Grossinger 12734	1	1	1	190	1420	2 slopes, 1 trail			100	GLM, lodging
Gunset	Richfield Springs 13439	2	2	1	330	1340	5 trails, 2 slopes				GLM
Hickory Ski Center	Rt. 418, Warrensburg 12885	3	3	1	1200	700	3 slopes, 12 trails			100	ATM, lodging
Hidden Valley	Lake Luzerne 12846	1			110	700	4 slopes			100	NS, ATM, lodging
Highmount	Highmount 12441	4	4		1050	2100	8 slopes, 3 trails			40	N, GLM, ATM; open Fri., Sat., Sun., and holiday weeks
Holiday Mt.	Box 629, Monticello 12701	2	4	4	400	900	30	40	30	100	NS, ATM
Holiday Valley	Box A, Ellicottville 14731	4	2	2	750	1500	25	50	25	75	NS, N, GLM, ATM, lodging
Hunter Mt.	Box 295, Hunter 12442	9	1	5	1600	1600	40	40	20	99.9	N, GLM, ATM, Nastar, lodging
Kissing Bridge	Glenwood 14069	3	5	3	500	1250	20	50	30	75	NS, N, GLM, ATM, XC, Nastar
Labrador	Truxton 13158	2	3		680		3 slopes, 13 trails			85	NS, N, ATM, Nastar
Mystic Mt.	New Woodstock 13122	1	2		590		12 slopes			75	NS, N
Oak Mt.	Box 206, Spectacular 12164	3	3		650	1600	13 slopes				ATM
Peek 'n Peak	Box 100, Clymer 14724	3	4	4	400	1400	20	60	20	85	NS, ATM, XC, Nastar, lodging
Plattekill	Roxbury 12474	1	1	1	1000	2350	14 slopes			90	ATM; open Fri., Sat., Sun., holidays, Christmas week, and mid-winter recess
Scotch Valley	Rt. 10, Stamford 12167	3	1	1	750	2200	20	60	20	25	GLM, ATM, XC
Shu-Maker Mt.	RD 2, Little Falls 13365	2	1	1	750	500	13 slopes			60	NS, Nastar
Wing Hollow	Allegany 14706	1	2		813	1540	7 slopes, 8 trails			60	NS, GLM, ATM
Snow Ridge	R.D., Turin 13473	3	3	1	500	1270	20	60	20		NS, ATM, XC, Nastar, lodging
Song Mt.	Box 149, Tully 13159	1	4		700	1298	6 slopes, 12 trails			85	NS, N, Nastar

NAME OF AREA	ADDRESS	GONDOLA/TRAM	CHAIR	SURFACE	TOW	VERTICAL RISE (IN FEET)	BASE ELEV. (IN FEET)	ADV.	INTER.	BEGINNER	PERCENTAGE OF AREA COVERED BY SNOW-MAKING	OTHER FACILITIES
NEW YORK (*cont.*)												
Sterling Forest	Box 608, Tuxedo 10987		4			450	950	10	70	20	100	NS, GLM
Swain	Swain 14884		3	2		650	1300	15	45	40	80	NS, ATM, XC, lodging
West Mt.	RD 2, West Mt. Rd., Glen Falls 12801		3	1	2	1010	450	15	70	15	50	NS, ATM, Nastar
Whiteface Mt.	Wilmington 12997		6	3		3216	1220	44	33	23	65	GLM, ATM, lodging
Willard Mt.	Greenwich 12834		1	2		465	950		2 slopes		33	N, NS
Ski Windham	Windham 12496		4		1	1550	1500	40	40	20	90	N, ATM, Nastar, lodging
NORTH CAROLINA												
Appalachian Ski Mt.	Box 617, Blowing Rock 28605		2	3		365	3635		8 runs		100	NS
Beech Mt.	Box 277, Banner Elk 28604		5	2	1	809	4675	20	30	50	100	NS, N, ATM, Nastar, lodging, Skiwee
Cataloochee	Rt. 5, Waynesville 28786		1	1	1	740	4660		8 runs		85	NS, ATM
Sapphire Valley	Sapphire Valley 28774		1		2	325			3 slopes		80	NS
Seven Devils	Hwy. 105, Boone 28607		2		2	600	4219		5 slopes		100	NS, GLM
Sugar Mt.	Box 369, Banner Elk 28604		3	2	1	1200	4100	30	30	35	yes	NS, N, GLM, Nastar, lodging
NORTH DAKOTA												
Trestle Valley	Minot 58701			2	1	195	1315		10 trails		80	NS, ATM, XC
OHIO												
Boston Mills	Peninsula 44264		5		4	240		10	40	50	100	NS, N, GLM, ATM
Brandywine	Box 343, Northfield 44067		6		10	241		10	40	50	100	NS

414

Area	Address										Facilities
Clear Fork	Box 308, Butler 44822	3	2	4	300		30	40	30	90	NS, ATM
Snow Trails	Box 163, Mansfield 44901	3	2	5	300	990	10	70	20	90	NS, ATM
Mad River Mt.	Bellefontaine 43311	3	1	4	300	1160	1 slope, 3 trails			100	NS, ATM, lodging
OREGON											
Anthony Lakes	Box 1045, Baker 97814	1	1		850	7125	25	50	25		N, GLM, XC
Cooper Spur	Box 335, Hood River 97031		1	1	500	4000					NS, GLM, XC
Hoodoo	Box 20, Hwy. 20, Sisters 97759	3		2	1000	4668	32	39	29		NS, GLM, XC
Mt. Ashland	Box 220, Ashland 97520	2	2	1	1150	6350	65	25	10		N, ATM, GLM, XC, Nastar
Mt. Bachelor	Box 828, Bend 97701	9		1	1700	6000	20 (+10 expert)	40	30		NS, ATM, XC, Nastar
Mt. Hood Meadows	Box 80, Govt. Camp 97028	7		1	2777	4523	20 (+10 expert)	40	30		NS, XC
Multorpor-Ski Bowl	Govt. Camp 97028	4		8	1500	3700	30	50	20		NS, GLM, XC
Spout Springs	Rt. 1, Weston	2	2	1	550	4950	4 slopes, 5 trails				NS, N, GLM, ATM, XC, Nastar, lodging, Skiwee
Timberline Lodge	Govt. Camp 97028	4		2	3500	5000	20	50	30		N, NS, GLM, ATM
PENNSYLVANIA											
Big Boulder	Lk. Harmony 18624	6	2		475	1725	20	40	40	100	NS, N, GLM, ATM, lodging
Blue Knob	Box 184, Claysburgh 16625	2	2		1052	2100	15	70	15	75	NS
Boyce Park	675 Old Frankstown Rd., Pittsburgh 15239	2	2		170		2 trails				
Buck Hill	Buck Hill Falls 18323	2	2		320	1600	2 slopes, 1 trail			yes	lodging
Camelback	Box 168, Tannersville 18372	7	3		800	1200	20	40	40	100	NS, N, GLM, lodging
Doe Mt.	RD 1, Racungie P.O. 18062	3	1	1	500	600	4 slopes, 1 trail			100	NS, ATM

NAME OF AREA	ADDRESS	NO. OF LIFTS				VERTICAL RISE (IN FEET)	BASE ELEV. (IN FEET)	RUNS (IN PERCENTAGES)			PERCENTAGE OF AREA COVERED BY SNOWMAKING	OTHER FACILITIES
		GONDOLA/TRAM	CHAIR	SURFACE	TOW			ADV.	INTER.	BEGINNER		
PENNSYLVANIA (*cont.*)												
Elk Mt.	RD 2, Union Dale 18470		5			1000	1693	40	30	30	95	NS, GLM, ATM
Hidden Valley	RD 6, Somerset 15501		2	4	1	400	2550	25	50	25	80	NS, N, ATM, XC, lodging
Jack Frost Mt.	Box 37-A-1, White Haven 18661		5	1		500	1500	25	50	25	100	N, NS, GLM, ATM
Laurel Mt.	P.O. Box 527, Ligonier 15658		1	2	2	900	2000	30	50	20	80	NS, ATM
Little Gap	Palmerton 18071		2	1	1	801	631	40	40	20	100	NS
Mt. Saint Onge	Crystal Lake Camps, RD 1, Hughesville 17737			1	1	250	1850	2 slopes, 3 trails				GLM, XC, lodging; open weekends
Seven Springs	RD 1, Champion 15622		9		4	865	2075	20	65	15	80	NS, GLM, XC, lodging
Ski Liberty	Fairfield 17320		4	1		570	580	20	50	30	100	NS, N, GLM, lodging
Ski Roundtop	RD 1, Lewisberry 17339		5	2		550	650	30	30	40	100	NS, N, GLM, ATM, Nastar
Spring Mt.	Box 42, Spring Mt. 19478		3		2	455	45		2 slopes		100	NS, GLM, ATM
SOUTH DAKOTA												
Deer Mt.	Lead 57754		1	2		600	6000		25 trails		100	NS, GLM, ATM, XC
Great Bear	Box 545, Sioux Falls 57101				4	250			9 runs			NS, ATM
TENNESSEE												
Ober Gatlinburg	Box 387, Gatlinburg 37738	1	4		1	600	2700		4 slopes		90	NS, GLM, ATM, Nastar
UTAH												
Alta	Alta 84070		8		3	2000	8550	40	35	25		GLM, ATM, XC, lodging
Beaver Mt.	124 N. Main, Logan 84321		3	1		1540	7235	40	35	25		NS, GLM, ATM

	Address										Facilities
BrianHead	P.O. Box 38, Cedar City 84720		5		1200	9800	20	60	20	64 acres	N, GLM, XC, Nastar, lodging
Brighton Ski Bowl	Brighton 84121		4		1140	8730	25	50	25		NS, GLM, XC, lodging
Deer Valley	Box 889, Park City 84060		5	1	2200	7200	37	50	13		N, ATM, lodging
Mt. Holly	Box 697, Beaver 84713		1	1	1000	9200		1 wide trail			GLM, ATM, XC, lodging
Nordic Valley	Box 285, Eden 84310		2		900	5700					NS
Park City	Box 39, Park City 84060	1	11		3100	6900	37	46	17	yes	NS, N, GLM, ATM, XC
Park West	Box 308, Park City 84060		7		2000	7000	35	45	20	5	NS, ATM, XC, Nastar, lodging
Powder Mt.	Box 117, Eden 84713		3		1300	7600	20	70	10		NS, ATM
Snowbasin	4921 Kiwana Dr., Ogden 84401		6		2400	6400	33	46	21		ATM, XC
Snowbird	Snowbird 84070	1	7		3100	7900	50	30	20		N, ATM, Nastar, lodging
Solitude	P.O. Box 17315, Salt Lake City 84117		4	1	1700	8100	33	42	25		NS, GLM
Sundance	Box 837, Provo 84601		3		1700	6100	40	50	10		NS, GLM, ATM, lodging
VERMONT											
Bolton Valley	Bolton 05477		4		1100	2150	20	60	20	yes	NS, N, ATM, XC, lodging
Bromley	Box 368, Manchester Center 05255		5	1	1334	1950	24	50	26	83	N, GLM, ATM, Nastar, lodging
Burke Mt.	E. Burke 05832		2	3	2000	1200	24	38	38	25	N, XC, lodging
Carinthia	W. Dover 05356		1	1	800	2000		8 slopes			GLM, ATM, lodging; open weekends and holidays
Jay Peak	Jay 05859	1	2	6	2153	1815	25	55	20	44	N, XC, Nastar, lodging
Killington	Killington 05751	1	11		3060	1060	33	23	44	yes	N, lodging
Mad River Glen	Waitsfield 05673		4		2000	1600	40	40	20	15	N, GLM, Nastar
Magic Mt.	Londonderry 05148		3	1	1600	1400	25	50	25	50	N, ATM, lodging
Maple Valley	W. Dummerston 05357		2	1	850			11 trails		30	NS, N, ATM
Middlebury Snow Bowl	Middlebury 05753		1	3	1100	1500		4 slopes, 12 trails			GLM, ATM
Mt. Ascutney	Box 29, Brownsville 05037		2	3	1480	800	30	40	30	yes	NS, N, GLM, ATM, XC, lodging

NAME OF AREA	ADDRESS	NO. OF LIFTS				VERTICAL RISE (IN FEET)	BASE ELEV. (IN FEET)	RUNS (IN PERCENTAGES)			PERCENTAGE OF AREA COVERED BY SNOWMAKING	OTHER FACILITIES
		GONDOLA/ TRAM	CHAIR	SURFACE	TOW			ADV.	INTER.	BEGINNER		
VERMONT (*cont.*)												
Mt. Snow	Mt. Snow 05356	2	11		1	1680	1900	10	72	18	41	N, GLM, ATM, Nastar, lodging, Skiwee
Norwich Univ.	Northfield 05663		1	2		902	850	11 trails, 3 slopes				ATM
Okemo Mt.	RFD 1, Ludlow 05149		3	6		2100	1200	20	50	30	50	N, ATM, XC, Nastar, lodging, Swikee
Pico Peak	Sherburne Pass, Rutland 05701		7	2		1967	2000	20	60	20	35	N, GLM, ATM, Nastar, lodging
Round Top	Plymouth 05056		2	1	1	1300	1300	35	35	30	yes	N, ATM, Nastar, lodging
Smugglers Notch	Jeffersonville 05464		4		1	2610	1100	34	41	25	15	N, ATM, XC, Nastar, lodging
Stowe (Mt. Mansfield, Spruce Pk.)	RD 1, Stowe 05672	1	5	3		2150	1300	15 (+5 expert)	70	10	120 acres	N, ATM, XC, Nastar, lodging
Stratton Mt.	Stratton 05155		8	3		1900	2125	25	28	47	90 acres	N, GLM, ATM, XC, Nastar, lodging
Sugarbush	Warren 05674	1	10	3		2600	1483	31	45	24	140 acres	N, GLM, ATM, Nastar, lodging
Suicide Six	Woodstock 05091		2	1		650	550	30	40	30	50	GLM, ATM
VIRGINIA												
Bryce Mt.	Basye 22810		2		3	500	1250	33	23	34	100	NS, GLM, ATM, Nastar, lodging
Homestead	Hot Springs 24445		1	1	1	695	2500	30	40	30	100	GLM, ATM, lodging
Massanutten	Box 1227, Harrisonburg 22801		4	1	2	795	1730	25	50	25	100	NS, N, GLM, ATM, Nastar, lodging
Wintergreen	Wintergreen 22958		3			500	2925	16	66	18	100	NS, N, GLM, ATM, lodging
WASHINGTON												
Alpental	Box 1038, Snoqualmie Pass 98068		4	1	4	2200	3200	40	40	20		NS, ATM

Area	Address				Vertical	Summit	% Beg.	% Int.	% Exp.	Snowmaking	Features
Crystal Mt.	Crystal Mt. 98022	7	1	10	3102	4400	40 (+30 expert)	20	10		NS, N, GLM, ATM, XC, Nastar, lodging
49° North	Box 166, Chewelah 99109	4		3	1845	3928	40	30	30	yes	N, GLM, Nastar, lodging
Mission Ridge	Box 542, Wenatchee 98801	4		4	2140	4600	20	50	30		NS, GLM, ATM, XC
Mt. Baker	2014 Moore St., Bellingham 98225	6		2	2074	3500	25	60	15		GLM, ATM
Mt. Spokane	Rt. 1, Box 41D, Mead 90021	5		2	1514	4367	30	50	20		NS, N, GLM, lodging
Ski Acres/Snoqualmie Summit (one area linked by shuttle bus)	Box 1068, Snoqualmie Pass 98068	15	2	15	900	3000	35	45	20		NS, GLM, ATM, Skiwee
Stevens Pass	Star Route, Leavenworth 98826	8		6	1800	4000	47	39	14		NS, ATM
White Pass (Sno-Country)	Box 354, Yakima 98907	3	1	1	1500	4500	20	60	20		NS, ATM, XC, lodging
WEST VIRGINIA											
Alpine Lake	Box 22, Terra Alta 26764		2	1	400	2500				yes	NS, GLM, lodging; open weekends and holidays
Canaan Valley	Box 368, Davis 26260	2	1	1	850	3430	28	44	28	70	N, NS, GLM, ATM, lodging
Oglebay Park	Wheeling 26003		2	1	330		40 acres			yes	N, ATM, XC, Nastar, lodging
Snowshoe	Snowshoe	5		5	1500	3250	20	55	25	95	NS, GLM, ATM, lodging
WISCONSIN											
Alpine Valley	Box 615, East Troy 53120	12		5	288		20	60	20	100	NS, GLM, ATM, lodging
Cascade Mt.	Box 138, Portage 53901	2	1	3	460	817	28	36	36	100	NS, ATM, Nastar, lodging
Christmas Mt.	Rt. 1, Wisconsin Dells 53965	2		2	205		7 runs			yes	NS, XC
Deepwood	Wheeler 54772		2	4	300		13 runs			yes	open weekends and holidays
Devil's Head	Merrimac 53561	8		4	495		20	60	20	100	NS, GLM, ATM, Nastar, lodging

NAME OF AREA	ADDRESS	GONDOLA/ TRAM	CHAIR	SURFACE	TOW	VERTICAL RISE (IN FEET)	BASE ELEV. (IN FEET)	ADV.	INTER.	BEGINNER	PERCENTAGE OF AREA COVERED BY SNOWMAKING	OTHER FACILITIES
WISCONSIN (*cont.*)												
Little Switzerland	Rt. 1, Slinger 53086		5		3	200		15 slopes and trails			100	NS, GLM
Mt. La Crosse	La Crosse 54061		2		3	516	620	30	50	20	100	NS, N, GLM, ATM, XC, Nastar, lodging
Navarino Hills	Rt. 1, Shiocton 54170		1		5	106		10 trails, 1 bowl			100	NS, GLM, ATM
Playboy Club	Lake Geneva 53147		3	2		211	1085	20	60	20	100	NS, N, GLM, XC, lodging
Port Mt.	Bayfield 54814			1	4	317	963	13 slopes and trails				NS, GLM, ATM, XC
Rib Mt.	Wausau 54401		2	2	1	600	1242	25	50	25	100	NS, XC, Nastar
Sheltered Valley	Three Lakes 54562			1	3	200		10 runs				
Sky Line	Friendship 53934		2	1	2	335		7 slopes and trails			100	NS
Telemark	Cable 54821		3	2	1	370	1400	20	40	40	100	NS, GLM, XC, Nastar, lodging
Timberline	Rt. 1, Arena 53503		1	1	1	390	820	7 runs			100	NS, GLM, XC
Trollhaugen	Dresser 54009		3		5	250		27	40	33	100	NS, N, GLM, ATM, XC, Nastar
Tyrol Basin	Rt. 1, Mt. Horeb 53572		1	1	3	280	850	12 runs, 1 trail				NS, ATM, Nastar
Whitecap Mts.	Montreal 54550		5		4	400		25	50	25		NS, N, GLM, ATM, XC, lodging
Wilmot Mt.	Wilmot 53192		8		6	230		40	30	30	100	NS, ATM, lodging
WYOMING												
Antelope Butte	Box 551, Grayball 82426			2		900	7900	3 slopes				open weekends and holidays
Grand Targhee	Alta 83422		3		1	2200	8000	20	70	10		N, ATM, XC, Nastar, lodging
Jackson Hole	Teton Village 83025	1	6			4139	634	50 (+5 expert)	35	10	25 acres	N, ATM, XC, Nastar, lodging, Skiwee

Resort	Location					Vertical	Elevation	5 slopes			yes	
Meadowlark	632 Bighorn Ave., Worland 82401			2	1	600	8500	30	40	30	yes	GLM; open Wed., Fri., and holidays
Medicine Bow (Happy Jack)	Box 121, Centennial 82055		2	2	2	600	9000	35	45	20		open Wed.–Sun.; daily during holidays
Snow King	Box R, Jackson 83011		2			1571	6237					N, XC, lodging
ALBERTA												
Fortress Mt.	Calgary		3	3		1100	6700	30	40	30		N, XC, Molstar
Lake Louise	Box 5, Lake Louise, Banff	1	5	3	1	3250	5400	35	45	20		N, XC, Molstar
Mormot Basin	Box 1300, Jasper		3	2		2300	5680	30	35	35	yes	GLM, CTM, Molstar
Mt. Norquay	Box 40, Banff		2	4	1	1350	5700	50	15	35	yes	N, Molstar
Sunshine Village	Box 1510, Banff	1	5	3	1	3514	5440	20	60	20		NS, N, CTM, Molstar, lodging
Westcastle	Pincher Creek			3		1700	4800	48	35	17		CTM
BRITISH COLUMBIA												
Apex Alpine	Penticton		2	2	2	1800	5450	39	46	15		lodging
Big White Ski Village	Kelowna		4	3		1850	5450					N, NS, GLM, XC, Molstar, lodging
Blackcomb	Whistler		5	1	1	4019	2214	30	50	20		GLM, lodging
Fairmont Hot Springs	Fairmont Hot Springs		1			1000	4200	15	60	25	yes	NS, XC, Molstar
Fernie Snow Valley	Fernie		1	3	1	2100	3500	35	40	25		N, GLM, XC
Forbidden Plateau	Courtenay		1	3	2	1150	2300	10	65	25		N, GLM, XC, lodging
Gibson Pass	Manning Parc	2	2	1	1	1388	4339	20	50	30		GLM, XC
Grouse Mountain	Vancouver	2	4	2	2	1200	2800	40	40	20		N, NS, GLM
Harper Mountain	Kamloops		1	2	1	1400	4000	25	50	25		NS, GLM, XC
Hemlock Valley	Harrison Mills		3	3	2	1200	3300	13	65	22		NS, GLM, XC, lodging
Kimberly Ski Resort	Kimberly		2	1	2	2300	4200	25	60	15	15	N, NS, GLM, XC, lodging
Panorama	Invermere		3	2	1	3200	3700	15	63	22		GLM, XC, lodging
Red Mountain	Rossland		3	1	1	2700	3800	40	40	20		NS, GLM, XC, Molstar, lodging
Silver Star Vernon	Vernon		3	4		1600	4680	15	50	35		N

NAME OF AREA	ADDRESS	GONDOLA/ TRAM	CHAIR	SURFACE	TOW	VERTICAL RISE (IN FEET)	BASE ELEV. (IN FEET)	ADV.	INTER.	BEGINNER	PERCENT- AGE OF AREA COVERED BY SNOW- MAKING	OTHER FACILITIES
BRITISH COLUMBIA (*cont.*)												
Tod Mountain	Kamloops		3	2		3100	3963	50	25	25		N, GLM, XC, Molstar
Whitewater	Nelson		2	1	1	1300	5400	50	30	20		GLM, XC
Whistler	Whistler	1	10	2	1	4280	2140	15	47	38		N, XC, Molstar, lodging
MANITOBA												
Holiday Mountain	La Riviere			3	2	380	1250	9 slopes			90	NS, lodging
Mt. Agassiz	McCreary		1	2	2	505	2302	30	50	20	100	NS, GLM, XC; open Tues.–Sun.
Stony Mountain Winter Park	Winnipeg			2	2	125		5 slopes		20	100	NS, GLM, XC; open
SASKATCH- EWAN												
Blackstrap Recreation Site	Saskatoon			1	2	290		12 runs			100	NS, GLM; open Wed. and Fri.–Sun.
White Track	Moose Jaw			1	2	300					100	NS, XC; open Wed.–Sun., daily during Christmas
NEW BRUNS- WICK												
Poley Mountain	Waterford			2	1	750		8 slopes			40	XC
Silverwood Winter Park	Fredericton			1	1	305		3 trails				NS, GLM
Sugarloaf Provincial Park	Atholville		1	2		507	150	7 trails				NS, GLM, CTM, XC
NOVA SCOTIA												
Ben Eoin Recreation Centre	Sydney			1	1	470	30				80	NS, ATM, XC

Area	Location											Notes
Martok Ski Area						610	90					80	NS, GLM
PRINCE EDWARD ISLAND	Charlottetown	2	1	3	180	120		6 slopes				NS, XC; closed Mon. and Tues. except holidays
ONTARIO												
Blue Mountain	RR 3, Collingwood	12	7	5	800	625	17	56	27	12 trails	85	N, NS, XC, Molstar, lodging
Calabogie Peaks	Calabogie	1	3	1	760	505	40	35	25		40	XC, lodging
Candiac	Dacre		3		600			7 trails				XC; open Wed., weekends, and holidays
Carlington Park	Ottawa			1	70							NS; located in center of Ottawa
Devil's Elbow	Bethany	3	3		350	1200		7 slopes			100	XC
Echo Ridge	Box 137, Kearney		1	1	350							GLM, lodging
Happy Valley Ski Resort	Walkerton		1	1	175							NS, XC, lodging; open Wed.–Sun.
Hidden Valley	RR 2, Huntsville	2	1	1	335	945	20	50	30		90	GLM, XC, lodging
Horseshoe Vy.	Box 607, Burrie	4	2		400	1000	20	50	30		80	N, XC, Molstar, lodging
Loch Lomond	RR 4, Thunder Bay	3	1	1	800	975	35	40	25		90	NS
Mansfield Skiways	Mansfield		4		400		10	60	30		75	
Moonstone	RR 4, Coldwater	3	3	1	450	150	20	60	20	7 slopes	100	N, GLM, ATM, XC
Mountain View	RR 2, Midland		2	1	150							XC; open weekends and holidays
Mount Pakenham	Pakenham	1	1	1	275	450	25	25	50		50	NS, GLM, XC; open Wed.–Sun.
Searchmont Vy.	Searchmont	1	2	2	700	900				15 slopes	90	GLM
Ski Dagmar	Ashburn	1	2	2	200		5	85	10		90	NS, GLM, XC
Talisman	Kimberley	3	1	1	600	775		50	50		75	NS, N, XC, lodging
Tally-Ho Winter Park	Huntsville		2	1	208	992		50	50			GLM, XC, lodging
QUEBEC												
Alta	Val-David	1	1		775	1100	50	25	25		70	N, CTM, lodging
Belle Neige	Val Morin	1	3		507	550		10 slopes			30	XC, lodging
Bromont Ski Center	Box 29, Bromont	3	1		1300							NS, GLM, XC
Edelweiss	RR 2, Wakefield	2	4	1	625	570	30	40	30		100	NS, CTM, XC, lodging

QUEBEC (*cont.*)

NAME OF AREA	ADDRESS	GONDOLA/TRAM	CHAIR	SURFACE	TOW	VERTICAL RISE (IN FEET)	BASE ELEV. (IN FEET)	ADV.	INTER.	BEGINNER	PERCENTAGE OF AREA COVERED BY SNOW-MAKING	OTHER FACILITIES
Gray Rocks	Box 1000, St. Jovite, Mt. Tremblant		3	2		610	830	38	29	33	60	XC, lodging
Le Relais	Lac Beauport		1	4		750	600	9 trails and slopes			25	N, NS, CTM, lodging
Mont Alouette	Ste. Adèle			4		509		20	50	30	yes	GLM, XC, lodging
Mont Blanc	Saint-Faustin		1	5		900		9 runs			yes	XC, lodging
Mont Carmel	Valmont		2	3		495			50	50	35	NS, GLM, XC
Mont-Gabriel	Mont-Gabriel		1	9		750	570	40	50	10	50	NS, XC, lodging
Mont Grand Fonds	La Malbaie			2		1200		10 trails				XC
Mont Habitant	St. Sauveur des Monts		4			500	700	30	40	30	80	NS, XC, lodging
Mont Olympia	Piedmont		1	4		800	605				40	NS, ATM, GLM, XC
Mont Orford	Magog		3	3	1	1650	1200	27	33	40	15	N, XC, Molstar
Mont-Plante	Box 17, Val David				2	450	1075	11 slopes				NS
Mont Ste. Anne	Box 40, Beaupré	1	4	8	1	2050	2625	6 slopes				N, XC, lodging
Mont St. Castin	Lac Beauport		2	4	1	550	617	10	67	23	yes	NS, lodging
Mont Ste. Marie	Lac Ste. Marie		3	1		1250	655	16 slopes			40	N, XC, lodging
Mont St. Sauveur	St. Sauveur des Monts		4	3		700		30	40	30	66	NS, N
Mont Sutton	Sutton		5	2		1550	1400	28	56	16	3	N, lodging
Mt. Tremblant	Mt. Tremblant		8	3		2131	879	20	60	20	40	XC, lodging
Owl's Head	Mansonville		5	1		1770	680	21 trails				GLM, XC, lodging
Ski Morin Heights	Morin Heights		5	1		700	680					
Vallée Bleue	Val David		1	3		365	1100	12 trails				lodging
Vallée du Parc	Blvd. du Parc, Grand'Mère		1	3		550	500				75	NS, XC

Glossary

For convenience, this glossary is divided into five sections: Technique, Equipment, Terrain and Ski Area Terms, Competition, and General. Terms listed in each of these areas are in alphabetical order.

TECHNIQUE

Abstem   A stemmed turn in which the lower ski is stemmed instead of the uphill ski. Archaic.

Angulation   A body position in which the knees and hips are rolled into the hill in order to edge the skis. The upper body is angled outward and down the hill to compensate for this action. Also called Comma Position at its extreme.

Anticipation   Rotation of the upper body in the direction of the turn before unweighting and edge change. Distinguished from rotation inasmuch as anticipation can be followed by counterrotation or a reversing of the shoulders as the turn is carved.

ATM   Accelerated Teaching Method.

Avalement   An action in which the skier retracts the legs to stay in contact with the snow when going over a bump. Derived from the French *avaler* ("to swallow"). The skier swallows up irregularities in terrain or any tendency of his own skis to leave the snow. Action is characterized by a momentary sitting back.

Boogy To ski all out.

Carved Turn A turn arced by a skier with little or no sideslip or skidding.

Certification The method used in the United States and Canada to test instructors. A certified instructor has passed both written and practical examinations administered by a board of examiners who are experienced ski instructors. In order to remain certified, an instructor must attend an "up-date" clinic every two or three years, depending on the division.

Check Any maneuver to slow down the skis with an Edgeset (*q.v.*).

Christie A contraction of the word Christiania; any turn in which the skis are in a parallel position as the turn is completed.

Comma Position *See* Angulation.

Counterrotation A means of initiating a turn by quick unweighting, twisting the feet to turn, with the shoulders turning in a direction opposite to that of the turn. Also referred to as Reverse Shoulder.

Daffy Jump into the air, splitting legs as in a space walk. Freestyle term.

Downhill Ski The lower ski or the one that will become the lower ski in any turn. Also known as the "outside" or "turning" ski.

Down Unweighting The removal of the body's weight on the snow by "dropping" the body sharply.

Edgeset Increasing the holding action of the edges. The skier may set edges or create a "platform" before the turn by increasing the angle or weight applied to the edges.

Edging A means of controlling the sideward slippage of the skis by setting the skis at an angle to the snow so that they "bite" the surface.

Fall Line The shortest distance down the slope; the steepest gradient.

Garland An exercise in which the skis are alternately slipped downhill and traversed across the hill.

Geländesprung A German term meaning terrain jump; an aerial maneuver to clear obstacles by springing into the air.

Glisser, Glissement French for sliding. In ski racing, refers to a subtle "second sense" by which the skier senses the speed or sliding of his skis on the snow and through this intuition manages to increase his speed.

GLM Graduated Length Method. A system of ski instruction in which the novice starts on shorter-length skis and graduates to longer skis as he progresses in skill and speed.

Heel Thrust   The pushing of the tails of the skis down the hill in order to complete a turn or to check speed.

Herringbone   A climbing step in which the skis are edged and held in a reverse-V position in order to prevent them from slipping back.

Inside Ski   The ski which is on the inside of the turn or will become the inside ski in any turn.

Jet Turn   Refers to an edge-set turn in which the skier uses the resultant reaction from the edge set on his legs and skis to project his feet forward in the turning direction. Accompanied by Anticipation.

Kangaroo   An extreme Avalement turn.

Kick Turn   A means of reversing direction on skis when in a stationary position.

Killy Start   A racing start in which the skier attempts to build up as much upper-body speed down the course as he can before allowing his feet to pass through the starting wand to set the electric clock running. Idea is credited to Jean-Claude Killy.

Mambo   A series of turns using both overrotation and counterrotation to produce a light, dancelike movement on easy slopes.

Moebius Flip   Single somersault with a body twist.

Parallel Christie   A turn in which the skis remain parallel throughout the turn; usually a skidded rather than a carved turn.

Prejump   A maneuver in which a skier jumps before he reaches the crest of a bump so that his trajectory follows the contour of the bump.

Reverse Shoulder   *See* Counterrotation.

Rotation   A means of initiating a turn by rotation of the shoulders in the direction of the turn.

Royal Christie   A christie executed on one ski, with the other ski elevated and behind the skier. Also called Revel.

Ruade   A parallel turn made by diving forward and unweighting the skis by retracting the tails, by pulling up the legs in the manner of a horsekick.

Rücklage   A German word meaning backward lean.

Schuss   Skiing down the fall line without turns or checks.

Schwups   Austrian term describing wide-track approach to skidded beginner turns. From a wide, partial stem stance, the skier brings one ski parallel to the other in the completion phase.

Short Swing   A continuous series of parallel turns down the fall line with checks.

Sideslip   Sliding of the skis sideways by flattening the skis.

Snowplow A basic means of checking speed accomplished by opening the tails of the skis into a V position and edging the skis. Also called a double stem.

Snowplow Turn A turn made out of the snowplow position by shifting the weight to the ski that will be on the outside of the turn.

Split Rotation A turn initiated with rotation and completed with counterrotation, or vice versa. *See also* Anticipation.

Spread Eagle Jump with arms and legs spread out. Freestyle term.

Steered Turns Turns of the stem variety in which one of the skis is pointed in the new direction in the initiation phase of the turn.

Stem The basis for a series of turns in which the tail of one ski is pushed out so that the turn is started from a half-V position.

Stem Christie An advanced form of stem turn in which the ski is stemmed only slightly and in which the other ski is immediately brought alongside so that most of the turn is completed with skis parallel.

Stem Turn A turn in which the uphill ski is stemmed and then weighted, and then held in that position until the arc of the turn is well established. The turn can be finished either in the stemmed position or the skis can be brought back to a parallel position in the completion phase.

Style The individual interpretation of technique.

Technique A formal exposition of ski instruction from the beginning stages to the advanced maneuvers. Also called a teaching system or a teaching method. Hence American Technique, the Official Modern Austrian Ski System, the French Method.

Traverse Skiing across the slope at some angle to the fall line.

Unweighting A means of reducing the weight on the skis before turning so that the skis turn more easily.

Uphill Christie A turn up "into" the hill with skis parallel. The completion phase of all christie turns.

Uphill Ski The upper ski or the one that will become the upper ski in any ski turn.

Up-unweighting Unweighting by means of rising sharply. When the rising motion slows or stops, the skis are unweighted.

Vorlage Forward lean or shifting the weight forward before a turn.

Wedeln A series of parallel turns made in the fall line with a minimum of edge set.

Weighting The application of weight to the skis in order to set the edges. Usually accomplished by angulation or by rising sharply.

Weight Shift   A transfer of weight from one ski to the other, specifically from the downhill ski to the uphill ski in the initiation phase of steered turns.

Windshield Wiper   A sloppy, heavily skidded turn.

EQUIPMENT

Antifriction Pad   A mechanical device or antifriction material placed between boot and ski to promote binding release, especially in forward falls when friction load builds up near the toe.

Arlberg Strap   A leather strap attached to the ski and wrapped around the boot to prevent the ski from running away when the binding releases. Archaic; also, dangerous.

Base   A protective layer of plastic covering the running surface of the ski and designed to make the ski slide easier.

Bear Trap   Any nonrelease binding, specifically toe irons. Archaic.

Camber   The arch built into a ski so that the ski can distribute the skier's weight over the entire length of the ski.

Chatter   The tendency of skis not to grip on hard snow or ice, caused either by the inability of the ski to damp vibration or by the skier's not weighting the ski properly and sufficiently.

Cracked Edge   Type of steel edge on a ski that is neither segmented nor one piece, but consists of a partially segmented steel strip.

Damping   The quality in a ski that prevents it from vibrating excessively after it is deflected by a bump. Skis insufficiently damped have a tendency to be unstable.

Double Boot   A ski boot with a soft inner boot for improved fit and warmth built into a stiff outer boot that provides control over the skis and support for the ankle.

Edges   The strips of metal, usually made of hard steel, on the outer edges of the running surfaces of skis.

Effective Torsion   Combined mathematical relationships of a ski's torsional rigidity and its side camber dimensions. One of the measurements in the SKIpp Test (*q. v.*).

Flexibility, Flex   A ski must be flexible enough throughout its length to float in powder, to absorb bumps, and to get a maximum amount of edge on the snow, yet stiff enough so that it provides a grip on hard snow and ice. Skis tend to do one thing better than the other, which defines their "flex."

Forward Spring   The characteristic of touring skis to spring forward and upward when unweighted. This aids the kick.

Front Throw   A device for tightening the cable assembly that holds the boot to the skis. Archaic.

Groove   The channel that runs almost the full length of the running surface of the ski and used to be regarded as essential to keep the skis running straight when they are flat on the snow.

Heel Release   A device that enables the heel to release upward from the ski in the event of a forward fall.

Highback   Refers to the extension of the back of the boot up the rear calf of the skier's leg. It has become an integral part of the boot, although it began as an optional attachment.

Hook(y)   Condition of a ski when it wants to continue turning after the skier has ceased any turning action of his own. Instability in traversing. Often caused by concave bottoms or warpage.

Long Thong   A binding consisting of a long leather strap fastened to the ski and then wound around the boot in a special pattern to provide maximum support. Widely used in 1940s and 1950s in connection with a turntable. Archaic.

Notching   Two vertical notches in front of the ski boot sole spaced to engage two projections in the toe unit of the binding. Archaic.

Polyethylene   A plastic available in various degrees of hardness and used for the running surfaces of skis. It is very fast on snow. Usually on skis under the trade name of P-Tex.

Release Binding   Any Heel or Toe Release or a combination thereof that releases the skis from the boot in the event of a bad fall.

Rotamat   *See* Turntable.

Safety Binding   A misnomer for a Release Binding.

Safety Strap   A strap attached or wrapped on the boot and fixed at one or two points on the ski to prevent it from going dangerously down the hill after a skier has come out of his binding. Another misnomer; more accurately called a leash. *See also* Windmilling.

Shovel   Area near front tip of the ski.

Side Camber   The arc built into the sides of skis to assist in turning. Also known as side cut.

Sidewall   The side of the ski.

Ski Brake   An attachment to the ski or binding that prevents a ski from sliding after the binding has released.

SKIpp Test Ski Performance Prediction Test. A system of bench testing skis correlated with on-snow performance.

Step-in Binding Usually, a release binding consisting of an integral toe and heel unit that snaps the boot in place as the skier steps on the ski.

Tail Rear end of the ski.

Toe Release Any unit that holds the toe of the boot to skis but releases in the event of a twisting fall.

Torsion A quality in skis that determines the ability of the skis to twist in the vicinity of the tip when passing over uneven terrain. Also referred to as torsional stiffness.

Tracking The quality of skis to maintain a given direction firmly without wandering.

Turntable A rotation heel binding. Rotamat.

Warmup Pants or Suit Insulated or down-filled clothing usually worn over regular ski clothes. Easily unzipped when the skier, or the weather, has warmed up.

Warp A twist in a ski.

Windmilling Flailing about of a ski after a skier has fallen. Considered dangerous because it may cut or otherwise injure skier. Caused by a "Safety Strap."

TERRAIN AND SKI AREA TERMS

Aerial Tramway A large lift in which two large cabins are suspended from heavy cables. As one cabin goes up, the other comes down, jig-back fashion. Usually found only in very large areas with steep approaches to the top of the mountain. An aerial tram car may accommodate as many as a hundred or more passengers.

Base A firm layer of hard-packed snow covering the bare ground. Necessary to prevent ski bottoms from being damaged by rocks and dirt.

Boiler Plate A covering of solid ice resulting from a hard freeze following thawing conditions or rain.

Breakable Crust A condition in which the surface of the snow freezes into a crust when there is loose snow beneath it. This condition is most frequently encountered in spring and following warm wind on new snow.

Chairlift A form of uphill transportation in which a series of chairs is suspended permanently from a continuously moving cable. Each chair can accommodate one to four skiers, depending on design.

Corn   A type of snow found in spring or warm weather and formed by alternating thawing and freezing. This action removes the sharp edges off the snow crystals and gives the skier the illusion that he is skiing on ball bearings.

Crud   *See* Breakable Crust or Mashed Potatoes.

Frozen Granular   A type of snow often confused with ice but which is often made up of crystals of frozen snow.

Gondola   A lift consisting of a series of enclosed cars or cabins suspended from a continuously moving cable. Unlike the chairlift, the cabins are loaded while they are stationary and then are clamped on the cable by means of a special mechanism.

Grooming   Improving snow conditions for skiing by machinery: rolling, packing, cutting down bumps, breaking up ice.

J-Bar   A lift in which a series of J- or L-shaped bars is suspended from a continuously moving cable. The skier leans against the bar and is pulled uphill.

Lift Line   A line of skiers waiting to load onto a ski lift. Also the straight cut through trees where the lift ascends the mountain.

Mashed Potatoes   A type of snow that gets wet and heavy as a result of warm weather.

Mogul   A bump formed by the turning action of skiers. Usually found in quantity on steeper slopes, particularly following a heavy snowfall.

Packed Powder   A condition of snow that is packed either by skiing across it or by machinery. Packed powder is firm but has a soft, almost fluffy surface, which makes it ideal for skiing.

Piste   A term used in all Alpine countries of Europe meaning a hard-packed trail or slope.

Pomalift or Platterpull   A lift consisting of a series of steel bars, usually retractable, that can be suspended from a continuously moving cable. The bars have disks attached. The skier straddles the disk and is then hauled uphill.

Powder   Light, dry snow.

Rope Tow   A form of uphill transportation consisting of a continuously moving rope. The skier is pulled uphill by grasping the rope.

Sitzmark   A hole made in the snow by a skier's fall.

"Ski!"   A warning that a loose ski is coming down the hill.

Snowcat   Actually a trade name for Tucker over-the-snow vehicles, but used generically by skiers to designate all over-the-snow, tracked vehicles.

Spring Conditions   A catch-all phrase used in snow reporting to designate constantly variable conditions due to freezing temperatures at night and above-freezing temperatures throughout most of the day.

T-Bar   A lift consisting of a series of T-shaped bars suspended from a continuously moving cable. The T accommodates two skiers who sit partially on the bar and are pulled uphill.

"Track Left" or "Track Right"   A warning a descending skier shouts to someone in his path whom he intends to pass, "left" or "right" indicating on which side the skier will pass.

Transition   A change in ski terrain, as when going from a steep pitch to a flat section on the trail.

COMPETITION

Alpine   All competitive events whose basic element is down-mountain skiing: Downhill, Slalom, Giant Slalom (*q.v.*).

Citizen's Race   An FIS term used to distinguish a race for recreational skiers from regular, sanctioned competitions for card-carrying, seeded racers.

Closed Gate   A Gate whose line between the two poles is in the Fall Line.

Combined   The result of two or more races arrived at by converting the results of each into points and then adding them together. *See also* FIS Points.

Downhill   A race essentially down the mountain in which control gates are used only to check unsafe speeds and to guide the racer around dangerous obstacles.

Dual Course or Parallel Course   Head-to-head racing in which two courses are set parallel down the mountain and two racers start simultaneously out of a dual starting gate. Since no two courses can be exactly the same, dual slaloms usually are decided by taking two runs in which the racers switch courses on the second run; or a timer is used to decide close races.

Elbow   A slalom figure in which a Closed Gate is followed by an Open Gate set off to one side.

Europa Cup   A series of Alpine races, patterned after the World Cup, conducted each winter in the European Alpine countries, principally among racers not on the more difficult World Cup circuit.

FIS Points A mathematical system used to convert times and distances to points, both to determine the skier's ranking in the combined standings and to determine his seeding position.

Flush A slalom figure made up of three or more Closed Gates in succession.

Four-way Competition Ski competition that involves Downhill, jumping, Slalom, and cross-country. Rare if not archaic.

Gate Any arrangement of two flags or poles through which a skier must pass in a race.

Geschmozzel Start A start in Alpine racing no longer used. All racers started at once.

Giant Slalom A form of Alpine racing in which the racer passes through a series of gates connected by relatively long traverses. Giant Slalom combines elements of both Slalom and Downhill.

Hairpin A slalom figure made up of two successive Closed Gates.

H-Gate (Seelos Flush) A three-gate slalom figure in which a Closed Gate is sandwiched between two Open Gates.

Hot Dog Contest Acrobatic skiing contest scored with points for difficulty, style, etc. Hot dog or hotdogger refers to a daring, acrobatic, or fast skier.

Nastar National Standard Race. Skiers compete in easy, open Giant Slalom courses at many areas across the United States. Their results are comparable because pacesetters who set the standard at the areas have met in preseason and are mathematically equalized.

Nations Cup FIS trophy awarded annually to the national ski team that earns the greatest aggregate number of World Cup points in a season.

Nor-Ams A series of Alpine races, patterned after the World Cup, conducted each winter in North America, principally among American and Canadian racers who are not in Europe with their national teams.

Open Gate A gate whose line between the two poles is across the Fall Line.

Riesenslalom German word for Giant Slalom.

Section Timing A racer's time over a given section of a slalom, giant slalom, or downhill course. Section and interval timing are used extensively by coaches and ski journalists to analyze where a racer won a race, e.g., on the flat, in a tricky combination of gates.

Seeding A method of classifying racers in a given race according to ability. Racers are usually seeded in groups of fifteen, each racer's group being determined by the number of FIS Points he has. Within each group, a racer's starting number is determined by draw.

Ski Meister A German term meaning ski master; in four-way competition the competitor who has the best combined score in Downhill, Slalom, jumping, and cross-country.

Slalom   An Alpine form of competition in which the racer must run a course designated by a series of gates set in various combinations so as to test his technique, speed, and agility. Failure to pass through the gate properly results in disqualification.

World Cup   Overall awards given annually to the man and the woman skier who earn the greatest number of World Cup points in a season. World Cup circuit usually consists of an equal number of Downhill, Giant Slalom, and Slalom races during the winter. Awards are also given to the top scorer in each discipline and the combined.

GENERAL

American Plan   A method followed by some lodges and hotels in which the per-day cost includes both meals and lodging.

Charter Flight   A flight (usually to Europe or a major resort) in which a group charters a plane for the purposes of skiing.

European Plan   A method followed by most lodges and hotels in which the per-day cost includes only lodging, meals (if available) being to order and charged separately.

High Season   A time of the year when the resorts are busiest, specifically the two weeks over Christmas–New Year's, from mid-February to mid-March, and over Easter if Easter falls within the ski season. European hotels usually raise their rates during these periods.

Joring, Ski-Joring   A skier, without poles and holding on to a rope, is pulled by a horse, snowmobile, or other motive power along the snow.

Low Season   That part of the ski season when most resorts are relatively quiet, usually before Christmas, in January, and in late spring.

Modified American Plan   Hotel accommodation including room, breakfast, and dinner, but not lunch. Favored at many ski resorts.

Package Tour   An arrangement whereby the skier pays for everything—transportation, lifts, rooms, and meals—at one time. Some package tours are somewhat less comprehensive.

Powderhound   A skier who loves and seeks out deep powder skiing.

Schussboomer   Also known as a boomer, a skier who skis recklessly and indiscriminately.

Snow Bunny   A new or beginning skier.

Ski Organizations

ASA (American Ski Association)   The largest recreational-skier organization in the United States.

ASF (American Ski Federation)   Washington-based lobbying and umbrella organization for the ski industry.

CSA (Canadian Ski Association)   The Canadian equivalent of USSA (*q.v.*). It makes the rules for the sport throughout Canada, sanctions races, promotes safety on skis, and raises funds for the Canadian teams.

CSIA (Canadian Ski Instructors Alliance)   The Canadian organization for ski instructors. CSIA determines the technique that will be taught by Canadian instructors and publishes a manual to that effect. It also certifies instructors through boards of examiners who give written and practical examinations.

FIS (Federation Internationale de Ski)   This is the world body governing competition. Through its committees and its annual congress it makes the rules for the various ski races, determines eligibility, approves courses for international competition (through its technical delegates), sanctions events eligible for FIS points, selects the sites for the biennial FIS World Championships, and approves the courses for Olympic competition.

NSAA (National Ski Areas Association)   A professional group for ski area managers in the United States. It deals with such common area problems as trail marking, safety, insurance, marketing, and legal matters.

NSPS (National Ski Patrol System) A volunteer organization of skiers who patrol the slopes and render first aid to the injured. NSPS is organized along the regional lines of USSA and each region has several subregions. Members must be experienced skiers and highly proficient in first-aid skills.

PSIA (Professional Ski Instructors of America) An association of professional ski instructors in the United States. This group is responsible for the American Technique and other matters of concern to professional ski instructors. PSIA does not certify instructors. This is left to divisional certification groups whose geographic locations roughly correspond to those of the amateur divisions (*see* USSA).

SIA (Ski Industries of America) A professional group that consists of manufacturers, distributors, and importers of ski clothing and equipment. SIA conducts one major trade show annually in the spring, studies tariffs, and generally promotes the sport.

USSA (United States Ski Association) The ski organization in the United States charged with implementing the FIS rules in this country, raising funds for the national teams, sanctioning national championships and other major races, and concerning itself with almost every aspect of competitive skiing. However, an "independent subsidiary," the United States Ski Educational Foundation, really controls the ski team.

A Chronology of Ski Developments

1850–51 The organization of first "snowshoe" clubs reported among prospectors in the "Lost Sierras" in California.

1853 First downhill races by showshoers, in Onion Valley, California.

1856 "Snowshoe" Thomson, a Norwegian immigrant, makes the first of his ninety-mile mail runs on skis between Placerville, California, and Genoa, Nevada, setting off a "snowshoe" rage. He continued the runs until 1869.

1860 Sondre Nordheim makes the first officially measured jump (30.5 meters) in Morgedal, Norway.

1866–75 Peak of racing enthusiasm in California. Races are of the downhill type with money prizes for the winners. "Dope" (wax) becomes a factor in racing.

1868 The first public discussion of ski technique (in Norway) following the use of the Telemark turn by the skiers of Telemark in a competition with skiers from Christiania (Oslo).

1877 Christiania (Oslo) Ski Club founded.

1882 Nansen Ski Club, Berlin, New Hampshire, becomes first ski club in America organized along modern lines and remains the oldest ski club in this country with a continuous history.

1887 First jumping competition in the United States, at Red Wing, Minnesota, won by Mikkel Hemmesveit, a Norwegian immigrant.

1888 Fridtjof Nansen, a Norwegian, traverses southern Greenland using skis. The event itself and the book he subsequently published resulted in a tremendous interest throughout Europe in skiing. The two combined are usually considered responsible for opening the Alpine skiing era.

Skis first reported used in New York City, during blizzard of '88.

1891 Group of eleven clubs forms the Central Ski Association, an unsuccessful forerunner of the National Ski Association (now United States Ski Association).

1892 First Holmenkollen meet (jumping and cross-country).

First German books on ski technique.

1894 Fritz Huitfeld produces the first toe irons, a significant invention that made positive control over the skis feasible and greatly speeded the development of skiing on the more difficult Alpine slopes.

1896 An Austrian, Mathias Zdarsky, publishes the first methodical analysis of the stem turn and its application to Alpine skiing. The method advocated by Zdarsky involved a single pole.

1903 Ski Club of Great Britain founded.

1904 National Ski Association founded at Ishpeming, Michigan. Carl Tellefsen elected its first president.

Montreal Ski Club, Canada's first, founded and a few days later conducts first Canadian jumping meet.

1905 Zdarsky sets first slalom course. This required the competitors to go around a single pole, not through a gate made up of two poles.

1907 First U.S. cross-country championships, held at Ashland, Wisconsin, won by Asario Autio.

Hannes Schneider starts the ski school at St. Anton, Austria.

1909 Dartmouth Outing Club is founded and Fred Harris elected first president.

1910 First International Ski Congress held at Christiania, Norway.

Alpine skiing takes on a distinct identity of its own with the publication of ski technique books in English and German.

1911 First Dartmouth Winter Carnival.

First ski factory in the United States opened by C. A. Lund in St. Paul, Minnesota. It remains in continuing operation as the Northland Ski Company.

The stem christiania first described as such by Carl Luther, a German writer, although Hannes Schneider had developed the turn as early as 1908.

1913 Dartmouth defeats McGill in the first intercollegiate ski meet at St. Sauveur, Quebec.

1917 First community winter carnival held at Newport, New Hampshire. First Canadian cross-country championships are staged by the Montreal Ski Club.

1920–24 Hannes Schneider formalizes his technique into an instruction system, which subsequently became known as the Arlberg Technique. The first truly Alpine technique, it advocated the abandonment of the Telemark.

1921 Canadian Amateur Ski Association formed. First Canadian national championships in jumping and cross-country held.

First modern slalom set at Muerren, Switzerland, by Arnold Lunn. The following fall, the first systematic exposition, complete with diagrams, of two-gate slalom was published by Arnold Lunn.

Dr. Arnold Fanck, a German documentary film maker, makes the first ski movie. Hannes Schneider is the major participant in the film.

1922 United States Eastern Amateur Ski Association formed.

The first Vasa race held in Sweden.

1923 First American slalom set by Prof. Charles Proctor of Dartmouth College.

1924 First Olympic Winter Games held at Chamonix, France, with Nordic ski events only.

The International Ski Congress is made into a permanent organization: the Federation Internationale de Ski (FIS); Col. Ivar Holmquist named first president.

Cash prizes outlawed by NSA in American amateur competitions.

1925 NSA recognizes USEASA as an affiliate.

1926 First modern downhill race in the United States, held at Mt. Moosilauke, New Hampshire, and won by G. Michelson of the University of New Hampshire.

First ski shop opened in the United States, by Oscar Hambro in Boston. NSA recognizes U.S. Western Ski Association as affiliate.

1927 First snow train in North America, from Montreal to the Laurentians by the Canadian Pacific Railroad.

Central U.S. Ski Association founded. Recognized as an affiliate of NSA in 1928.

1928 First Arlberg–Kandahar race held, at St. Anton, Austria.

Second Olympic Winter Games held, at St. Moritz, Switzerland. Ski events are confined to Nordic competition.

1928 (*continued*)

FIS provisionally recognizes Ski Club of Great Britain downhill and slalom rules.

1928–30 Rudolf Lettner of Salzburg develops and perfects the attachment of steel edges to skis.

1929 First ski school in the United States organized at Peckett's in Franconia, New Hampshire, by Sig Buchmayr.

First ski train in the United States runs from Boston to Warner, New Hampshire.

An experimental downhill race is run in connection with the 1929 FIS World Championships at Zakopane, won by B. Czech of Poland.

1930 The first speed trials inaugurated, the so-called Flying Kilometer, at St. Moritz, Switzerland. Gustav Lantscher of Austria is the winner at an average speed of 66.4 miles an hour. (Ralph Miller of Dartmouth College was clocked at over 109 miles per hour at Portillo, Chile, in 1955, but this speed was unofficial, because there was no electric timing. The figure has been surpassed both by American and European racers since that time.)

Pacific Northwest Ski Association formed and recognized by NSA.

California Ski Association, predecessor of the Far West Ski Association, recognized by NSA.

FIS gives full recognition to downhill and slalom.

1931 First official FIS World Championships in downhill and slalom at Muerren, Switzerland, won by Walter Prager and David Zogg, downhill and slalom respectively; and Esme Mackinnon, both women's downhill and slalom.

1932 Third Olympic Winter Games held at Lake Placid, New York, with downhill and slalom still excluded from the ski events.

The first rope tow installed, by Alex Foster at Shawbridge, Quebec, Canada. This invention was to have a major effect on the development of skiing in North America.

First Quebec–Kandahar is held, at Mt. Tremblant, Quebec.

1933 First National Downhill Championship is held, at Mt. Moosilauke, New Hampshire, and won by Henry Woods.

Hollis Phillips wins first American Inferno race at Tuckerman's Ravine on Mt. Washington, New Hampshire.

1934 The first rope tow in the United States installed on Clint Gilbert's farm at Woodstock, Vermont.

Dick Durrance wins second American Inferno race.

1934 (*continued*)

First public ski shows held at Madison Square Garden and Boston Gardens. These events draw thousands.

Otto Furrer becomes first three-time winner of Arlberg–Kandahar.

1935   American women participate for the first time in FIS World Championships at Muerren, Switzerland.

First U.S. National Downhill and Slalom Championships held at Mt. Rainier, Washington, and won by Hannes Schroll.

First counterrotational technique introduced by Toni Ducia and Kurt Reindl, two Austrians who worked as trainers for the French team.

The first Kandahar cable binding holding the skier's heel to the ski introduced.

First snow reports published in New York City.

The first overhead cable lift, a J-bar, built at Oak Hill in Hanover, New Hampshire, by the Dartmouth Outing Club. The lift is still in operation.

1936   Fourth Olympic Winter Games at Garmisch-Partenkirchen includes downhill and slalom for the first time. The rotational technique of Toni Seelos receives first worldwide attention when, as forerunner, he beats the slalom gold medalist by over five seconds.

Development of Mt. Mansfield begins after arrival there of Sepp Ruschp from Austria.

Sun Valley opens for its first season, installing the first two chairlifts ever made.

1937   First American ski team visits Chile.

First chairlift installed in the East, at Belknap (now Gunstock), New Hampshire.

First parallel technique introduced to North America, by Fritz Loosli.

Dick Durrance wins first Harriman Cup race at Sun Valley.

1938   First aerial tramway in the United States installed, at Cannon Mountain, Franconia, New Hampshire.

First skimobile built, at Mt. Cranmore at North Conway, New Hampshire.

First Canadian chairlift built by Joseph Ryan at Mt. Tremblant, Quebec.

National Ski Patrol established with Minot Dole named as chairman of national committee.

First certification examination of ski instructors held at Woodstock, Vermont. Sepp Ruschp becomes the first certified instructor in the United States.

1938 (*continued*)

Canadian Ski Instructors Alliance formed.

Arlberg–Kandahar cancelled when Germany annexes Austria and Hannes Schneider imprisoned by the Nazis.

1939   Hjalmar Hvam introduces first workable release bindings.

Hannes Schneider arrives in the United States and takes over leadership of the ski school at Mt. Cranmore, New Hampshire. Schneider also developed the first groomed slope, by cutting down trees and completely clearing the south slope of Mt. Cranmore.

Toni Matt schusses Headwall of Tuckerman's Ravine in third and last American Inferno race.

First National Women's Downhill and Slalom Championship, at Stowe, Vermont, won by Marian McKean and Grace Carter Lindley, respectively.

1940   First T-bar in the United States installed, at Pico Peak, Vermont.

1941   87th Mountain Infantry Regiment activated, at Fort Lewis, Washington, and trains on Mt. Rainier; later merged into the 10th Mountain Division, which trained at Camp Hale, Colorado.

1946   Aspen Skiing Corporation formed under Walter Paepcke.

Platterpull (Pomalift) developed in Europe by Jean Pomagalski.

First successful metal skis made (but never marketed) by the Chance Vought Aircraft Corp. The skis were designed by Wayne Pierce, Jr., Art Hunt, and Dave Richey, who subsequently developed another metal ski design, the Alu-60.

1947   First double chairlift installed at Berthoud Pass, Colorado.

Howard Head begins first experiments with metal skis.

First Learn-to-Ski Week promoted by Sun Valley.

1948   Gretchen Fraser is first American skier to win Olympic medals (gold in slalom, silver in Alpine Combined) at fifth Olympic Winter Games at St. Moritz, Switzerland.

KLM runs first ski flight to Europe.

First chairlift in Midwest is built, at Boyne Mountain, Michigan.

A sharp swing toward reverse-shoulder technique noted among the younger racers of Europe.

1949   Mad River Glen, Vermont, and Squaw Valley, California, are opened.

1950   First postwar FIS World Championships are held at Aspen (Alpine) and Lake Placid (jumping) and Rumford, Maine (cross-country).

1952   Andrea Mead Lawrence wins gold medals in giant slalom and slalom at sixth Olympic Winter Games at Oslo, Norway. This is the first

1952 (*continued*)
Winter Olympics at which giant slalom is recognized as a separate event.

First artificially made snow used at Grossinger's Resort in New York; Fahnestock, New York, two years later, becomes first ski area to make snow on regular basis.

1953 Modern Austrian Technique using counterrotation introduced in Austria by Prof. Stefan Kruckenhauser.

1954 NCAA recognizes skiing as an intercollegiate sport.

Ski Hall of Fame dedicated at Ishpeming, Michigan.

First FIS Women's Nordic Championships.

1955 Modern Austrian Technique first internationally demonstrated at International Ski School Congress at Val d'Isere, France.

Hannes Schneider dies.

First buckle boots introduced by Henke.

First stretch pants introduced by Bogner.

First polyethylene base introduced by Kofix.

1956 Toni Sailer wins downhill, slalom, and giant slalom at Cortina d'Ampezzo, Italy, the first time that a skier made a "grand slam" of all three Alpine events at an Olympic Winter Games.

Austrian Technique makes heavy inroads in American skiing after its introduction here.

1958 Buddy Werner becomes first American male racer to win a major European race when he wins Combined at the Lauberhorn.

Lucille Wheeler of Canada wins gold medals in giant slalom and downhill at the FIS World Championships at Badgastein; Sally Deaver of the United States wins silver medal in giant slalom.

First gondola installed, at the Wildcat area in New Hampshire.

1959 Buddy Werner becomes first American male to win a major European downhill, winning at the Hahnenkamm in Kitzbuehel, Austria.

1960 French become the first team to use metal skis successfully in winning several major European downhills prior to the Olympics.

Eighth Olympic Winter Games, at Squaw Valley, California. Canada's Ann Heggtveit wins slalom; Penny Pitou wins silver medals in downhill and giant slalom; Betsy Snite wins silver medal in slalom. France's Jean Vuarnet wins men's downhill on metal skis.

1961 Professional Ski Instructors of America (PSIA) organized at Whitefish, Montana.

Christian Pravda wins first professional ski race at Aspen, picking up $1,500 in prize money.

1961 (*continued*)

Ski Industries of America (SIA), the first nationwide trade organization, opens New York City offices.

Bob Beattie, University of Colorado ski coach, named head coach of the U.S. Alpine team for the 1962 FIS World Championships. Two years later he became the first American coach to succeed himself when he was named to lead the 1964 Olympic team.

1962 Chuck Ferries wins Hahnenkamm slalom.

NSA changes name to United States Ski Association (USSA).

PSIA formulates American Ski Technique.

1963 National Ski Areas Association (NSAA) founded.

1964 Billy Kidd and Jimmy Heuga become the first American men to win Olympic medals for skiing, being second and third, respectively, in the slalom at the ninth Olympic Winter Games at Innsbruck, Austria. Jean Saubert ties for second in the giant slalom and places third in the slalom.

Buddy Werner killed in a Swiss avalanche shortly after announcing his retirement from racing.

Uniform trail marking system adopted by NSAA.

1965 First American International Team Races (a memorial to Buddy Werner) held at Vail, Colorado, and won by Austria (men) and France (women).

David Jacobs named first full-time Canadian ski coach.

1966 First FIS World Alpine Ski Championships held in the Southern Hemisphere, in August, at Portillo, Chile. France dominates.

First World Cup season begins in December in Europe.

GLM, first successful experiment in Graduated Length teaching method, introduced at Killington, Vermont.

Gjermund Eggen, Norway, wins FIS World Championship 15 km., 50 km., and relay gold medals.

1967 Jean-Claude Killy and Nancy Greene win first World Cup. France wins Nations Cup.

Avalement "sitting back" technique of racers analyzed.

Nastar recreational ski-racing program introduced at eight areas.

1968 America hosts its first International Congress of Ski Instructors (Interski) at Aspen. Austria's Kruckenhauser introduces wide track and schwups to teaching.

Snowmaking spurs growth of Thanksgiving skiing, near city hills.

Theft problems mount at ski areas.

1968 (*continued*)

Jean-Claude Killy captures all three gold medals in Alpine skiing at the Olympics at Grenoble, matching Sailer's triple gold of 1956. Furor over Karl Schranz's disqualification from slalom. Killy and Nancy Greene retire, sign lucrative product-endorsement, personal-appearance contracts.

"Killy start" technique introduced.

Helicopter skiing gains in popularity.

1969 Bob Beattie retires as director of U.S. Alpine racing program, heads new pro racing circuit.

Warmup pants, cracked edges, plastic boots gain with consumers.

1970 Billy Kidd wins combined title of world championships at Val Gardena, first American male gold medal winner in history of Alpine skiing. He turns pro. Willy Schaeffler named U.S. Ski Team coach.

Denver wins bid to be 1976 Olympic Winter Games site.

Karl Schranz wins his second World Cup.

Custom-fit boots by injection foaming introduced in ski shops.

Summer ski camps attract hundreds of youngsters to western United States, Europe.

1971 Boots get higher and stiffer. Boot canting is found to prevent falls as well as aid technique. Antifriction pads improve safety of bindings. SKI Magazine introduces Ski Performance Prediction Test (SKipp). Acrobatic "hot dog" skiing makes big gains in United States; first tournaments held.

Snowbird opens in Utah. Environmental concern seen halting new area construction in Vermont.

Nastar expands to eighty ski areas.

1972 Barbara Ann Cochran wins America's first Olympic gold medal in Alpine skiing in twenty years. International Olympic Committee bars Austria's Karl Schranz from competing in Sapporo Winter Games.

Spider Sabich wins over $50,000 in prize money on ISRA American pro racing circuit.

Avery Brundage retires after twenty years as President of International Olympic Committee, succeeded by Lord Kilanin of Ireland.

Gustavo Thoeni of Italy wins World Cup for second year in row.

Toni Sailer takes over coaching of Austrian ski team; Jean Vuarnet and Georges Joubert named to head French team.

Denver loses 1976 Winter Olympics; they are awarded to Innsbruck.

1973 Jean-Claude Killy wins Grand Prix pro circuit, five years after Grenoble.

1973 (*continued*)

Austria wins Nations Cup, France slumps in Alpine skiing. Thoeni and Proell win their third World Cups.

Hot dog, acrobatic skiing draws huge crowds, purses grow.

Short skis boom.

1974 Lake Placid gets approval to host 1980 Games, offsetting the disappointment following the ouster of the 1976 Games from Denver.

Energy problems, combined with recession and poor weather, deal eastern ski-area business a body blow and reshuffle the order of popularity, underscoring the need for serious snowmaking and grooming.

1975 Colorado edges into national skier-visit lead, but new Gov. Richard Lamm, who had led the anti-Olympics movement, declares moratorium on construction of new resorts.

Ingemar Stenmark emerges as a major force in Slalom (SL) and Grand Slalom (GS), narrowly losing the World Cup as Thoeni wins his final trophy.

Proell wins her fifth World Cup.

Hank Kashiwa wins men's professional title.

1976 U.S. fares poorly at Innsbruck Olympics.

Ingemar Stenmark wins first of three World Cup titles and spread-eagles the world in SL and GS with radical new techniques. Phil Mahre finishes fourteenth in first season.

Henri Duvillard wins first of two men's pro titles.

1977 Killington buys Mount Snow, takes commanding lead in eastern skiing, and underscores the future need for large capital base to continue expansions.

Sunday v. *Stratton* decision on liability, a $1.5-million judgment in favor of injured skier, terrorizes ski-area business.

Stenmark widens domination of SL/GS competition.

1978 20th Century-Fox buys Aspen Skiing Corp. for nearly $50 million; emphasizes fact that major corporations will play an increasingly important role in ski-resort development.

Andre Arnold wins first of four men's pro racing titles.

1979 World Cup rules revised to penalize Ingemar Stenmark's refusal to race Downhill (DH); despite winning a record fourteen SL and GS events he finishes fifth in World Cup. Phil Mahre finishes second.

Proell wins sixth (and final) World Cup.

Lange, innovator in sixties, regains role in ski boot market.

1980   Phil Mahre recovers from serious 1979 injury to win silver at Lake Placid; otherwise, U.S. Ski Team does poorly at Olympics, prompting a further overhaul of the team's organization.

Tyrolia catches Salomon in battle for bindings market leadership in United States.

1981   Chuck Lewis, last major "independent" in Colorado, sells Copper Mountain to Apex Petroleum Co. Overall, Rockies struggle with snow drought, second in five years, that slashes business severely.

Phil Mahre, in last race of season, overtakes Stenmark for overall World Cup title, first ever for U.S. skier, but Stenmark wins WC titles in SL and GS and leaves open the question of who's the better skier.

Tamara McKinney wins World Cup title in GS.

Andre Arnold wins fourth men's pro title but circuit self-destructs in "strike" at final race at Mammoth, California.

Toril Forland outlasts Jocelyne Perillat of France and Viki Fleckenstein of United States in tight battle for women's pro title as circuit grows in purse and visibility.

Vail finally opens Beaver Creek, $50 million in the building.

Geze unveils upward-release toe.

1982   Phil Mahre refines his new style and wins four WC titles: overall, combined, SL, and GS, the last two narrowly over Stenmark in heated battle. Stenmark finishes second overall as well, while Steve Mahre, fourth in 1981, finishes third.

Canadian Steve Podborski wins DH title, producing clean sweep of all men's World Cup trophies for North America.

U.S. Women's Team wins Nations Cup and shows first-seed strength in all WC disciplines.

Rockies continue to sag in skier visits despite good snow season as East begins to regain prior leadership with solid growth and Europe again becomes competitive.

Forland wins women's pro title again; Fleckenstein and Perillat tie for second. Circuit continues to grow in popularity.

Deer Valley, with Stein Eriksen deeply involved, opens in Utah.

Bibliography

No attempt is made here to present a complete bibliography of ski literature. Only those books that have had unusual influence on the skiing of their time or that are unique for one reason or another are listed below. For those interested in delving further into ski literature, Baker Library at Dartmouth College has the most comprehensive collection of ski books and journals in the United States.

BOOKS

ALLAIS, EMILE; GIGNOUX, PAUL; and BLANCHON, GEORGES, *Ski français*. Grenoble, France: B. Arthaud, 1938.

AURAN, JOHN HENRY, *The Ski Better Book*. New York: Dial Press, 1975.

BARTHEL, BRUCE; HILTNER, WALT; and MOHAN, JOHN, *Freestyle Skiing*. New York: Winchester Press, 1976.

BAYS, TED, *Nine Thousand Years of Skis*. National Ski Hall of Fame Press, 1980.

BEAR, RUEDI, *Pianta Su Ski Like the Best*. Boston: Little Brown, 1976.

BEATTIE, BOB, *Guide to Ski Racing*. Boulder, Colo.: World-Wide Ski Corp., 1971.

BERRY, I. WILLIAM, *Kids on Skis*. New York: Charles Scribner's Sons, 1980, 1982.

451

————, *The Skier's Almanac*. New York: Charles Scribner's Sons, 1978.

————, *Where to Ski*. New York: Signet, 1974.

BILGERI, GEORG, *Der Alpine Skilauf*. 1910.

BRADY, MICHAEL, *Nordic Touring and Cross-Country Skiing*. Oslo, Norway: Dreyers Forlag, 1971. New York: Dial Press, 1972.

BRADLEY, DAVID; MILLER, RALPH; and MERRILL, ALLISON, *Expert Skiing*. New York: Grosset and Dunlap, 1960. (Revised edition 1964.)

BRANDENBERGER, HUGO, *Methodik des Skilaufs und Skimechanik*. Rapperswil, Switzerland: Verlag Gasser & Co., 1958.

BROWER, DAVID (ed.), *The Sierra Club Manual of Ski Mountaineering*. New York: Ballantine Books, 1969.

BRUNER, HANS, and KALIN, ALOIS, *Ski-Langlauf fur Meister und Geniesser*. Bern, Switzerland: Benziger Verlag, 1969.

BURNABY, SARA, and LAWRENCE, ANDREA MEAD, *A Practice of Mountains*. New York: Seaview Books, 1980.

BURTON, HAL, *The Ski Troops*. New York: Simon & Schuster, 1971.

CAMPBELL, STU, *Ski With the Big Boys*. Tulsa, Okla.: Winchester Press, 1974.

CASEWIT, CURTIS, *The Compleat Skier*. New York: Popular Library, 1974.

CAULFIELD, VIVIAN, *How to Ski*. 1910.

CEREGHINI, MARIO, *5,000 Years of Winter Sports*. Milan: Edizioni de Milione, 1955.

CHONTOS, STEVE, *The Death of Dover, Vt*. New York: Vintage Press, 1974.

CLIFFORD, PEGGY, *To Aspen and Back*. New York: St. Martin's Press, 1976.

COUTTET, JAMES, and GIGNOUX, PAUL, *Christiania Leger*. Paris: Libraire Hachette, 1961.

COVINO, FRANK, *Skier's Digest*, 2nd edition. Northfield, Ill.: D.B.I. Books, 1976.

DERCUM, EDNA, *It's Easy, Edna, It's Downhill All the Way*. Carbondale, Colo.: Sirpos Press, 1981.

ENZEL, ROBERT, *The White Book of Ski Areas*. Washington, D.C.: Inter Ski Services, 1981.

EVANS, HAROLD; JACKMAN, BRIAN; and OTTAWAY, MARK, *We Learned to Ski*. New York: St. Martin's Press, 1974, 1975.

FOEGER, WALTER, *Skiing for Beginners: The Natur Technik Method*. New York: Ronald Press, 1963.

GILLILAND, MARY ELLEN, *Summit*. Silverthorne, Colo.: Alpenrose Press, 1980.

GREENE, NANCY, *An Autobiography*, with Jack Batten. Toronto: General Publishing, 1968.

HALL, MARTY, *One Stride Ahead*. Tulsa, Okla.: Winchester Press, 1981.

ISELIN, FRED, and SPECTORSKY, A. C., *Invitation to Skiing*. New York: Simon & Schuster, 1947. (Revised editions 1958, 1966, 1968.)

JAY, JOHN, and the Editors of SKI, *Ski Down the Years*. New York: Award House, 1967.

JEROME, JOHN, *On Mountains*. New York: McGraw-Hill, 1979.

JOUBERT, GEORGES, *How to Ski the New French Way*. New York: Dial Press, 1967.

KIDD, BILLY, and HALL, DOUGLAS KENT, *Ski in Six Days*. Chicago, Ill.: Regnery, 1975.

KILLY, JEAN-CLAUDE, with Al Greenberg, *Comeback*. New York: Macmillan, 1974.

———, *Skiing . . . The Killy Way*. New York: Simon & Schuster, 1971.

KRUCKENHAUSER, STEFAN, *The New Official Austrian Ski System* (translated by Roland Palmedo). New York: A. S. Barnes & Co., 1958.

LANG, SERGE, *Le Ski et Autres Sports d'Hiver*. Paris: Larousse, 1967.

LEDERER, WILLIAM J., and WILSON, JOE PETE, *Complete Cross-Country Skiing and Ski Touring*. New York: W. W. Norton, 1970.

LIEBERS, ARTHUR, *The Complete Book of Cross Country Skiing and Ski Touring*. New York: Coward, McCann & Geoghegan, 1974.

LOBITZ, W. CHARLES, Ph.D., *Skiing From the Head Down*. Philadelphia: J. B. Lippincott, 1977.

LUND, MORTEN, *Ski GLM*. New York: Dial Press, 1970.

LUNN, SIR ARNOLD, *The Story of Ski-ing*. London: Eyre & Spottiswoode, 1952.

LUTHER, CARL L., *Der Moderne Wintersport*. 1911.

MAJOR, JAMES, and LARSSON, OLLE, *World Cup Ski Technique*. Park City, Utah: Poudre, 1978.

MANN, BOB "BOOGIE," *Hot Dog Skiing*. New York: W. W. Norton, 1973.

McCLUGGAGE, DENISE, *The Centered Skier*. Waitsfield, Vt.: Vermont Crossroads Press, 1977.

McCULLOCH, ERNIE, *Ski the Champion's Way*. New York: Harper & Row, 1966.

———, *Ski Easy, The New Technique*. New York: McGraw-Hill, 1973.

MILLER, PETER, *Ski Almanac*. New York: Doubleday, 1979.

———, *The 30,000-Mile Ski Race*. New York: Dial Press, 1972.

MILLER, WARREN, *In Search of Skiing*. Albuquerque, N.M.: Hermosa Publishing Co., 1980.

NANSEN, FRIDTJOF, *Paa Ski Over Grönland*. Oslo, Norway, 1890. (German and English editions, 1891.)

PFEIFER, LUANNE, *Ski California*. San Rafael, Calif.: Presidio, 1980.

PFEIFFER, J. DOUGLAS, *Skiing with Pfeiffer*. Riverside, Calif.: A to Z Printing, 1958.

———, and the Editors of *Skiing*, *Skiing Simplified*. New York: Grosset & Dunlap, 1971.

PROCTOR, CHARLES N., *Skiing*. New York, 1936.

RAND, ABBY, *A Ski Guide to Europe*. New York: Award House, 1968. Updated Charles Scribner's Sons, 1970.

———, *Ski North America, the Top 28 Resorts*. Philadelphia: J. B. Lippincott, 1969.

ROTHAFEL, ROXY, *Roxy's Ski Guide to New England*. Charlotte, N.C.: The East Woods Press, 1978.

SANDERS, R. J., *The Anatomy of Skiing*. Denver, Colo.: Golden Bell Press, 1976.

SCHNEIDER, HANNES, and FANCK, ARNOLD, *Wunder des Schneeschuhs*. 1926. English edition, *Wonders of Skiing*, New York, 1937.

SCHNIEBS, OTTO, *Skiing for All*. New York, 1936.

SIMONTON, JUNE B., *Beaver Creek—The First One Hundred Years*. Beaver Creek Resort Co., 1980.

SKI Magazine, Editors of, *Encyclopedia of Skiing*. New York: Harper & Row, 1979.

———, *Expert Tips for Better Skiing*. New York: Harper & Row, 1972.

———, *Skier's Handbook*. New York: Harper & Row, 1966; Award House (paperback), 1967.

———, *Ski Pointers by the Experts*. New York: Harper & Row, 1961; Universal Publishing & Distributing Corp. (paperback), 1964.

Ski Racing, Editors of, *The Interview Book*. Paper House, 1974.

SLANGER, ELISSA, *Ski Women's Way*. New York: Summit Books, 1979.

SLUSKY, DEE, *The Skier's Year Round Exercise Book*. New York: Scarborough, 1979.

SMITY, PHILIP, *Total Breathing*. New York: McGraw-Hill, 1980.

SNELLMAN, WALT, *Mastering The Mountain*. New York: Ziff-Davis, 1980.

SONNENFIELD, MARTHA, and SNYDER, FRANK V., *The Stratton Story*. Stratton Corp., 1981.

STENMARK, PAM; ABRAHAM, HORST; and LIGHTHALL, NANCY, *Skiing for Women*. Palm Springs, Calif.: ETC Publications, 1979.

TAYLOR, CLIF, *GLM, The New Way to Ski!* New York: Tempo Books, 1973.

———, *Ski in a Day*. New York: Grosset & Dunlap, 1964.

Tinker, Gene, *Let's Learn Ski Touring*. New York: Walker & Company, 1971.
Zdarsky, Mathias, *Lilienfelder Schilauf Technik*. 1896.

JOURNALS

American Ski Annual (no longer published).
British Ski Year Book, published annually by the Ski Club of Great Britain.
Der Schnee Hase, published annually by the Swiss Academic Ski Club.
Der Sport, published three times weekly in Zurich.
L'Equipe, published daily in Paris.
Powder, published six times a year in Dana Point, California 92629.
Sci (Italian), published seven times a year. Via Padova, 35, 20127 Milano, Italy.
Ski (French), published six times a year. 63, Champs Elysees, Paris 8, France.
Skier's Advocate, published four times a year between September and March by the American Ski Association, 6900 E. Belleview Avenue, Denver, Colo. 80111.
Skiing, published seven times a year between September and March by Ziff-Davis Publishing Company, 1 Park Avenue, New York, N.Y. 10016.
SKI Magazine (incorporating *Ski Life*), published seven times a year between August and March by Times Mirror Magazine Co., 380 Madison Avenue, New York, N.Y. 10017.

TRADE JOURNALS

Ski Area Management, published bimonthly by David Rowan, N. Salem, N.Y.
Ski Business, published monthly by Nicholas Hock, Darien, Conn.
Skiing Trade News, published monthly by *Skiing*.
The Ski Industry Letter, published biweekly by Washington Business Information, 235 National Press Building, Washington, D.C. 20045.

Photo Credits

Index